Teaching Online

Teaching Online: A Practical Guide is an accessible, introductory, and comprehensive guide for anyone who teaches online. The fourth edition of this bestselling resource has been fully revised, maintains its reader-friendly tone, and offers exceptional practical advice, new teaching examples, faculty interviews, and an updated resource section.

New to this edition:

- entire new chapter on MOOCs (massive open online courses);
- expanded information on teaching with mobile devices, using open educational resources, and learning analytics;
- additional interviews with faculty, case studies, and examples;
- spotlight on new tools and categories of tools, especially multimedia.

Focusing on the "hows" and "whys" of implementation rather than theory, the fourth edition of *Teaching Online* is a must-have resource for anyone teaching online or thinking about teaching online.

Susan Ko, Director of Faculty Development and Instructional Technology, CUNY School of Professional Studies.

Steve Rossen, Instructional Technologist and Electronic Librarian, formerly Manager of the Faculty New Media Center at UCLA.

Teaching Online
A Practical Guide

Fourth Edition

Susan Ko and Steve Rossen

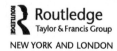

Routledge
Taylor & Francis Group

NEW YORK AND LONDON

Fourth edition published 2017
by Routledge
711 Third Avenue, New York, NY 10017

and by Routledge
2 Park Square, Milton Park, Abingdon, Oxon, OX14 4RN

Routledge is an imprint of the Taylor & Francis Group, an informa business

© 2017 Taylor & Francis

First published 2004 by Houghton Mifflin Company

Third edition published 2010 by Routledge

Library of Congress Cataloging in Publication Data
A catalog record for this book has been requested

ISBN: 978-0-415-83242-7 (hbk)
ISBN: 978-0-415-83243-4 (pbk)
ISBN: 978-0-203-42735-4 (ebk)

Typeset in Utopia
by Wearset Ltd, Boldon, Tyne and Wear

Download the eResources from: www.routledge.com/9780415832434

Once more with Steve...

Brief Contents ● ● ● ● ●

Contents ● ● ● ● ●

Preface   ● ● ● ● ●

When the first edition of this book emerged in 2000, communication via the internet and the rapidly expanding Web was already popular but the online environment was not nearly as ubiquitous as it has become today. Now, connecting to information, services, and to others is something we take for granted to do our banking, read (or make) the news, order and pay for nearly every type of merchandise, post our vacation photos, chat with friends from around the world, seek advice about what ails us, listen to music, watch videos, and share our thoughts, creations, and mutual interests. And we now access the internet not only from our desktop and laptop computers but also from a rapidly expanding array of mobile devices. We are increasingly able to depart from the Web and its browser-based programs to access programs we wish to use via mobile "apps" that we download to our smartphones, optimized and personalized for our quick and ready access. Thus our ability to connect and to communicate online has become an inseparable and seemingly necessary part of our lives.

But while nearly everyone lives some part of his or her life online these days, this does not necessarily indicate familiarity with the techniques of online teaching and learning. Even though teaching and learning online is no longer a new phenomenon, it still makes many instructors both anxious and apprehensive. They still harbor some basic questions such as: What is the difference between teaching "on the ground" and teaching online? What are the fundamental techniques? Where can you learn them? What kind of equipment or software do you use? How do you measure how effective you are? How do you assess the success of your students?

While many instructors have long since taken the plunge, some are still asking those basic questions, and we find that many others worldwide continue to regard the prospect of teaching online with trepidation and anxiety. Even those who have acquired quite a bit of experience may still find themselves challenged by the unique demands of teaching online. And both neophytes and experienced online instructors are sometimes charmed and bewildered by the astonishing array of new tools that have appeared in the wake of each successive edition of this book. Some of the questions these instructors are likely to ask are: How can I manage my time better when I teach online and not feel so overwhelmed? Which of the new technologies are worth the effort for me to learn? Do you know of any different teaching and learning activities I might try to better stimulate and motivate my students?

This book is written for the rapidly rising population of instructors who want to teach online, who have been told to teach online (sometimes in conjunction with on-the-ground classes), who are currently teaching online (but want to improve), or who are training or encouraging others to teach online. It is also for the administrator or support staff who assist instructors in their endeavor to teach online. In other words, it is intended for lecturers, professors, tutors, teaching assistants, department chairs, academic deans, program planners, instructional designers and technologists, and information technology support personnel at both the administrative and departmental levels.

The book is as much for the tenured professor as for the adjunct, part-time instructor or teaching assistant. Those in the K–12 education field may also find that much of the advice given here is relevant for their teaching circumstances. It is also aimed at the growing number of students enrolled in programs in educational technology, computers in education, or similarly organized programs focused on technology in education. It is for the college administrator who is trying to convince a skeptical and unwilling faculty member to adopt this mode of instruction, as well as for the part-time instructor who drives seventy miles a day to teach four courses at four different institutions. It is for the training staff and those in faculty development who work with a wide array of instructors, ranging from those to whom life online is second nature to those who struggle to keep up with the constantly evolving technologies.

The book is written from the unique perspective of two authors who have taught online themselves and have trained thousands of other faculty to teach online. It is more concerned with the "whys" and "hows" of implementation than with theory, not because we do not value pedagogical theory but because such topics are discussed and critiqued more effectively elsewhere. While our advice is congruent with research findings in the field of online education, we will only refer to that research in passing (avoiding footnotes while providing some carefully selected references for you to pursue in the Guide to Resources section). Unlike other books you may have read on the subject, this is not a collection of essays, not a general overview, not a focused look at one particular aspect of online teaching and learning, not a treatment of the subject based primarily on one institutional model, nor is it—strictly speaking—a technical handbook. Rather, it is intended as a practical and concise guide both for instructors teaching completely online and for those supplementing or fully integrating a traditional classroom with online elements. It will help reinforce what you may learn at your institution if you are lucky enough to have such instructor-development resources, but it will also serve as a survival manual for those who are operating largely on their own.

Our goal is to immerse instructors in this new environment as quickly as we can, using plain language and illustrating our points with case studies from colleagues or students that we have worked with or known, representing a wide variety of different disciplines and institutions. We hope to get you up and running as quickly as possible and then provide a resource for you to refer back to at critical junctures in your future teaching practice.

●●●●●

Organization of This Book

The book is divided into three parts.

In Part I, "Getting Started," we define and describe the world of online teaching and learning and introduce the skills, training, and support you will need to become part of it. These two chapters are aimed especially at those new to online teaching, but those with experience may find it helps provide a context of online teaching as it exists today and lays out the parameters for the book to follow.

Part II, "Putting the Course Together," covers the process of converting or developing course content for the online environment while discovering new possibilities for your course. We help you take inventory of your existing course and suggest areas for innovation, while guiding you through the development process and the creation of an online syllabus. We provide advice on using different types of software environments and offer a detailed look at opportunities for incorporating diverse activities and internet resources. We shed light on the often-confusing issue of making effective use of multimedia, explore some of the new tools of the Web 2.0 world, and explore matters of copyright and intellectual property as they relate to the online classroom.

Although we strive to make the topics in Part II easy enough for beginners to grasp, we believe there is much here to offer even experienced online instructors. Carefully chosen examples from real-life instructors help illustrate the approaches and solutions outlined.

In Part III, "Teaching in the Online Classroom," we focus on some of the techniques you will need to become an effective instructor, whether you teach totally online or a blended course, or are enriching classroom instruction with online activities. We discuss how to make sure your students are prepared for online classes, provide suggestions on the topic of online classroom management, and describe ways to integrate online activities into the face-to-face classroom. We explore the challenges of teaching those giant-sized online classes called MOOCs. Finally, we discuss how online teaching can revitalize your career and how to keep current with the pace of change.

As a handy reference, resources are collected together and augmented with additional materials in the Guide to Resources at the end of the book. We have included a section concerning online education theory and research for those who would like to pursue such topics. Because internet addresses change so frequently, we urge you to consult the publisher's website for updates, corrections, and any new references.

Terminology is often a barrier for those unfamiliar with the internet or computer software. Thus, there are numerous short definitions and boxed sidebars throughout the text to help you understand the narrative. A Glossary at the back of the book includes those terms and offers additional assistance. When a term is introduced and appears in bold font that indicates you can find it in the Glossary even if there is no sidebar definition given.

●●●●●

What's New in This Edition

While we have maintained the original approach, outlines, and many of the same topics of this book, and you will find most of your favorite chapters are still present, some chapter numbers and many chapter dimensions have changed and we have an entirely new chapter on teaching in a MOOC. Past readers of our book will recognize some familiar stories from instructors whose cases are as relevant now as they were in the third edition, while they will also encounter entirely new voices joining us for this fourth edition. New technologies, the greater availability of video and mobile apps, and the pedagogy needed to exploit these new tools have resulted in many other updates and revisions to this edition.

Some illustrations of learning management software and processes have been eliminated due to the greater familiarity of current readers with basic internet technologies and the wide availability of such examples on the internet.

All chapter resources are still subsumed into a convenient and accessible location at the end of the book in an expanded Guide to Resources section. This resource section is also available online at the book's companion website.

● ● ● ● ●

Acknowledgments

We would like to acknowledge the special assistance of our editor for this edition, Alex Masulis—his patience, encouragement and, of course, timely invitations to discuss our progress over lunch. I would also like to acknowledge the help of editorial assistant, Daniel Schwartz.

We would also like to thank the many accomplished instructors—our colleagues in online education—old and new, who generously shared their experiences and whose many contributions have enriched this book.

A nod is due to my academic home at City University of New York—to all the faculty I have encountered while conducting workshops to prepare faculty to teach online and to CUNY School of Professional Studies in appreciation of the dedication of its faculty and staff alike to students in our online programs.

Finally, we would like to thank those readers who have continued to enthusiastically greet each new edition and whose many emails and queries about the whereabouts of the fourth edition encouraged us to persist in writing this latest version. Here it is at last!

Susan Ko

I

Getting Started

1

●●●●●

Teaching Online:
An Overview

While online education delivered via the internet has been around for about two decades, many people still don't know exactly what it is, or how it's done, or even what some of the terms used to describe it mean. The **MOOC** craze of recent years heightened the awareness of many to the possibilities of online learning, but muddied the waters when popular commentators, in debating the merits or perils of online learning, often failed to distinguish between the pre-existing model of small-scale online courses led by instructors and these new opportunities in which thousands or even tens of thousands of would-be learners might be involved.

> **MOOC**—Massive Online Open Course—an online course in which large numbers of people (hundreds, thousands, or even tens of thousands) may freely enroll without charge. Some MOOCs are not really open in that they are either limited to certain users or charge a fee.

Some faculty may now have a general notion of what's involved in online education, but they don't know how to get started, or they feel some trepidation about handling the issues they may encounter. And there are now many who have taught online, but feel that they have barely scratched the surface in terms of learning how best to adapt their teaching to the new environment. Perhaps this range of feelings exists in part because the online environment is so different from what most instructors have encountered before.

Teaching online means conducting a course partially or entirely through the internet—either on the Web or by way of mobile **apps** that allow one to manipulate the online course elements. You may also see references to online education as **eLearning** (electronic

app—mobile apps are application software that are downloaded to a tablet or smartphone and designed to perform specific functions. These functions may duplicate those that can be performed in the internet browser version of a program but are generally optimized to operate in the mobile environment.

learning), a term often used in business. It's a form of **distance education**, a process that traditionally included courses taught through the mail, by DVD, or via telephone or TV—any form of learning that doesn't involve the traditional classroom setting in which students and instructor must be in the same place at the same time.

What makes teaching online unique is that when you teach online, you don't have to be someplace to teach. You don't have to lug your briefcase full of papers or your laptop to a classroom, stand at a lectern, scribble on a chalkboard (or even use your high-tech, interactive classroom "smart" whiteboard), or grade papers in a stuffy room while your students take a test. You don't even have to sit in your office waiting for students to show up for conferences. You can hold "office hours" on weekends or at night after dinner. You can do all this while living in a small town in Wyoming or a big city like Bangkok, even if you're working for a college whose administrative offices are located in Florida or Dubai. You can attend an important conference in Hawaii on the same day that you teach your class in New Jersey, logging on from your laptop via the local café's wireless hot spot or your hotel room's high-speed network. Or you may simply pull out your smartphone to quickly check on the latest postings, email, or text messages from students, using a mobile app for your course site or to access other resources.

Online learning offers more freedom for students as well. They can search online for courses using the internet, scouring their institutions or even the world for programs, classes, and instructors that fit their needs. Having found an appropriate course, they can enroll and register, shop for their books (whether hard copy or ebooks), read articles, listen to lectures, submit their homework assignments, confer with their instructors, and access their final grades—all online.

They can assemble in **virtual classrooms**, joining other students from diverse geographical locales, forging bonds and friendships not possible in conventional classrooms, which are usually limited to students from a specific geographical area. Online learning activities may be conducted in **asynchronous** format, allowing for access and posting by students at different times during the week, or via **synchronous** sessions or a combination of both.

The convenience of learning online applies equally well to adult learners, students from educationally underserved areas, those pursuing specialized or advanced degrees, those who want to advance in their degree work through credentialed courses, and any students who simply want to augment the curricular offerings from their local institutions. No longer must they drive to school or remote classroom, find a parking space, sit in a lecture hall at a specific time, wait outside their instructors' offices for conferences, and take their final exams at the campus. They can hold a job, have a family, take care of parents or pets, and even travel. As long as they can get to a computer or other device connected to the internet, students can, in most cases, keep up with their work even if they're busy during the day. School is always in session because school is always there.

So dynamic is the online environment that new technologies and techniques are emerging all the time. What's commonplace one year becomes old hat the next. The only thing that seems to remain constant is people's desire to transmit and receive information efficiently, to learn and to communicate with others, no matter what the means. That's what drives people to shop, invest, and converse online, and it is this same force that is propelling them to learn online as well.

Online education is no longer a novelty. In the United States alone, over 27 percent of college students took at least one distance learning course in fall of 2013, according to the National Center for Education Statistics, while the Babson Survey of February 2015 noted that even while the overall rate of growth had slowed in recent years, online education remained at high levels in public four- and two-year institutions, with both public and private four-year institutions exhibiting the highest levels of growth (see www.onlinelearningsurvey.com/reports/gradelevel.pdf).

Worldwide, online learning is taking place in a variety of environments and combinations. There are students using mobile devices to communicate and collaborate with instructors and classmates, others gathering in local computer labs to connect with central university resources to bring previously unavailable classes to far-flung portions of a nation, and there are degree programs offered fully online for which students need never set foot on a physical campus. Open or "mega" universities providing alternate routes for higher education to hundreds of thousands of students in such countries as India, Indonesia, Turkey, and other nations use a variety of different distance education methods, online increasingly among them, to deliver courses, certificates, and degrees.

But all this freedom and innovation can sometimes be perplexing. If the conventional tools of teaching are removed, how do you teach? If school's open twenty-four hours a day, seven days a week, when is school out? What is the role of the instructor if you don't see your students face to face? Do you simply deliver lectures and grade papers, following in the traditional pattern, or do you take on other roles, for example, that of a facilitator, moderator, or mentor?

And what if you're among the many instructors who teach face to face but maintain an internet site or blog as well? Does making your course notes available online mean that coming to class will become obsolete? How do you balance the real and virtual worlds so that they work together? And if information can be presented readily online, what should class time be devoted to: Discussions? Student presentations? Structured debates? Even more challenging, if your course is conducted and class activities occur both online and in face-to-face sessions, how do you create a blended learning experience for your students that is integrated and coherent?

There is no prototypical experience of teaching online. Some instructors use the internet to complement what they teach in class or to replace some of the "seat time." Others teach entirely online. Some institutions offer the latest software, support, and training to instructors; others offer little more than the bare bones to instructors.

You will get a sense of these differences in the chapters that follow. For the time being, take a look at two hypothetical instructors working online.

● ● ● ● ●

The Range of Online Experiences: Two Hypothetical Cases

The first of our hypothetical instructors, Jim Hegelmarks, teaches philosophy entirely online. The second, Miriam Sharpe, teaches a first-year physics course in a conventional classroom but uses a **learning management system (LMS)** to replace some face-to-face class time and to help her students review material and get answers to their questions.

Western Philosophy, a Course Taught Entirely Online

Jim Hegelmarks's course in Western philosophy is now in its third week, and the assignment for his class is to read a short commentary he has written on John Stuart Mill's *Principles of Political Economy*, portions of which the class has studied. He has asked the students to read his commentary and then respond in some detail to a question he has posted on the online discussion board for his course.

Connecting to the internet from his home, or sitting in a local coffee shop with his laptop and wireless connection, Hegelmarks types the **URL** of his class website into the location bar of his Firefox browser and is promptly greeted with a log-in screen. He types in his user name (jhegelmarks) and his password (hmarks420); this process admits him to the class.

Hegelmarks's course is conducted using a learning management system (or **virtual learning environment**) which his university has adopted for all online courses.

> **Learning management system or software (LMS), also known as virtual learning environment (VLE), learning management system (LMS), learning platform, online delivery system** A software program that contains a number of integrated instructional functions. Instructors can post lectures or graphics, moderate discussions, invoke chat sessions, post video commentary, and give quizzes, all within the confines of the same software system. Not only can instructors and students "manage" the flow of information and communications, but the instructor can both assess and keep track of the performance of the students, monitoring their progress and assigning grades. Typical examples of an LMS are those produced by Blackboard and Canvas, or adopted from "open source" products such as Moodle or Sakai. Your institution may have yet another proprietary system of its own, and there are many others in use or being developed all over the world. These systems, as well as many of the tools which are continually being added to these systems, are discussed in more detail in Chapter 6.

Subject*

Week 3 Discussion

Message*

Based on this week's readings and my commentary, please comment on the influence of **John Stuart Mill** on 19th century philosophers. What application to social philosophy can be drawn from his Political Economy?

Figure 1.1 Jim Hegelmarks creates a discussion topic using Moodle software. Reproduced by permission from Moodle.

The main page of Hegelmarks's course contains a number of navigational links on a class site menu that he can use to manage the course. His commentary is posted in a section that is set up to display text or audio lectures, but the area he's interested in today is the discussion board, so that's where he goes first. With his mouse, he clicks on the menu link that leads to the discussion board and reviews the messages that have been posted there. Several of the students have posted their responses to the assignment. He reads through the responses on-screen thoughtfully, printing out the longer ones so that he can consider them at his leisure. Each posting is about fifty words in length although he has a few students who post more lengthy replies.

After evaluating the responses, Hegelmarks gives each student a grade for this assignment and enters the grade in the online gradebook, which can be reached by clicking another navigational link on the course's main page menu. Each type of graded assignment, including participation, has a section reserved for it in the online gradebook. He knows that when students log on to the class website to check their grades, each student will be able to see only his or her own grades—no one else's grade will be visible. Hegelmarks also knows that those who have failed to complete this assignment will be able to monitor their progress, or lack of it, by looking at the gradebook online.

What concerns Hegelmarks now is that only five of his fifteen students have responded so far. Because it's already Friday, and there's a new assignment they must do for the next week, he decides to take a look at some of the statistical information that the learning management system offers for tracking student progress. What he finds is that of the ten students who haven't responded to the question, eight have at least clicked on (and one hopes, actually read) the commentary for that lesson, some spending more than sixty minutes at a time in that area. Two haven't looked at it at all.

Hegelmarks's first concern is with the two students who haven't even looked at the assigned commentary. It isn't the first time they've failed to complete an assignment on time. Hegelmarks sends both of them a low-key but concerned email asking whether they're having any special problems he should know about, gently reminding them that they've fallen behind.

The lengthy time the other students have been taking to read his commentary concerns him as well. From experience, he knows that students often struggle with some of the concepts in Mill's *Political Economy*. He had written the commentary and created the homework assignment in an attempt to clarify the subject, but taking a second look, he now realizes that the commentary was written far too densely. He makes a note to rewrite it the next time he teaches the class.

While Hegelmarks is still online, a student instant messages him, using that feature of this learning management software, and Hegelmarks takes a few minutes to answer a question about the upcoming assignment. The question had been addressed in the classroom Q&A area, and in fact, the student seems to know the answer already, but he is grateful to receive Hegelmarks's further affirmation. Hegelmarks has the ability to make himself unavailable to the students via instant messaging but he usually maintains his presence because he feels that those few students who like to contact him in this manner may need this individualized attention and reassurance.

The last task Hegelmarks completes before logging off is to comment on the student responses that he has just read and graded. He doesn't comment on each one—that would take far too long—but he composes a summary message touching on the main points his students have made, and he posts this on the discussion board for all to see.

Introduction to Physics, a "Blended" Course

Our second instructor, Miriam Sharpe, teaches an introductory physics class at a large public university. Her course, a prerequisite for anyone majoring in physics, is what we call **blended**, that is, combining both online and face-to-face activities, and is one in which the online activities are required rather than optional.

The class is large, with eighty students enrolled, and Sharpe has two teaching assistants (TAs) to help her. Before this course was designated a blended class, Miriam used to meet with students on campus in a large lecture hall two times per week and used a very basic website to post online readings and resources. Now she lectures to her class on campus once per week, using PowerPoint slides projected onto a screen to elucidate her points. Because she relies on so many slides, she has decided to post them on the course website for students to review.

Although some of her colleagues disapprove of this practice, arguing that it will dissuade students from coming to class, Sharpe contends that relieving students of the tedium of taking copious notes during her lectures makes it easier for them to comprehend and remember the material. More important, by posting her slides online, she gives students the opportunity to review the material before coming to class. As a result, she has found that the questions raised in class, and the discussions they provoke, are far more relevant and lively.

> **Blended course** (also known as hybrid)
> A course which includes both face-to-face meetings and online components. Definitions of blended courses vary from one institution to another. For example, a blended course may be defined as one in which some "seat time" is replaced by online activities, or this term may be applied to those courses in which both the face-to-face and online components are required, to differentiate the course from one in which online elements are merely supplementary. The Online Learning Consortium has defined a blended or hybrid course as one in which 30–79 percent of the content is delivered online.

Sharpe also uses the course website for discussion groups. Each TA leads a discussion group of thirty students, with Sharpe handling the remaining twenty herself. In these virtual discussion groups, students can post their queries and concerns and receive a response from Sharpe, a TA, or other students. Sharpe and her TAs make a point of checking the **discussion boards** at least once a day. Sharpe has one more major use for the website: to post sample exams. When she first started using the site, she simply posted the exams as documents that her students could read. But after her university adopted a new learning management system, she was able to offer the sample exams in such a way that students could take an exam online and receive both feedback and a score. This trial assessment, she has discovered, is quite popular with her students.

Since first beginning to supplement her class with online materials two years ago, she has gone from a rudimentary website which was maintained by her TAs to software that easily permits her to upload most materials on her own. The greater ease of using today's software has actually encouraged Sharpe to more readily conceive of activities that can be implemented online. Now that all her students are readily able to access the internet and many are using the new mobile app to access the learning management system, she has no qualms about requiring students to perform certain activities online. This year for the first time she has begun

> **Wiki** Software which allows for the collaborative creation and editing of content in web page format without knowledge of programming code. Various built-in controls allow for the setting of different authoring permissions and the tracking of each contribution and different versions over time. The online encyclopedia, Wikipedia, is a prominent example of the wiki format.

to require students to use the university's **wiki** software to compose their group project reports rather than have them use valuable time on campus to accomplish that portion of their work. By using the wiki software rather than simply having students post projects to the discussion board, Dr. Sharpe gains another advantage—she is able to track each individual's contribution to a group project through the wiki's recording of each edit.

• • • • •

Teaching Online: The Basics

Now that you have some idea of what it's like to teach online and what some of the basic terms and concepts are, you may be thinking about how to teach your own class online. Later chapters will go into detail on many specific aspects of the task. Here we comment on some of the basic pedagogical considerations involved in teaching courses like those of our two fictional instructors, Jim Hegelmarks and Miriam Sharpe.

Teaching a Course Entirely Online

Perhaps the most daunting task is to plan a new course that will be taught entirely online, particularly if you've never taught online before. Composing the syllabus, assembling the exercises and quizzes, weighing the criteria for grades—all this presents a set of unfamiliar challenges.

Yet closer inspection reveals that the approach to solving such problems is similar to what you would use "on the ground." The same instructional strategy you've learned for a live classroom—setting the goals of the course, describing specific objectives, defining the required tasks, creating relevant assignments—applies online.

Where the online course differs is in technique and in discovering the new teaching and learning opportunities afforded by the new online environment. In a classroom, you have your physical presence—your voice, body language, intonation, expressions, gestures—to help you communicate with your students. Online, at least for the majority of the time, you don't. In a classroom, a smile can be a powerful signal of approval. Online, it's reduced to a ludicrous little **emoticon or emoji**—small images like smiley faces or other images that provide a kind of short-hand for other types of emotions. In a classroom,

Emoticon A graphic symbol created with text like the smiley face :), used in online communications to express emotions that might otherwise be misunderstood when relying only on text. The word comes from combining emotion with icon.

Emoji A picture image rendered by code, which may differ in appearance based on the particular browser or app being used. As successors to emoticons, they have become increasingly a part of online communication. Large versions of emojis are known as stamps or stickers. Most emojis are freely available, integrated within communication tools, whereas others can be purchased by users as specialized sets. Emoji originated in Japan and they remain especially popular as an adjunct to electronic communications throughout Asia.

the instructor is often the "sage on the stage." Online, the instructor is more like the "sage on the page." It is the written word, at least for now, that conveys the crux of what you want to say. Increasingly, there are opportunities to inject audio or video to relieve that burden of text.

While these opportunities existed in previous years and were discussed in earlier editions of this book, the pace of change has picked up so that the easy-to-use tools for instructors to produce audio and video are now more widespread and cheaper (if not free) than ever before. Also, many more students are able to access these audio and video communications than was previously the case. However, for most readers of this book, these non-text methods for communicating, providing feedback, and presenting are likely still secondary to the ubiquity of text-based communications.

The fact that the majority of online teaching is still done using the written word puts an inordinate emphasis on style, attitude, and intonation as they can be expressed in print. A sarcastic aside, a seemingly innocent joke, shorn of an apologetic smile or a moderating laugh, can seem cold or hostile to the student reading it on the screen. The occasional use of an emoji aside, none of the conventional ways of modifying ambiguous or ironic statements—the wink, the raised eyebrow, the shrug, and the smile—is available with online text. Thus an instructor communicating with the written word must pay particular attention to nuances.

In a physical classroom, moreover, you're always there to listen to your students or observe their interactions. Online, you're there only sporadically, at the times when you log on, whereas your students may post their comments at any time of day. These circumstances modify the instructional role you play, making you more a facilitator or moderator rather than only the expert from whom all knowledge flows. Indeed, online courses depend heavily on the participation of students. As an instructor, you need to step back a bit from the spotlight in order to allow the students to take a more active part. Perhaps you will intervene only when the flow of conversation strays too far off the mark or when you need to summarize the conversation in order to progress to another point.

Conversely, online participation is just as important to the student as it is to you. What makes the internet such an attractive medium—the ability to communicate instantly with anyone in the world—is what drives students to the internet rather than to a conventional classroom. If, when they log on to the course, all they can do is read the voluminous course notes you have posted there, they will soon become frustrated and drift away. And given your students' propensity to upload photos and videos, while keeping up a continuous stream of communication via text messaging, Twitter, Instagram, Facebook, instant messaging apps, using both text and voice-enabled chat, they are likely already acculturated to being active participants in the online world. Increasingly, students are comfortable (maybe more than you are) communicating and accessing information online, but it's good to keep in mind that this doesn't mean that they are sophisticated participants in an academic online setting or discerning consumers of content.

It's your responsibility to bear all this in mind when devising your course. You will fashion tasks and exercises that emphasize student collaboration and de-emphasize the traditional role of the instructor as the central figure in the pedagogical play but you will also try to provide the rules and protocols that will facilitate learning, and find ways to give students the benefit of your expertise and guidance.

This doesn't mean that an online syllabus should include only tasks that must be performed online: hunting for online material, for example, or linking to a host of other websites. In fact, such tasks can often prove counterproductive, requiring that students stay online an inordinate amount of time. Indeed, the sort of tasks you have your students perform need not, and perhaps should not, differ from what you would have them do on the ground. They still need to go to libraries to perform the functions of sound research, albeit many institutions provide databases and full-text resources online, and they still need to investigate, examine, and observe phenomena on their own. What's different is how they communicate what they have learned, how they talk to each other, and how you talk to them. A successful online course often includes challenging assignments that lead to publicly conducted discussions, moderated and guided by you. An online course will also find a meaningful way to incorporate the increasingly rich mix of resources available on the internet.

For instructors like Miriam Sharpe, who teach face to face but use the internet to augment the work in class, there's a somewhat different set of criteria. For these instructors, the internet may be a place to post information before class in order to inspire a meaningful in-class discussion. Or the information on the internet may help give students the proper context for a lecture, so that the lecture falls on well-informed ears rather than becoming a mere oration accompanied by the sound of pencils furiously scribbling notes (or the clicking of laptop keyboards, or fingers tapping on tablets, as the case may be).

Conversely, the online class site might be used to elucidate or elaborate a point that was brought up in class. Students may begin a group project in a face-to-face session, continue it online for a number of weeks, then return to present it on campus, integrating the two modes in a series of tightly woven transitions. Online may become the venue where students can comment, critique, or analyze material in a leisurely and thoughtful way, instead of having to contend with other students in impassioned face-to-face debates. Indeed, the online environment can provide a safe place for students who ordinarily might not chime in, too timid or shy to take part in discussions with those who are louder, more aggressive, or domineering. In this sense, using the internet as a means of communication can often provoke more thoughtful and reasoned discussions than might be possible in a classroom.

Later chapters will describe the options in more detail. Here, our point is straightforward.

Important! *There's no need to start from scratch to teach online. You can apply what you already know and add to it by using new tools and techniques adapted for the online environment.*

What about Support Personnel and Training?

It may have occurred to you that mastering new software and techniques is a task that ought to be handled by someone else—by computer support personnel, or instructional designers, for example, or by graduate student teaching assistants. On many campuses, however, neither the expertise nor the funds are available to provide the level of support each faculty member might like to have.

Most of the time, computer support personnel have to deal with problems concerning infrastructure, networks, and servers that shut down. When they respond to an individual faculty member, they're typically concerned with hardware or software problems: "I can't type the letter k on my keyboard"; "I can't download this video." Teaching assistants, for their part, may have more advanced computer skills than faculty members, but may not be familiar with the learning management system or other tools from the instructor perspective. Instructional designers and instructional technologists are often specially hired to assist instructors, but they are seldom numerous enough to replace all of faculty's own efforts.

Many instructors who have painstakingly acquired computer skills and familiarity with the internet may even feel intimidated by the increasing ease and frequency with which their students communicate via smartphones, socialize on social networking sites like Facebook, Instagram or Twitter, create and upload videos to YouTube, and, in effect, live comfortably with technology occupying a major portion of their daily life. Some instructors struggle to keep up with the ever-increasing number of technology tools available, while others worry about looking foolish to their students through a too "faddish" and superficial adoption of these tools. (Do your students even want you to "friend" them on Facebook or follow them on Twitter, Instagram, or other social media?)

Increasingly, online programs do offer ongoing support to their instructors. But even in these comparatively proactive programs, there's a limit to how much attention and help can be offered to each faculty member, particularly as the number of online courses continues to grow. Of course, instructors who aren't based on a campus have even fewer resources to help them troubleshoot problems.

While more prevalent than in the early years of online education, still scarce is the availability of reliable and effective training for online instructors. A hodgepodge of different workshops, brown-bag lunches, and self-paced online materials may be cobbled together to ease an instructor's progress, but there are still a great number of instructors who must learn on the job. Often this means that the first course you teach is beset with errors, miscues, and miscalculations, much as may have happened when you taught your first class face to face.

Even for those who enroll in a formal training course, the results can be disappointing. Some tend to betray the idiosyncrasies of the particular person who delivers the training while others may be taught by technical staff with little teaching experience of their own. Some tend to deal with the subject as if it were a phenomenon to be researched rather than a new set of skills to be mastered and employed. To make matters worse, training is often offered in a conventional classroom or lab setting, depriving faculty members of the experience of learning online or learning online in a real-life teaching situation, i.e., alone, at their own computer.

The situation isn't entirely bleak, however. Even if your institution doesn't provide much in the way of preparation for online teaching, there are some reliable training programs offered to the public, several of which are mentioned in Chapter 15. We will also discuss with you how you might network with other online instructors for mutual support and learning. In addition, the amount of technical know-how you need before you begin is less than you may suppose. Newcomers to online teaching are likely to exaggerate the computer and overall technical expertise required. Let's address that question directly.

● ● ● ● ●

Do You Have to Be a Computer Expert?

Instructors often wonder what qualifications—especially what level of technical computer skills—they need to consider teaching online. Do you have to be an expert or an advanced computer user? In other words, a "techie"? The answer is a resounding "no."

In terms of technical computer skills, an instructor needs little to start with. A very basic familiarity with computers and the internet will more than suffice. That means knowing how to do the following:

1. Set up folders and directories on a hard drive.

2. Use word-processing software properly (for instance, cut, copy, and paste; minimize and maximize windows; save files).

3. Handle email communications, including attachments.

4. Use a **web browser** such as Chrome, Safari, Internet Explorer, or Firefox to access the internet, including multimedia resources like YouTube, and to navigate between windows and tabs.

5. **Download** and **upload**: that is, retrieve a file from your institution's computer network or from the internet or learning management system and save it on your own computer, and having made changes or created a new document or image, be able to transmit it back to your online class site.

If you lack some of these skills, you can pick them up on campus or in online workshops. Once you're comfortable with these basic skills, you should, with experience, be able to build on them and become more skilled. Your main task will then be to learn to use the learning management system or other software tools with which your university expects you to teach. Most campuses will regularly offer training sessions or self-paced tutorials for instructors to learn the adopted tools. Because software may be regularly updated and new tools adopted, expect periodic retraining or the need to set aside some time for practice with technology.

With the advent of more user-friendly and menu-driven software, it is actually getting easier for instructors to learn to teach online. For example, it is no longer necessary for most instructors to learn HTML in order to format the text they post online because the advent of **WYSIWYG ("what you see is what you get")** editors that operate very much like word-processing software are increasingly built right into the software programs instructors use to teach.

Faculty of all ranks who are enthusiastic about the possibilities offered by online teaching—and who are willing to invest some time in learning new technology and methods for the sake of personal and professional growth—are good candidates for teaching online.

This raises a question we are often asked—what kind of people make the best online instructors? **Surprisingly, it is "people-oriented" people who make the best online instructors.** Though these people-oriented people may initially feel the most anxiety about teaching online, their desire to reach out to their students, their empathy and interest in others, and their urge to bridge communication gaps mean that they have the aptitude and motivation to become the very best online teachers.

Important! *"Techies" don't necessarily make the best online instructors. An interest in teaching should come first, technology second.*

What Can Teaching Online Do for You?

Beyond the case we have made for the greater flexibility and accessibility of online teaching, the rich and diverse world of resources that becomes available, and the fact that online learning is becoming more expected and even demanded by students, is there anything else that we might say to those of you who come to this book with one arm twisted behind your back, unconvinced of the desirability of teaching online? Although teaching online presents many challenges to the instructor, there are many more benefits to be gained from the experience. Let us highlight two major benefits you may not have considered.

Heightened Awareness of Your Teaching

Among instructors who have taught online, the advantage of the process that they most commonly express is that it makes them better teachers—not only online, but also in their face-to-face classes.

Traditionally, few of us in higher education have any training in teaching methods or instructional design. We learn chiefly from osmosis (being in a classroom), from mentoring by more experienced colleagues (if we're lucky), or through time spent as teaching assistants as a sort of apprenticeship in graduate school.

Teaching online heightens our awareness of what we're actually doing in the classroom. The interactions between our students and ourselves—which often consist of fleeting occasions in the on-campus classroom—are recorded for us online, available for our review and reflection. We also have the opportunity to observe and review how our students respond to our assignments and to track the growth of understanding or incomprehension as they respond to the lessons and activities we set in motion for their learning. Some learning software even may provide us with detailed data about the individual student's progress through the assigned activities.

This heightened awareness can be both illuminating and humbling. We find that the instructional design process becomes less implicit and more of a deliberate enterprise. Sometimes this leads us to make changes in the way we do things or to try out new approaches, not only in our online courses but in our on-campus classrooms as well.

As you reconsider your instructional methods, you may find that the rapid and flexible communication afforded by the internet fosters some creative new approaches. Isabel Simões de Carvalho, teaching mechanical engineering at the Instituto Superior de Engenharia in Lisbon, Portugal, began to use the online classroom to support her traditional face-to-face classes and soon found herself introducing entirely new types of learning activities, taking advantage of the way that face-to-face meetings and online activities could be paired to deepen immersion in a learning activity. She was surprised by the way students seemed to rise to the occasion—"a really interesting discovery was that by asking them to do quite a bit of challenging work, one can get students to more readily engage in learning and they even enjoy it!"

When you teach online, you, too, may experience that serendipitous moment when the possibilities of the medium and your course objectives suddenly come together. Grasp that moment and shape it to enliven and enrich your students' learning!

New Connections with the Wider World

A great fear among many instructors is that all human interaction online is inevitably superficial and that such a learning environment leads to more alienation between students and instructors, and less meaningful communication among colleagues.

Communication online isn't the same as in person, but it can be both effective and satisfying. It also brings us new opportunities to communicate with, and even to get to know, people we would have no other chance to meet—either because they live at a great distance from us or because their schedules wouldn't otherwise allow them to take our classes.

This is different in nature from the sometimes superficial or fleeting exchanges of social media in that we are engaged in extended and often very profound interactions online with students. At the risk of sounding heretical, we will venture the proposition that meeting online is sometimes the ideal way to get to know a student or colleague. The by-now-old joke goes, "On the internet, nobody knows you're a dog," and by the same token, nobody knows whether you're under twenty-one or over sixty-five years old, Latino or Asian, unless you choose to self-identify or post a current photo or video. Because communication online requires a great deal of "listening" it can be the very best way to get to know another's ideas and way of thinking without the distractions of often unacknowledged biases and preconceptions.

Teaching online does not preclude meeting face to face. Many instructors, including the authors of this book, arrange to meet online students at conferences. Online students will also network among themselves, carry on long correspondences, and sometimes meet in person. In fact, talking extensively with another online, observing that person's interaction with others, and perhaps collaborating on a project can often form the basis of a solid friendship.

New connections with distant colleges also become possible. An instructor residing in Missouri may teach for an institution based in New York, and a professor on leave from a college in California may teach a class from a temporary post in France. In this way, instructors are often able to continue their institutional associations with their former colleges after they have moved far away from the home campus site.

With online education, cross-cultural and international collaborations become possible, without the expense and difficult logistics of travel, allowing students from different lands to exchange ideas and work in concert on projects and topics of interest to both parties.

For those who teach blended courses, one benefit that will be immediately obvious is the greater number of students heard from in your class—in a face-to-face class of fifty students, an instructor is lucky to get the active participation of more than a small handful of students. Many more lack the confidence to speak up in the classroom, while others may nod off or distractedly text friends on their smartphones during the in-class time. Online, especially if you establish a participation requirement, you are likely to "hear" from nearly all your students. That shy student in the back row of your classroom might end up being the most loquacious or even most eloquent contributor to your online discussion forum.

Your Students Need You More than Ever

Students today are bombarded with an excess of information, communications and messages via photos, videos, and news delivered in short bursts of commentary. Increasingly, the sources of information are obscured and filtered through branded channels. Many people confuse the accessing of information with the process of learning. With everyone online a self-appointed authority, and so many apparent paths to learning available, critical thinking and discernment are more important than ever. Faculty are trained to be critical observers, questioners, curators, sense-makers, and mediators of content and communications. This aspect of our experience is more and more a valuable set of skills that can be brought to bear to assist our students. Students online are no less in need of our attention and concern than the student attending a traditional class on campus.

In the next chapter, we will begin preparing you for online teaching by showing you how to explore your institution's resources and make practical sense of what you find.

2

●●●●●

Scouting the Territory: Exploring Your Institution's Resources

In Chapter 1, you learned a bit about how online learning functions. Now you're ready to begin planning the online environment of your course.

But where should you start?

A good first step is to scout the territory in which you plan to operate—that is, explore the technological and administrative environment in your institution to ascertain what is possible and desirable to do. The tools an institution uses, the policies that might constrain or enable you, and the support it offers very much influence the choices you'll need to make. Before you sit down to sketch out your course, you must be certain that what you're planning can actually take place.

Colleges and other institutions, after all, don't exist in a vacuum. They have administrators, department heads, and computer support personnel, all of whom have budgets, agendas, and rivalries. Investments have been made (or are on the planning board) in computer hardware, software platforms, computer labs, maintenance, support, and instructor training. In addition, your academic program may stipulate that you use particular tools, templates, or approaches to create your online course and there may also be a set of guidelines or standards that govern the development of online courses on your campus. All of these factors, in one way or another, may affect the shape of the course you plan to teach.

Uncovering all this information probably isn't as formidable a task as it may seem. If you've been working at your institution for some time, you already know much of the information. What you don't know you can usually find out by visiting the institution's website or by scheduling a few informal interviews with your department head, chief administrator, or computer support person. Perhaps your institution has a special unit dedicated to helping faculty learn about teaching online or, at the very least, a unit that offers some technical training on using whatever software tools your institution may have adopted. If you know what questions to ask and what to look for in advance, you should be able to walk away with most of the information you need.

●●●●●

Questions to Ask about Your Institution's Resources

The following sections describe some useful questions you can ask in our equivalent of a walk-through survey.

What's Already in Place?

This question is the most important of all. In practice, you'll break it down into a number of subordinate queries, such as these:

- Does your institution already provide courses online, either as completely online or blended format?
- If so, which courses?
- Who teaches them? Is there anyone in your academic program already teaching an online or blended course?
- What software platform(s) or tools do they use?
- Who put the courses together? Are there special staff available to help with course design and development?
- How long did it take to put them together?
- Is there a policy in place for those who want to teach an online or blended course? Is there release time or payment available to faculty? How does one go about proposing to teach a new online course?
- Is there a set of standards for course design or expectations for teaching online or blended courses that faculty are expected to follow?

■ Are there any restrictions on how much of a course can be required to be accessed online, on whether synchronous tools can be used as well as asynchronous?

■ Is there any training in place for those who want to teach online? If so, who offers it—faculty development, academic departments, academic technology, instructional design units?

■ Is there an orientation to prepare students for online learning and technical staff to support them?

Once you find out about online courses already being taught at your institution, make an effort to contact other instructors and talk to them at length. Tell them what you plan to do and solicit their reactions. Find out what their experiences have been. Ask about potential pitfalls you ought to avoid. Talk to your administrator and any other gatekeepers to the process to find out about the applicable policies.

Information gained in this way is the most valuable you can collect. Not only will you learn first-hand what's going on, but you may, if you're lucky, forge a few strategic alliances with some of the pioneers or leaders of online teaching at your institution or even gain a mentor.

What Kind of Software Is Available at Your Institution to Run Online Courses?

It is easiest to work with the software that your institution has already made available—that way you have probable sources of technical support, and are least likely to propose using software that your students will have difficulty accessing. Some institutions offer the choice of more than one learning management software system to instructors while others are amenable to supporting additional tools and programs that an instructor might wish to use.

What Is the Profile of Student Users?

Imagine, for instance, that your university has an adequate network on campus, with a high-speed connection to the internet and perhaps subscribing to a variety of **cloud-based services** whereby software can be easily accessed via browser. But if a considerable number of your students live in rural areas where they are limited to dial-up access from off-campus, you won't want to create the type of course exercise in which they're required to go on extended searches online for material or information. Nor will you want to schedule a lot of synchronous chat sessions or include video resources when you know that the connectivity is tenuous. Your student body may also include military students or other workers who are restricted by firewalls that make it difficult for them to use any programs that require downloading to their own computers. The computer support units on campus or those in charge of online programs generally have information on how, when, and from where students are accessing online course sites and this information is valuable for your planning. You will also want to find out which library services or other student services, like tutoring, are available online.

If, on the other hand, there are adequate on-campus labs or laptop computing programs that can be accessed by students who will be on campus at regular periods to take a blended course, you may be able to use a certain amount of more sophisticated resources and software by taking advantage of and planning ahead for students to avail themselves of these campus-based computing resources.

What other facts do you know about the students taking online or blended classes at your institution? Do they have the same profile as those taking face-to-face courses on your campus, do they include a greater proportion of adult learners, or do they fall into the 18–22 year old age range? Do most work more than twenty hours per week and likely need the weekend to complete major assignments? Answers to such questions can help you better prepare and organize instruction for your students.

What Kind of Technical Support Does Your Institution Provide?

Technical support comes in various sizes and shapes. Some colleges have computer support personnel who are strictly network maintenance types, with no time for wild-eyed academics. Still other institutions have well-meaning but somewhat inexperienced administrators in charge who aren't thoroughly familiar with what an online or blended course can provide. The best have personnel who know their trade and are able to communicate what they know to faculty members.

So get to know your local technical support personnel or instructional technologist and ask the appropriate questions. Are there separate staff available to deal with the LMS issues versus multimedia tools or computing problems? Will the individuals assist you in an instructional media lab or come to your office to help you with such mundane details as improving a scanned graphic in Photoshop? Will they capture your on-campus lecture and then post it online for you? Or perhaps there are extensive online tutorials or workshops that you can avail yourself of to learn specific skills? Perhaps you don't even need to be on campus to get help because support staff can assist you completely at a distance via phone and screen sharing when necessary?

Will your students receive support and advice during office hours only or through a 24/7 tech help desk service? Or will you and your students be essentially on your own?

The answers to such questions will help you determine just how complex and demanding your online work can be, as well as which methods and software programs might best accomplish the task. Above all, you will want to avoid making choices that force you to be the main source of technical support for your students. While this was quite common during the early years of online teaching, it was never an ideal situation for an instructor to be spending a good deal of time doing something other than teaching.

You also need to consider where you yourself will be working most of the time. If you'll work mainly at home you will want to obtain reliable and unlimited high-speed internet service. Also, if you anticipate spending part of the class time away from your normal environment, make sure that you find out about arrangements for access when traveling. Check ahead with your hotel to find out if there is wireless (also known as **wifi**) or other high-speed connection service for your laptop or mobile device, or if there is a business center that offers reasonably priced internet access. Finally, you may be able to use a smartphone, that is, one that allows you to access the internet, class email, and your university websites, to keep up with your class during a trip of relatively short duration. Because the mobile versions of software may differ from those for the desktop, be sure to test out the mobile version of your class software before traveling to make sure you have all the requisite controls you will need.

What Kind of Instructor Training and Support Is Available?

Learning how to teach online is an ongoing process that includes not only mastering new skills, but also a cycle of review, reflection, and continual revision of one's online course. By finding out what's already available at your institution in terms of training and support in the technical aspects as well as the pedagogical approaches to teaching online, you can devise a plan for sustaining your efforts. As mentioned in Chapter 1, sometimes there is a hodgepodge of different resources on campus offered to instructors, while other institutions may have well-organized paths for attaining the expertise to teach online and the support personnel in place to guide you along the way.

Support for online teaching may be found in faculty development units, or it may be lodged within a special academic technology, online teaching and learning unit, or instructional design group. It may be scattered about in several different units on campus, or there may be centralized university system-wide resources available for training instructors on multiple campuses. Finally, your institutions may make funds available to support your learning from sources outside your institution.

Beyond the help you may find at your institution through workshops and contacting those colleagues who have pioneered such efforts, you may also find help in the online "global village." Now is the time for you to discover one of the great benefits of teaching on the internet—the incredible creativity and generosity of a vast percentage of its citizen proprietors. For the instructor like yourself, willing to take the technological plunge but wary of sinking too deep, there are numerous resources available to buoy you up. Some of these are fellow educators who are happy to share their experience, and some of these are internet resources that are free, or that cost so little that either you or your institution may decide they are affordable.

Even if you are fortunate enough to work at an institution that seemingly provides everything you and your students need for online or blended instruction, it is imperative for you to keep up with what is happening in the world of online education.

Academic institutions can be notoriously rigid. Having installed a learning management system, they often begin to act like poker players nursing a good hand. They tend to stand pat, not drawing any cards and not discarding any either. When new software becomes available or new technologies come into being, they tend to dismiss these developments as too expensive, too difficult to implement, not practicable, or not necessary "at the present time." Often they would like to be more flexible, but costs and staffing as well as the need to prioritize on behalf of the greatest number of students make them slow to respond to developments. There is also the fact that as the emergence of new technologies gathers momentum, it is often hard to tell which tools have long-term promise and which are simply a passing wave. As an instructor, you are most concerned with teaching and even if you are not much of a "techie" you are paradoxically more likely to spot a new tool that will have relevance for you than are many of your technical staff or administrators.

Important! No one knows everything, not even your technical support personnel. Even in a high-tech world, you have to do a little homework of your own to stay on top of new developments and be sure that those around you are on top of things as well.

One other word about living in even the highest tech institutional environment: No institution will ever be able to provide the level of support to which you may think you're entitled. The fact that your university has purchased fancy equipment and software doesn't mean that you won't have to learn some skills. Sooner or later, you'll have to learn how to use updated or new features of that learning management software, how to find and download graphics, and how to record an audio or video file, just as instructors once had to learn to use the overhead projector, tape recorder, or yes, how to navigate the internet.

In the following chapters you'll learn about these skills and how to master them or how to find some free or low-cost software tools that can enhance the resources available to you at your institution. We will also tell you how to find the training and resources you need to keep up with the dizzying pace of new technology.

Now, let's get started with the nitty-gritty of putting your course together.

II

Putting the Course Together

3

● ● ● ● ●

Course Design and Development

All right. You've taken the grand tour of your campus and are familiar with the lay of the land.

You're ready to get down to work, to convert your on-the-ground class to a blended one. You open your syllabus and stare at it. It reads just like it always did: It has your name, a description of the class goals and objectives, your grading policy, a schedule of your office hours, and a week-by-week listing of assignments and quizzes.

Nothing very exciting—just the same old stuff. You take your syllabus, which you wrote using a word-processing program, perhaps convert it into an HTML page (or ask instructional support staff to do so), and upload it to be displayed online. Or perhaps your learning management system requires you to do little more than fill in the text fields with the appropriate information. You upload an outline version for all the PowerPoint slides you will deliver in the lecture hall into the LMS content area, and even add a cheery welcoming announcement. You ask a colleague to have a look at your site. He tells you that it looks just fine. Once the course starts, your students, on the other hand, never look at it twice. Why should they, once they've printed out your syllabus, your slides outlines, and read your initial announcement? Everything for the online elements of your course appears to be optional while everything for the face-to-face portion remains mandatory. Students quickly discover that the online portion is neither vital to nor particularly instrumental to their success in the course.

Our point is this:

> **Important!** *Putting your course online means more than merely copying your content into an online format.*

Rather, converting your course to an online environment means adapting it to use some of the tools available in the new environment and taking advantage of some of the capabilities offered by online. If you teach a blended class (one that's both face to face and online), the conversion involves using online to complement what you do in class. If you're teaching exclusively online, it involves recasting your entire class into a new online format. And perhaps you are not converting your face-to-face class at all, but creating an entirely new course for delivery online. In any of these cases, if you want the resulting class to be a coherent and effective learning experience, you need to think about purposeful design and development of your course.

● ● ● ● ●

Some Examples of Course Design and Development

Let's have a look at some actual instructors who have gone through this process. Here are three different situations: a speech course delivered completely online, an Italian language and culture course delivered in hybrid format, and an engineering course that's a blend of face-to-face and online components.

A Speech Course Taught Entirely Online

Mary Jane Clerkin developed a speech course for delivery as a completely online course at Berkeley College. Clerkin had taught Oral Communication in a face-to-face delivery format for many years before developing the online version. The challenge as she saw it was to promote the same type of interaction, "the same give and take" in the online course as had always been present in the on-site version. Another concern she had was to establish a sense of community in the online class. Finally, she needed to find a way to demonstrate to students that it was not necessary to have a live, face-to-face audience apart from their classmates in order to learn to speak effectively.

While learning objectives and the core syllabus remained the same as in the on-site version, the use of technology was key to transforming this course for online delivery. Beyond the Blackboard learning management system used at Berkeley, there was a need for tools that could provide the essential elements of speech—voice and body language. While the course was almost entirely asynchronous, Clerkin also made limited use of a tool that allowed for both the instructor and students to speak to each other using their own voices in an asynchronous mode. Students were required to have use of a webcam along with their textbook so that they could see themselves as they presented and practiced until they were ready to post their speech for peer review in the Blackboard discussion forum. Clerkin noted that "the opportunity to practice and improve their delivery skills after viewing their videos makes a difference—they practice until the background, lighting, and delivery are to their satisfaction." She structured the course to provide three types of review. First, there was the self-review involved in the student perfecting the speech video before submitting it to the discussion forum. Second, there was the peer review in the discussion area, using a rubric created by Clerkin for this purpose. Finally, after each speech was presented, she emailed the student to provide individualized instructor feedback as well.

Mary Jane Clerkin viewed the asynchronous elements of the course as benefiting students in many ways, allowing for reflection before responding,

> *More thoughtful and comprehensive dialog is promoted and modeled by the professor. Online students can practice diction exercises and listen to themselves and their peers as they attempt exercises that promote good enunciation.*

She also expressed that the lack of a "live audience" was more than out-weighed by the communication and community that took place in her online class,

> *Every night our television newscasters inform us of the day's events. They are excellent public speakers, and their content and delivery is no less effective because their audience of millions of viewers is not personally present. So too, our students reach all of the members of the class no matter where they are located. Overall, this asynchronous speech course permits a heterogeneous group of students from different parts of the world to come together in a learning environment that encourages and facilitates active participation.*

A Blended Course in Italian Language and Culture

While one might think that teaching a language or speech class online or in blended format might constrain the ability of students to speak, listen, and practice their language and communication skills, the proliferation of new and easy-to-use social, media rich, and sharing tools are actually providing new opportunities for students to stretch themselves and have more in-depth learning experiences. So while many people have tended to focus on overcoming a perceived deficiency of real-time communication in comparison to the traditional classroom, by using these rich online resources and tools (often accessible via mobile devices), language learning, public speaking and other "live action" skills may actually be enhanced. When students can be asked to create and review videos of themselves and others, to annotate and provide audio commentary on media, or to create multimedia-enhanced stories, essays, and blogs or other lively demonstrations of what they have learned, instruction gains an added dimension.

Elda Buonanno is an innovative comparative literature instructor who was faced with numerous challenges in transforming her face-to-face Advanced Italian Conversation course for Iona College into a blended format. As is the case with other courses in which one must demonstrate speaking or presentation skills, finding the right multimedia tools was crucial to success. But given that this course also features an exploration of Italy through regional food, history, and culture, the ability to integrate the many resources available on the internet held the promise that a blended format might truly enrich the learning experience for her students.

In this blended format, the course met face to face once weekly for seventy-eight minutes and once a week online in a real-time session, using Blackboard Collaborate, with the rest of the activities carried out by students in an asynchronous online environment, using the Blackboard LMS (including its blog feature) and a host of other tools and resources. In the face-to-face portion, Buonanno spent the time introducing the content for the week, in discussion and in speaking and listening activities like role play or individual performance. She closed each face-to-face class session with a written self-assessment of what was learned by the student and a quick oral quiz, asking students how they would explain to another, in Italian, what they had learned. A real-time online class session was also conducted each week using Blackboard Collaborate, following a similar set of activities, but taking advantage of the online asynchronous environment to ask students to post materials and prepare work prior to the real-time online session.

Buonanno made use of audio and video tools not only to provide tutorials and instructions to students online but also asked her students for daily audio artifacts via Vocaroo.com, a free online audio recording program. Or, she asked them to work individually or in pairs to compile audio and video presentations using image annotation, blogs, or screencasting programs. For example, for a lesson on Italian food, students were asked to use a tool called Thinglink. com to annotate images they had collected and to demonstrate their knowledge of specific vocabulary for food ingredients and regional dishes. For a final project, students were given the option to present a multimedia presentation via Prezi (Prezi.com, presentation software), Glogster (glogster.com, multimedia posters), or Storybird (Storybird.com, a visual story building program).

The richness of materials available on the internet was fully exploited by carefully structured assignments. For example, students were asked to watch video interviews with Italian chefs and then discuss these online in real time as a way to assist them in identifying differences in regional cuisine. They were also asked to review multiple websites and videos on the subject of the Slow Food movement and work in pairs during the real-time online session to compare Slow and Fast food concepts, continuing this work with partners by putting together a Glogster poster presentation before the next face-to-face session. By using such internet resources, Buonanno felt that she was enabling students to

> *develop a wider and contextualized knowledge of the Italian culture … the more the contents were presented in a communicative and "real" contextualization, the more evident the learning progress becomes.*

In thinking back over the development of this course, Buonanno reflected,

> *The fact that I had already taught the course and had a previous knowledge of the contents and the feedback from my students, made the journey smoother and easier. The students*

responded well to the hybrid format and the obstacles of learning and practicing a language online were overcome by the audio that students had to produce.

There was a lot of material that I had to develop but due to the format of the course, the students had to produce more, and with more frequency than in the traditional course. The extra work involved did not seem to affect the interest or the pace of the class, and the students eventually realized that they had learned more and actually had a "better" learning experience through this format.

A Blended Mechanical Engineering Course

Isabel Simões de Carvalho is currently an Associate Professor with IPE–Military Institute of Portugal but previously taught an Energy Production and Management course at an engineering school, Instituto Superior de Engenharia, in Lisbon. Her students were in their first year of a mechanical engineering Master's degree program.

Her institution was committed to face-to-face instruction and generally followed a traditional lecture format, but Carvalho had been gradually adding web-enhanced approaches to the course, working on her own initiative. Not only did she incorporate appropriate topical resources available on the internet, but she also augmented her course, first by adding class email, and then an online discussion forum, and eventually adding elements that were provided with true learning management software.

Her class evolved into a true blended class only through trial and error. Initially, in introducing email and discussion forums, she found herself swamped by the extra work involved in responding to students outside the face-to-face class (F2F) meetings.

I remember thinking "what did I get myself into?" Time management was really an issue what with trying to read all the messages and get back to the students. So I also started to provide some feedback at F2F. This and other "small" issues led me to recognize the power of delivering a blended course.

The students in the classes responded enthusiastically to the addition of this online activity, but she began to realize that merely adding online elements was not sufficient, and that what was needed was a true redesign of her course to effectively blend and integrate face-to-face and online elements.

> *I began to try different structured activities. A more effective integration of the F2F with the online became an objective. I worked a lot of different assessment formulas and tried them for a couple of semesters. This was a challenge!*
>
> *I started to take some time at the beginning of the course to explain to students the objectives of such a teaching and learning methodology. This has proven to be important in ensuring their engagement and success in the course.*

Carvalho had a strong philosophical bent toward active learning approaches. Based on her past experimentation, she evolved a set of assignments that seem to work well within this framework. Among these were an individual assignment that required students to perform a "home energy audit," and a group assignment that required students to collaborate online and present their final projects in the face-to-face classroom.

Carvalho used the online discussion for a number of purposes. For example, case studies were presented in the online forum as part of the sharing of current events related to class topics. After field trips and guest speakers, students were asked to reflect on what they learned by posting in the discussion forum. For another assignment, each group was asked to post a peer review of two other groups' presentations.

She began to realize that she could encourage attendance in the face-to-face meetings and focus attention on lectures or other content delivered in that format by introducing online activities that could not easily be accomplished without experience of those face-to-face activities.

Carvalho noted that many of her students simply were not used to the types of methods she had implemented. Therefore, not only did she need to explain how the class operated, she also needed to invest quite a bit of time in the first weeks of each class, carefully facilitating online discussions and heightening awareness of the connections between face-to-face and online components of the course.

> *The first 4 to 5 weeks required a lot of effort from my side to explain (better even, exemplify) how it worked. These first weeks*

I used a lot of visual information and concentrated on the most "appealing" subjects that usually promote a lot of debate and student participation. Fora moderation was quite time consuming during this period. There was a need to start things moving and I needed to be "present" quite often both to give them examples and to promote motivation with positive and encouraging messages. After this period, the process seemed to feed itself and my work online did decrease.

In order to guide students and clarify what is expected of them for each task, she introduced a series of rubrics that detailed what students needed to do in order to fulfill the terms of each assignment. Her approach to assessment gradually became more complex, as she sought to make students more self-directed in their education. By providing a variety of different activities to accomplish the same learning objectives, she created a kind of assessment matrix that allowed students more choice in how they approached learning.

Isabel gradually adopted new methods to communicate with her students. For example, she began to regularly send text messages to student cell phones to provide reminders about upcoming due dates and class events.

She found some solid formulas for success and accumulated some well-tested methods in her repertoire, permitting her to simply apply these structured course elements each time she taught. However, Carvalho viewed her course as a constantly evolving project as she challenged herself to find new ways to promote deeper learning. As she faced each new group of students who brought their own dynamic to the class, she tried new activities and researched new approaches, trying to "improve and adapt to the needs of each specific group of students."

● ● ● ● ●

Initial Steps in Course Design and Development

Now that you've had a look at these examples that introduce you to the process of converting or designing a new course, you're probably wondering where to begin.

Take a look at the resources you have available to you. In addition to your syllabus, you probably have some goals and objectives, a list of assignments, required readings, quizzes, papers, and grading policies. Do you also have lecture notes that you created using a word-processing program? PowerPoint slides, overheads, or slide transparencies that you regularly show to your class? Audio or video materials? Some internet-resource sites that you consider essential for the course? All of those elements comprise the potential raw material you'll use to convert your course to one that you can teach online.

It would seem at first glance that the essential task to be accomplished is to convert these materials into digital files to be posted on the internet. But the fact that someone has transformed all of his or her lectures into electronic files and transferred graphics to web pages doesn't mean that a course has been converted. In fact, this isn't even the first step! It's only the mechanical aspect of the job. We'll discuss some of the mechanics further in later chapters, but here we want to focus on more basic considerations.

As our three scenarios demonstrate, a strict translation of what you normally do on the ground into the online environment isn't always desirable. Like the art of translation, course conversion should not merely strive for a word-for-word equivalency, but should allow the new language of communication to be fully exploited. Just as there are some things one can say only in Chinese or Spanish, there are new and different forms of expression that can be attempted in the online medium. Although the communication of content and the achievement of course objectives will naturally be the aim of any course conversion process, there's a great deal more to be gained than a mere transfer from one medium into another.

Important! *If you simply post your lectures and syllabus on the internet, you haven't necessarily created a viable tool for your students. The missing element here is instructional design.*

Without necessarily becoming an expert in instructional design principles, you need to become aware of what you normally do to create a course for the face-to-face classroom and then think about applying these steps to the online course. The following sections provide a simplified view of this process, along with some additional elements that apply to the online environment.

In approaching the design and development of your course, the idea of "backward design" promoted by Wiggins & McTighe in *Understanding by Design* (1998) might prove a helpful concept—it means to design your course or each unit or lesson with the "end" in mind. They described the three necessary stages of design as

1. Identify desired results
2. Determine acceptable evidence
3. Plan learning experiences and instruction

In other words, start with your learning outcomes and what you hope students will learn, then determine what learning activities are needed for students to arrive at those results and what evidence of student learning you would need to assess those results. Wiggins & McTighe decried a focus on planning learning activities without full consideration of the purpose of those activities and the tendency for secondary and higher education instructors to unduly focus on "coverage"—what the teacher will be able to get students through in however many weeks the course lasts.

It's important to plot out the basic structure of a course before building it out, whether face to face (F2F), blended, or online. But this takes on special importance in the case of an online course because everything in an online course must be structured and apparent to the learners. Building out your online course as you are teaching it is not an approach that results in a well-integrated and cohesive learning experience, and it is also a method that is sure to contribute to the stress of teaching online.

Perhaps you will be working with an instructional designer to create your course. In Chapter 4, we will provide some tips on how instructors and designers can achieve a smooth and productive relationship but even if you are lucky enough to have support from designers or other personnel, it makes sense for you to familiarize yourself with the whole process and to think deeply about what you are trying to achieve with the course. After all, you probably know your existing course better than anyone else, and even if it is a new course, you will still want to tap into the teaching expertise you possess to help shape the course.

Here we will look at three elements of converting to or creating an online course: the process of analysis, course goals and learning objectives, and design.

Analysis

You'll need to have some idea of whom your course is for, what role it is to play in the program curriculum, what the basic student learning outcomes are, and what resources will be available to you and your students. Here are some additional questions you might want to ask, building on some of the issues discussed in Chapter 2:

1. Who is your student audience? For example, is this course for 20 or 120 students? Is the course for beginners or advanced students? For majors or primarily non-majors? What is the average age range of students and the percentage of working adults? Are all students local or do some reside at a considerable distance?

2. Will new students have an orientation to online prior to taking your course? How much information will you need to provide to manage expectations?

3. What types of materials must be made available to students only online? For example, will any on-campus activities or labs be available? Or must all class activities be delivered online?

4. What support will you have available to assist you in creating online course materials?

5. Is there an established suite of tools or learning management software available to house your course, or will you have to create everything on your own web pages or use free resource sites?

Course Goals and Learning Objectives/ Outcomes

You are probably familiar with your academic program level goals and objectives and know that these broad goals and objectives are meant to be realized through the goals and objectives of the many individual courses that comprise a program. Here we will focus only on what are known as "course level" goals and objectives.

The difference between goals and objectives is basically the difference between things that can be known but not easily measured and those that can be demonstrated! So a goal in Ancient World History 101 may be for students to attain a good grasp of the cultures, forces, and events that helped shape the ancient world but a more precise objective would be for a student "to identify the causes of the decline of the Roman Empire." Goals, like purposes, set the parameters of what we expect to gain from the learning experience, but objectives tell us how we will be able to know, not merely intuit, whether or not a student has learned. Learning objectives are also referred to as learning outcomes and they are usually expressed as expected outcomes—what we can expect students to be able to do as a result of learning. (Even though there are some differences in the meaning of these two terms—objectives and outcomes—we will use them interchangeably in our discussion in this chapter to mean the specific and observable evidence of student learning.)

On some campuses, goals are now being expressed as **competencies**. Competencies are usually more general than objectives/outcomes and often relate to skill or knowledge required for a job or profession. (David Gosselin of the University of Nebraska-Lincoln has provided a helpful definition and examples of the differences between outcomes and competencies at http://serc.carleton.edu/integrate/programs/workforceneeds/competencies_and_LO.html).

Perhaps you are asking "why do we need to write/take note of learning objectives? No one even pays attention to them."

From the point of view of the instructor engaged in the process of designing and developing a course, we would say that paying attention to course level learning objectives keeps you focused on what is to be taught, what is to be learned, and helps you in planning. (At the very least, it prevents you from going off on a tangent. However clever, amazing, and interesting that reading, resource, or activity may be, if it doesn't really serve a purpose in the course, you may want to save it for another, more appropriate occasion.) From the point of view of the students, it tells them what is expected of them and explains why in the world they are being asked to do X and Y.

You may have already been given the learning objectives or expected outcomes for your course from your academic department or institution. But if you have not, we suggest that you take the time to articulate how it is you will be able to recognize that students have learned what you want them to learn.

For each unit and objective of the course, jot down some corresponding readings, activities, and assessments that you are planning to use for students to accomplish that objective. For example, unit 2 may cover the decline of the Roman Empire. Perhaps your objective is for students "to evaluate the different theories concerning the decline of the Roman Empire." This might be achieved by having students stage a debate; individual projects based on research into each theory, then presented in the discussion forum and critiqued by students; or writing an essay on the exam asking students to compare and contrast two theories. Or you might assign a combination of these activities.

Many instructors have no difficulty expressing their goals for the class but find it very frustrating to write learning objectives, especially if asked to do so on the sub-unit or activity level. We would discourage instructors from tasking themselves to write learning objectives for every activity, and instead concentrate on the overall course objectives and how they can be applied for one or more units of the class. A particular set of learning objectives related to research skills might be satisfied by a major project, while an objective involving critical thinking and writing might apply to several assignments distributed over a number of different units or modules of the course. And while an objective should not be overly broad, it is not beneficial for it to be too picayune either ("the student will be able to name all the Roman emperors"). The words know, learn, and understand belong in the realm of goals and if you can avoid using such terms when writing objectives, you are well on your way to accomplishing the task. Another tip is to keep overall course learning objectives to no more than a dozen—this will keep you focused on the essentials.

One approach for coming up with learning objectives we have found that is easy to use and apply for most instructors is that based on **Bloom's Taxonomy**, a hierarchical system of classifying different levels of thinking. Bloom's Taxonomy for the cognitive domain is familiar to K–12 educators as well as instructional designers as a hierarchical classification of learning objectives and the verbs that correspond to each task level. There are many charts and graphic representations of Bloom's Taxonomy. (See the Guide to Resources for some of these.)

Table 3.1 is a simplified version of these correspondence charts, showing sample verbs for writing learning objectives, and some types of assignments that students might be expected to produce.

A more recent version of Bloom's Taxonomy relabels these levels as Remembering, Understanding, Applying, and Analyzing, and swaps the two top levels so that Creating is at the top, with Evaluating just underneath. (See http://edorigami.wikispaces. com/#Bloom's Taxonomy for some nice graphic representations

Table 3.1 Bloom's Taxonomy

Domains	Sample Verbs for Writing Learning Objectives	Sample Assignments
Knowledge or Remembering	Recall, tell, show, match, list, label, define, cite, name, brainstorm	Test, worksheet, quiz, labeling, table
Comprehension	Compare, contrast, demonstrate, identify, report, outline, summarize, review, explain, catalog	Outline, summary, test, identifications, review, compare-and-contrast exercise
Application	Develop, organize, use, select, model, choose, construct, translate, experiment, illustrate	Report, diagram, graph, illustration, project, video, case study, journal
Analysis	Analyze, categorize, classify, distinguish, dissect, examine, differentiate, calculate, solve, arrange	Model, report, project, solution, debates, case-study solution
Synthesis	Combine, compose, solve, formulate, adapt, develop, create, validate, design	Article, report, essay, experiment, composition, audio or video product, drawing, graph, design
Evaluation	Assess, evaluate, determine, measure, select, defend, score, rank, discriminate, judge, justify, conclude, recommend	Peer and self-evaluations, chart, critique

of the old and new versions.) Nevertheless, the verbs associated with these levels remain much the same.

Sharon Guan, an experienced instructional designer and Director of Faculty Instructional Technology Services at DePaul University, advises that faculty should not become overly concerned with writing ever more precise objectives. She notes that:

> Sometimes objectives are very subtle in the faculty's mind and if a faculty member has no designer to work with, that faculty member should just ask herself, "What do you want students to be able to do as a result of this class and how would you know that students have learned or know how to do this?"

She also cautions that it is possible for someone to write very precise learning objectives and yet have a poorly designed course!

It is necessary to provide follow-through from articulating those learning objectives to devising the actual instructional activities so that the latter align with the former, as we discuss in the next section on design.

If you are interested in the topic of learning objectives, or want to learn how to write better objectives, there are some selected websites under the Course Design, Instructional Design category in the Guide to Resources section of this book.

Important! Don't drive yourself crazy trying to write ever more precise learning objectives—the main point is to express as clearly and plainly as possible what it is you want students to learn and how they can best demonstrate that they have learned it.

If you are teaching a course for which the learning objectives have already been set, then you can focus on how to design learning activities that will be in alignment with those objectives. And you can refer to Bloom's Taxonomy to clearly locate the level or way of knowing in which that objective is grounded. This will help you design the most appropriate way of fulfilling that learning objective.

Design

"Design" really means the shape and direction you want your course to take. It means purposefully planning the course, rather than simply letting it happen. In thinking about the design of your course, you need to consider your course objectives, the preferred teaching strategies and approaches to the material that you want to preserve, and any new approaches you would like to try in the online environment. Always keep in mind two design principles: Make sure that your course objectives are defined in terms of the learning outcomes that you want students to be able to demonstrate and that you align all activities, assignments, and assessments with those expected learning outcomes. Even if you have never consciously planned all these aspects of a face-to-face course, as an experienced instructor, you likely have an internal guidance system that has directed you in making instructional choices over these many years. So feel confident that you can do the same thing now, but in a more explicit fashion.

Here are some of the types of questions to ask yourself.

1. If you are designing a blended course, how can you best take advantage of each format, online and face to face? Are there some activities that must take place face to face, or do you have the option of reenvisioning how each activity will be carried out? How will you ensure that the face-to-face and online elements are complementary, reinforcing, and integrated? (See Chapter 13 for more in-depth considerations for blended courses.)

2. Is collaborative work among students and/or peer review appropriate or desirable?

3. What are the best ways to assess your students in the context of your course or discipline?

   a. Portfolios?

   b. Multiple-choice quizzes? Self-assessment exams or graded exams?

   c. Essays, journaling, or research papers?

   d. Fieldwork reports or other experiential learning documentation?

   e. Individual projects and presentations?

4. What will be the balance of student-centered versus instructor-led activities? Will you mainly facilitate discussion and research, or does the course have a strong component of lecturing and instructor commentary as well?

5. How central is discussion or student presentation to achieving the objectives of the course? Do you want to take advantage of the many new tools that would allow students to generate content in text, audio, or video?

6. What are your preferred methods of presenting content?

   a. Do you have graphics or slides that you want to utilize in some way?

   b. Do you use lecture notes or commentary and will these be converted or substantially revamped?

   c. Is it important for you to accommodate as many different approaches (visual, auditory, project based, collaborative) to learning as possible?

7. How might your available resources affect the implementation of your design?

   a. Do you have online testing capabilities? If so, would these be mainly for self-assessment or do they possess the necessary security for graded tests?

   b. What forms of communication are options—for example, do you have a discussion board, a chat or other synchronous software?

   c. Is audio or video an option for presentation or activities in your online classroom and do you have the necessary tools to create such media? Will you need some training or support?

Language and speech courses, as demonstrated by the case studies presented at the beginning of this chapter, present a number of unique challenges when delivered solely online. Yet, for those teaching these types of courses, there are luckily more and more software options available, both within the learning management software or outside it. The ubiquity of recorders in the many devices we own, the availability of video chat, as well as sophisticated "language lab" software by textbook publishers present a growing number of ways to allow students to communicate orally as well as through video.

Perhaps this is the time to revisit whether a direct "translation" is either possible or desirable. Say that you have PowerPoint slides with lots of text on them. These probably won't translate very well to an online setting except as a framework for notes, although simple figures and images may be directly convertible. But look at the other side of the question as well: Do you really want to replicate the combination of lecture and slides that you've always used, or would it be possible to consider some new combination of presentation methods? For example, when you deliver a PowerPoint in class, unless you are just reading off the slides, you are likely "filling in" the contextual information as well as adding commentary to enhance your slides. Delivered as just a stack of slides online, such slides are now devoid of much interest. But by trying a new approach such as narrating your slides as part of a screencast video (see Chapter 9 for more ideas on creating content), you might find that students will actually pay attention to your content!

Important! *The move to an online format offers you opportunities to try out new methods and approaches. Preserving the quality of your course need not mean finding an exact translation of what you've always done in the past.*

● ● ● ● ●

Rubrics and Guidelines for Online Course Design

There are a number of systems that have been developed to guide and evaluate quality design in online courses. While some of these are intended for use only within a particular network of institutions, others have been aimed at general standards which can be adopted by any institution and then supplemented with other criteria specific to that institution. These systems can be used both to guide the design of an online course and to evaluate the quality, and if your institution does not have its own rubric or guidelines for online course design, you might find it worthwhile to consult one of the following considered here. Not all rubrics include criteria that apply to the course teaching and learning stage, but all include elements related to the design phase.

The Illinois Online Network's **Quality Online Course Initiative** (QOCI) rubric (www.ion.uillinois.edu/initiatives/qoci/index.asp) comprises six main areas: instructional design; communication, interaction, and collaboration; student evaluation and assessment; learner support and resources; web design; and course evaluation. The checklist under instructional design includes such aspects as whether content is sequenced and structured, whether information is chunked, and whether course objectives are clearly presented and explicated.

California State University, Chico has its **Rubric for Online Instruction** (www.csuchico.edu/eoi/the_rubric.shtml) which is designed to be used as a guide for course design as well as a set of evaluation criteria. The rubric is organized into six categories: Learner Support and Resources; Online Organization and Design; Instructional Design and Delivery; Assessment and Evaluation of Student Learning; Innovative Teaching with Technology; and Faculty Use of Student Feedback.

The **open SUNY COTE Quality Review (OSCQR) Rubric** was developed by Open SUNY Center for Online Teaching Excellence (COTE) to address instructional design and accessibility of online courses.

The Illinois, Chico, and Open SUNY rubrics all bear a Creative Commons license allowing free educational use by providing attribution.

Quality Matters™ began as a project with MarylandOnline and has grown into a widely adopted system for design and evaluation of online courses as well as a sophisticated training and peer-review program. The Quality Matters™ rubric contains forty elements categorized into eight major standards: Course Overview and Introduction; Learning Objectives; Assessment and Measurement; Resources and Materials; Learner Engagement; Course Technology; Learner Support; and Accessibility. You can have a look at a simplified version of their rubric at https://www.quality-matters.org/ by registering on their site. The rubric is available to subscribing institutions or individuals.

Many institutions use the Quality Matters™ standards to guide their course design and others have made this rubric part of a larger system, based on their institutional needs and resources. For example, at the College of Arts and Sciences at Seton Hall University, Senior Instructional Designer Renee Cicchino explained that they developed an online course template built upon the Quality Matters™ rubric to serve as the foundation for faculty developing online courses. She describes how this became included in the course development process:

> *Before development occurs, faculty meet with the Quality Matters™ certified reviewer and their instructional designer to discuss the elements of the rubric and create a project plan and timeline for deliverables to ensure that the course is completed on time. Once development has been completed, the course is reviewed, feedback and recommendations are given to the faculty and instructional designer for review and if need be, for revision. Our online course template includes sample grading rubrics for discussion postings, sample participation requirements, as well as minimum technology requirements and tutorials. The template is populated with materials, documents, and samples that are updated on a regular basis. An exemplar course is available for new faculty course developers to use as a*

reference. Faculty are enrolled as students so they can experience the course from the student perspective.

If your institution or program does not have a set of guidelines for you to follow, we strongly recommend using one of the free rubrics and set of guidelines included here as a checklist as you design and develop your course. At the very least, you may find that these resources serve to broaden your thinking about the course design process.

●●●●●

Other Design Considerations

Universal Design and Accessibility

While many still think in terms of accessibility factors for online content solely as a way to accommodate students with hearing or vision disabilities, it is perhaps a more advantageous approach to think in terms of "universal design in learning (UDL)." Universal design in learning means to design so that course content and instructional activities can be utilized by the greatest number of students to the greatest extent possible without having to make special adaptations. Additionally, universal design for learning principles are informed by the idea of providing multiple paths, perspectives, and approaches to learning. For example, video captions not only allow visually impaired students to access the video, but also help students who may find it is easier to absorb the contents of video when they are able to review the transcript of what is said. Allowing for some judicious choices in how an assignment might be fulfilled—for example, oral delivery of a speech vs. writing a paper—can also help to engage greater numbers of students.

From the outset as you begin designing your online course it is best to create content so that it is easily readable by eyes and screen reading software for the visually impaired, also keeping in mind how you might provide logical alternative ways to process content. Some very basic tips are:

■ create documents using 12-point font and use Styles to ensure consistency and ease of scanning by students using screen readers;

- create text descriptions (alt-text) for all images;
- create captions or transcripts for all video and audio files;
- create meaningful titles or descriptions for all hyperlinks;
- test out all external sites and tools to ensure they are accessible. Be prepared to provide alternate sites or assignments when they are not accessible to all.

While we are not suggesting you become an expert on all the details of universal design and we understand that you may have instructional technology staff who can assist you in making sure your online or hybrid course is compatible with universal design principles and is accessible, we do recommend that you educate yourself in a general way about universal design (such as the tips provided above) so that you a) do not waste time having to redo or undo your work, b) can use your expertise in teaching to devise the most skillful and beneficial approaches to learning for your students.

There are some easy to use and easy to understand websites to consult before you embark upon course design. For a quick overview and some guides, see the Colorado State University site on

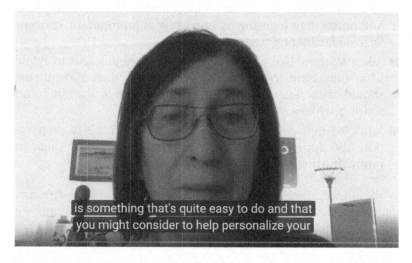

is something that's quite easy to do and that you might consider to help personalize your

Figure 3.1 Miriam Sharpe, our physics instructor, makes an introductory video to show her colleagues how easily it's done, recording with her iPad, then uploading her video to YouTube and using their Transcript Synchronization feature to add captions.

UDL at http://accessproject.colostate.edu/udl/ or the quick guides and tutorials for faculty at CUNY School of Professional Studies at https://spsfaculty.commons.gc.cuny.edu/accessibility/.

For more information, and to better understand UDL, check out the CAST site for UDL guidelines at www.udlcenter.org/aboutudl/udlguidelines_theorypractice.

The above site itself provides a good example of how information can be presented and apprehended in a variety of different ways.

Adult Learners

If your students are mostly working adults, it's a good idea to incorporate some key adult learning principles, not only into the design of learning activities, but also to factor these into your approach to communicating and providing feedback to your students. Perhaps most important to keep in mind are that:

■ Adult learners tend to be self-directed and independent, even as they need guidance, examples, and feedback from instructor and peers in order to progress. Organize your course to provide adequate feedback intervals, opportunities to share with peers, and rather than focusing on imparting of information, concentrate on facilitating student discovery.

■ Adult learners like to draw on their experience and to relate what they learn to real-world applications, thus assignments should allow for reflection, application, active learning, and sharing of ideas with others.

■ Adult learners come to the class with varied levels of preparation and appreciate just-in-time resources to assist them in improving their skills or background knowledge.

While these principles may be beneficially implemented in any college class, they are particularly valuable when your students are adult learners.

Scaffolding

To **scaffold** an assignment or assignments means to incrementally arrange the tasks (or a series of assignments) so as to allow students to gradually build on their knowledge and skills and to provide the necessary support resources at each stage. For example, a major research paper can be scaffolded into a series of smaller assignments—selecting a topic, creating an outline, writing a review of the literature, and producing a first draft before finalizing the paper. As part of this scaffolding, provide guidelines, examples of exemplary work as appropriate, and allow sufficient time for instructor feedback and questions so that students may become more skillful with each task and incorporate what they have learned throughout the course into their final work. Scaffolding is an effective method for nearly any subject matter and by breaking down a major task into smaller incremental steps, can even be a way to demonstrate the proper procedural approach in a particular discipline.

Low-Stakes Assignments

A low-stakes assignment is one that is ungraded or comprising a relatively low percentage of the grade. Low-stakes assignments are valuable ways to build confidence and can be the first small tasks in a scaffolded series of assignments, worth no more than 1–10 percent of a grade. As they often correspond to the lower levels on Bloom's Taxonomy, they can provide a foundation for higher-level thinking. When they serve to reinforce memory of facts or help in retention of basic principles, they can lay the groundwork for more complex tasks. Low-stakes assignments can be almost any type of assessment, but see the later section of this chapter on low-stakes testing.

●●●●●

Course Development

The development stage involves the actual creation of a syllabus, class schedule, content, and exams, as well as the fleshing out of the learning activities the class will undertake. Having assembled your materials and analyzed the needs of your class, with your course objectives and basic design considerations in mind, it's now time to make a few decisions about what you're going to do.

Some Help in Getting Organized

Even before you begin to create your syllabus, you should draft the course goals and objectives along with a general outline of the major units of your course and their topics. In some cases, you may want to follow the order of your main required textbook, while in others you may have more freedom to organize the units.

Some institutions supply their instructors with course planning tables or forms, but it is easy to create one on your own. And you really do need one! There is an enormous amount of detail involved in planning an online course and it is difficult to try to juggle it just in one's head.

A basic table should include columns and rows to list your course objectives, each weekly unit or module of the course, major content (main readings, instructor presentations, web resources), types of interaction and activities (discussions, group work, blogging, weekly email or announcement, etc.), and any major assignments and exams that you already know about at this point. For those teaching a blended course, the template should specify what is to be accomplished online and what is to be done in the face-to-face classroom, and stipulate if these need to be done in a particular order. Such a simple template as this can help supply the basic building blocks you need to create your syllabus and to actually build out your course.

Table 3.2 is an example of this type of simple planning template for a unit of a course on Cultural History of Ancient Rome.

One can add a column for a timeline of development, and for those developing a course with the assistance of others, the roles played by each person and any due dates can be indicated as well. If there are particular skill attainment objectives that need to be embedded throughout the course, one might add a column; see the Guide to Resources section of this book for links to some course design and development planning charts from a variety of institutions.

The instructional sequence of activities is something that you need to consider when planning your units. *Sequencing* means to arrange your assignments and activities into a logical order that will allow students to attain the learning objectives. For example, students will read the text and the instructor commentary prior to discussing all topics in an asynchronous forum prior to writing a

Table 3.2 Example of Simple Course-Planning Template

Course Objectives and Targeted Skills as Applied to a Unit and Time Period	Instructor-Generated Content, Communications, and Feedback	Class Interaction and Activities	Readings, Web Resources	Assessments—Graded Assignments, Exams, Projects, etc.
Unit 3: Age of Augustus (time span: four weeks)	Audio lecturette and text transcript providing commentary on historical, social, and cultural aspects of Augustan Rome—in three fifteen-minute segments	Discussion in weekly forum based on readings and resources	Textbook, pp. 12–65 Electronic full-text articles on Augustan society	Participation credit for weekly discussion according to rubric
Course Objectives that apply to this unit: 1. Identify key historical events and persons of the period	Weekly announcements in the online classroom; biweekly reminder emails and text messages; weekly office hours via chat	One weekly discussion involving debate on social or political issue of the period, with students assigned to argue a particular position	Web resource on literature of the period focusing on primary texts: Ovid, Virgil, and Horace	Short essay based on questions related to readings from either Ovid, Virgil, or Horace
2. Analyze the social and political framework of the period	Feedback in the form of comments and follow-up questions in the weekly discussion	Formation of study groups and initial organizational meeting; group creates outline in wiki		Short online self-assessment quiz on key events, dates, and persons—students get credit for taking quiz
3. Critique representative works of literature from this period	Automated feedback preloaded by instructor for self-assessment quiz			
Targeted skills: Critical thinking, essay writing	Individual feedback from instructor on short essay			

reflective essay—all steps but the last to take place in Week 2 of the course with the essay due at the end of Week 3. While this sequencing is something you naturally do when planning a face-to-face course, it requires a bit more forethought in the case of an online or blended class. Whether your units comprise one week or several, you will need to work out the sequence in terms of weekly units, because that is how students approach an asynchronous online class and the week remains the basic building block of an online syllabus, as explained in Chapter 5. So, if your units are each of multiple weeks, you will want to further break down your planning template by weeks, either by adding columns to the above sort of template or simply transferring that task to your creation of the syllabus schedule to nail this down.

The content and activities in most college classes can probably be divided into a few large categories:

■ *Instructor-generated content and presentation.* Typically this includes lectures, simulations, charts, and graphs, as well as PowerPoint, Prezi, or the creation of audio or video files.

■ *External content.* Textbook or other assigned readings (hard copy or increasingly ebooks, online articles), video or audio resources, library and internet-accessed content. Guest lecturers may also be included in this category.

■ *Discussion/interaction/communications.* Small-group, guided discussion sections run by teaching assistants are a common format for discussion in large classes. So are question-and-answer sessions as adjuncts to lectures, labs, and exams. In seminars, instructor presentation and discussion are often combined during one class session.

■ *Group-oriented work and student-created content.* Collaborative, cooperative, and other peer activities are included here. These might include a group project, peer-reviewed compositions, journals, and an independent project presented to the entire class.

■ *Research.* Research may be conducted either by individuals or in groups. A separate category may be carved from research to encompass practical applications, experiments, fieldwork, interviews, apprenticeships and other forms of experiential learning.

■ *Assessment.* Assessment activities typically involve exams, essays, and projects; all graded assignments; peer-based strategies; portfolios that combine different types of work; and evaluation and credit for participation. Rubrics serve to guide students as they undertake an assignment as well as provide the basis for grading that assignment.

Let's look at some of the factors you need to consider in converting these various types of course activities to an online format.

● ● ● ● ●

Instructor-Generated Content and Presentation: Lectures and Commentary

Lectures and commentary are probably the most common method of presenting content in a traditional college classroom. Often they're accompanied by slides, blackboard/whiteboard writings, or computer-assisted PowerPoint presentations.

To translate this type of activity into an online environment, you can use several different online formats alone or in combination. Here are some notes on these possibilities, along with their advantages and disadvantages.

Text

Text in the form of web pages or PDFs or other documents or a blog format is still a logical choice for converting lecture materials. Compared to a conventional lecture, text on a web page or online document has the advantage that students can copy the materials and make their own notes; in addition, they have more time to reflect on what you've said.

The main pitfall here is trying to transcribe your speech without taking into consideration that the lecture will be read, not listened to. You don't want to create documents that are tediously formal or that appear as overly long blocks of text when viewed online.

Also take into consideration the readability level of your lectures and commentary—make sure your text is appropriate for the student audience in regard to level of course offering, and the expected proficiency that students will bring to the subject. If you only have experience giving informal lectures to your students in the face-to-face classroom, give your written lectures a bit more scrutiny. Without your voice and body language and pauses for questions, the text must carry the full freight of what you are trying to say. Some instructors have been introduced to the idea of submitting their text through a "readability index" (these include the Gunning Fogg, SMOG, and Flesch-Kincaid systems), software for which is often available online (see our Guide to Resources under the Readability and Learning Styles subsection for some links to these). These indicate the relative ease of reading, in some cases providing an indication of the number of years of education that a person can be expected to need in order to easily comprehend your text. Keep in mind that these provide only an estimate based on a formula, but if you find that your text aimed at freshmen is judged to be closer to graduate student level, you might want to take another look at your text with an eye to making some revisions. Taking readability into account does not mean that you must "dumb down" your content—only think about how you can communicate it more clearly online.

Tips for Writing Online Text

■ Strive for a style midway between casual speech and formal writing.
■ Chunk your writing into short paragraphs with space between them.
■ Use headings, italics, formatting, and other indicators to allow the eye to quickly take in the gist of the presentation but don't overwhelm the viewer with multiple colors and a hodgepodge of styles.
■ Intersperse text with graphics or present graphics via links.

PowerPoint Slide Shows

As we mentioned earlier, remember that in the face-to-face classroom, the students have you to observe, but online the slides themselves must carry the entire presentation. Therefore, design, images, and graphics are essential to the success of such presentations.

Keep in mind, too, that slide presentations, when they involve a large number of slides and click-throughs, can be very tedious to the viewers. If you wish to use slide-show presentations, divide up your slides and test them so that each segment takes no more than ten minutes. That will make it easier for students, not only to initially absorb, but also to find particular segments for review. Don't try to directly replicate long PowerPoint presentations that are mainly bulleted text. If your slides are primarily of this type, consider converting them into short text paragraphs with bulleted items. This web page or document format can replace your slides.

Narrated Slides, Audio or Videotaping, and Screencasting

Narrated slides can be an effective way to present materials online. However, you should avoid simply narrating bulleted text. Here are some tips for using narrated slides effectively online:

- Make sure each narration extends over a series of slides rather than stopping for five or more minutes on one slide.
- Use a casual narration with lots of color in the voice.
- Use graphics, arrows, video snippets, or other visual means to enliven the presentation.

A narrated slide presentation is particularly good for taking students through a series of steps—say, the steps for learning a computer software program. Audio alone or in narrated slides can also be a very effective instructional method in foreign languages, art, and music. Audio might be used to replace a short lecture or a guest lecture. Audio can also serve as a personalized introduction to the course or to the instructor. In the latter case, a short audio welcoming message might be combined with a still photo. How to create audio is discussed in more detail in Chapter 9.

Some online programs feature lectures that have been captured live in a face-to-face classroom and then converted into streaming video files. You can still see some examples of these on YouTube. Although this is indeed an option, it isn't a particularly desirable one if the videos are not optimized for online viewing—for example, they consist of far away or static views of the instructor at the lectern or when students asking questions cannot be clearly heard.

Even though most students no longer have a problem accessing video from off campus, you will see that there is a downside to just having staff record you in a classroom, however tempting that may be from the standpoint of saving time. What happens in the on-site classroom does not always translate very well to the computer screen, unless the institution has the appropriate equipment and knowledge about how to do this and the instructor adapts his or her techniques. It's a little like watching a video of a theater production or pirated movie filmed by someone in the audience. You might find that while you enjoy listening to the lectures, the video portion doesn't add much to your comprehension. Best are those in which the video production has sought to present the lesson with the remote viewing audience in mind (close-up shots, reproduction of what's written on the board, and questions from the classroom student audience repeated by the instructor for the benefit of the remote audience).

More and more institutions are investing in studios where faulty can create lectures that are optimized for online delivery. However, if your institution does not provide that sort of resource, you will find that it is increasingly easy to do this on your own. There are even advantages to creating videos that are not overly produced and more casual in approach.

Effective uses of video aside from full lectures might include a demonstration of a science experiment or a presentation of vignettes for a language course.

Many demonstrations can be created on your computer using screen-casting programs, like Jing or Camtasia, that capture the entire sequence or an edited version of what you display on a computer screen. This is discussed in greater detail in Chapter 9.

Or, if you have access to a collaborative synchronous program like Adobe Connect, or Blackboard Collaborate, you can record a presentation, and place the link in your classroom so that the presentation can be accessed asynchronously. These types of demonstrations allow instructors to be both focused and customized in their approach.

When offering audio and video, you should also take into consideration students' disabilities as well as learning preferences. Create captions or prepare a text transcript or summary for the benefit of those who have sight or hearing disabilities. This will also serve to give all students other options for accessing the material, including those who have technical problems and those for whom the text option is a learning preference. You can best prepare your transcript or summary before making your video or slide narration. Preparing transcripts for formal lectures after recording can be quite labor intensive. By creating the text materials ahead of time, you also generate, in effect, a script or storyboard from which you can more efficiently produce your audio or video. See Chapter 9 for more information on creating these types of multimedia presentations and on accessibility issues.

Instructor Presentation: Simulations and Experiments

Before you go to the trouble of creating these yourself, you may want to see if there is an online subscription service or publisher website that already has the kinds of simulations you want. These are increasingly available for many different courses.

If you already have your own computer simulations and experiments, or want to create them, it may be possible to have students access them via a web page. But you should test any simulations under the real conditions in which students will access them. If they involve long download times they may prove less effective than you wish. In that case, if your class is a blended one, you may want to continue using a computer lab for these activities.

But what if no actual lab is available, and you have a large number of computerized simulations to demonstrate? In such cases, you might consider distributing your simulations as short videos uploaded to your video hosting service or YouTube channel. You may need some support from your instructional technology services to do this. In the past, instructors often made and distributed such materials on DVD, but DVD players are less ubiquitous among students today as many computing devices are no longer even equipped with them.

See Chapter 7 for more discussion of simulations.

Using External Content

You will want to check textbook and ebook availability as always, but it is worth looking into whether there is a good **open educational resource** (OER) version of readings available. When appropriate, selecting OERs can provide considerable cost savings to students and thereby help ensure that everyone actually accesses the assigned readings. (Students will often not even purchase the required book when it is particularly expensive.) Sometimes these OERs are also more up to date and have greater currency for a particular subject.

In regard to guest lecturers, you will need to find out whether it is even a possibility for someone outside your campus to be given permission to access your learning management system, and if it is, what procedures are needed to provide permission. You can also ask a guest to create a video or audio lecture and simply make that available to students in the online class site. Whether you teach a blended or online class, you can use the online discussion area as a way to complement the guest appearance, providing opportunities to pose questions ahead of time or to hold follow-up discussion. These methods of enriching guest lectures must be planned in advance to work most effectively.

Open Educational Resources (OER)

Resources available on the internet that allow for free educational use subject to attribution. Some OERs may also allow for remixing or adapting or even commercial use, while others limit such repurposing to non-profit use only. To clarify the conditions of use, many OERs bear a Creative Commons License (see more about this in Chapter 8).

Discussion/Interaction/Communications

Earlier, we mentioned the following types of discussions that are normally held on an on-the-ground campus: those facilitated by teaching assistant as small-group guided discussions; question-and-answer sessions as adjuncts to lectures, labs, and exams; and seminar models in which instructor presentation and discussion are often combined. All of these may be successfully transported to the online environment.

In planning these activities, however, you'll need to decide which can best be carried out in an asynchronous (not-in-real-time) forum and which in a real-time, synchronous mode. Here your audience and course analysis comes into play. If you're conducting a primarily face-to-face class, for example, you may want to have all real-time discussion carried out in the live classroom and utilize an asynchronous forum for follow-up discussions that allow for more reflection. Or you may want to utilize an asynchronous forum for preparatory exploration of topics before the face-to-face discussion takes place.

If your course is entirely online, a synchronous mode of discussion might seem to offer the best parallel to face-to-face interaction. Yet if students are logging in from multiple time zones or are primarily working adults, the synchronous mode will allow too little flexibility in scheduling. In that case it may be a good idea to think of how you might create the best mix so that your synchronous communication sessions might be augmented by asynchronous discussion.

Later chapters will discuss specific strategies and techniques for getting the most out of both asynchronous and synchronous discussions. The following sections look at factors you need to consider when planning your course discussions.

Asynchronous Discussion   To prepare for your use of asynchronous discussion opportunities, you should first decide on how you want to use discussion in relation to your presentation and assignment elements in the course. In other words, decide whether discussion topics will closely follow the questions you raise in your lectures and other presentations, or whether the topics will provide opportunities to introduce additional materials and further applications of ideas you've presented.

For example, one instructor we know ends each short online lecture segment with two or three questions. The discussion scheduled in coordination with this lecture starts out by repeating these questions and having students respond to them. After the discussion based on the questions, one may then open up the forum to additional questions.

What about a seminar type of discussion? Even though a face-to-face seminar is synchronous, you will find it possible to organize the same type of activity in an asynchronous mode. To do so, you need to create a segmented lecture or dialogue. First, you create some initial or topic questions to pose, or short mini-lectures followed by a series of questions. After allowing an interval of time (say, two or three days) to permit students to respond to the initial mini-lecture or question, you proceed to ask some open-ended questions, such as, "What other ramifications might there be to this set of circumstances?" or simply, "Are there any other aspects of the lecture that you want to comment on?" Questions may be prepared in advance and used or not used as you deem appropriate.

Asynchronous Discussion in Math and the Sciences

Some instructors we know in various sciences—including some of the social sciences, computer science, and math—have told us that discussion isn't an appropriate activity for their students. Their idea of discussion is that it's connected to the realm of the soft, fuzzy, inexact, and ambiguous fields of the humanities. We believe, however, that all instructors can utilize discussion forums in online environments.

A good example of a "hard" use of online discussion is a question-and-answer forum. From such a forum a "frequently asked questions" (FAQs) page can be created to serve as review material. In fact, posting a FAQs page can eliminate some of the chit-chat and elementary questions that, however essential, are time-consuming for the instructor to answer; thus, it can permit the instructor to broach new or more in-depth topics.

Another use of the discussion forum is to ask students to offer possible solutions to problems. Discussion then consists of analysis of these solutions, with the instructor contributing comments as well. Some instructors have a slightly different approach to this process: First, they receive and evaluate the solutions; then they choose the best ones to post and discuss with students online. John Beyers, who teaches Developmental Math for the University of Maryland University College, uses the discussion area to have students choose a "problem of the week." Each week all students are responsible for posting their solutions to math problems and Beyers gives feedback concerning process and answer, all right in the discussion forum so that all students get the benefit of seeing these sample problems resolved.

The discussion area may also be used to post student homework or to allow students to present projects. Questions may then be posed by other students, and the instructor may offer his or her input for the benefit of the entire class. Students in the sciences can benefit from seeing how others approach the material.

Discussions that are coordinated with assignments must be scheduled to allow enough time for reflection and response. If assignments are presented in the online classroom and students are asked to comment on them, guidelines and procedures must be set up in advance to make sure that the discussion is structured and focused. Even though this activity may be asynchronous, you will probably not want to allow unlimited time for participation, especially if one of your goals is giving students feedback that they can apply to their subsequent assignments.

You'll also have to decide who will lead discussions—you, the instructor; the teaching assistant; or a student or group of students appointed for this purpose each week? What guidelines will you use for teaching assistant or student facilitated discussions?

Synchronous Discussion   Synchronous discussion as an instructional activity may be text-based chat, or it may include audio or video. It may be webinar-like in that it is mostly the instructor delivering content, with students permitted to ask questions via chat or voice. Or it may be an opportunity for students to work in online groups. For example, if a small group needs to come to consensus on an issue, it can often be faster to do this via a real-time session than to wait for the back and forth of several days of asynchronous decision-making.

In chat and all synchronous conferencing, everyone participating must log on to a particular site at the same time. The entire conversation then takes place in real time, although your synchronous program may allow for saving the chat transcript or video so that it can be read (or listened to) after the actual event.

Your learning management software package may already include a real-time chat tool which can be used for both class instruction as well as individual office hour sessions. Most allow for avatars or photos of participants which adds to the personalization. Because the features of these software programs vary greatly, you need to become familiar with the functions afforded you by these programs—for example, can the leader of such discussions be students as well as instructors? Are there options for phoning in as well as using a microphone? (The latter makes use of **VOIP**, Voice over Internet Protocol. VOIP is convenient but can sometimes result in time lags during synchronous conversations. One of the most common VOIP service providers familiar to readers is probably Skype.)

While synchronous sessions can be more spontaneous than asynchronous communication, adequate preparation and forethought are still essential to its success, especially if they are to be used to deliver instructional content. The timing of synchronous sessions, for example, is an important factor in planning.

If your students reside in different time zones, you'll need to make multiple times available for the same discussion topic: Say, topic A will be discussed on Tuesday at noon US Pacific time and the same subject repeated on Thursday at 7:00 p.m. US Pacific time. (A website like the World Clock www.timeanddate.com/ worldclock can be a helpful resource for students to ensure schedules are synchronized.)

You might indicate to students that you'll be surveying them to find the most convenient times for all. Or you may set up two or more real-time meeting times and require that each student sign up for a particular time slot so that you can control the number participating in each session. You need to decide all of this ahead of time.

Chat is fast-paced and has the potential to be a confusing format for instruction with multiple students. A specific topic and the response to it often may be separated by other questions and comments, making it difficult for an instructor and students to follow a train of thought.

Important! *To get the most out of instructional use of synchronous tools, we recommend that students be given adequate preparation by announcing the topic to them ahead of time and publicizing the rules for the conduct of the session.*

For example, you may have a series of questions that you want students to think about before the chat. Or you may have students view a web resource or read a particular passage before the chat. See Chapter 11 for tips on how to facilitate synchronous discussion in an effective manner.

Some synchronous tools are accompanied by a whiteboard or other types of shared display spaces. The whiteboard is an online version of the traditional blackboard that allows an instructor or student to draw or write on the whiteboard in real time (and in some cases to use math and science symbols as well) while students can type in their questions using the chat function. The questions appear, chat style, in the space below the whiteboard. Other types of shared display spaces permit instructors to guide students to view an external website or an uploaded document. The instructor can then write on the displayed web page, initiate chat discussion, and encourage student questions about the site being viewed by all.

Collaborative real-time programs such as Adobe Connect, Blackboard Collaborate, Go-to-Meeting, and Join.me provide chat space for students who may wish to ask questions during a presentation or who do not want to use audio tools. They may also allow for application sharing, that is the software may allow the instructor or student to give access to the computer desktop of the other party and provide assistance in real time. For example, the student may be asked to share his desktop to show the instructor how he has worked out a problem on his spreadsheet, allowing the instructor to enter corrections while discussing the errors the student has made. Or the instructor may display a document on which she has highlighted certain features and examples in order to better discuss these with the students.

Because synchronous tools may vary in their features, may vary based on what plan the subscriber has, and because tech companies are continually updating their options, before developing an activity, the first step is to thoroughly test out your software to make sure you are able to accomplish what you desire. If you plan to use a synchronous tool, you must plan ahead carefully to coordinate synchronous sessions with your topics and assignments. Students will need to know the protocol to follow for such an activity. For example, you might want students to first visit on their own the URL of a site to be discussed, or you might ask students to work on some preliminary problems before using the whiteboard or application sharing to show them the correct solution. While support sessions may be spontaneously scheduled in response to need, if you think some of your assignments or instructional units may call for such sessions, you may want to include those in your syllabus schedule.

●●●●●

Group-Oriented Work and Student Presentation

All types of group activities, from peer review to true cooperative learning exercises, are possible in the online environment. To be effective, however, group activities must be well organized and properly paced. In Chapter 7, we'll discuss how to conduct specific types of group activities and presentations. Here we'll outline the considerations related to planning and implementation.

In terms of your planning, consider how many group activities will be included in your course. Also, if you decide to reconstitute groups during the course (that is, not have students remain with the same group throughout), make sure that you allow enough time for students to get to know each other and develop working relationships.

Important! **Group organization and working procedures take longer to develop in the online environment.**

Always consider in your planning how, where, and when groups will be able to meet and work together online. Also consider how you will monitor and evaluate individual contributions if this is an element you're concerned about.

Groups will need specific guidelines for working together and even for initial formation. It's generally a poor idea to allow groups to evolve naturally. This isn't likely to happen online in a way that will be satisfying to the entire group of students. (When we see the words "Group yourselves" on a syllabus, we tend to shudder.) If it is appropriate for the particular activity, you may allow for some choice in group formation by asking students to let you know of a preference for joining certain classmates. Or if you are asking students to choose a group based on the topic of interest that may be workable.

In regard to group internal organization, you may want to specify a method of group organization or particular roles to be filled; for instance, a rotating chair plus a keeper of a group log or a spokesperson.

If you are teaching a blended class, take advantage of that combined delivery format by scheduling time for students to hold their first group meeting during a face-to-face class session. While not a necessity, many have found that it can provide a boost to and lay a solid foundation for the future online group communications.

Allow student groups as many avenues for communication as possible, with an emphasis on asynchronous discussion forums, synchronous chat, whiteboards, and document sharing areas in a learning management system. If an asynchronous discussion board is available to students, that's preferable to relying only on email and listservs. Email and listservs aren't the most efficient forums for group work, because documents and comments can't be viewed in sequential order without creating unwieldy email messages.

If you allow groups to decide how to communicate, make sure to request that groups seek consensus on how they will carry out communication. If there are working adults or those who reside in another time zone within a group, those students may not be able to communicate synchronously and should not be forced to do so. For those who do not have a full set of tools for organized group activities, it may be advantageous to use a third party service like a wiki provider or Google documents or spreadsheets. See Chapter 9 for some possibilities.

For each group, recommend an ice-breaking, getting-to-know-you activity as early as possible. This can include an initial casual get-together opportunity—in a face-to-face class, for example, or in a totally online setting.

Decide how you'll determine the composition of groups. For example, will groups be chosen by you via random assignment? Will they mix male and female students? Special practical considerations may apply. For instance, if students will rely heavily on real-time communication, it would be wise to factor in time zone residence when constituting the groups. Another consideration is the task itself—there are types of projects for which you may want as great a mix of diverse backgrounds as possible, while other group assignments may call for students of the same discipline or related background to work together.

How will students be graded on group work? Some instructors give a grade for the entire group, and others for each individual. This is easier to arrange online because you may specify that all group work be done in an asynchronous area visible to you or that the transcript of all chat sessions be saved and sent to you. You may want to prepare a grading rubric for students to see, in order to clarify your criteria for grading.

What role will student presentations by groups or individual students play in your course? To which assignments, activities, or topics will the presentations be connected? What will be the structure of each presentation? Will it involve a simple presentation of text, such as posting a paper or a group summary of the week's lessons? Or will the presentation involve the display of multimedia projects, an increasingly more feasible option with the advent of Web 2.0 technologies?

There are more examples of these types of activities in Chapter 7, but here we want to emphasize that such activities must be carefully planned, and areas for their implementation must be chosen or organized.

Research

Research activities, including fieldwork, may be carried out in a number of ways in an online class.

Web-Based Research Web research is an obvious option. There are open-ended activities, and there are guided activities. In the former, instructors typically propose web searches in which students are told to go find information on a particular topic. But in these open-ended research opportunities, it's vitally important that you give students some guidelines for both evaluating and searching out web resources. Because of the enormous growth of the internet, open-ended research is becoming increasingly frustrating and difficult. Search engines typically discover only a small percentage of the sites actually available.

We suggest that you not only give students some training in web search and evaluation, but also consider providing them with initial home-base sites from which they can fan out to find others. You could offer this guidance in the form of edited or reviewed collections of hyperlinks. For example, there may be an economics department at a university that maintains a site of the best links related to economics. Or a reputable and well-established association or journal might provide a selective list of relevant sites in its field. These provide reliable starting points for students to begin their searches.

Another way to approach this problem is to give students your own list of pre-evaluated sites to use for their research. This is similar to distributing a bibliography for research papers in an on-the-ground class. You might want to enlist the help of your campus librarian in assembling a list of websites for your students. Or you might encourage students to consult with their local librarians. Librarians are increasingly engaged in the review and evaluation of websites and electronic reference materials, and they can be a great resource for students who are doing research on the internet.

Social Bookmarking Free tools like Diigo (www.diigo.com) or Evernote (www.evernote.com) can be part of your design for research activities on the internet, providing ways for students to work singly or in groups to tag (give a searchable term or topic label to a bit of information), sort, annotate, and store their web links. While social bookmarking thrives on open sharing, depending on the particular social bookmarking tool, it is possible to keep links private or confine sharing to a particular group. Social bookmarking tools vary in features, but most permit users to view how others in their selected group or the vast number of users in that bookmarking system have bookmarked the same links, how those users have annotated and categorized links, and to see what other related links those users may have discovered. Such social bookmarking tools permit students to keep their collection of links housed on the internet so that they may access them from any web browser or mobile app without being tied to a particular home or work computer, and to easily widen their circle of references and pointers to research topics. Diigo also offers a premium but still free account to educators that provides additional controls and features and ability to create student accounts.

Library Research   Library research for a fully online class will depend on the facilities, materials, and services that your library or those in your consortium make available online. If your school subscribes to an electronic full-text service, that will make library research much easier for your students. There are a few databases available online free of charge, as well as many others that charge for their services.

If full-text documents aren't available to your students, you may still be able to direct students to databases that will help them expedite their in-person research at nearby libraries. Here's another case in which it's vitally important to consult with your librarian and survey the resources that will be available to your students, as well as the costs of accessing them.

Fieldwork, Internship, or Other Experiential Learning   Fieldwork isn't as obvious an option for an online class, because it implies experimentation or apprenticeship in a live, on-the-ground environment. However, although the fieldwork itself may be accomplished outside the online classroom, its results may be presented online, and a discussion and evaluation may also be accomplished online. Online teacher-education and professional practice programs may incorporate periodic reports from the mentor or supervisor at the student teaching site, as well as videos capturing the teaching assignment, while those providing oversight at a lab or internship can be asked to help evaluate students.

Students themselves may be asked to report on, interpret, or incorporate their on-site experience in the context of their other course activity.

If you're using field studies or internship periods as part of your class work, it's essential that you carefully schedule the before-and-after activities that will take place online. Any prerequisites, such as a secured internship position or a prearranged work site, should be stated in your course description at registration time and in any catalogs that list your course, but should also be thoroughly explained in your syllabus.

If a proctor or supervisor's report is required for fieldwork, this should also be clearly indicated. You will need to create the necessary forms and make any arrangements required to allow this aspect of the course to be implemented if your institution or department has not already organized this.

Assessment Considerations

As part of your planning, you will need to make some choices about the types of assessment you'll use. Any type of assignment is a potential assessment, either "formative" (part of the instructional sequence, for the purpose of measuring progress and giving appropriate feedback, not graded) or "summative" (a graded assignment or test that takes place at the end of an instructional sequence or as a final assessment of the course). Chapter 7 of this book will provide some ideas about the multitude of different ways in which you might assess your students. What matters most is that the assessment:

■ is relevant to the objectives and goals of the course;
■ is appropriate for the level and scope of the course content;
■ is easily enough accomplished online;
■ is clearly outlined to students via logically organized instructions that include the how, when, and where of online logistics.

Next, make sure that you vary your mix of assessments so that:

■ there are a variety of different types of assessments, allowing students to be assessed from a number of different perspectives, using a diverse set of skills;

- the number and pacing of the assessments are appropriate for the course length and format;
- there are some options for student choice and different levels of challenges.

The importance of assignment design A poorly constructed assignment can contribute to a lack of student success. Few instructors are familiar with instructional design principles for writing up assignments and, in an online course, you must provide more information than you normally would for a face-to-face class. If you are fortunate enough to be able to call on instructional designers to review your new online and blended course assignments, don't hesitate to do so. If you are without such resources, here are a few tips for writing better assignments for online and blended courses.

Before faculty write up the instructions for an assignment, they should:

- anticipate how their students will understand the assignment and actions they are asked to take;
- reproduce the steps and logical sequence and grouping of tasks associated with the assignment.

An assignment write-up should typically have the following components:

1. A title and descriptive, introductory, or contextual portion that sets forth the background details that students need to know before attempting the assignment. For example, "Having read chapter 10 and engaged in discussion on the early modern era in Japan, you are being asked to write a research paper on a major innovation of the Meiji period so as to further explore the implications of the issues covered in your text." Or, "building on the class practice exercises in X, you are now being asked to tackle a major problem using the skills you acquired during weeks 1–3."

2. The instructions—the main tasks or elements the assignment must cover or include, in logical order, along with directions for how and when to submit the assignment. The latter is not obvious in online and blended classes. For example, "please

submit as an Excel document labeled with your name and assignment number (e.g., Joe Student #2 via the week two assignment link in our class site," or "post an abstract of your paper in the discussion forum for week two by March 25th, adding the title of your abstract in the subject line, post a comment by March 30th on at least one classmate's posted abstract, and then bring a hard copy of your full paper to the class meeting on April 2nd." When expressing the required length of a written assignment, state the number of words, rather than pages (e.g., 500 words, not 2–3 pages).

If the assignment requires a number of steps, be sure to list these in the order they are best completed, as in "solve problem X and then explain your solution," or "discuss two divergent theories, select the theory you consider most valid and explain why, and write 2–3 paragraphs concluding what the ramifications would be of adopting that theory." Or for a multimedia assignment, "after watching the interview with X, write a 350–600 word review of the interview, comparing the content of the interview to one of the case studies from Week 3. See the criteria below for points to cover. Post your review to the class blog by March 10th."

3. Assessment criteria—these can be clearly listed criteria (best as numbered or bulleted list) or may be in the form of a rubric. Late submission policy, if not stated in the syllabus, should be included as well. Bear in mind that students will use your assessment criteria as guidelines for completing their work, so put some careful thought into what you include and what you leave out. Include any definitions that might not be obvious to students. For example, if you haven't already explained what is meant by a "persuasive essay" or "position paper," "peer reviewed articles," "analytic," or "substantive," be sure to do so, and when appropriate, provide examples, models, or resources to assist students. For example, "see the sample under our resource section of how to write a review of the literature for a research paper in history."

For more detail on writing up instructions, see this tutorial module from CUNY School of Professional Studies at http://spscourse design.commons.gc.cuny.edu/writing-up-an-assignment-and-using-rubrics/.

● ● ● ● ●

High-Stakes, Low-Stakes Testing

If online testing is available to you, you'll have to decide which types of questions to create and whether a specific test will be used for self-assessment, review, and practice, and for either a low percentage of the grade or ungraded (that is, low-stakes testing), or for a significant percentage of the final grade (high-stakes). If you are using low-stakes self-assessment, determine whether it will be possible for you to see the results of the self-assessment or just to record that the student has accessed the self-assessment.

Low-Stakes Testing

While in the traditional face-to-face classroom, low-stakes multiple choice tests do not enjoy a stellar reputation as an effective teaching technique, research into online learning has shown that they can be a very effective method to help students in an online course to attain a grasp of factual information and that such tests enable the repeated practice needed for students to proceed to tackle more complex assignments that involve higher-level thinking. By building in automatic feedback, and allowing multiple attempts for no or little credit, retention of foundational material and a gain in confidence are promoted.

High-Stakes Testing

Some online testing programs allow for relative security. They may be set so that students can access them only at a specific time, after obtaining a password, and they may be timed or made to record any pause in execution. Even so, if students aren't taking such tests in a proctored environment, there's naturally some possibility of fraud and cheating. However, this is also true for many testing situations on the ground. (How many large lecture classes check student IDs before exams?) To cut down on fraud and cheating in graded online high-stakes testing, in cases in which a campus-based or proctored test is not an option, you should consider the following techniques in your planning:

1. When using close-ended questions such as multiple choice or short answer in a timed and high-stakes test, the test should be

sufficiently lengthy or difficult enough that it isn't easy for students to look up information and still complete the test on time. Always, always randomize questions, drawing from a larger pool of questions.

2. A good proportion of questions should relate directly to in-class discussions or other in-class activities, including instructor lectures or case studies. Even if students can access the transcripts of such discussions, these aren't easy to locate in time to respond to timed tests. In addition, this type of question isn't easily answered by "stand-ins" who haven't actually participated in the whole class.

3. Don't rely only on online testing for grading individuals. Make sure you have at least two other methods of evaluation, such as essays, projects, or discussion participation. You can even include one real-time online "debriefing" via video chat that can serve as a basis of comparison with the student's other work.

4. Find out if other security measures are available through your learning management or specialized software and learn how to use them. You may have options such as issuing a password to access a test, automatic randomization of questions, setting time limits for tests, or you may be able to arrange that a student contact you before gaining access to the test or answer personal challenge questions to authenticate identity. At the very least, every instructor should assume the responsibility for not reusing the same test questions semester after semester. This is actually much easier to accomplish in online testing by creating a very large pool of questions from which to draw your exam and recreating that exam from the pool each semester. This not only prevents students from sharing exam questions within a class, but also guards against students colluding over more than one semester of the same course.

While some institutions with online programs still rely on old fashioned on-campus proctoring or allow students who live outside the area to arrange ahead of time for a proctor at another university, testing service or library in their area to monitor their test, a more sophisticated approach to electronic means of security is found in the recent introduction of a number of technology solutions to online testing that have emerged involving biometric (verification of physical characteristics of an individual) authentication of a student via eye scan, fingerprint or keystroke analysis, and/or monitored webcams and software. Some of these methods are being used to test students in on-campus computer labs. Remote proctoring solutions can involve live monitoring, recording for later review, or other methods. These proctoring solutions are implemented on an institution- or system-wide basis, and involve considerable costs on the part of either/or the institution and students, coordination, and planning. Some companies who offer these remote proctoring solutions are ProctorU, Proctortrack, and Software Secure Remote Proctor Now.

If you happen to belong to an institution that makes this sort of remote proctoring possible, you will need to attain a clear understanding of how it works and how it will impact the way you develop your exams.

For the vast majority of instructors, such biometric or other high-security testing arrangements will not be available. Therefore, instructors need to be purposeful in devising assessments, whether exams or papers, so that it is not easy for students to simply plagiarize. The more open-ended the paper topic assigned, the easier it is for students to plagiarize and the harder it is for instructors to detect cheating. For example, asking a student to "Write a ten-page paper on Augustan Rome" simply leaves too much room to forage among websites and fulfill the assignment. A more plagiarism-proof assignment would be:

> Write a ten-page paper characterizing the major trends in the literature or art of the Augustan era, using at least three primary source documents or images presented in our class, as well as five additional library resources. In presenting your characterizations, incorporate at least one topic from our class discussions.

Many institutions subscribe to services or have learning management software that incorporate tools like Turnitin.com or SafeAssign which provide feedback to the faculty member on possible student plagiarism. Feedback from these tools which includes a percentage of the student's work which matches work from other students must be carefully reviewed to eliminate those matches resulting from proper citation of the same sources or other "false" matches. Or, an instructor can use a simple method like choosing an odd or unusually eloquent turn of phrase and inserting it in Google, which will often turn up the source for a plagiarized assignment. But in some cases, it is just not possible to find the evidence of plagiarism, or to detect self-plagiarism, like students reusing their papers from another class. Beyond that, it is a terrible waste of an instructor's time to continually play policeman. Using Turnitin or SafeAssign in a regular and consistent way, and letting students know you will be using it, makes your job a bit easier.

Another measure of protection is to make sure that in setting up your grading criteria, responsiveness to the assignment requirements is made a major determinant of the grade. "Responsiveness" means that you can often avoid having to make a difficult determination about plagiarism. For example, no matter how erudite that suspect paper is, the fact that it discusses the Roman poet Ovid without any of the class reference points as stipulated by the assignment directions means that the student has simply not met the full set of criteria for a good score.

Portfolio methods of assessment are yet another way in which to measure student learning, ensuring that the student is assessed over time, by a progressive series of work products. It isn't difficult to assemble a portfolio of work in the online environment. The key is planning an adequate variety of activities from which students can assemble portfolios of their work. You can create a special online area, equivalent to a folder, where student work and evaluations of student work can be stored. Find out if your institution provides some sort of electronic portfolio software.

A more difficult to detect and defend against form of cheating has evolved wherein students contact a "tutoring" company whose main line of business is not to assist students but to actually do entire assignments or even take an entire online class while assuming the identity of the student. The most brazen of these companies actually bear names that spell out their aims in their website names—like "letmetakeyouronlineclass" or "writeyouressayforyoulazyone" and even brag about their notoriety. It is very difficult to detect students who are cheating on more than the occasional assignment and guarding against such schemes really cannot be an individual instructor's undertaking but rather the concerted effort of an institution to provide the strategies and measures to counter such dishonesty.

Now that video chat has become so much easier for all, some are beginning to include this medium into at least one high-stakes assessment. It can be the equivalent of an oral exam and then the grade is divided up between the oral and written portions. This can work especially well for a final project or paper.

● ● ● ● ●

Assuring Academic Integrity among Your Students

For instructors who suspect that the elegantly worded phrases they suddenly encounter in their students' essays may have been borrowed from something the students discovered online, a simple search on Google will often result in the identification of the plagiarized portions.

As mentioned, institutions now provide access to plagiarism detection services like Turnitin or SafeAssign, either through student submission of work to these sites or through integration of these tools within their LMS. If you have access to one of these services, set up your assignments to incorporate submission by all students rather than to use these to submit suspect work only. Get to know how these sites work and how you can accurately interpret the results produced after a student submits work.

But again, as students spend more and more time online and students themselves increasingly engage in production on the internet, assurance of academic integrity and guarding against plagiarism is something that should start well before the work is produced. A more holistic approach may be to emphasize emphasizing the concept of academic integrity rather than simply telling students "not to cheat."

Here are some other tips for encouraging academic integrity through design:

■ Make sure that paper or essay topics are sufficiently specific, rather than so broad that any borrowed text could meet the requirements.

■ Include an element that requires students to refer to discussions or other content specific to the class activity.

■ When allowing for choice in picking topics, either provide a set of choices or require that students provide an outline, bibliography, and rough draft of their papers so that you can monitor the development of the work. Include a real-time video discussion of the topic or a debriefing if feasible.

- Make sure that rubrics or listed criteria for grading the assignment include responsiveness to the assignment requirements and questions. While you may not be able to prove plagiarism, you can easily see what's relevant and what is not.

- Ask students to give examples and evidence to support their arguments and theses.

- Insist on clear citations and a reference list that matches those citations.

- For group work, ask students to clearly label each person's contribution or make sure to have students work in an area wherein each student's work is visible to you.

- If students are creating multimedia products, ask them to read about fair use guidelines and document what they have borrowed from elsewhere.

- Remind students at the beginning of the course of your institution's policy on plagiarism, and give examples, if not provided by your institution, of what constitutes plagiarism.

There are some excellent publicly available resources such as the Academic Integrity tutorial site (www.umuc.edu/students/academic-integrity/ai-tutorial/academic-integrity-tutorial.html) at University of Maryland University College or the Academic Integrity Quiz (https://www.reed.edu/registrar/academic_integrity/quiz.html) at Reed College (provides automatic feedback) that may a good starting point for your students. Or perhaps your institution may have its own tutorial or handbook.

Requiring students to take such tutorials or quizzes or devising exercises that cover academic integrity as part of the introductory materials in your course can help students get off on the right foot. It is very helpful when institutions include something on this order in their orientations but it bears repeating by you in each course. Students do not always realize that they have plagiarized or otherwise offended the rules of academic integrity. Exposing all your students in a systematic way to such resources, creating a short assignment around such a resource, or simply discussing the rules are frank, non-threatening ways to raise awareness of the issues before any offense occurs.

• • • • •

Choosing Textbooks, Coursepacks, and Software for Your Course

Even though your course may be totally online, there's no reason to discount the idea of ordering a textbook for your students. A textbook may provide the most effective and most easily procured source material for your course. (It can usually be ordered and purchased online.) Increasingly, textbooks are available both in hard copy as well as in the form of ebooks (electronic books). Hard-copy textbooks may be useful for those who don't want to read book-length materials completely online, and it allows them to avoid the expense and time of printing out copious amounts of text. But it is unwise to order a textbook from which you will only require students to read a few chapters. Students increasingly refuse to buy expensive textbooks that they know they will be used only sparingly in the course. Rather than assign such a textbook, choosing a less expensive ebook option or assembling an electronic "coursepack" or anthology of different writings provide better solutions. Ebooks increasingly come in a variety of delivery modes, from access on a website or downloadable versions for ebook readers and other mobile devices. Ebooks often provide features that allow the student user to annotate and highlight the text electronically, adding to the attractiveness of this option.

A coursepack anthology of writings from different sources can also be ordered and is essential when you wish to make use of copyrighted materials to which the library does not have full-text electronic versions. Perhaps your library provides a service by which these can then be placed directly in your online classroom. Some will still want to reproduce a coursepack in print but others will find it sufficient to secure electronic rights. A hard-copy coursepack may make sense when the instructor's own authored materials aren't easily scanned into an online format or when students are best served by having a hard-copy reference.

Depending on your subject matter, you may find that you are increasingly able to assemble the equivalent of a "coursepack" from open educational resources available on the internet that allow for free educational use. These open educational resources (referred to as OERs) range from courseware made available by such universities as MIT to freely shared podcasts from an individual biology instructor at a community college. We will discuss more about how to find open educational resources in Chapter 8.

Some publishers provide companion websites to support their textbooks, and the best of these can furnish your students with valuable resources. In some cases, there is a companion DVD but increasingly, these are materials made available online with a key supplied after purchase. Again, it makes little sense to require students to purchase access to such materials if you are not really going to make full use of them. Additionally you may want to inquire as to the accessibility of the materials (for example, some include videos that have no captions) and whether they can be accessed via mobile apps.

Remember that you can also create your own online resources that will help students get the most out of the text, for instance, self-assessment quizzes, guideline questions for use in discussion, and website reference lists for further exploration of the textbook topics.

In ordering software applications for use in a particular class, the pricing and compatibility of programs are important issues, as well as the analysis of your student audience. If price and lack of consistency among students are issues for your students, using Google Docs or another software program freely available on the internet may be the answer. Or your learning management software may include math editors that make it easier to deliver instruction.

Look to a specialized blog or a social bookmarking site like Delicious or Diigo to see what sites educators are recommending, then try out and evaluate them for your own course needs.

●●●●●

Redesign

As institutions become more involved with online education and try out new delivery formats, course lengths, or class sizes, faculty increasingly find themselves being asked to redesign an online course to meet the new specifications. While we discuss the issues involved with different class sizes in Chapter 11, we will take a moment to address the overall issues involved in redesign of term length here.

Whether a course is shortened from fifteen weeks to ten or is lengthened from six weeks to twelve, redesign is what is required, rather than simply truncating, chopping, or stretching to try to fit the new dimensions of the course. As part of this redesign, you must revisit the course objectives because it is those intended learning outcomes that should be the main determinant of the design changes you will make.

Start with some practical steps. If you have previously taught the course, plot out the new term length on a weekly calendar alongside the schedule of your previous class (or another's syllabus) as a reference. Where do exams, term breaks, and holidays fall in the new schedule? How much time was previously devoted to introductory activities, wrap-up, review, small-group formation, visiting speakers, or library-related activities?

Try to understand your institution or department's rationale and purpose for the new course length—is it to provide more time to cover complex material? A function of student demand for shorter courses and more variety in courses? Understanding the purpose behind the change may help you as you approach redesign.

If the length of the course is shortened, be certain to find out whether the new version of the course will be considered an "intensive" or "accelerated" course—that is, is the course now expected to cover more credit hours, the same number of credits, and what is the expected time on task required of students per week?

Redesign from Longer to Shorter

Course Content   Calculate the prior weekly reading load for students, including textbooks, online lectures, etc., and now examine how many hours per week that translates to under the new schedule. Assuming the course is not now considered an accelerated version, if you expected students to read sixty pages of a textbook each week and the readings now work out to ninety pages a week, is it possible for you to trim some of the reading without negatively affecting the attainment of learning objectives?

Consider being more selective. Perhaps there are entire topics or subtopics that have proved non-essential and could be eliminated, along with their corresponding readings? If you cannot in good conscience cut any of the topics or textbook reading, consider reducing other content such as your online lectures and commentary and additional web resource readings. You may also choose selected chapters that you can assign to students—singly or in pairs—to read, analyze, and then present in summary to fellow students in the conference area, using a special template for this activity. Sometimes a change in pacing will do, with longer reading assignments reserved for times when students are not busy with major projects and papers. When altering reading assignments, consider all text elements of the class, including any library reserved readings, or external website materials. Make sure any cuts you make in one element or another of the reading do not undermine support for the learning objectives, assignments, or exam questions.

While "coverage" of a subject remains an important considera-tion, a rushed and superficial learning experience is sometimes the result when one attempts to pack too much into a shorter period. Again, the core learning objectives should be the main determinant of your redesign choices.

Discussion Activities   If you have created one or more discussion fora for each week of the course, start by reducing the number of separate fora to the new reduced number of weeks. Review past discussions; are there particular topics and questions that seemed to stimulate the most productive discussion in your students? If so, those are the ones you want to make sure to preserve. Are there some topics and discussion questions that might be consolidated within another forum? Finally, are there any discussion questions or topics that are not really essential and could be eliminated in their entirety?

You may want to slightly reduce the number of responses stu-dents are required to make each week while retaining the peer-to-peer responses built into your design. For example, if you require students to respond each week to three or four faculty-posted dis-cussion questions as well as to two responses from other class-mates, you might reduce that requirement to two responses to faculty-posted discussion questions and one response to a class-mate. If you use a rubric or other clearly stated criteria to judge the quality as well as quantity of postings, you can probably preserve the desired level of interactivity in discussion.

Assignments   What are the major graded assignments and how much time on task is required for students to accomplish each?

The three main choices you have in redesigning assignments involve reworking, consolidation, or elimination.

Reworking: It may be possible to narrow down research topics or reduce the number of words/pages required for papers. Get started early on group projects, asking students to meet for the first time earlier in the course, and make all group projects more explicit and directed so that students can quickly engage in the project without spending a lot of time organizing themselves or coming to a decision about the path to take.

Consolidation: You may be able to combine two assignments that address different learning objectives or skills so that both are fulfilled in a single assignment. For example, you may have had one assignment in which you asked students to come up with their own imaginary marketing plan and another in which you asked students to analyze a company's approach to marketing. It may be possible to combine these two assignments into one in which students are asked to devise a plan to improve the company's approach to marketing. Both analytic and planning skills will come into play in the newly consolidated assignment.

Elimination: Eliminate what is no longer current for your field or does not have a good time/benefit ratio for students. That is, if an assignment has really not proved effective in the past, consider why it was ineffective. Calculate whether it can be revised, eliminated, or even replaced by something better yet less time-consuming. Perhaps in the past you asked students to write three papers on three or more related topics. This task might be replaced with an activity in which students write one longer paper that incorporates those three topics.

In redesigning assignments, be careful to ascertain any limitations to your choices. For example, if a particular assignment has been designated a key part of a program's outcomes assessment plan, or is related to prerequisites for future courses, the consequences of making changes to that assignment may have an effect beyond your own course.

Feedback and Interaction   With a shorter course, you may be concerned that you will not have sufficient turnaround time to give high-quality feedback on assignments or to engage with students in discussion. Maintaining high levels of interaction and quality feedback should remain a high priority—this is not likely to be the case if you try to maintain exactly the same assignments and numbers of discussion fora that you had in your previous longer course. The best approach is to prioritize and rank your assignments and discussion topics. By consolidating assignments whenever possible, you will have fewer but more focused opportunities to give feedback. Use detailed rubrics to speak for you and conserve your time to make those individualized comments that are necessary to help your students improve their performance. For example, it may be that you can address such elements as grammar, structure of an assignment, required parts of an assignment, etc. through a rubric, freeing up your time to write comments that address the student's specific problem, shortcomings, or strengths.

Redesign from Shorter to Longer

Course Content   Avoid the temptation presented by a longer course that seems to invite the addition of more and more content and activities to a course. Determine whether adding readings and activities will enhance the course or whether they simply add up to "filler." Look for those readings and activities that will add a vital new dimension to the course.

Assignments and Feedback   A longer course provides a great opportunity to diversify approaches to learning. You may find that you now have time for a major project or research paper, or to structure a group project over a number of weeks.

Depth and relevance rather than simply "more" should be the goal. For example, if you previously assigned a final project, you might now find there is sufficient time for students to not only complete the final project but for you to ask them to provide an outline, first draft, or bibliography at an early stage of the project, so that you gain an opportunity to provide feedback to students before the final version is due. Or, you might allow students to share their final projects with their classmates and participate in a spirited give-and-take discussion concerning their projects.

Being able to assess students in an early stage of an assignment, to take the temperature of the class via short surveys and to use that student feedback to inform the remainder of the course, or to simply have the leisure to guide students through a more comprehensive preparation and review for a final exam are all possible advantages that come with a longer course.

A Redesign Template   Table 3.3 is a simple template that might prove useful for planning the redesign of a course. The example shown is for redesign of a course that is moving from fifteen weeks to a shorter ten-week course.

● ● ● ● ●

Some Final Tips on Course Development

Before you begin to convert or create a new online or blended course, here are some final tips:

1. Devise some sort of simple chart for yourself as provided earlier in this chapter to plot out the major units, their objectives, content, and assignments if your institution does not supply one. There are a lot of moving parts in an online course, and a table, chart, or other planning document can help you bring these all together in the initial planning stages, make it easier to discern what is missing, and facilitate the creation of your syllabus. Read more about planning and follow the link to a fillable planning tool provided by CUNY School of Professional Studies at http://spscoursedesign.commons.gc.cuny.edu/planning-out-your-course/.

2. Even though you may ultimately create web pages written in HTML or post materials within a learning management system, make sure you save all content that you create, whether it be lecture notes, quizzes, or announcements, in some electronic, word-processed format, so that you'll be able to reuse or revise it for a future course. In other words, don't simply post your materials online without saving them in clearly marked files on your own hard drive, to the cloud, or flash drive. Include the date of the latest revision of your documents. This warning is particularly relevant for those who may use an external hosting service for their main classroom content and services.

3. When you do create your course materials, you may place them in one of the integrated learning management systems or in

Table 3.3 Example of a Redesign Template

Learning Objectives for Course	Previous Assignments to Meet Objectives/New Assignments	Previous Course Content Coverage to Meet Objectives/New Content	Previous Discussion Topics and Questions/New Topics and Questions
Describe the major cultural, political, and social elements of China from 220 BC–AD 200	Three two-page essays on three different dynastic periods/One 5–6 page paper that compares and contrasts the major elements of three different periods	200 pages of textbook readings over a period of four weeks/An instructor lecture and three focused articles of 20–30 pages each in a period of two weeks	Discussion questions distributed over four weeks/Focused discussion questions included in two weekly discussion fora

some combination of web pages, discussion forum software, or other online software tools. Be aware that each system and tool is different. Therefore, be sure to give yourself enough time to experiment with different ways of organizing the material. Try out all major features of the system; knowing the limitations of your software will save you time in the long run. Also be sure to try out a sample unit in your course from the students' perspective, or ask your teaching assistants or colleagues to play this role and give you feedback. Then go back and make changes in your syllabus. More information on building out a course is provided in Chapter 6.

4. Be sure to develop a schedule or project plan for preparation and delivery of any materials that need processing by teaching assistants, technical support staff, instructional designers, or librarians. Make sure you ascertain the turnaround time necessary for anything you'll be doing that requires some mediation by others. Draw up a time line and then work backward from your due dates to plan your own work.

5. Find out if there are any institutional or departmental policy restrictions that might affect your choices for course activities, materials, online communication tools (especially the use of external hosting services and free tools). Another issue is the preservation of course data and student records. Perhaps your university wants you to preserve a record of communications or work posted on third-party sites. It is essential to know these restrictions up front.

4

●　●　●　●　●

Working with Others to Develop a Course

While many instructors worldwide operate largely on their own when it comes to development of online courses, a growing number of institutions committed to online education have increasingly turned to a team approach for course development. The "team" may be as small as an instructor paired with an instructional designer, instructional technologist, or other technically oriented person providing assistance, or it may be a larger group of individuals—technologists, designers, graphic artists, and programmers, along with a project manager—joined in their efforts by an instructor who most likely serves as the content expert and perhaps plays other roles as well. There may be peer reviewers from the ranks of fellow instructors, or external subject matter experts.

In some cases the resulting course is meant to be reproduced without many alterations as it devolves to each new instructor to teach. In other situations, the team is devoted to creating only some core materials or a skeletal syllabus that are incorporated within the larger course, taught by successive instructors who each add their own materials and craft all or some of their own assignments.

From the point of view of an institution, standardization of portions (or the entirety) of online courses may be seen as a way to ensure consistent quality and scalable coverage of required content over multiple sections of a course. From the point of view of an instructor who was not involved in the development of that course, it may be difficult to force one's own shape into the existing structure modeled by others.

If you are the instructor charged with developing and teaching a course, what are the secrets of developing a course within a team approach? If you are an instructional designer or other team member, how can you most successfully approach your work with the originating instructor? And how can an instructor most effectively develop and teach a course which is completely or largely authored by others and still experience professional satisfaction?

● ● ● ● ●

A Model of Instructor–Designer Collaboration

Sharon Guan is an instructional designer, currently Director of Instructional Technology Development at DePaul University in Chicago but previously at Indiana University, where she worked with Pete Mikolaj to develop a course for the School of Business at Indiana, Commercial Liability Risk Management and Insurance. Previously offered only face to face, the course was converted to the online format and along with changing the delivery format, it was decided to take advantage of the opportunity to alter the teaching approach. In working with Mikolaj, Guan proceeded by first choosing an appropriate learning theory and then allowing the course development flow from that imperative.

Prior to working with Guan, Mikolaj had been using group projects in most of his courses, but was not always satisfied with the quality of team participation. He had tried a number of different techniques, including peer evaluation, but was still not satisfied and was looking for "a better way for building cohesion within the team and a way to build motivation." He was also concerned about how to evaluate the teams so as to assign individual student grades.

While Mikolaj had considerable industry and teaching experience, he said that he tended to be a lecturer and considered himself a rather boring lecturer at that! He credits Guan with helping him to change to a more learner-centered approach, and showing him the value of including examples, graphics, as well as guest experts in the class. He commented, "I was relieved to find that there were other ways to convey information so that students can actually enjoy learning!"

As Guan described it, she:

played the role of a typical designer with Pete being the content expert. He brought to me his syllabus, lecture notes, assignments, and other course materials. After going through these,

I suggested major surgery of course structure from chapter-by-chapter coverage to one that centered around one group project. Pete welcomed the suggestion and we worked together to fit the content into the new structure.

Sharon Guan also helped Pete Mikolaj with his questions about motivating and evaluating team members by designing a project rubric and measures for assessing individual contributions to the team.

Guan and Mikolaj shared the work along with some student workers who were available to digitize materials and create graphics. While Guan generally utilizes a formal work-flow development chart in working with instructors to ensure that all stay on schedule, she and Mikolaj met weekly and his commitment to close cooperation meant that such aids were not needed to the same degree.

In regard to working with Guan to redesign the course, Mikolaj noted that his greatest difficulty had probably been in:

accepting the need for a more formalized evaluation than I was accustomed to using. I was not familiar with much in the way of assessment and Sharon jumped in and helped me organize an evaluation plan that fit the particular objectives we had set out for the course.

Mikolaj even found that his collaboration with Guan produced another unexpected benefit—the experiences he had with this first course resulted in ongoing discussions and analysis as he introduced additional components of learner-centered design into his subsequent courses and sought to learn from those experiments. Guan also encouraged Mikolaj to incorporate new technologies in subsequent courses, patiently coaching him through his hesitation to try out appropriate tools.

Thus what began as a collaboration to develop a new online course turned into a professional quest for Mikolaj in becoming a more effective online instructor:

I am learning more about how to be an effective teacher, which I feel is the ultimate reward. In close second place is the education I am getting—it's quite exciting to be learning new concepts and feel that one is at the forefront of the educational process.

● ● ● ● ●

Advice for Instructional Designers on Working with Instructors

Sometimes instructional design seems theoretical and abstract to instructors and they may feel that the realities of teaching don't match up with the systematized and idealized instructional design principles. This can be particularly true when what's involved is designing a student activity as opposed to instructor presentation materials. Some designers may have more experience designing for self-paced instructional activities rather than instructor-led online classes. And designers who lack experience teaching may not understand the dynamic nature of teaching and classroom interaction. As Pete Mikolaj said, "I discovered that not all designers were like Sharon Guan! They don't know how to motivate students, don't have that first-hand and direct teaching experience." Sharon valued the experience she had as a teaching assistant during her graduate school days as well as her engagement as a tutor, working with students one-on-one. She commented,

> I often hear complaints about designers from instructors. That designers are too demanding and can't put up with the fact that instructors like to be creative, that they have different working styles. It's important that designers have the experience of teaching so that they understand that perspective.

Renee Cicchino, the instructional designer at Seton Hall University in New Jersey, echoes that sentiment:

> I believe that the online course design process is easier for those designers with some online teaching experience. In addition to being able to draw from our own online teaching experiences, I find that instructors are often able to relate better to a fellow instructor. During the course development process I share techniques that worked for me as an instructor as well as the things I look for as a past online student.

The writing of learning objectives is an aspect of design that can cause conflicts between designers and instructors. The fact is that instructors are rarely trained as part of their preparation for teaching to write precise learning objectives. Typically, they end up

> **Advice to Instructional Designers on Working with Instructors on the Writing of Learning Objectives**
>
> ■ Discuss the objectives with instructors in terms of what instructors want students to learn and the ways that students could demonstrate that learning in the context of class assignments, readings, etc.
> ■ Expose instructors to some simple examples of ways to express learning objectives but do so without pressing them to comprehend complex systems—avoid jargon!
> ■ Help instructors in a collaborative way to refine the learning objectives so that they would be reasonably clear to both the instructor and his or her students (there's really no value in the objectives being understood only by design professionals).

writing more general learning goals. And they may find it hard to match up those learning objectives, whether written by themselves or designers, with the actual course activities that they want to occur.

Sharon Guan emphasized that rather than pressing the instructor to write ever more precise objectives, and, in the process, sometimes humiliating the instructor, the designer needs to simply discuss with the instructor what it is that students should be able to demonstrate so that the instructor knows that the student has learned. She added, "and having someone else write the objectives for you is not really that good," as much of value can get lost as the expert tries to hone the language. For example, Guan also teaches Chinese language and said, "One of my goals is that students fall in love with the language." That sort of goal is a valid one, but not easily conveyed in a precise learning objective! Each instructor has his or her goals and the designer needs to strike a balance so that the objectives emerge with clarity without being overly pedantic about the process or producing learning objectives that really do not reflect the realities of the classroom dynamic.

There are resources that can assist instructors in improving their writing of learning objectives (see the Guide to Resources section) but bear in mind that for most faculty, a little goes a long way. As Sharon Guan has characterized it, "it's an important subject, but tends to be boring for faculty." One simple way to get the concept of different levels of learning and their expression in objectives is to help the instructor locate the level of learning taking place and appropriate verbs to express that level. Instructors can readily understand the difference between rote memorization and analytic thinking. So that if the level of learning is at the basic level of demonstrating reading comprehension and memorizing facts, the learning objective might be expressed with the verbs "to identify or name" while at a higher level of thinking, the learning objective might be expressed as "to reflect on or to analyze."

Renee Cicchino finds that instructors often write learning objectives from a conceptual perspective rather than a measurable perspective, but she hastens to add, "99% of the time the objectives are actually there—they just need to be reworded in a measurable way." At Seton Hall, instructors are often given a list of action verbs based on Bloom's Taxonomy as an aid to developing measurable learning objectives. (For some online resources that use this same approach, see the Guide to Resources in this book.)

Many instructors are particularly put off by the use of jargon and designers would be wise to avoid the use of jargon in working with instructors. Guan noted, rather than use such terms as "goal driven, assessment driven and outcomes based," sit down with instructors and ask "What do you want students to be able to do as a result of this class?" and "How would you know that your students had learned this?" Even the term "deliverable," which is handy in its application to so many different types of assignments, can seem off-putting to instructors—better, says Guan, to express this by asking "What do you want the students to present to you—something concrete—to show they understand?"

Another factor which may give rise to misunderstanding is the inherent difference that exists between interactive online classes and self-paced computer-based training (often known as CBT). Some designers have in the past focused on self-paced learning modules in which the instructional content and activities must carry the entire weight of learning, because there is no teacher mediating the experience. The content is sequenced and the directions specifically oriented toward the student's completion of a series of tasks on his or her own, with perhaps interaction occurring through built-in automatic feedback and response. An instructor-led online course is different in that the instructor is expected to facilitate learning and the interaction with classmates also contributes to the learning experience—therefore there are multiple layers of interaction—with content, with the instructor, and with classmates. While sequence is still important, there must be room to breathe for the instructor to play a role and to respond to the needs of students. Sharon Guan advises, "Designers need to take on the student perspective and I would recommend that they take an interactive online class to be exposed to both synchronous and asynchronous modes."

Good teaching is dynamic and designers can benefit from having had teaching experience of their own, whether in a face-to-face or online context. Short of attaining that teaching experience on their own, the designer can perhaps best make up for that lack by carefully interviewing the instructor as to what he or she would normally do in the classroom to accomplish a particular end, then helping the instructor translate that into an appropriate online mode or introducing a new approach to accomplishing the same goals. This means that the designer must accept that good instructors are more than content experts—they are also teaching experts. The designer should seek to draw out that often latent knowledge so that it is clearly manifested in the online course as it is developed. Renee Cicchino mentions that as the designer begins to work on online course design with an instructor, if possible, one way to better grasp the teaching methods of an instructor is to visit the instructor's face-to-face class to observe and analyze the instructor's teaching style first-hand.

Three Suggestions for Designers from Sharon Guan

- Act more as a support than a consultant.
- Always do more show than tell! Earn instructors' trust by showcasing a piece of work you have accomplished such as a course, learning object, or a simple reader-friendly digital document.
- Be flexible in your way of serving the diverse clientele of university instructors—get to know their personalities, working habits, and view of instructional design.

● ● ● ● ●

Advice for Instructors Working within a Team Approach

When teaching in the face-to-face class, instructors are accustomed to responding to body language, questions from students and other cues that students are in need of further clarification, explanations, or assistance about what they should be doing in the course. For an online class, a good deal of this needs to be anticipated, so that students are clear about what they need to do and when and where, and the instructor can provide additional emphasis, reminders, and referrals to other resources as needed. Therefore, if you are working with an instructional designer, or within an even larger team framework, it's best to approach the experience as a way to become more aware of your teaching while at the same time taking advantage of the opportunity to try out new approaches to teaching arising from the multiple perspectives afforded to you by the team.

Juanita Pardo González taught two blended courses in English as a Foreign Language to undergraduates at Universidad de Los Andes in Bogatá, Colombia. Each course involved students meeting 4.5 hours per week face to face, with the expectation of an additional 3 hours per week spent online. During the first year, having had no more than a technical training course in her LMS, González began to apply information and communication technologies to one of her courses, but:

> I would just assign students to go to the course web page to do an activity that I formerly did in the face-to-face class. The activity was a basic drill, consisting of listening and repeating phrases or words. These online drills were not required for students but just provided an additional opportunity to practice listening and speaking the language.

Not being satisfied with that first effort, she sought help in an attempt to determine the needs for a blended course. González was fortunate to belong to an institution like Los Andes which provided extensive support for the use of technology in teaching and learning. She was soon assisted by an instructional designer in creating some observational criteria and guidelines to examine what had gone on in that first class, looking at the student behavior and underlying approaches to teaching inherent in her instruction, along with the degree of consistency between the course content and her pedagogical practice. As González put it, "the goal of the process I went through was to design a blended course where I would not have to change my essential teaching style, but to find ways to apply my style of teaching to the new environment."

With these investigatory resources, she came to realize that she needed to apply a different strategy the next time the course ran:

> First, I integrated the course content to the work online, instead of simply using the web page—I devised a cycle in my teaching that allowed me to insert the online portion into one of the steps of the teaching cycle. In this way the online component did not seem added to the course, but a part of the course.

At the same time, she also received help from another part of the Los Andes team. Their technology services provided some additional software programs to meet the particular needs of each of the courses. For example, early on, she discovered that most of the practice exercises could be done at home by students via an online lab program and that they did not need the instructor for immediate supervision of this activity. With the help of technology, she realized that with online drill and practice exercises "the students could get a faster response from the machine than from me." This freed up her time to give better and more detailed feedback to students in other activities.

Then she realized that some of her presentation could be delivered online as well, and that through the use of video, she could "allow other voices into the classroom" than just her own, and include students as sources of information as well. She also began to add self and peer evaluation to her course, establishing clear criteria, and after demonstrating in the face-to-face class meeting how to perform these assessments, she found that students could perform these assessments quite well given clear limits and guidelines.

Later on, the instructional designer and graphics designer suggested a further remodeling of the course to bring a fresh look to the courses. That resulted in numerous sections of the original course teaching the same content. González went on to train new instructors in the use of technology for the course. She also created videos to prepare students on the proper use of the online components of the course. González thus moved from trying to operate entirely on her own to becoming part of the team effort to support blended classes in her discipline.

One of the most important things she learned about designing and teaching a blended course is that:

You must dare to let your students teach you! You have to feel comfortable with the tools and with the structure of the class in order to be able to teach it. You need to be willing to monitor and accompany your students in paths you had never planned. You need to be willing to give your students more freedom and responsibility than you have in traditional face-to-face classes and you need to accept the different forms in which students will take that freedom and responsibility.

John Beyers, an instructor and currently program chair for math and statistics at University of Maryland University College described his past experience working with a team to transform a pre-existing course in development math into an online course that could be offered to as many as twenty-five sections of students in one semester. Starting out, Beyers had the syllabus, schedule of class meetings and activities, and some model assignments. It took multiple weeks and feedback from a half-dozen veteran instructors to create the new syllabus for an online course. Beyers also chose the three main textbooks before work began on creating course modules with a larger team. This larger team consisted of instructional designers, a graphic designer, a programmer, a peer reviewer, and a project manager. John Beyers played the role of both content expert and curriculum expert. Beyers described the collaboration,

At the initial meeting, we set up goals and a timeline. The project manager was really key to the whole endeavor. Instructional designers, graphic designers and programming created learning objects to add interactivity to the math content. I was comfortable working with the team. When there was an issue of pedagogy, the others tended to listen to me as content and curriculum expert. They suggested learning objects and I would work with them on the design. Some of the advantages of working in a team are that you tend to stay on task, there's accountability in a team, more staff resources, and multiple eyes on the project.

In the role of content expert, you must recognize how a lack of content expertise can affect the ability of other team members to provide their own expertise. For example, John Beyers found that he needed to do as much rendering as possible of graphs and equations before turning these over to the graphic artists. In math, accuracy is a major issue, and graphic artists are not usually mathematicians, so the task of helping the artists more easily adapt the design and also reviewing their work for errors fell to Beyers. In the same way, Beyers had to be attentive to changes in wording suggested by the instructional designers—in math, words like "and" and "or," "equal" and "congruent" are not interchangeable!

John Beyers noted that instructors also need to appreciate the limitations of the course development enterprise when it comes to programming difficulty and expense. "I had great ideas," he noted, "but such limitations could drive what the team could and could not do. Dynamic graphs, simulations, animations—that sort of work was really the potentially most expensive and complex part of course development."

The rewards of a team approach to create course elements that can be scaled to multiple sections can be great. Beyers noted that when the course first went online, the university suddenly had 4,000 new students who wouldn't have otherwise taken the course—previously they would have had to take it at a community college and transfer the credits in. Beyond that, attrition was actually cut in half,

> *in part due to the consistency in the syllabus and course modules. Previously the attrition rate was very high, students would take different versions of the course and then as they advanced to the next course in the series, they sometimes discovered that they had missed important elements and were not well prepared. So both student retention and student success (as measured by passing and enrolling in the next course in the series) have gone up as a result of this change.*

While you may be playing the role of content expert, do not hesitate to assert your teaching expertise when you sense that something devised by the team is unlikely to be workable in the classroom situation. We advise all instructors to, at the minimum, take an online class or online teaching training before attempting to act as a content expert for the design of an online course. You are unlikely to contribute much to the course if you have neither taught online nor have experience as a student in an online class.

Renee Cicchino suggests that instructors avoid becoming fixated on an exact one-to-one transformation of face-to-face into online activities. One can avoid this problem, she says, by focusing on what you want students to achieve by the activity. Cicchino states that "when we run into a problem trying to replicate exactly what the instructor wants created, we show them an alternative that creates the same outcome." For example, in developing a science course, the instructor, never having taught online, could not see how anything could replace a face-to-face classroom activity in which she had students label and color different geologic samples. The designer presented a variety of different alternatives, until reaching a resolution by which a matching exercise was created using images of the geologic samples and the learning management system quizzing software.

The instructor should not hesitate to ask the designer to share examples of what other instructors may be doing in their online classrooms to accomplish similar objectives. Seeing how concrete examples work in the context of a real class or talking with other instructors who have implemented such elements can do much to facilitate understanding between instructor and designer.

Instructors should beware of harboring unrealistic expectations of the designer. Sometimes instructors expect designers and other team members to perform all remotely technical and even routine cut-and-paste work for them, handing over a rudimentary syllabus and even handwritten notes from past lectures and exams and expecting the team members to simply "upload" and format everything for them. Some instructors even demand designers edit their content and correct their spelling! While it's unreasonable to expect all instructors to perform all technical tasks without assistance, if an instructor at the very least does not learn how to use the class software fairly well, does not review or format their materials or try to grasp the concepts of online teaching, the resulting classroom performance of that instructor is often disastrous. Students readily apprehend when an instructor seems lost in the online classroom. Renee Cicchino emphasizes, "It's so important for instructors to understand that it's not the designer's course, it's the instructor's course. Designers are there for support and guidance but instructors must take responsibility for their course, content and knowing the technology."

• • • • •

How to Best Approach a Course You Did Not Develop but Are Asked to Teach

When you are asked to teach a course you did not develop but are asked to retain any major elements of that course, you are, in effect, still working with "others." That is, what you do in the way of design and development to modify that course must be done in the context of and with respect for what those before you have created.

In traditional face-to-face teaching, it is not at all unusual to be handed a syllabus created by another instructor and be asked to teach the same class. In some cases, one is expected to follow the syllabus very closely while in other cases, much leeway is afforded the new instructor. And in the traditional classroom there are courses (especially those of lower division, multiple section offerings) that go beyond a common syllabus to those in which particular class activities are mandated (ranging from specific lab and language exercises to writing and library assignments) or a common midterm and/or final are expected as well.

Online, because everything in a classroom may be preserved and observed, standardized elements of a course are even more easily replicated. This has led to the possibility of standardizing instructor lectures, activities, and discussion topics, as well as other class resources. Some have decried and fear what they derisively refer to as a "canned course," but most institutions have avoided such extremes of repurposing content ad nauseam and keep the courses "fresh" through constant revision and updating, as well as depending on instructor input and feedback, interpretation, and facilitation in the classroom.

Many institutions have rules governing what can and cannot be repurposed in subsequent sections of a course. In some cases, the originating instructor has created materials for the course as work for hire with the express idea that the subsequent instructors are required or permitted to reuse any portions they wish. In other cases, only certain basic course content modules and assignments are to be reproduced, and instructors must ask permission to reuse any other materials.

Therefore, upon being asked to teach an online course that you did not develop, it would be wise to quickly determine what must be retained, what you have the option to reuse, and what you can freely develop on your own to add to or replace elements of the course. For example, can you add your own lectures? Change all or some of the assignments? Is the textbook predetermined or can you substitute another or supplement it with other readings? And what about coverage of the content? Is it possible to eliminate, consolidate, or add other topics or shorten the chronological reach of a survey course?

Before making any changes, do consider the reasons behind existing course requirements and the expectations of students taking the course, as well as whether the course is part of a series or constitutes a prerequisite. For example, if the registration description causes students to expect the course to cover eighteenth-century European history or the course is intended to prepare students for advanced physics it would be doing a disservice to students to arbitrarily truncate the course.

Most instructors like to add something of their own to a course they have been handed. There is always a point of view and an approach behind every course developed, whether that development was in the hands of one instructor or a team of course developers. Being handed a course in which little or nothing can be changed may feel like being asked to wear a suit of clothes measured on another. There is seldom an exact fit and in any case, the instructor may find the style itself difficult to carry off.

When instructors are able to develop some part of the courses they are asked to teach, it is highly motivating—increasing their engagement in the class. Therefore, even if you are new to teaching a course, once you have determined the departmental or institutional requirements for altering the course, strive to enhance the course, whether through the artful shaping of discussion questions, the addition of new internet resources or ways to communicate, or subtle twists on the structure of assignments.

John Beyers spoke of his approach to motivating instructors who were assigned to teach one of the many sections offered each semester of a developmental math course:

> It can be difficult for some who don't like any standardization. I created a model classroom for them to review and they can see my approach. I explain the benefits of standardization of certain elements—those that must be the same for all sections are the textbook, course module content, and learning objectives. The weight and content of the final proctored exam (worth 30 percent) must remain the same, but how quizzes and

the main project are approached can be handled differently by instructors and the way in which the discussion area is used can vary as well although participation weight remains at 10 percent. A few instructors will try to do everything based on my model, but if the fit isn't quite right, they can include additional software or develop a resource website where students can get additional practice. I also encourage instructors to find their own creative ways to connect math to everyday life.

● ● ● ● ●

Suggestions for Approaching the Teaching of a Highly Standardized Course

If you are an instructor whose institution has determined that you cannot change anything in a standardized course, don't be disheartened.

First, make a point of carefully studying the course well ahead of the time you will teach and explore the points of view and approaches you find in the course so that you can intelligently help students do their best in the class. If you are uncertain about why a certain approach is taken, talk to other instructors, the course developers (if available), or your administrator. If, after sincere efforts, you cannot believe in the basic premises of the course, it will be hard to convince students of the same and you are better off not teaching such a course. If you find errors in the course, report these to the course developers or departmental administrator. Distinguish between a valid point of view and a mistaken one. While your own approach may differ from the former, only the latter is one that you cannot teach.

Once you have thoroughly absorbed the reasoning, approach, and principles of the course you will teach, you can look to providing feedback to the students as your main route to contributing to the course. Through feedback, you can contribute instructor commentary, encourage higher-level thinking, and point the way to additional resources. These should enhance, perhaps widen the scope, or provide clearer focus, but not undermine the course principles. For example, in responding to a student's posting in the discussion on some themes of the textbook, you may skillfully weave in commentary that you might otherwise have included in a lecture:

John, your response is a thoughtful exploration of the more subtle aspects of X. And you have noted some of the shortcomings of this theory. Some contemporary scientists have tried to explain some of these shortcomings. I have noted these with an asterisk next to their listing in the selection of recommended further readings for this week. This is also a topic that is possible for some of you to explore as part of your second assigned paper.

Or, "Jack, Lorena—in regard to the difficulty you noted in arriving at the answer through this process—you may find that this internet resource which provides a visual simulation of the process is helpful to you."

While your feedback will necessarily be situational, dependent on the kinds of questions and comments arising during the class, you can also do some preplanned development. When familiarizing yourself with the course content, assignment directions, and other features of the course, jot down notes about any topical areas, issues, or assignment directions that you think are likely to require some further explanation or additional resources. If you are permitted to create additional discussion questions, draft these for each week of the course so that they enhance those discussion questions that already exist. Note any types of issues you anticipate might arise as a result of the pre-existing discussion questions.

Another way you can make a contribution is through weekly announcements and emails which are usually left to the discretion of the instructor. Weekly announcements can be used to summarize the week's activities and point out areas that students successfully navigated or continued to have difficulty in comprehending. You can also preview the week ahead and draw attention to focal areas of upcoming course materials. Such announcements can be delivered via text, video, or audio, depending on your preferences. Or they might be in the form of a weekly instructor's blog commentary. If you feel that students may need more than the required textbooks are supplying, you may be able to suggest additional resources for background or further exploration.

Finally, if you feel that you have some ideas about how to improve the course, you might contact your administrator and signal your interest in joining the course development team assigned to the next update to the course. By articulating what you have found to be shortcomings in the course and suggesting how it might be improved, you may well persuade your institution of your approach. To bolster your case, indicate specific examples of student work that demonstrate the need for revision, greater clarity, or other changes you are proposing.

● ● ● ● ●

Competency-Based Education and Adaptive Learning Modules

Competency-based education (CBE) is a hot topic nowadays. What is called CBE varies by institution and program, but in the context of higher education it almost always includes:

■ a personalized approach for students, with an emphasis on scaffolded paths for the student to demonstrate mastery of skills, knowledge, or behavior—students are provided with support at each incremental step;

■ assessments which provide evidence of attainment of each competency, set forth as learning objectives or outcomes, a set of skills, specific knowledge or behaviors;

■ rapid feedback to students available at each step of the learning path;

■ a curriculum which is focused on attainment of clearly articulated learning objectives;

■ standardized content or adaptive learning modules are often included, although there can be project-based approaches which do not involve standardized course content;

■ instructor role may be confined to feedback and evaluation or mentoring and these roles may not be combined in one instructor—there may be evaluators, teaching assistants, mentors or other unbundled instructor roles.

CBE is almost always the product of a team-based approach to development of course content. If there are not sufficient automatic feedback loops within the course content and assessments themselves, the course design will include key entry points for instructor guidance, evaluation of student work, and feedback. There is usually some sort of time limit for completion of courses, although students likely will work at their own speed within those outer time constraints.

If you have been asked to be part of a team developing CBE courses, your expertise in the course content, and your help in identifying these key points for instructor intervention will be vital to the success of the team effort. If you did not develop but have been asked to teach what is identified to you as a CBE course, you should:

■ Study the learning objectives and content, assessments. Try some sample lessons yourself to get a better feel for what students will experience.

■ Ask how feedback will be provided at each stage and what kinds of feedback you as instructor are expected to offer.

■ Find out how formative and summative assessments are evaluated and how the student's final status in the course is evaluated.

Most importantly, find out what your exact instructional role will be. Instructors are used to imparting knowledge, providing feedback, evaluating student work, mentoring, to name just a few tasks they may undertake. Some institutions using CBE are disaggregating instructor tasks and may hire you to play only one or more of your customary teaching roles. Find out how you will interact and coordinate your role for the benefit of students. Such disaggregation can only work well when all those who assume these different roles are part of a system for working together.

Adaptive learning software modules may or may not be included in competency-based education. They are modules that provide immediate feedback at each step to the learner and present carefully calibrated challenges to incrementally advance the student's level of attainment of the learning objectives. If a student falters on a particular lesson, the software provides feedback, review, or support to the student to assist him or her in meeting that challenge and allowing progress to continue. Most adaptive learning software is commercially produced (although some originated at universities) and requires a great deal of programming and design expertise. Some names you may have heard of in connection with adaptive learning are Knewton and ALEKS. The Open Learning Initiative (OLI) free and open courses developed at Carnegie Mellon and now at Stanford have been a widely adopted and successful example of courses using adaptive learning techniques.

While you as an instructor may never be involved in the development of adaptive software unless selected to serve on the initial development team as subject matter experts (or as part of an initial research team at a university), you may be exposed to it through your textbook publisher's "online lab" or be asked to use one of the open and free courses by OLI to teach a foundational course. While there is much promise in the adaptive approach, the software has not yet attained the level of sophistication and subtlety that many would wish. Therefore, most adaptive software is still used in the context of curriculum which also provides for instructor intervention and facilitation.

Our advice for anyone who will be using adaptive software within the context of a regular online or hybrid course or within a CBE context is to get some first-hand experience of the adaptive learning content by attempting some sample lessons on your own. Carefully note any limitations you may see in regard to content, approach, or assessments.

Finally, a bit of philosophical advice for those who have misgivings about standardization and view with alarm what may seem the shrinking dimensions of instructor prerogatives—some of the more idealistic motives behind this trend in online education are the desire to create a more consistent learning experience for students, to produce measurable student learning outcomes and common assessments that will let us know if institutions are doing a credible job of preparing students for the world of work or further education, and to ensure quality of online offerings. The focus is on student learning and that is something with which few instructors would disagree. However, despite all these commendable objectives something all long-time educators know is that students still look to instructors to play an important role in their learning experience and there is often a correlation between how high they rate their course experience and the esteem they feel for the instructor. So do keep that in mind whether you are helping others to develop a course or teaching a course developed by others. Make a space for the instructor!

5

●●●●●

Creating an Effective Online Syllabus

Whether working alone or as part of a team to develop a course, the syllabus is an important part of course development, regardless of delivery format—online, in blended format, or face to face. Defining syllabus broadly here, we assume the traditional syllabus should include not only a schedule of topics, readings, activities, and assignments, but also such elements as goals, objectives, or expected outcomes for the course, grading policies, procedures, and any other information necessary for students to succeed.

Some instructors separate these various elements and call them "Course Information," "Course Requirements," "Grading," "Schedule," and so on. For the purposes of this chapter, however, we'll cover all these essentials with the term syllabus.

Although the details of course requirements, expected outcomes, schedule, grading, and procedures are staple elements of any course syllabus, they are perhaps even more important for an online class. Students tend to feel somewhat disoriented without the familiar first-day speeches from the instructor, and they may wonder if any of the same old rules will apply in this new online territory.

It's typical for first-time online instructors to include too little detail in their syllabi. One instructor we know changed nothing in his regular on-the-ground course syllabus except to add the words, "This course is delivered completely online." Unfortunately, students had a hard time even finding his syllabus, as he posted no welcome at the "entrance" to his online course, and then they were puzzled by his schedule, which still listed "class sessions" as once a week. Some students reasonably thought this phrase referred to online, real-time chat. Others wondered if the phrase meant that their asynchronous communications should be posted only once a week, on the particular day named in the schedule. As a result of this lack of clarity, the first week's discussion forum was dominated entirely by questions about where, when, and how to do the assignments, and the main topics for that week were nearly forgotten in the confusion.

Even after the instructor's hurried explanations, students continued to experience confusion about dates and times, procedures, and grading. They could refer back to the first week's forum and search through the various discussion threads in which these questions had been raised, but they had no clear reference document to which they could turn. One student even had a grade dispute with the instructor that arose from an ambiguity in the syllabus. In the syllabus, the instructor had declared that all late assignments would be penalized at the rate of one-quarter grade point each day, but hadn't clearly specified that the due dates for assignments were based on the instructor's time zone, not the student's. Thus, the student claimed that, when he posted an assignment at 11:00 p.m. Pacific time, on the due date, he was unfairly penalized because the server on which the course was housed, located (like the instructor) on the East Coast of the United States, had recorded the time as 2:00 a.m. the following day. These examples, both serious and trivial, illustrate some of the problems that can ensue if online syllabi (and, naturally, subsequent directions) aren't thorough and detailed.

In blended courses clear directions are equally vital. It's important, for instance, to explain to students how the mixture of different venues will be integrated. Which course activities will take place in the on-campus classroom, which in the online classroom, and what's the sequence of procedures students should follow each week? Imagine that, before the face-to-face class meeting on Wednesday, you want students to read the online lecture and post a preliminary report, but you want them to wait until after the class meeting to take part in that week's online discussion. In many cases, they won't understand that sequence unless it's carefully explained to them.

There are three aspects of an online syllabus we want to emphasize in particular: the contract, the map, and the schedule.

● ● ● ● ●

The Contract

Increasingly, the syllabus has come to be the contract between students and instructor, laying out the terms of the class interaction—the expected responsibilities and duties, the grading criteria, the musts and don'ts of behavior. Let's look at some features of the contract that are especially important for an online course.

Class Participation and Grading Criteria

What's meant by "participation" in the online setting won't be obvious to students. Participation should be defined. For example, is it posting, that is, sending messages to the classroom discussion board? Or is it just logging on and reading (an activity revealed to an instructor only when course management software has the capacity to track students' movements online)? Perhaps participation includes taking part in an online group presentation or showing up for a real-time chat.

Important! *Whatever kind of participation you expect in your course, you should make that explicit in the syllabus.*

If you're going to count participation toward the final grade, you should define how that will be calculated. We recommend, in fact, that you always give a grade for active participation in the class, that is, for contributing to discussions and asking or answering questions. The plain fact is that if students aren't graded, the great majority won't actively participate. For a blended class, you will want to decide whether students are given participation grades for both face-to-face meetings as well as online participation, and how the grade for one, the other, or both should be divided up. Besides judging the quality of students' contributions in the class, you may want to set a minimum level for quantity of participation or require that a portion of postings be responses to classmates.

Another consideration in asynchronous courses is the degree of self-pacing allowed. Must students follow a chronological order of topics in their participation, or can they go back and respond to previous weeks' topics?

Can they complete assignments at different times during the course? The answers to these questions really depend on the nature of your course. For example, if your course has a set number of tasks, which can be completed at any time or in any order within the twelve weeks of the course, then you may not be concerned about students skipping about or restarting conversations about previous weeks' topics.

Managing Student Expectations

The task of managing student expectations is very important in the online classroom. Some students enroll in an online course expecting it to be much easier than a regular course. Others imagine that the course will be something like independent study. Still others think the instructor should be available for twenty-four real-time hours a day. Your syllabus as well as your introductory comments can help manage such expectations, correct false impressions, and set the stage for the smooth unfolding of your course.

It's also helpful if your institution has a general student orientation (or at least a student handbook or web tutorial) that explains how the online course will work, how much student–instructor interaction can be expected, and so forth. If your institution doesn't have such an orientation, or your class has a unique approach that goes beyond the typical online offerings at your institution, you may need to supply some of this information in your own syllabus. Michelle Pacansky-Brock, currently serving as Teaching and Learning Innovation Specialist at CSU Channel Islands previously taught an online Art Appreciation class for Sierra College that was unusually rich in its use of technology and multimedia. In her syllabus she cautioned students about that fact, "Important!!! This online class is image intensive. Due to the visual nature of the content of this class, you will regularly download large files containing high resolution images and movies…"

A continuing-education instructor we know, who has a busy professional practice, complained after a few weeks of her online class that students had "unrealistic expectations." When pressed to explain this remark, she commented that if she didn't reply to each and every student comment in the discussion forum or if she appeared not to be in the online classroom every day, she would receive plaintive email queries or even classroom postings inquiring about whether she had read a particular message. She further explained that she had expected students to work on their own during the first part of each week and only then to post their thoughts in the discussion forum. Unfortunately, neither her syllabus nor her introductory comments ever mentioned these teacher expectations.

This case shows that managing student expectations can also require an instructor to communicate her expectations for herself to the students. This type of problem can be handled by a simple statement in the syllabus to the effect that the instructor will look in frequently during the week but may not be in the classroom every day, or that students should work on the week's assignments during the first part of the week (say, Monday through Wednesday) and then post their responses later in the week (Thursday through Sunday).

For her blended class, Isabel Simões de Carvalho, teaching at Lisbon's Instituto Superior de Engenharia, expressed her availability online in the following manner:

> *Your teacher will be online with all of you at least every two days and will provide feedback within forty-eight hours maximum. However, if you have an urgent subject that you need to discuss with your teacher ... then you should send an email to the instructor and in this case, do not forget to fill in the course name within the subject line.*

Other information of a "contractual" nature that you might want to incorporate in your syllabus includes the following:

- your policy on late assignments;
- whether due dates are calculated by your time zone or the student's (or the server's, as that might actually be in a third time zone);
- your availability for real-time chat appointments (which some call "virtual office hours");
- overall specifications for writing assignments (Formal essay? Informal journal? Of how many total words? MLA or APA style?);
- your institution's policy on plagiarism and cheating.

• • • • •

The Map

In this new territory of the online classroom, students will seize upon your syllabus as if it were a map. Students will want to know how to proceed and where everything is located. So, one of the first things you must do, whether through the syllabus or in an introductory message, is to explain the "geography" of the course.

In fact, if the syllabus isn't visible on the first level of the course, but instead can be arrived at only by one or two clicks of the mouse, then this introductory set of directions must be given in an announcement area or even delivered prior to the course, by email. For example, an announcement with explicit directions to the syllabus might say:

> *Welcome, please click on the Class Information tab at the upper left hand corner of this web page to find the links labeled syllabus, and weekly schedule. These will guide your work in this course, so I recommend that you print these sections out for handy reference. If you have any questions about these documents, please post a question in the Q&A forum portion of the discussion area.*

What else does "explaining the geography" mean? If your course consists of various web pages plus a discussion forum, you'll need to let the students know where to find the component parts of the course and under what headings: "Lectures will be on the page whose link says 'Lectures,' and these are arranged by weeks." If the discussion forum, a blog, or other software is hosted on an outside site, students need to be told that this link will take them off the university server, or that they must use a password given to them, and so on. If you've created a discussion forum dedicated to casual communications and socializing for students, let them know that the area you have imaginatively labeled "Café Truckstop" is intended to be the online equivalent of a student lounge.

This is particularly important when using learning management software that has its own unique and not easily customizable category headings or when your institution or department does not have a common classroom template. Students will need to know what you have stored behind each of the online classroom headings or where a particular link might lead.

While not essential, a narrated guide or video tour to the syllabus can be created by an instructor to reinforce the importance of the syllabus and to draw attention to it from the very first day of the course. You can use a simple series of screen shots within a PowerPoint narration or use screencasting video software to capture your movements as you click about the syllabus to point out the various sections of the document.

In a blended course that combines face-to-face and online components, it's essential that you specify where to do each activity. For example, in Isabel Carvalho's blended course syllabus she clearly stated, "Besides the weekly face-to-face sessions, this course has an online learning environment. The face-to-face and online components are not independent but instead are considered to be complementary." She added,

> We will be together face-to-face 4.5 hours per week and I will expect you all to spend at least 2 hours a week online using the discussion forum, viewing and downloading course resources and materials, and interacting with your peers.

Such general statements are then further detailed in the class schedule.

Other procedural and "geographical" issues you might want to cover in the syllabus include these:

- the URL for your home page, the companion website for a text, or other resources;
- where to access and how additional technology tools will be used in the class;
- how emailed assignments or those submitted via the LMS are to be labeled in the subject line;
- which file types you'll accept for attached documents (for instance, Microsoft Word, Rich Text Format, PowerPoint, PDF, Excel);
- any contact information for technical and administrative support;
- the proper sequence for accomplishing weekly activities and assignments (for example, do the exercises before taking the quiz, post a message in discussion before emailing the assignment).

• • • • •

The Schedule

The course should be laid out by weeks for students, because this is commonly the unit by which students gauge their own participation and work. If your class starts on a Wednesday, then Tuesday will become the last day of your week unless you state otherwise. If your first week of class is a shorter than usual one, say, starting on a Thursday, you can, if otherwise allowed by your department, let students know that the first week is a shorter than usual one, running Thursday through Sunday, and that subsequent weeks will all run Monday through Sunday. Arranging for weeks to end over a weekend can be very helpful for adult students in particular.

We recommend that you think in terms of subdivisions of two- or three-day spreads. For example, if you post your lecture on Monday, allow students through Wednesday to read and comment on it rather than asking them to do so by Tuesday. Students can be told to log on every single day, but it is perhaps wiser to take advantage of the asynchronous flexibility of the online environment. Assume that some students will log on and read on Monday night, some on Tuesday morning, and others at midnight. The Monday reader may return on Tuesday night to reread and post. The Tuesday reader may respond with comments at once. This scheduling flexibility is even more important for those who have students in different time zones or in foreign countries.

It's also good to gauge your students' access to computers or mobile devices and their probable work schedules. This goes back to what we discussed in earlier chapters. If your students are accessing the course website from a campus lab, the dorms, or branch campus libraries, then they'll follow a different pattern than will typical working adults or continuing-education students, who may want to use the weekends to do most of the time-intensive assignments. A Monday or Tuesday due date for assignments will allow working adults to make the most of their study time out of the office.

Using Specific Dates

Instead of simply listing the course schedule for "Week One" and "Week Two," your schedule should include the specific dates for

A Checklist for Your Online Syllabus

Here, in summary form, is a checklist for creating your online syllabus. You needn't include all of these items (some may be more appropriate for your class than others), nor do you have to include them all in one document called a "syllabus." You can distribute this information among several documents if desired.

■ Course title, authors' and instructor's names, registration number, and term information; syllabus web pages should bear creation or "last revised" dates if the term date isn't included at the top.

■ Course instructor's contact information, indication of instructor availability in classroom, for "office hours" and private communications. Contact information for technical support.

■ Course description, perhaps the same as the description used for a course catalog listing, but probably more detailed; should list any prerequisites or special technical requirements for the course; if blended course, define what is meant by blended in regard to face-to-face class meetings and required online work.

■ Course objectives or expected outcomes; what students can expect to learn by completion of the course.

■ Required texts or materials: any books or other materials, such as software, not made available in the course but required for the course.

■ Explanation of grading criteria and components of total grade: a list of all quizzes, exams, graded assignments, and forms of class participation, with grade percentages or points; criteria for a passing grade; policies on late assignments. More detailed instructions for assignments should be included elsewhere but at the very least, the outlines and due dates of each major assignment should be listed first in the syllabus.

■ Participation standard: minimum number of postings per week in discussion and any standards for quality of participation. If a rubric will be used to evaluate participation, reference to the rubric and where it may be found can be provided rather than including the whole rubric in the syllabus.

■ Explanation of course geography and procedures: how the online classroom is organized; how students should proceed each week for class activities; how to label assignments sent by email; where to post materials in the classroom; any special instructions.

■ Week-by-week schedule: topics, assignments, readings, quizzes, activities, and internet resources for each week, with specific dates.

■ Any relevant institutional or program policies, procedures, or resources not mentioned above. These may be available as links to institutional web pages.

Sometimes it's difficult to anticipate every issue that may arise during the class and to include that in your syllabus. There's obviously a balance between readable brevity and a syllabus so voluminous as to be intimidating. Whatever you do not include in your initial documents can be referenced for further examination—for example, "Discussion Participation is worth 20 percent of the grade. See the rubric for participation posted in the Major Assignments section of the online classroom"—or may still be introduced by means of announcements, weekly emails sent to all students, or postings in an appropriate forum. You will also want to use these means to reinforce important elements of your syllabus as the course progresses.

each unit, week, or topic area covered. This is particularly important for asynchronous courses in which students may be logging on at diverse times and days during the week. It's quite common for students to lose track of the weeks in the term when following an asynchronous online schedule. (And it's not unheard of for instructors to forget the dates, either!)

If you don't want to include dates on the main syllabus web pages because you want to reuse it for subsequent terms, and worry about making mistakes in updating it, then send students an email version of the syllabus or post a downloadable document version with the relevant dates inserted. Some learning management software includes a calendar feature that you may use to reinforce the dates for each segment of the course. However, don't assume that all students will check the calendar, especially if it is only available when they are inside the LMS. It is generally more effective to include the dates in a downloadable syllabus schedule if you want to ensure that students will have something at hand that they can consult with relatively greater frequency.

Schedule Format   It is vital that your schedule is readable and easily scanned by the eye. That means you need to have clear and consistent headings and spacing that allow one to grasp the *what* and the *when* and how of each week, task, or assignment. If your schedule is complicated, with many contingent tasks or contains many different readings or activities, a table is often the best solution. Tabular format is particularly helpful for blended classes in which the coordination of face-to-face meetings and activities and those performed online requires clarity and precision. We have provided examples of two display formats here, with the list view for the online syllabus example and the tabular view for the blended syllabus example.

Supplying Information More than Once

It's easy to lose track of where and when something was said in threaded discussions or by email. When you give directions, it may not be possible for students to simply link back to them at a later date. For that reason, you should provide important instructions in more than one location. However, to maintain consistency and accuracy, you will either need to repeat that information in full or refer students back to the complete directions in the syllabus or other central document. Be very careful not to truncate your instructions for an assignment—in posting reminders, always refer students back to the most detailed version. For example, an announcement can note an upcoming due date for an assignment mentioned elsewhere, "Remember, papers are due this week and must be a minimum of 1,000 words and based on at least three scholarly resources. Please review the assignment details for this paper found in the syllabus and under Major Projects." Or you may respond to a question in the discussion area, "John, your paper must be on one of the topics listed and Wikipedia may not be one of the three scholarly resources. Please refer to the Major Projects area for full details on topics and resources for this assignment."

Important! **In an online environment, redundancy is often better than elegant succinctness.**

Although students in some learning management platforms may be able to use a search function to find your instructions, in many cases students will have to waste energy and time to sift through materials before they can locate that one crucial sentence of direction. Therefore, even if you intend to explain assignments and procedures later in the course, it's best to state them up front in the syllabus as well. Then, if your course is laid out entirely in web pages, make sure that each page permits students to link back easily to essential information in the syllabus.

• • • • •

Sample Syllabi: Online and Blended Course Versions

The following is a composite syllabus based on courses in Modern China taught by Susan Ko at a variety of institutions. The first is a syllabus for the fully online version, followed by one representing a blended version of the same course. Both are designed as ten-week courses, but only the first five weeks of the course are provided here in the schedule portions.

Modern China: History and Culture

HISTORY 415

Delivered online, SomeUniversity Spring term, **** year

Course Description

This online course provides a survey approach to the history and culture of China in the modern period, from the mid-nineteenth century through the year 1990.

Contacts and Communications

Instructor: Dr. Susan Ko, sko@someuniversity.edu

See my instructor's bio in the classroom link under my name. Please contact me via the email address above or feel free to use the classroom instant message (IM) tool when you see me among the names of those currently logged in. I am also available by appointment on Skype.

I will log on to the classroom nearly every day and the discussion area Q&A forum is generally the best place to ask most questions. But if you need to contact me on an individual basis, please use email and I will try to reply within twenty-four hours. Your communication is important to me! To ensure that I see your message among my email, please use the class name and number HIST 415 in your subject line. For those of you halfway across the world from the instructor's eastern US location, given the time differences you may have to allow up to thirty-six hours for a "prompt reply."

Technical support is available 24/7 by contacting tech24@7help.edu or calling 1–800-TECHELP.

Your Online Classroom and Procedures

Each class week begins on Monday and ends on Sunday. Although all students will have taken the software orientation, at any point you may review the learning management software features by clicking on the Guide link.

The Announcements area of the classroom that you see each time you log in will be used on at least a weekly basis to post updates and comments on class matters. The instructor will also email the class to remind students of important due dates. (If you prefer to receive text message versions of these emails, please let the instructor know by following the instructions posted in the classroom.)

The **Course Materials** area, arranged in folders by week, houses the content for the course. All materials for the course are posted and can be reviewed from the start of the class. There is also a folder within Course Materials labeled **Detailed Assignment Instructions** that provides full information, criteria, rubrics, and samples for completing each assignment.

The **Discussion area** contains at least one discussion forum for each week of the course. Each discussion forum will be opened for posting on the Saturday before each new week begins. There is a forum labeled "Student Lounge" for casual conversations as well as a general "Q&A" forum where questions about class requirements or other questions that do not fit into a weekly discussion may be asked. It is recommended that you "subscribe" to the Q&A forum so that you can receive notification via email each time a question is posed or answered.

The **Assignment area** is the place to submit individual assignments unless otherwise indicated in assignment instructions.

Click on the link for each assignment to submit your work. Remember that our classroom server is set to US Eastern time. Therefore all due dates are noted as of US Eastern time. Use the World Time Clock link available in the classroom to convert all times and dates.

Introduction

This ten-week course provides a general survey of Chinese history and culture in the modern period, from the Qing dynastic period through the founding of the People's Republic and post-Mao China through 1990. We will try to trace the continuing themes as well as changing conditions that mark China's tumultuous modern history.

This course is conducted completely online. To do your best in this course, it is recommended that you download or print out this syllabus to keep as a reference, log on frequently (at least 3–4 times a week) to the online classroom and keep up with all assigned readings and internet work.

Course Objectives

- Describe the major cultural, political, and social elements of traditional China.
- Trace recurring themes and concepts in Chinese history.
- Identify the major historical figures and events that have shaped modern Chinese history.
- Analyze the underlying themes and issues in the modernization process, including those in the economic, political, and social spheres.
- Differentiate the characteristics of the Chinese state in the Mao and post-Mao era.
- Demonstrate an appreciation for Chinese arts or literature as a reflection of Chinese society and values in different historical periods.

Course Textbook and Materials

Main textbook: J. Spence, *The Search for Modern China*, 3rd edition only. See the link to **Buy Textbooks** in the classroom if you have not already obtained your book or check on Amazon.com for used copies.

If you are not already familiar with Chinese names and their pronunciation, you may find that in the beginning, you may have a little trouble remembering and identifying the names of people, places, and events.

I recommend that you take notes while you read and refer often to the Glossary contained at the end of the textbook. When referring to Chinese names, places, and events, I will try to include short identifications whenever possible. If you are ever in doubt about what I am referring to in my commentary or in the conference discussions, please don't hesitate to ask!

We will be using many internet resource readings as well as periodical articles available through our electronic reserves of the library. The latter are labeled Library Electronic Reserve Readings and are also found under Course Materials for the week indicated. The instructor will also introduce numerous multimedia resources from the internet, especially during the last half of the course. (There will be alternative assignments for those who are unable to access any of the third-party multimedia resources.)

Finally, the instructor will provide short commentary on a weekly basis to help elucidate the issues from our readings and provide additional perspectives. These commentaries are posted in the Course Materials area of our classroom.

Grading Information

Grades are based on a scale of 100 points and are distributed among major assignments as follows:

- Participation on a weekly basis: 30 points
- Group summary and question based on reading: 10 points for group work, 5 for individual contribution
- Short essay paper: 10 points
- Proctored exam: 25 points
- Final analytic paper or project: 20 points
- Grading scale:
  - A: 90–100
  - B: 80–89
  - C: 70–79
  - D: 60–69
  - F: 59 points or below

Timelines

Participation in discussions must be completed within the week assigned.

Other assignments are due according to the posted dates and as described in instructions, either submitted via the assignment submission link or posted in a designated discussion forum.

Unless otherwise noted, grades will be posted in the Gradebook no later than the end of the week following the due date of the assignment.

This university maintains a strict academic integrity policy. Please follow this link to read the policy related to plagiarism.

Assignment Descriptions

1. Participation

Students are expected to participate by responding to the instructor's questions as well as to ask questions or comment on the responses of their classmates. A good question is as valuable as a comment. See the Participation Rubric posted under Course Materials to understand grading criteria and expectations. There are ten graded weeks of participation. **Please make your first posting in each week's forum by Thursday.**

2. Group summary and question based on reading

Each student will be assigned to a group by the beginning of the third week of class and group postings will begin in Week 5. You will work within groups of four or five inside your group wiki to prepare a weekly summary ending in one or more discussion questions based on one of the weekly chapter reading assignments from the Spence text. The group will post the summary as pasted-in text and discussion question(s) in the weekly conference, creating a thread with the subject line, *Reading Summary, Chapter* ___. The group members will then be in charge of conducting the discussion.

Up to **ten points** will be awarded based on the criteria posted under "Group Summary" in the Course Materials, Detailed Assignments Instructions folder. This also includes some tips for organizing your group.

The summary and question must be posted in the online classroom no later than each Wednesday of the week assigned to your group. This will allow for sufficient discussion time. You will receive a grade of up to **five points** for your individual contribution. This grade will be based on the instructor's observation of your work in the group wiki as well as a peer evaluation. See under Course Materials for the Peer Evaluation Rubric. You will be asked to evaluate yourself as well as your peers.

3. Short essay paper

This is a short essay, 2–4 pages in length, due at the end of Week 4, February 20 of this course. Submit your assignment through the Dropbox and label the file **Firstinitial+Lastname+ShortE**.

The choice of topic questions and some guidelines are posted under the Course Materials area, Detailed Assignments Instructions folder. The style of this paper will be very much like the type of essay questions you will encounter in the proctored final exam.

4. Proctored exam

There is a mandatory proctored exam that must be completed no later than April 23. To schedule your proctored exam on campus or with an approved proctor near you, see the classroom link for "Exam Appointments."

Our exam will be short-essay and identification questions. Short-essay questions will ask you to reflect on what we have learned and draw connections between different events, themes, and facts. Identification questions require a short paragraph to explain the who, what, when, or importance of something we have studied. My own philosophy is that students shouldn't be surprised or "tricked" by what they encounter on the exam—if you have paid attention and kept up with your reading, discussion, and assignments, the questions should not be unexpected.

5. Final analytic paper or project

This assignment is an analysis of a continuing issue or theme that you have followed since the beginning of the course. For example, you may want to concentrate on economic development in China, the status of women, local officials versus central party control, China's relationships with its neighbors in East Asia, role of intellectuals and artists, etc. A full list of possible topics and issues as well as format and other requirements is contained under the detailed instructions for this assignment in Course Materials. This paper is due the end of the ninth week of this class but you must submit your topic for approval at the end of Week 5. There is a multimedia option for those students who may prefer to work in audio or video. See detailed instructions under Course Materials, Detailed Assignments Instructions folder for more information. Once you have submitted your project or paper, you are invited to share it online with your classmates during Week 10.

Other Resources

Need Some Review of Skills or Assistance?

For help in navigating the various types of writing assignments, follow the link to the Writing tutorial center in the resource list at the top right of the online classroom.

See the links in the classroom to **Library** and **Student Advising** for additional support if needed.

Schedule

Week 1, January 24–January 30

Traditional China under the Qing

Readings:

■ Spence, Chapter 3, bottom page 53–top page 69, Chapters 5 and 6, pp. 96–137

■ Instructor commentary under Course Materials for Week 1

■ Visit web resources indicated under Course Materials for Week 1

Discussion forum:

Introduce yourself in the Introductions forum, then participate in Week 1 discussion forum.

Week 2, January 31–February 6

China's Dual Crises, External and Internal

Readings:

■ Spence, Chapters 7 and 8, pp. 141–191, and pp. 202–214

■ Instructor commentary for Week 2

See list of topic questions for Short Essay assignment under Course Materials, Detailed Assignment Instructions folder.

Participate in Week 2 discussion forum.

Week 3, February 7–February 13

The End of Dynastic China

Readings:

- Spence, Chapters 10 and 11, pp. 215–263
- Instructor commentary for Week 3
- Library electronic reserve reading #1

Participate in Week 3 discussion forum.

Locate and check in with your group in the designated Group area.

Week 4, February 14–February 20

The New Chinese Republic

Readings:

- Spence, Chapters 12 and 13, pp. 267–313
- Instructor commentary for Week 4
- Visit web resources for this week

Participate in Week 4 discussion forum.

Short essay due end of this week, via assignment submission link. Label the file Firstinitial+Lastname+ShortE.

Week 5, February 21–27

Union and Disunion

Readings:

Topics under Course Content

- Spence, Chapters 14, pp. 314–341 and Chapter 15, pp. 342–374
- Instructor commentary for Week 5
- Library electronic reserve reading #2

Participate in Week 5 conference discussion. Group presentations begin.

Submit your final paper/project topic choice to instructor via email for approval by the end of this week.

Put HIST 415 and Final Topic in the subject line of your email.

Modern China: History and Culture

HISTORY 415

Delivered in blended format, Some University Spring term, **** year

Contacts

Instructor: Dr. Susan Ko, sko@someuniversity.edu

Office hours, Tuesdays 3–5 p.m. in Room 210 of Miller Building. Phone: 321–568–3987

Please contact the instructor via the email address above, or by phone, or feel free to use the online classroom instant message feature when you see the instructor among the names of those currently logged in to our online classroom.

The instructor will log on to the online classroom nearly every day, whether or not the class is meeting face to face in a particular week. The Q&A discussion forum is generally the best place to ask most questions. But if you need to contact me on an individual basis, please use email and I will try to reply within twenty-four hours. Your communication is important to me! To ensure that I see your message among my email, please use the class name and number HIST 415 in your subject line.

Technical support is available 24/7 by contacting tech24@7help.edu or calling 1–800-TECHELP.

Course Description

A survey approach to the history and culture of China in the modern period, from the mid-nineteenth century through the year 1990.

Introduction

This is a **blended** course. That means we will meet face to face every other week and for the last class meeting in Week 10, but that we will meet online only during the other weeks. Attendance at the face-to-face meetings and participation in all online activities is required. You will find that the online and face-to-face elements of this course are interdependent and integrated. Online participation is required every week, even in weeks when we are meeting face to face—you will be expected to go online, preferably within seventy-two hours of a face-to-face meeting, to continue discussion or complete other activities.

The dates during which we meet face to face are clearly indicated in bold font on the syllabus schedule.

This course provides a general survey of Chinese history and culture in the modern period, from the Qing dynastic period through the founding of the People's Republic and post-Mao China through 1990. We will try to trace the continuing themes as well as changing conditions that mark China's tumultuous modern history.

Course Objectives

- Describe the major cultural, political, and social elements of traditional China.
- Trace recurring themes and concepts in Chinese history.
- Identify the major historical figures and events that have shaped modern Chinese history.
- Analyze the underlying themes and issues in the modernization process, including those in the economic, political, and social spheres.
- Differentiate the characteristics of the Chinese state in the Mao and post-Mao eras.
- Demonstrate an appreciation for Chinese arts or literature as a reflection of Chinese society and values in different historical periods.

Information and Procedures

Each class week begins online on Monday and ends on Sunday. Our face-to-face on-campus meetings all take place on

Tuesday evenings, 6:30–9:30 p.m. in the Seely Center, room 2009. The Center is equipped with wifi and you are welcome to bring your laptop to class.

Face-to-face meetings will be a combination of instructor lecture, discussion, and student presentations. If you miss a face-to-face meeting you will be required to do additional makeup work online.

Online Classroom

A brief overview of the online classroom will be given at the first class meeting. At any point you may review the learning management software features by clicking on the Guide link. Here is a quick guide:

The **Announcements** area of the classroom that you see each time you log in will be used on at least a weekly basis to post updates and comments on class matters. The instructor will also email the class to remind students of important due dates. (If you prefer to receive text message versions of these emails, please let the instructor know by following the instructions posted in the classroom.)

The **Course Materials** area, arranged in folders by week, houses the content for the course. All materials for the course are posted and can be reviewed from the start of the class. There is also a folder labeled **Detailed Assignment Instructions** that provides full information, criteria, rubrics, and samples for completing each assignment. As noted below, read the instructor commentary before attending the face-to-face class.

The **Discussion area** contains at least one discussion forum for each week of the course, whether or not we are meeting face to face in a particular week. Each discussion forum will be opened on the Saturday before each new week begins. There is a forum labeled "Student Lounge" for casual conversations as well as a general "Q&A" forum where questions about class requirements or other questions that do not fit into a weekly discussion may be asked.

Important: Do not wait till the class meets face to face to ask a question! Post it online!

It is recommended that you subscribe to the Q&A forum so that you can receive notifications by email whenever a new question has been posed or a question answered.

The **Assignment area** is the place to submit individual assignments unless otherwise indicated in assignment instructions. Click on the link for each assignment to submit your work. *Please do not bring assignments to the face-to-face class meetings to hand in to the instructor.*

Course Textbook and Materials

Main text: J. Spence, *The Search for Modern China*, 3rd edition only. See the link to Buy Textbooks in the classroom if you have not already obtained your book, or check on Amazon.com for used copies.

If you are not already familiar with Chinese names and their pronunciation, you may find that in the beginning, you may have a little trouble remembering and identifying the names of people, places, and events.

I recommend that you take notes while you read and refer often to the Glossary contained at the end of the textbook. When referring to Chinese names, places, and events, I will try to include short identifications whenever possible. If you are ever in doubt about what I am referring to in my commentary or in the conference discussions, please don't hesitate to ask!

We will be using many internet resource readings as well as periodical articles available through our electronic reserves of the library. The instructor will also introduce numerous multimedia resources from the internet, especially during the last half of the course. If you are unable to access the multimedia resources from home, you are expected to use the campus labs to complete this work.

Finally, the instructor will provide short commentary on a weekly basis to help elucidate the issues from our readings and provide additional perspectives. These commentaries are posted in the Course Materials area of our classroom. During weeks that the class meets face to face, it is recommended that you read the instructor commentary **before** coming to class.

Grading Information

Grades are based on a scale of 100 points and are distributed among major assignments as follows:

- Participation on a weekly basis: 30 points
- Group summary and question based on reading: 10 points for group work, 5 for individual contribution

- Short essay paper: 10 points
- Proctored exam: 25 points
- Final analytic paper: 20 points
- Grading scale:
  - A: 90–100
  - B: 80–89
  - C: 70–79
  - D: 60–69
  - F: 59 points or below

Timeliness

Participation in online discussions must be completed within the week assigned.

Other assignments are due according to the posted dates and as described in instructions, either submitted via the assignment Dropbox or posted in a designated discussion forum.

Unless otherwise noted, grades will be posted in the online gradebook no later than the end of the week following the due date of the assignment. This university maintains a strict academic integrity policy. Please follow this link to read the policy related to plagiarism.

Assignment Descriptions

1. Participation

Students are expected to participate by responding to the instructor's questions as well as to ask questions or comment on the responses of their classmates in the online classroom. A good question is as valued as a comment. See the Participation Rubric posted under Course Materials to understand grading criteria and expectations.

Additionally, during weeks in which we meet face to face, you may receive credit for participation in either the face-to-face class and/or the online classroom. This is detailed in the Participation rubric.

2. Group presentation and facilitated discussion

Each student will be assigned to a group during the face-to-face class meeting of the third week of class and will be able to hold their first organizational meeting face to face. Students will work online in the Groups area within a group wiki to prepare a five-minute presentation and at least three discussion questions based on an assigned topic from one of the weekly chapter readings from the Spence text, a Library reserved reading, or an internet resource site. The group will present and facilitate a discussion (with help from the instructor) during a fifteen-minute period at each face-to-face meeting, starting with Week 5.

Up to **10 points** will be awarded to each group for their live presentation, facilitation of discussion, and online preparation based on the criteria posted under "Group Summary" in Course Materials which also includes some tips for organizing your group. You will also receive a grade of up to 5 points for your individual contribution. This grade will be based on the instructor's observation of your preparatory work online, the presentation and discussion on-campus, as well as a peer evaluation. See under Course Materials for the peer-evaluation rubric. You will be asked to evaluate yourself as well as your group peers.

3. Short essay paper

This is a short essay, 2–4 pages in length, due at the end of Week 4, February 20, of this course. Submit your assignment via the Dropbox and label the file **Firstinitial+Lastname+ShortE.**

The choice of topic questions and some guidelines are posted under the Course Materials, Detailed Assignment Instructions folder. The style of this paper will be very much like the type of essay questions you will encounter in the proctored final exam.

4. Proctored exam

In Week 11 there is a mandatory proctored exam on campus in our regular meeting room. See the university website in February for the examination schedule for this course.

Our exam will be short essay and identification questions. Short essay questions will ask you to reflect on what we have learned and draw connections between different events, themes, and facts.

Identification questions require a short paragraph to explain the who, what, when, or importance of something we have studied. My own philosophy is that students shouldn't be surprised or "tricked" by what they encounter on the exam—if you have paid attention and kept up with your reading, discussion, and assignments, the questions should not be unexpected.

5. Final analytic paper/project

This paper is an analysis of a continuing issue or theme that you have followed since the beginning of the course. For example, you may want to concentrate on economic development in China, the status of women, local officials versus central party control, China's relationships with its neighbors in East Asia, role of intellectuals and artists, etc. A full list of possible topics and issues as well as format and other requirements is contained under the detailed instructions for this assignment in Course Materials. This paper is due at the end of the ninth week, April 10, of this class but you must submit your topic for approval by the end of Week 4. Final projects will be shared with the class at the last face-to-face meeting. There is a multimedia option for those students who prefer to work in audio or video. See detailed instructions for more information.

Other Resources

Need some review of skills or assistance?

For help in navigating the various types of writing assignments, follow the link to the Writing Tutorial Center in the resource list at the top right of the online classroom.

See the links in the online classroom to **Library** and **Student Advising** for additional support if needed.

Schedule

Due dates are end of week unless otherwise noted. F2F meeting dates and assignments due are in bold font.

 This chapter is available as a downloadable eResource from:
www.routledge.com/9780415832434

Table 5.1 Syllabus Schedule in Tabular Format

Week/Topics	F2F Meeting	Online Activity and Assignments Due	Readings and Materials
Week 1, January 24–30, *Traditional China under the Qing*	**Tuesday, January 25, 6:30–9 p.m., Seely Center, Room 2009** In-class intro to our LMS class site	Introduce yourself in Introductions forum, **first posting in Week 1 forum by January 28**	Spence, Chapter 3, bottom page 53–top page 69; Chapters 5 and 6, pp. 96–137 Instructor commentary under Course Materials Visit web resources under Course Materials for Week 1
Week 2, January 31–February 6, *China's Dual Crises*	No face-to-face meeting	Participate in Week 2 discussion forum and make first posting no later than February 4 Review list of topic questions for Short essay assignment under Course Materials	Spence, Chapters 7 and 8, pp. 141–191 and 202–214 Instructor commentary for Week 2
Week 3, February 7–February 13, *The End of Dynastic China*	**Tuesday, February 8, 6:30–9 p.m.** Assemble with your group, receive your topic and date for presenting	Participate in Week 3 discussion forum and make first posting no later than February 11 **Start work in group wiki after February 8 meeting**	Spence, Chapters 10 and 11, pp. 215–263; Library electronic reserve reading #1 Instructor's commentary for Week 3
Week 4, February 14–20, *The New Chinese Republic*		Participate in Week 4 discussion forum and make first posting no later than February 18 Continue work in group wiki **Short essay due end of this week via Assignment link. Label file submitted Firstinitial+Lastname+ShortE**	Spence, Chapters 12 and 13, pp. 267–313; Instructor's commentary for Week 4; Visit web resources for Week 4
Week 5, February 21–27, *Union and Disunion*	**Tuesday, February 22, 3–5 p.m.** Groups 1 and 2 to present and lead discussion	Participate in Week 5 discussion forum, first posting no later than February 25 Groups 1 and 2 be prepared to respond to questions after F2F presentation **Submit your final topic choice to instructor via email for approval by end of this week. Put HIST 415 and Final Topic in your subject line**	Spence, Chapter 14, pp. 314–341 and Chapter 15, pp. 342–374; Library electronic reserve reading #2 Instructor commentary for Week 5

6

●●●●●

Building an Online Classroom

Now that you've done the necessary design, planning, and development work on your course and fleshed out your syllabus, it's time to actually build your course.

This means that it's time to put your work online—compose web pages, set up discussions, post assignments, create quizzes—in short, start learning more about and working with the software you will be using to run the class.

EDUCAUSE Center for Analysis and Research surveying over one hundred institutions in more than a dozen different countries reported in 2014 that while nearly all institutions have a learning management system in place, the greatest use faculty make of their LMS is just to push out content. Granted, only one-third of those in this faculty survey had taught an online course within the last year of responding to the survey, but the report highlights that a majority of the surveyed faculty admitted that they did not have a deep knowledge of their LMS features and agreed "that they would be more effective instructors if they were better skilled at integrating LMS technology into their courses." (See www.educause.edu/library/resources/study-faculty-and-information-technology-2014.)

While you can make a start with basic knowledge of your LMS or other tools available at your institution, a deeper familiarity is only gained from actual use. If you have only a hazy grasp of your LMS or other tools you need, consider signing up for some additional training at your institution that will cover those features beyond the fundamentals you already know. Once you have an overview of their potential and understand a few of the functions, you can try out and then practice using a few of those features and tools that interest you.

With some training and practice under your belt, and a greater awareness of the capabilities of your software, you can then begin to **build out a sample unit**, generally a week, for your course, based on whatever course development planning documents you have already put together to map out the units of your course (as recommended in Chapter 3). You will want to build out a sample of each of the different tools or areas you propose to create. As you begin to build or perhaps even later as you move to the implementation or teaching stage, you may find that some of the features you planned to incorporate don't work as well as you thought they would. You may also find a few new functions in your software that you didn't know existed. The fact is that the initial stage of preparation and the first time teaching the course involves a bit of trial and error. As you experiment with sample units to create a prototype for your course, you will soon learn how to get the most out of whatever learning management system or other software tools you are working in—whether it be a fully developed and integrated set of tools or some combination of blogs, discussion forum, social media, or online testing. In fact, as you become more familiar with the particular software environment you will be using, you may find that you want to go back and revise your original course plan (before you start teaching or when you revise the course after the first time teaching it) to reflect the opportunities or limitations that you have discovered.

In this chapter we will be discussing the various types of functions and features available in some of today's software and how best to exploit these features. In doing this, we will use examples from a variety of different existing software platforms, both learning management systems as well as some of the standalone types of tools or mobile apps.

The good news is that those instructors whose institutions do not have a learning management system will have little problem finding free tools and remote servers on which to set up their online and blended classrooms. Even those who have a learning management system available may choose to supplement what they do with the some of these free tools. As you examine the features of learning management systems or tools, be aware that this is a rapidly changing field. When we wrote the first two editions of our book, there was intense competition among many different learning management systems. By the third edition of 2010, there had been many acquisitions, consolidations, as well as a few new systems that really caught on, like Canvas, and Schoology, but there had also emerged open-source systems like Moodle and Sakai, new versions of existing software like BrightSpace (formerly Desire2Learn) as well as a wildly proliferating set of Web 2.0 tools that could be used in conjunction with others for online education. Our descriptions of particular features for software correspond to the versions existing at the time of this writing. Our purpose is not to tout one software platform or tool over another, but to show 1) the opportunities presented by certain types of features and 2) how you can adapt and implement your favored teaching strategies.

This is not to say that a particular software or learning management system may not be better suited to your pedagogical needs than another or seem more pleasing to you in terms of ease of use. But there is scarcely an existing LMS nowadays that doesn't possess sufficient tools for you to adequately teach your online or hybrid course so it is best not to get too obsessed with a quest for the perfect LMS but instead to focus on how to exploit the strong points and work around the deficiencies of any LMS or set of tools. The trend in recent years is for an institution to be able to swap out one tool for another while still using the basic features of a learning management system. For example, an institution might be able to substitute a different chat or discussion board for the one that comes with the system—either by having its own technical staff write a program or adopting a tool from a software vendor whose products are designed to be compatible with a particular system.

Another trend is for the LMS itself to provide integration with tools from outside vendors so that the full or partial functionality can be captured within the LMS. For example, Pearson, Wiley, and McGraw Hill offer labs and texts with interactive resources and quizzes from which scores can be rendered in the grading areas of various learning management systems by partnering with Blackboard, Canvas, Moodle, and others. Other external application tools may also have this LTI (Learning Tools Interoperability) functionality within an LMS without full partnering—this allows tools to be more easily integrated with an LMS so that in some cases, the need for a separate access login is avoided. This new flexibility and interoperability of tools may make it easier for your institution to find the right mix it needs for its online classrooms without inconveniencing the student by requiring separate registrations and sign-ins. However, we do recognize that many instructors will not have the final say (or may not have any say at all) about which system or tools are chosen for the institution, so our intention is to help you make the best choices for your needs and make the most of whatever you have available.

So, by all means take advantage of any special features afforded by your software system, but don't feel that your system must dictate your choice of teaching methods and approaches. Generally, if you have the desire to include a particular kind of activity, you can find a way to implement it in almost any system.

If you were fortunate enough to receive special training on the software system you are going to use, you probably learned some tips and techniques for exploiting that system. If you haven't received this type of training, and it is not available from your center for teaching and learning or instructional technology or LMS training staff on your campus, we recommend that you join a user's group online or find an online resource guide devoted to users of that software. You can also share information and strategies informally with colleagues at your institution who may already have had some experience with the system. You may discover that a colleague at your own institution—or at one half a world away—has found a new approach to solving the same problems that you face.

● ● ● ● ●

Templates

Some institutions or programs have developed specific templates for the layout of an online course. A template for an LMS may be thought of as ready-made formatting or preselected functions to which you will add content. Templates for an LMS may go beyond a set of default settings in a new, blank LMS course site and may determine not only the general names and placement of menu item links in the LMS course site, but may also go so far as to determine the "containers" (folders, files, tables) in which that all content is organized and arranged. While set templates are to be expected for standardized or team-built courses (see Chapter 4) they may exist, albeit to a more limited degree, for otherwise non-standardized programs as well. So you will want to find out if your academic program has preferred or required elements for the layout of your course site. While you might feel a bit constrained by mandated templates, console yourself with the knowledge that while faculty often yearn to put their own stamp on course site design, the majority of online students commonly express a desire for more consistent templates in their online courses. Students like being able to figure out where everything is located from the start of a course so when site layouts vary greatly within an academic program or institution, students often grumble that this means they are constantly having to reorient themselves and find their bearings. Keep this in mind and make sure that however creative you may want to be, that the logic of your course organization is evident, and at the very least, be prepared to explain the course site "geography" to your students on the first day and remind them as needed thereafter.

• • • • •

Dividing Up and Organizing Your Material and Activities

In building your course, no matter which system you use, you will have to make decisions about organizing and dividing your materials. A basis for many of these decisions will have been worked out already during your design and course planning phase, but others must be adjusted to fit into the framework of the actual software structures within which you are creating your course site(s).

For example, in terms of your overall organization, do you want to divide the course into units according to week or topic or some combination of both? Your ability, based on the way you have divided up material, to receive student tracking data reports from your LMS for a particular piece of content or activity might be one consideration. Such a consideration might cause you to separate rather than group together particular items of content. Other, more obvious factors include how many topics you will cover each week, how large your documents or media files are, and whether the portions you create will be easy to digest (and, if necessary, download) for your students.

Another basic question must be whether you want all presentation materials to be housed in areas apart from discussion and conferencing areas and, if so, what coordination you wish to have between these areas. For example, if you present a "lecture" in

Unit 1, do you want to create a discussion forum that will match it and provide direct reference to it? Will your LMS allow you to then create a direct link to it? Or do you want to post mini-lectures directly in the discussion forum thread, culminating in questions to which students must respond?

Perhaps you have units of content and assignments that must be completed before allowing students to move on to the next unit of study. In this case you would want to make use of any forced sequencing of content that your LMS permits.

How many assignments are to be delivered to you alone, and how many are to be shared with the class as a whole? Do you want students to work in small groups? If so, you need to give them a space to work as a team and a place to present their work to the entire class as well if desired.

Important! The overall guideline here is to create or make use of a space for every activity you devise and to find the best space for every activity.

Timing of Access

Before you actually begin to build your course, find out exactly when students will first be able to access your classroom and whether they will have access to the entire course at that time. For example, will they be able to enter your course site two days or even two weeks before the class officially starts? At that point, will they have access to an outer web page or "front door" but not to the discussion area, or to the announcements and syllabus only?

Also, find out if and how your software allows the instructor to work on a section of the course without making it available for students to see. Most learning management systems allow you to set specific dates for the release of a section or document or simply to toggle an on/off switch to determine the availability of a specific area. But if you have no way to control the timing of your students' access, you should consider laying out and arranging your course on paper or in a practice course shell, and making all changes in your word-processed and HTML documents prior to posting the final version.

This will prevent students from becoming confused if you need to revise your materials at the last minute. However, no matter your situation, do post at least an announcement or syllabus for students to access on the first day available to them, and remember to give detailed guidance about how and where to proceed. There's nothing more discouraging to students than entering an empty, unattended online classroom!

How much of your course materials should you actually make available to students at one time? This is a tough question to answer, because there is no one response that will suit all teaching situations and approaches. If you post all the presentation materials for all the weeks of your course so that students can review all content, this does offer two advantages:

1. Students can gain a more detailed understanding of what the course involves.
2. If they choose, students can work ahead.

The disadvantages are that, in an asynchronous class, even one with defined start and stop dates, you may be detracting from the sense that the class as a whole moves and learns together. If you also allow students to post in discussion forums as many as two or three weeks ahead, you further lose the sense of class cohesiveness. Such an approach would also prevent you from adapting to the class's needs with timely supporting materials and feedback. You may find, too, that simultaneously keeping an eye on two, three, or four discussion forums adds significantly to your workload and frustrates your students' ability to follow class conversations. Therefore, this is not an approach we recommend.

Often, a good compromise is to restrict the advance posting of materials and the opening of new discussion forums to no more than one or two weeks ahead of the time when you expect the class as a whole to be ready for them. Or allow students to see all materials and discussion questions, but if your system permits you to do so, set the discussions to read-only status so that while students can read materials, they can only participate in the current week's discussion. If you have a lot of students working over the weekends, you can set the upcoming week's discussion to be accessible at the end of each current week—for example, if your class week runs Monday–Sunday, you can open Week 2 discussion for participation starting on the Friday of Week 1.

A different set of circumstances is present when your LMS offers the option to set up lessons in an **adaptive release** format. This means that you can set up a series of rules by which lesson units or tests are released only after certain triggering or qualifying actions—for example, students must make their own post before they can read discussion posts by others, students must score at a certain level on a quiz before they can access the next lesson, unit, or quiz, etc.

Pacing Considerations

A final important consideration is the method of pacing your students in your course. Everything takes longer online. Even if your students all enjoy high-speed internet or ubiquitous mobile access, you will still find that you must factor in the "click time"—the time it takes to open and close documents, to download and access documents and web pages, or videos and simulations. If the class is a very active one, or one in which there are twenty-five students or more, it will take time for your students to pick through the numerous discussion postings that accrue each week.

Even though you want your course to be as rigorous as its on-the-ground equivalent, you don't want to overload students with materials and tasks for which the payoff isn't worth the time expended. Leave students enough time to delve deeply into the material. Presumably, you will already have factored in these considerations when composing your online syllabus. However, these matters often become more apparent once you begin to lay out the course within your LMS software or web pages. In that case, don't be afraid to go back and make adjustments to your syllabus or schedule.

Presumably, if you have already done a particular activity in a previous face-to-face class, you will have some idea of the minimum amount of time needed to perform it. Then you need to factor in the additional time that might be needed to do the activity online. For example, students in a face-to-face class working in a group may be able to make their first group determinations in a few hours or to brainstorm their ideas in just an hour. Online, you will want to consider the asynchronous access and likely allow at least two days for the back and forth it may take for all to register their opinions.

If you are unsure how long it will take for students to complete an assignment that involves online work, we suggest that you try out a discrete portion of it and time yourself. For example, if you want to ask students to visit a particular internet resource with a view to answering certain questions and then to write a report based on the visit, you can surely time yourself as you undertake each step of the visit and jot down responses to the questions. Given that you probably have more expertise or are more familiar with the resource than your students, you can factor in the additional time you think students will need to achieve the same results. In the end, beyond finding out whether you have calculated a correct estimate of the time needed for students to do this, you may also discover that your instructions should be revised for greater clarity!

If you have little experience with online discussion, you might ask to visit a colleague's online class and time yourself on how long it takes you to read through and compose a meaningful response based on that class's weekly participation requirements.

Again, while you may have already factored in some of these considerations when composing your online syllabus, matters often become more apparent once you begin to actually lay out the course within your learning management software or web pages. If you discover that your estimates were wrong, don't be afraid to go back and make adjustments to your syllabus.

Now let's look at some of the structures, features, and built-in functions that are available in learning management systems and Web 2.0 tools.

Content Presentation Areas

Presentation areas are where you deliver your basic course content, lectures, and so forth. Web pages or content areas within an LMS are the most obvious presentation format but perhaps you also make use of a blog, wiki, or multimedia format.

If you are using LMS software, you will find that in some systems, presentation or content areas are clearly defined and set apart from other functions, while in other systems, multiple areas can be made to serve the presentation function. The presentation areas allow one to type or paste in text or to upload your text or media files into what is, in effect, a document storage area. This storage area, which can be filled by instructors only, may be entirely separate from the discussion forum and other areas where students can post or upload documents.

Learning management systems are increasingly sophisticated and nearly all now offer the option of built-in editors or plug-ins that permit elaborate formatting or conversion to HTML without you having to know any code. Many LMS also provide different options to create sequenced learning content, and such templated and sequenced content are often able to be reused and replicated in subsequent classes. There are also free cloud-based LMS systems (albeit with limitations as to file space or number of users) such as Blackboard CourseSites, and free services like Google that can offer a variety of substitutes for LMS features to present your content, with the ability to upload many different types of files. If your institution has no LMS, find out if it provides Google Apps for Education—this institutional version of Google applications provides many advantages over the publicly available Google programs but with equally rich functionality. For the many readers of this book who are not native English speakers, Google also supports a great number of different languages.

If, however, you are using software which has a limited number of areas in which you can present content, you may need to designate certain portions by name to serve as your presentation spaces. You might set these off by using special titles, bold text, or some other distinguishing marks, depending on what your software system permits. For example, if you wish to post materials in a discussion area, you might designate one forum for "Syllabus," another for "Lectures," and so on.

If you do not have learning management software, there are many free or low-cost versions of easy-to-create websites, blogs, or wiki software that can provide an adequate solution for your needs. All allow for copy-and-paste methods and include built-in formatting and templates designed to set your content off to best advantage. Some will allow you to set up discussions related to your content presentation.

One issue you may need to consider as you proceed to look for tools you can add on your own is that many of the free online tools incorporate advertising. While you may feel that advertising on these sites does not provide the most appropriate atmosphere, as long as your institution does not object, you will probably find that many of your students seem unbothered by the ubiquitous commercial features of free online services. Nevertheless, if you do want to use only non-commercial, advertising-free websites, look for resources designed specifically for educators, or those that offer special versions for educators like Edublogs (www.edublogs. org), PBworks (www.pbworks.com/education.html), Wordpress.

com (https://wordpress.com/classrooms/), or Weebly (http://education.weebly.com/) which have either limited advertising or none. All of these resources allow you to create materials without having to know HTML or possess special technical skills. Increasingly, these services provide a suite of tools or capabilities beyond just creating a website or blog or wiki, allowing you to customize the type of functionality you prefer. Note that beyond the free services offered there are often "premium" or "pro" subscription levels available at many of these sites. In those versions, a generally small fee allows users more features, more control, or more storage space. Let's look at just a few examples of these services and what you might be able to do with them, depending on the version selected.

Edublogs offers hosted blogging software for educators, whether K–12 teachers or university instructors. The service offers some simple how-to videos, and they also feature discussion forums where educators can post inquiries, help one another, and offer tips. Once you have set up a blog for your class, you will find that you have these capabilities, among others, depending on your service level:

- You can control who accesses your blog and who doesn't and moderate student postings.
- You can create course materials by uploading documents or simply copying and pasting your content into the blog.
- You can allow students to post their responses in discussions related to your content and receive emails letting you know when students have posted in the discussion, thus cutting down on the number of times you must log on to see if students are responding.
- You can allow students also to be notified when someone has posted a comment to the same piece to which they have responded.
- You can set up blogs for your students to create their own presentations.

With Weebly or Wordpress.com, you can create a website or blog, a place for your students to collaborate on a project or research and contribute resources or simply post responses for a series of different class topics. Such services like Weebly and WordPress.

com are continually adding features, but you may find that you are able to:

■ post your course materials by copying and pasting;
■ use ready-made templates;
■ add discussion forums;
■ set up blogs;
■ track statistics on student use of your site.

Through using one of these free tools, you may discover that you are able to use the online environment to enrich learning for your students and, after an initial investment of time in planning and creation of material, to relieve some of the burdens of teaching as well.

Adding Multimedia Content

Perhaps you want to present content via audio and/or video. Many learning management systems will allow you to upload such content for presentation. Perhaps your institution will allow you to upload a video lecture or demonstration to a site like YouTube and then you can simply provide a link to or embed the video so that it

Figure 6.1 Jim Hegelmarks experiments with creating a blog on Edublogs. Source: Edublogs.org.

ONE THOUGHT ON "WELCOME TO OUR CLASS!"

jhegelmarks on **July 18, 2016 at 12:51 am**
said: Edit

Please introduce yourself before
replying to my first commentary

Reply ↓

Figure 6.2 Hegelmarks invites students to participate by adding their comments to the class blog. Source: Edublogs.org.

plays within the site. Some free websites, blogs, or wikis will also allow for the direct uploading of files or embedding of external multimedia content.

If video is crucial to communicating your presentations, your first step is probably to contact your instructional technology or multimedia staff. It may be that video is easily inserted into your learning management system or is hosted on a special institutional server. There may also be staff who can help you create your video. Many institutions now maintain a channel on YouTube to host their video content or use a paid service like Kaltura, Ensemble, or Panopto. This underlines the point we have previously made that it is a good idea to find out what is available to you and how it is made available to you on your campus.

However, instructors who have no support at all for creating or hosting video materials are increasingly able to find ways to do this on their own. Chapter 9 discusses some of the available methods for accomplishing this.

Podcasting (or the video version, sometimes called **vodcasting**) has remained a very popular option for providing content as everyone from politicians to comedians and self-styled experts on every subject have offered audio commentary and made it available to an audience who can subscribe to receive automatic downloads of these commentaries. Mobile access to podcasts from smartphones and tablets has enlarged the audience and appeal of this format. Many educators have taken this approach to offering weekly lectures and commentary to their students who can download such materials to their mobile players for listening off-campus. Some learning management systems have built-in podcasting tools, enabling instructors (and/or students) to easily create and publish such audio presentations. A large number of institutions had grown accustomed to using iTunes U as a repository for their instructors' podcasts and, in 2015, Apple introduced a classroom-like suite of tools, designed for the iPad, to allow instructors to add discussion, assignment submission, and to post materials.

● ● ● ● ●

Announcement Areas

Some systems have a marked-off announcement area, that is, a special form of presentation area that students see as they enter the online classroom or even without entering the online class site, for example, on a home page of an LMS. The announcement may appear on the main entrance page of the course site or on an LMS home or landing page, or it may simply be a link to a document storage area that can be named by the instructor and accessed by students. There may be options to send announcements to students or for students to opt to receive announcements in other formats as well—via email, Twitter, or even RSS feed.

For the instructor, the announcement area offers a quick method of typing in announcements and updates for the course. Even if it is set up as a separate document storage area, students will know to consult it each time they enter the classroom. If you don't have a learning management system, you can always carve out your own announcement area set off from the rest of your content pages.

You can think of the announcement area as being like standing at the front of the room in a face-to-face classroom. Online, this is the stage upon which you call the class to attention, remind, cajole, encourage, and update students. Email, text messaging, and other communications may reinforce but cannot really replace classroom announcements. Therefore, plan to make full and regular use of this area if it is built into your software or to rig up an equivalent area in whatever you are using as an online classroom to serve this function. And keep in mind that announcements do not need to be limited to text and the occasional image—you can easily make your own short "on-the-fly" videos to serve as an announcement, embedding or linking such video announcements.

• • • • •

Syllabus and Schedule Areas

Depending on your software, you can post a syllabus and schedule in a document storage area, or you can create separate web pages for this purpose.

Important! **Make your syllabus available in a downloadable or easily printable document, because this is the "map" students will follow in your course.**

This means that, if you use graphics in your syllabus or if the syllabus is divided up into a group of hyperlinked web pages, you should also make it available in a text-only, scrollable document. This will permit students to print it out readily. Whether students print it out or just download it to their computing device, it provides a helpful reminder about upcoming assignments, and keeps them on track when they are offline or online, but not immediately accessing the online classroom.

In some learning management software, the syllabus area also serves as the chief organizing tool, the "home page" or outline for the course content. For example, each item on the syllabus may become a clickable link to respective sections of course material. If you have this sort of arrangement, make sure your headings accurately indicate the topics or content to which they provide links.

• • • • •

Threaded Discussion Forums

We will cover the management and facilitation of asynchronous and synchronous discussions in Chapter 11. Here, we will note that the asynchronous discussion areas in various software programs are structured in different ways, have different options for student use, and allow messages to be viewed or sorted in different ways.

Structure of Discussion Areas   Many systems have a hierarchical architecture. Forums, conference folders, or message groups form the highest level, with each containing a number of subordinate threads that together make up the discussion. In this case, it is important to decide how you want to divide up your forums—by week, by topic, by unit, or by some combination of categories. For example, you may decide not only to have weekly forums but also to create a forum that can serve as an open discussion or socializing area, a sort of "student lounge."

Take note of the arrangement of threads and responses within the system you are using. Within the limitations of a particular discussion software, the way you structure your discussion forums will probably affect your decisions about the number of topics you wish to introduce each week, whether to break down larger topics, and the instructions you need to give students about procedures.

User Options   In some discussion software, both students and instructors may initiate new topics; in other systems, only instructors may start new topic threads. Still other platforms may allow the instructor to set the options, using a switch that enables or prevents students from starting new topics.

Other user options in some systems include being able to add HTML files, use attachments, and change the subject line without having to create a new thread. Another user option you will need to investigate is whether or not students can edit or delete the messages they have posted (and see if this is something an instructor can set) and whether the instructor can intervene to do the same for student postings or their own. In some cases, a message may only be edited if a reply has not been posted to the message. In other cases, edits may be made but the system will indicate that an edit has been made on a certain date. Some institutions may even restrict use of the delete function because of their concerns about preserving the class record.

A feature that allows students to anonymously "rate" (for example, awarding a number of stars or thumbs-up to a posting) and/or comment on discussion items of their peers has increasingly become available in many learning management systems. You may want to use this feature to stimulate interest in discussion by allowing students to recommend and draw attention to the best postings. This can be a great feature in a large class with an abundance of postings.

Therefore be sure to familiarize yourself with user options in discussion software. As indicated above, these may influence the design of course activities, facilitation of discussion, as well as record-keeping and even strategies for handling student netiquette problems!

Viewing and Sorting of Messages   How are conversations viewed in your software? Do the messages have to be opened and shut one at a time in order to be read? Is it possible to open and read all messages in a linear fashion, one following the other in a scrollable page? Many systems have moved to a dual capability, allowing conversations to be viewed as both individual messages in threads and continuous conversations.

It is common for systems to also allow multiple ways for users to sort messages for their own viewing. For example, messages may be sorted by date, by topic, or according to the people who posted them. (This has substantial utility for classroom and time management, as explained in Chapter 11.) Some systems allow one to subscribe to receive email copies of new postings. While this can be useful for low-traffic discussion areas, it could obviously become overwhelming if one subscribes to email for a highly interactive forum. However, it is very useful for an instructor to be able to subscribe to a Q&A or Ask the Professor forum so that he or she is quickly alerted to questions posed by students and instructors should generally allow and may want to recommend that students subscribe to such a central Q&A area as well.

Blogs and Comment-Based Discussion

Traditionally, blogs are structured with text entries arranged in reverse chronological order, with the ability for the reader to post comments. Because comments were originally conceived of as comments on the blog posts, not on the comments of others, blog comments are sometimes displayed as a series of postings without threaded arrangement. If there is only a flat or continuous display view, it can be difficult to follow an intricate series of comments in which those posting are actually commenting mostly on each other's posts. Most blog software allows the author to choose between a flat or threaded view. If you are planning to use a blog for discussion in which responses among those posting is an important feature, you will want to use a blog structure that allows for threaded views. Another feature that can be helpful is when the blogging software allows the blog author's comments to be displayed with some sort of indicator that differentiates the comment of the author or administrator from those of the blog readers—this can be a different color font, a different color background for the name, a special icon, etc.

Other Types of Discussion

VoiceThread (http://voicethread.com) is a software tool that allows discussion to be centered on a visual element such as an image, video, or slides. (VoiceThread can also be thought of as a presentation tool.) Michelle Pacansky-Brock found this tool invaluable for facilitating discussion in her Art Appreciation course for Sierra College in California. Pacansky-Brock noted that before she began to use tools like VoiceThread, she had been "frustrated with my inability to truly engage my students with images. Their ideas and interpretations were distanced from the works of art. Using VoiceThread as a tool for discussions changed all of this." Using VoiceThread, students are able to draw (called "doodle") on top of an image as they leave an audio comment, and the resulting "doodle" is synced to the recorded comment in playback. Pacansky-Brock asked her students to "doodle" to circle examples of techniques or point out examples of key terms as she displayed images of artworks. Comments can also be made as text or by webcam, and photos of students may be uploaded to display alongside their comments. While no longer available in a free version, there is educator pricing available for both single instructor as well as campus. You may want to explore the Digital Library on the VoiceThread site for examples of faculty use in different disciplines. VoiceThread can now be integrated with some learning management systems. You may want to inquire about whether this tool is available at your institution.

The explosion of Web 2.0 tools has meant that instructors with access to little or no instructional technology support can easily find and apply tools that fit a specific pedagogical need. Pacansky-Brock comments about her approach to using such tools in an effective manner without overwhelming students, "I find that, first, it's critical to be knowledgeable about using the technologies before I introduce them to my students. More importantly, it's critical to explain to my students why they will be using the technologies."

● ● ● ● ●

Other Communication Tools

Internal Message Centers, Internal Tools for External Email

Some systems allow for their own internal message centers which is basically a private asynchronous messaging system which does not need to go to an outside email address. Students and instructors can use this mailbox exclusively for all correspondence within the course, sometimes by just typing in or selecting the name of the student or instructor. Another benefit of these systems is that instructors can maintain a full record of course communications. However, bear in mind that in most cases, students need to log in to the classroom in order to access this sort of message system. Unless there is an option for students to subscribe and receive these messages in their external email addresses as well, this sort of email can't be used to send reminders to students to log in to the class. Most learning management systems provide a convenient email roster, which allows students to send mail to all or part of the class from a central area that lists the addresses of all class members. These email tools also allow the sender to receive a carbon copy of sent mail at the sender's home email address.

Because many younger students tend to avoid email, it is important for institutions and instructors to remind students in online classes that they are required to regularly check their institutional email (or the email with which the online LMS account is associated if that is different) to keep updated about their online courses.

Instant Messaging and Texting

Instant messaging (IM) and SMS texting are two ways of communicating that are well known to all of us who possess smartphones and are particularly popular with younger students. IM may be a feature already bundled into your learning management system but if not, you can incorporate instant messaging by asking all students to sign up for a free IM service.

Be aware that you will need to set rules for interacting with students in this way—generally you can log in or out as you prefer, or you can leave it open on your computer but post messages indicating your availability status. IM apps allow for sending messages to single or multiple users, wherever they may be, and increasingly also allow for video or audio conversations.

There are a growing number of tools that allow instructors to send an SMS text message to all their students' phones or email addresses. Some instructors like to use Twitter for this purpose instead. Many universities have been experimenting with software programs that allow them to send text messages in a crisis situation, while others have also enabled instructors to use such software for instructional purposes. Because SMS messages are generally limited to 160 characters, they are not useful for imparting instructional content, but can readily be used for reminder notices and last-minute changes or corrections to class assignments and schedules. Most such software allows students an option to subscribe via email or to log in to a web page if they choose not to use text messaging or do not have a cell phone or a suitably inexpensive text messaging package plan for their cell phone or other mobile device.

Privacy issues related to use of SMS can be mitigated through use of a free application like Remind (remind.com) which allows instructors to set up unidirectional text messages to students without anyone having to share their phone numbers with the class.

Chat, Whiteboard, and Other Collaborative and Screensharing Tools

While IM is a form of chat, and like chat, a synchronous communication tool, the term chat is more often used these days to indicate that chat is used to talk with people on the same site, for example, to talk with others within your LMS or on another website. Also chat tools generally have the expectation that multiple people will be able to access and participate. There may be one or more chat "rooms" or spaces available for a particular class, depending on the software. As mentioned in Chapter 3, chat is sometimes combined with a whiteboard. There are also whiteboards that permit students to assume the role of presenter in order to share their work with classmates or that grant all students in a defined group the ability to collaborate on a project. If you have not included chat sessions in your course plan and syllabus, you still have the option to inform students that they are free to use chat for their social or group-project needs.

Synchronous tools like chat rooms and whiteboards are particularly appropriate for your class if your students live in the same time zone or are logging on from campus locations. If your students live in disparate time zones, careful schedule accommodation is required to make this a worthwhile and attainable learning experience.

If your software allows you to save and archive whiteboard and chat sessions, and make them available to view later, this can be a major asset. This feature enables students to refer to and reflect on chat and whiteboard activities, thus considerably increasing their value to your class.

Check, too, to see what options your software affords for student direction of whiteboard activities. If you can hand over the reins to students, this will allow you to arrange for individual student or group presentations in real time.

Depending on the nature of your course, you may find that past successful sessions that have been archived can be reused for future classes. For example, you may have used such software to demonstrate how to create a spreadsheet. Once you have archived it, you can share it with a new classroom as part of course content. If you teach a blended class, you may have access to a smartboard in your on-campus classroom that allows you to mark up, save, and upload content for later reference on the internet.

One usage that makes these meeting programs worth consideration is for holding office hours (Skype might be sufficient for this) or providing a student with extra help. So even if you do not intend to offer any instructional use of these tools, you may want to explore them for those potential purposes.

Tools like those in collaborative software such as Adobe Connect or Blackboard Collaborate allow instructors or students in online classes to meet in real time, using chat and/or audio/video and slides, share and interact with documents on another's desktop, etc. These are sophisticated tool sets and it is essential that you get some practice and familiarize yourself with their workings before you decide to include them in your course plan. We recommend that you avail yourself of training provided by your institution or the software vendor if such instruction is available, and also consult with colleagues or even instructors from other institutions who may already have used the software.

For those whose institutions do not provide collaborative software tools that allow for screen sharing, we recommend that you try out one of the free or inexpensive tools that fall into this category such as free versions of Join.me, Zoom, or Go-to-Meeting.

There are continually new entries into this category of tools (try doing a web search for free screensharing, meeting, collaborative, or conferencing applications) and the features of any particular software also vary over time, so you will want to try these out to see if they actually have the particular set of tools and capabilities you are seeking.

Group Activity Areas

Groups may be formed online when an instructor wishes to divide up the class for the purpose of certain tasks. Group activities may range from simple discussion to peer review to collaborative projects and cooperative learning activities, as explained in Chapter 7.

If you are using an LMS, you will probably be able to take advantage of its built-in group areas, each of which may contain its own asynchronous discussion, real-time chat, or document-sharing capabilities. This means that the members assigned to a particular group can engage in discussion and document sharing within their own small, private group environment, apart from other members of the class. Some learning management software includes built-in small group blog and wiki options.

If you are using software that does not have built-in group functions, you can still find ways to carve out group areas. For example, you can simply designate and label a particular discussion forum as a group area for asynchronous communication. To accomplish the document-sharing function, group members will attach or paste in documents in the appropriate discussion area. If you are using a system that consists mainly of web pages plus a discussion messaging system, you can assign topic threads within the system for use by particular groups. For example, you might name one threaded topic (or perhaps a whole forum) "Group A Discussion" and indicate to the class that this is only for a particular group of students to use. Students in that group can then post, read, and respond in that area.

Some software has additional special features, like randomization, that may be of value to you in setting up groups—such a feature has obvious advantages for trying to divide up students in large classes into small groups.

Again, if you do not have access to an LMS with group functions, there are free software resources outlined in this book that can provide the ability to create such set-aside areas for small-group activity. A social networking site like Facebook also offers opportunities to create private group sites that can include a number of different communication tools.

Any of the free wiki software sites will allow you to create an area in which students can collaborate as a group. One advantage of using wiki software for group projects is that it provides the instructor with a clear "page history" of all edits made, in order of most recent to oldest, noting who made each edit and when the edit was made. This means that you will be able to track the contributions of each student to the overall group project and it also gives you a sense of the direction and decisions that the group took in their collaboration. Being able to review this history might enable you to give better guidance to students about errors, missed opportunities, or even suggestions for more effective collaboration. To get a clearer picture of how this works, call up any page in Wikipedia and click on the View History tab or see the detailed explanation at https://meta.wikimedia.org/wiki/Help:Page_history.

Internet Resource Collections and Curation

Some software provides places where you can organize a reference list of relevant websites, making it easier for students to find and retrieve them as the course progresses. Curation means to not only collect but critically select and annotate resources, whether this curation is done by you on behalf of your students as part of course content, or whether you ask students to perform this activity as part of their research and analysis of sources.

Depending on your LMS software's options, you may want to organize your links according to each week of the class or in a topical fashion. Some systems allow both instructors and students to add web links in the resource area, while others limit this capability to instructors.

Visible groups [Group S ▾]

First name: **All** A B C D E F G H I J K L M N O P Q R S T U V W X Y Z
Surname: **All** A B C D E F G H I J K L M N O P Q R S T U V W X Y Z

Reflective journal · Feedback: Psychology in ... · Your course notes wiki ... · Survey: COLLES · Discussions about your ... · Group Project · Select your focus film · From Concept to Reality: ... · Course discussion · Video resources · Useful links · Let's make a date! · Course chat · Factual recall test · Prior Knowledge assessment · Announcements from your tutor

First name / Surname	Email address
Joseph Student	Joseph.Student@university.edu
Melanie Learner	Melanie.Learner@university.edu
Timothy Pedagogue	TP@university.edu
Lyndon Smartee	Lyndon.Smartee@university.edu

Figure 6.3 Tracking a group's activity in Moodle. Source: https://moodle.org/demo/.

Or, you may prefer to use a third-party social bookmarking service like Diigo, previously discussed in Chapter 3, which allows for tagging and sharing with "friends" or the formation of groups within which internet resources may be shared. Such a social bookmarking tool may be used as part of a research project. Other such curation and sharing tools which vary greatly in regard to features and emphasis but which have free versions available are Evernote (for text, internet resources, and private resources but which can be shared as well), Storify (good for curating from Twitter and other public social media sites, Pinterest (oriented to visual material), Padlet (padlet.com, similar to Pinterest but more oriented to education), and Scoop.it (topical, curated news sources).

ePortfolios

An ePortfolio is a way to create a portfolio online so that students can be assessed by carefully selected samples or evidence of their work, and may also serve as a way to showcase their work in one or more classes. Another way these can be used is to encourage students to evaluate their own work as part of the process of selecting which artifacts of their work they will choose to highlight in the ePortfolio. Increasingly, educators are looking to ePortfolios as a way that lifelong learning or student learning from multiple institutions or sources might be demonstrated. While ePortfolios may be used with fully online courses, they can be particularly attractive options for both blended and web-enhanced courses. Some portfolio software is integrated with an LMS, while others are untethered from an LMS. Digication (www.digication.com) is one of the better known, established platforms for ePortfolios.

Some instructors forego the sophisticated features of ePortfolio software and simply also use programs like WordPress to house student ePortfolios.

The ePortfolio provides a way to have students curate their own work, and it also permits students to use approaches other than papers and tests to demonstrate their learning. A student might display a paper next to photos, video, or music—most ePortfolio software allows for multimedia artifacts.

There is a rich history in the use of ePortfolios as a way to assess students. Those interested in the pedagogy and best practices of ePortfolios may want to browse through a free online journal like the *International Journal of ePortfolio* (www.theijep.com/about.html). Or check out the activities and resources of an international organization that is dedicated to ePortfolios and other evidence-based and experiential learning, AAEEBL (www.aaeebl.org/).

Searching Capabilities

Some LMS platforms provide extensive search capabilities. These can be very selective—for example, allowing users to search only in the discussion section. Or they can be comprehensive, allowing you to choose whether to search all sections of the course or to limit your search to a single area.

Search functions mainly come into play during the course, and can be useful not only for your students but for you as well. They permit you to find that one passage or comment you only dimly recall or to quickly find all postings on a topic or from a particular user. This can be particularly helpful for efficiency when grading discussion participation.

Quizmakers

Some systems make available multiple-choice, short-answer, and true/false exams. Even if you don't normally use this type of test, you may want to consider creating some assessment instruments that make use of the feature. For example, you might create self-assessment quizzes to help students review the material at the end of each unit, or you might ask students to take a diagnostic quiz at the start of your course. Such "low-stakes" quizzes can be helpful in reinforcing retention of content, keeping students engaged with material on a weekly basis and especially when provided with automatic feedback, assist students in identifying areas of knowledge they might need to review before progressing to the next unit of the course.

Important! **It is recommended that you rely on more than one form of graded assignment.**

From a security standpoint, it is better to be able to compare several different types of samples of a student's work than to base all the grades on a single type of assignment. Also, from the standpoint of multiple learning strategies, it is best to give students the opportunity to display their achievement and comprehension in a number of ways.

To increase security, find out the capabilities of your quizmaking system. As noted in Chapter 3, various features can help increase the security of an exam—for instance, timed, one-time access; password-protected access; and the ability to create pools of questions that permit individual randomization. There are many different approaches to quiz security issues. Some systems can limit access to a quiz to a certain IP address, thus allowing the instructor to control the student's point of access. Others may offer a posttest analysis that looks for similarity among student answers.

Another option available in some systems is the ability to give students automatic feedback. For example, in many quizmaking programs, students who answer a question incorrectly can receive automatic instructions for remediation: they can be told to review pages 10–15 in the textbook or to reread the instructor's Unit 1 lecture. Another handy feature of some software is the ability to postpone access to a quiz (for example, by withholding a password or blocking access) until the student has finished a particular section of the course.

Finally, there are options that permit an instructor to insert images or sounds into an exam. With these features, the instructor can pose questions based on graphs, charts, or bits of music and language. Depending on your subject field and teaching methods, these may be important features for you.

If you do not have access to a quizmaking tool, you may want to explore some of the free or low-cost (depending on the features you want, you may have to pay a small fee) online testing software sites. These sites allow you to create and will host the test-taking as well. As of this writing, some of the services include Zoho Challenge.com, SurveyMonkey.com (for surveys only), ProProfs Quiz School (www.proprofs.com/quiz-school), ClassMarker (www. classmarker.com) and EasyTestMaker.com. Each service varies in features offered, and the free versions will usually include advertisements on their sites. Some services may allow one to circumvent this by embedding the quizzes on your own website. In evaluating these quizmakers, you should consider the following:

- ease of use and reuse, templates available;
- types of quizzes one can make—multiple choice, fill in, essay, etc.;

■ what kind of automatic feedback is it possible to add for test-takers?

■ what types of media—images, video, audio—can be used in conjunction with test-taking;

■ scalability—how many users can accommodate?

■ can you create groups for each class of test-takers?

■ how scores are reported, what data are available;

■ ability to embed the quizzes into one's web page or LMS;

■ how readily quizzes can be saved;

■ time limits or security measures that are possible;

■ are the quiz products you create automatically made available to others to use?

■ does the site or the free version only include advertisements or non-educational materials that might be objectionable?

Student Progress Reports, Tracking and Alerts, Learning Analytics

Progress reports that can be accessed by the students themselves allow them to keep track of their own accomplishments. This is particularly helpful in courses in which the assignments may be accomplished in any order. If this feature exists, you won't have to be as vigilant in reminding students of their progress in the course. But you may also want to keep track of how students are faring in the course so if your LMS allows you to set up "alerts" to let you know if students have missed submitting by a deadline or have not accessed the course that week, this can allow you to intervene in a timely fashion. Remember to set up your "rules" for alerts before the class begins.

Student tracking by instructors—that is, obtaining statistics about when students log on, how long they remain in a specific area of the course, which specific documents or messages they have read, and so on—is increasingly recognized as an important feature for any learning management software suite. This ability to collect and review data on student use of the course may be referred to as learning analytics or performance dashboard or similar terms. Some systems allow tracking by the number of browser "hits" in a specific area of the course. Some give the duration of time spent in each area or reveal whether an area or item has been opened. A comparison of one student to others in regard to time on task or other measures may also be available. These tracking abilities can be valuable data in helping you assess participation. You will want to find out what portion of this data is available to you as instructor.

Bear in mind that these indicators are not always accurate, because they can sometimes be manipulated by students. For instance, a student can open an area of the course and simply let the clock run. This will give the appearance of the student having spent a great deal of time studying that section of the course.

However, if statistics reveal that the student hasn't even entered a certain area of the course that will tell you that he or she hasn't read the material contained within it. Or, if the student has spent only five minutes in an area of relative complexity, this is a sure sign that he or she hasn't dealt adequately with that portion of the course.

Finally, data may be relatively meaningless without analysis and evaluation of quality. Thus the best way to use tracking functions is as a contribution to a more comprehensive evaluation, including student assignments, student postings in discussion, student presentations, and objective quizzes and essays. Online courses do permit you to know a great deal more about a student's attendance and participation than is possible in an on-the-ground course but a true picture can only be compiled in the context of the student's entire record and with regard to the actual content of the activity being tracked.

Adapting to Your Software's Tracking Functions

If tracking is available in your software system, it's important to find out exactly how it functions, For example, if you can track the responses a student makes in discussion but can't tell whether the student is reading the topic messages you post, you might want to require a specific number of postings in specific threads each week. As another example, assume you can track students' access to your presentations, but only on a unit basis; that is, you can't tell whether students have read individual documents within a unit. In this case, you might want to place the most important documents in their own individual units.

If you have little or no tracking capability, then student work submitted to you directly by email or posted in the classroom will assume greater importance, as will quiz questions that test comprehension and familiarity with material.

Online Gradebooks

An online gradebook is a tool that allows you to record and compute grades for students and permits students to access their own grades. Just a few of the learning management systems that offer such gradebooks are Blackboard, Moodle, BrightSpace, and Canvas.

If you have an online gradebook available to you, we highly recommend that you consider using it and learn how to use it well. Online students really appreciate being able to track their own progress. Make sure that you take the time to access a gradebook in your LMS from the student view so that you will be aware of how much students can perceive of the record. There are often different options available to the instructor, such as setting a due date that will not permit late submissions without notification of the instructor, or areas in which feedback may be offered to the student. If the software permits, it is a good idea to build out your entire gradebook at the beginning of the course so that students are able to get a picture of the whole that complements what they will learn from the syllabus.

Whether or not you have an online gradebook as part of learning management software, you can create your own electronic gradebook in spreadsheet form for your own benefit. Even though you may feel that you can always refer back to the online classroom for a record of activity, it is easy to lose track of individual students in a busy class. Thus it is no less important to keep detailed records of student activity in an online setting than it is for the traditional on-the-ground class. See Chapter 11 for more information on record-keeping strategies.

● ● ● ● ●

Other Course Areas and Features

If your course is conducted completely online, think about creating an asynchronous "student lounge" discussion area—a place where students can socialize. Another useful discussion area is a forum designated something like "Q&A" or "Ask the Professor"—one in which students can address questions to you throughout the course, questions that are about the course as a whole, about some aspect of accessing a section of the course, are perhaps either "off topic" or concern ongoing procedural matters. These two types of messages—purely social and course related—can be combined into one area but are usually better separated. Having such areas available benefits the students, many of whom need the added interaction and feeling of camaraderie with classmates, as well as one central place where they know they can address urgent questions about the course.

Other helpful devices for personalizing a class include a discussion forum where students introduce themselves during the first week of class and student web pages where students provide some brief biographical information about themselves. Besides helping to break the ice, these areas provide an important service by allowing students to refer back to identifying details about their classmates as the course progresses. This is advantageous even in a blended class because it assists students in getting to know each other without having to continually ask, "What's your name again?" or "Where did you say you were from?" When using blogs or web pages for this purpose, always inform students whether web pages are open only to the class or can potentially be accessed by the public on the internet.

Most learning management systems, blogs, and social networking spaces make it easy for students (or you) to upload a photo to the classroom and, in many cases, a self-introduction video. Uploading photos or video of the self should always be voluntary. There are many reasons not to insist on this option. Although it does help give each student an identifiable face in the classroom, it under-cuts the egalitarian advantages inherent in an online classroom. Not knowing the race, ethnicity, age, attractiveness, or even gender of a student—except by that individual's own choice in self-identifying—often allows students (and you) to pay more attention to the ideas and words of class members without all the assumptions and subtle biases that we all harbor. We recommend that if a student does not want to upload a photo, that you suggest creating a cartoon avatar (there are many websites that offer this service) or using an image that the student considers characteristic of his/her interests or simply suggest the student use a photo in which he or she appears as a small figure in a favorite landscape.

Another desirable area to carve out is a technical support area or link to help. For instance, you may set up an area of the classroom or web pages that contain downloadable programs and

plug-ins (or hyperlinks by which one can access software), plus either a simple FAQ for the learning management software or a link to the instruction manual or "user guide." If support staff are available, they may monitor requests for help. In the absence of a full student orientation, a support area plays a vital function in providing self-help to students or a connection to support materials or staff. As a backup to these technical support areas, provide, via an initial email or message, some instructions for getting started and any other relevant information, such as phone numbers for support in the event that students have trouble logging on to the class.

Mobile Apps

If provided with the option for accessing the LMS via a mobile app, for smartphone or tablet, **many students will choose to do so at least part or even a majority of the time**. Therefore, it is important for you, as instructor, to become thoroughly acquainted with the mobile version of your online course site from both instructor and student roles. What we want to point out here is that the mobile app and the internet version of your course site are more likely to differ than not in many respects. So even if you, the instructor, do not normally use the mobile app version of your software to access the class, you will want to see what your content looks like in the mobile app, test out how easy or difficult it is for students to download, upload or access a portion of the course, and to see exactly what options in posting discussion or submitting assignments are available in the mobile version.

Connecting to Social Networking Sites

While many students might prefer to keep their Facebook or other social media accounts as a private realm apart from their classmates and schoolwork, many institutions have been taking advantage of the popularity of these social networking sites to give students an option to link up with what is happening in a course. Surmising that many of their students spend more time at these sites than they might be consulting their email, some institutions have arranged so that students can receive updates and reminders or notifications about what happens in the LMS class site from within Facebook.

Some instructors have also encouraged students to use Facebook as a way of presenting their self-introduction at the beginning of a class (or have presented their own self-introductions in this way) or to encourage social interaction among the entire class or small groups engaged in projects.

Finding the Right Tools and Keeping Informed

An assortment of tools has been mentioned in this chapter in conjunction with various course areas that one can utilize or improvise.

Because these tools are constantly in development, appear and disappear, it is necessary to find a way to keep up with the appearance and availability of these tools, as well as to take advantage of critical commentary on such tools from an educator's perspective so that you can quickly evaluate their suitability for your needs. A selection of blogs and other resource sites by educators devoted to evaluating new tools are included in the Guide to Resources. Depending on your interest, your favorite source might be the technology section of *The Chronicle of Higher Education* or *Inside Higher Ed*, it might be a personal blog from an online educator, or the instructional technology site of your own university.

Once you find some sources that you value, you may find it convenient to add these as "bookmarklets" to the toolbar of your internet browser for easier access. Most recent versions of browsers also have built-in **RSS (Really Simple Syndication) feed readers**, also known as **aggregators**. These permit you to subscribe to a blog, podcast, or other resource site so that you can receive the latest news or installment from that site without having to actually visit it each time. You may also find some of the previously mentioned curation tools useful as a way to collect and annotate resources and tools—since they are available on the internet or via mobile apps, it is easy to be continually updated on all your devices. Or you might try a popular personal aggregator like Flipboard which is designed to allow you to find and save resources or to subscribe to RSS feeds, or Feedly, which is mainly intended to provide for fast updating of those sites to which you subscribe. One thing to keep in mind when selecting an aggregator or curation tool—the default on some of these sites is public sharing so make sure that if you want to keep things private that such an option is available.

Virtual Worlds

Educators have been experimenting for many years with various types of **virtual worlds**, that is, online 3-D immersive environments that simulate reality and in which participants interact by using avatars, that is, representations of themselves (these can take the form of animals, cartoon-like characters, or images more closely based on their own appearance). Second Life for a time became perhaps the most widely known program for virtual world educational use. More recently, some institutions have been using an open source product, OpenSim, to create virtual worlds while K–12 teachers have been using an educational version of Minecraft, called Mindcraft Education edition (see http:// education.minecraft.net/) which is a combined game and virtual world environment and includes special class management controls for teachers.

Reasons for using a virtual world for educational activities range from simple curiosity, the coolness factor, and the desire to inject some fun into education to exploiting the virtual environment for role playing, interaction with objects, game-based learning, or complex simulations which involve danger or would incur prohibitive expense in the real world.

If your university or school is involved in using virtual world environments, and your subject matter seems to lend itself to this type of environment, we recommend the following steps as part of the planning, design, and development cycle:

■ Assess your students' likely ability to access the virtual world environment. Students who do not have access to the latest computer equipment are unlikely to be able to access these environments. Try out any student instruction manuals yourself to judge if they provide adequate directions for your students or whether you might need to augment the existing guides.

■ Allow sufficient time to practice your own skills in the virtual reality environment before you even decide to use the environment for instructional purposes. Clearly the time needed will vary according to the particular virtual world software, and the individual instructor. Even if you are not creating anything within the virtual world, allow sufficient practice time to feel comfortable in mastering the basic skills that enable you to move and communicate, and another dedicated period to be able to learn how to facilitate activities for your students.

■ Find out what materials are available from your university to assist students and run a required orientation for students to practice before you initiate any instructional activities in the virtual world.

■ If you decide to use the virtual world environment, draw up a detailed explanation of what students are expected to do there. Be prepared for the eventuality that some students may have difficulty or even dislike participating, and offer an alternative activity that might accomplish the same goals.

In Chapter 9 we explore simulations, games, and other tools that suggest other possible building blocks for your class. Now in the next chapter, let's look at all this from the standpoint of what students will do in your class.

7
● ● ● ● ●

Student Activities in the Online Environment

What kind of instructional activities are most effective for an online or blended course?

In this chapter we suggest some rules and guidelines to help you find the most suitable student activities for your course. We also present some concrete examples of activities that instructors have found to be effective, and we suggest how these might be organized and assessed.

You may well be familiar with theories of "learning styles," and perhaps you have applied these ideas in your on-the-ground classroom. An example of the learning style concept would be the idea that a visual/verbal learner prefers to read information, while a visual/non-verbal learner might learn best when there are graphics and pictures to supplement the text. Research has shown that a rigid concept of learners being locked into a specific way of learning is not really borne out by the evidence so it may be better to think of designing a course with diverse approaches that may have greater appeal to some learners and at the same time may stretch others to look at things from a fresh vantage point.

Because new educational technology tools are constantly emerging while at the same time becoming easier to use, it behooves instructors to allow their courses to develop and change as well. In thinking about student activities online, instructors should be alert to the possibilities for fresh approaches to learning that are inherent in some of these tools. How might such tools be used by their students to fulfill learning objectives in ways that are perhaps more engaging and, ultimately, how might they produce even deeper learning than that resulting from the traditional assignments of term papers and exams?

Bradley Gardener teaches a fully online course, Geography 301: International Migration & Ethnicity for CUNY School of Professional Studies. He reflected on how the assignments in this course have evolved over time to embrace more multifaceted approaches,

> *After teaching the same course for a while I start to get a feeling about how students will typically engage with the materials. Students are required to pick a topic from the course and elaborate on it in a final paper. I try to give them exposure to different types of migrations (refugees, forced migration, etc.) and different groups in different time periods (Irish, Chinese, African Americans in the Great Migration), so they can pick a research project that interests them. Diversity of assignments is important. Are they good talkers or writers? Do they demonstrate their expertise best through multimedia or sound? I try to give them as many opportunities as I can to engage with the course materials. At the end of the course, if they enjoyed themselves and got into at least one of these types of assignments and learned from it, I am happy!*

In this book, we think it best to emphasize the desirability of incorporating different types of learning opportunities and recognizing that there is more than one way to approach learning. Variety is as important online as in traditional on-ground courses, and using multiple approaches will both reinforce student learning and allow students to grasp the subject matter from different perspectives.

● ● ● ● ●

Group Activities

Group activities, meaning small groups rather than whole class activities, constitute an obvious strategy for large online classes, but they can be equally effective in classes of fifteen to twenty students. A mixture of individual and group-oriented activities can help provide a variety of contexts within which students may learn skills and concepts and demonstrate their mastery.

Group activities can range from the most informal small-group discussion to a highly structured and scripted arrangement. A group may include three or four students, or it may be just a pair of students who work out their own consensus about how to approach a mutual assignment. Some of this range of possibilities is illustrated in the discussion here that follows.

To organize group activities, you need to provide guidelines for each group's collaboration, set reasonable goals and objectives, and provide both a place for the group to work and a place or method to present its work. These matters often depend to some extent on the learning management system or other collaborative software you're using, a subject we discussed in earlier chapters. Here, rather than going into the mechanical details of setting up a communal online working space, we'll focus on general principles and on examples from actual courses.

You may have already learned a hard fact about collaborative activities in your on-the-ground classes: collaboration doesn't just happen. Many students have no idea how to collaborate on a task in a course. Thus it is vital to provide detailed guidelines on the responsibilities of each member of a group, as well as explanations of how groups are to proceed with their task. As mentioned earlier, you may want to define such roles as group recorder of the activities, group manager or leader, and group spokesperson.

It's also necessary to define clearly what the end product of each group's project should be, what it should include, and where in the online environment it should be presented. Timing may be critical here, if you want the entire class to have the chance to read and critique what a group has produced. Make sure you clarify the deadlines for each stage of the process.

Icebreaking Activities

As we mentioned in earlier chapters, online students need opportunities to get to know each other. By an icebreaking activity, we mean any activity that a) allows students to begin to form some sense of community online, and b) immerses students as quickly as possible into the class content.

We recommend that every online class—and every online component to a web-enhanced or blended course that includes a discussion forum—begin with an exercise in which each student introduces himself or herself to the class. This can be accomplished by a discussion thread or through the creation of student blogs or web pages. If you carve out a separate area for this activity or create a page of links to students' own blogs or web pages, your students will be able to refer back to the biographical information throughout the course.

It's best to keep the requirements for introductions simple: "Please say a few words about yourself and your reason for taking this class," or "Let us know from what part of the world you are logging on, and tell us a little bit about your background in this subject." Begin the process by introducing yourself to the class. Generally, you should include both the formal details of your career and academic interests and some informal information. How much of the latter you offer is up to you. You can also include information about how you prefer to be addressed, either explicitly ("call me Dr. Ko") or implicitly (for instance, signing off your introduction with just your first name).

In addition to these initial icebreaking activities, many instructors find it helpful to have the members of small groups engage in some sort of icebreaking team-building activity. This may involve asking each person for initial comments about how he or she visualizes the common project. It may include questions about people's typical online schedules and times when they might be available for a real-time chat. The more concrete and specific the icebreaking questions, the better, because specificity allows students to respond without worrying about whether they have stayed within the expected boundaries of the activity.

Some instructors encourage students to add photos, either by uploading them or by attaching or embedding an image file into a discussion thread or in a blog post. This is also an option for the instructor. Photos personalize the biographical information and help classmates form a clearer image of their fellow students. However, photos also have disadvantages as people naturally form impressions based on the images posted. Members of minority groups, older or disabled students as well as others may feel that preconceptions or even biases may result. Our only recommendation is that, if you encourage the use of photos, you always make it a voluntary matter. Students may end up using avatars or other alternative representations (images, icons, symbols), and in some cultures, it is not uncommon for students to post photos of themselves accompanied by family members, boyfriends or girlfriends. Again, instructors and students should feel able to post whatever representation (or no representation) of themselves they choose.

To quickly engage students into the subject matter of the course, students can be asked to a) answer a question or two about their prior knowledge of the subject, or what they hope to learn or b) attempt a simple initial assignment.

Questions about prior knowledge allow students to measure their progress later in the course as well as help the instructor gauge what support students might need, while asking students what they hope to learn, aids students in beginning to focus on aligning their personal goals with the course experience.

Dividing Students into Groups

Generally speaking, it's best for the instructor to play a role in dividing students into groups. It can prove difficult, confusing, and irritating for students when they are simply left to their own devices to form groups. Many online instructors don't realize how clumsy it can be for all but the most outgoing and determined students to join or form groups on their own. In addition, if the task will involve synchronous activities, the time zone in which each student resides becomes a major factor, and the instructor is often in the best position to take this into account. Also, depending on the nature of the group task, you may want a mix of students of differing characteristics or skills in each group. For example, you may want a mixture of male and female students in each group or those from diverse disciplines, or to combine students with relatively weak communication skills together with those who demonstrate a more fluid writing ability.

Nonetheless, you may want to include some measure of student volition in the process of setting up groups. Student choice may be desirable under three circumstances in particular:

1. The group activity involves a diversity of choices, and you would like as many students as possible to choose the area that truly interests them.
2. There are already "natural" groupings of students in the course that you would like to incorporate in your assignments in order to promote group camaraderie.
3. In the case of students in blended courses, it is more likely that they already know each other, especially if you have first given them the opportunity to get to know each other in one or more previous face-to-face class meetings.

An example of the second situation would be a course in which three students enroll from the same corporation or organization, and all of them have an interest in working together. Other examples might include mothers and adult children in the same course, or a husband and wife studying together. However, in some cases, you might want to break up these groupings to make it easier to distinguish the individual contributions or because you want students to work within groups of the greatest diversity possible.

When you would like to give students some measure of choice in forming their groups, one method is to ask students to email you their preferences. Tell them simply, "I'll try to take into consideration your preferences in forming the groups, but please be aware that it isn't always possible to satisfy everyone."

Stephen Rowe taught an advanced accounting course at Southern Cross University in Australia in which students addressed a case study and carried out their work in a group wiki. Each group represented the issues of a different character in the case study and had to address a different question. In order to form groups, Rowe instructed students that after they have read the case material they should "nominate which of the case characters you want to play." He then tried to match up students as much as possible with their preferred role, but let students know that it's "first in, first served—a maximum of five per group."

If you have strong beliefs about students forming their own groups, there are a few ways to facilitate this. One method is to create a discussion area where this formation can occur, and ask students to share some additional information that might assist them in making an appropriate selection. For example, Christine Appel of the Universitat Oberta de Catalunya noted that time availability was often a factor for her students who used both real-time chat as well as asynchronous discussion to communicate. With a large percentage of working students, those who work days versus evenings are able to sort themselves out fairly quickly in selecting a group.

In the case of blended classes, we recommend that you take advantage of the opportunity to meet face to face to enable groups to conduct their first meeting in the on-site setting.

Size and Duration of Groups   Don't make the groups too large. The ideal number will vary based on the task. A group formed only for the purposes of discussion can easily accommodate ten or more, but when the group members must collaborate on even a very simple assignment, a group of four or five is probably the optimum size and for some tasks, you might want no more than three. For online collaboration, any number larger than these risks creating problems of organization and communication that will consume valuable time.

Try to maintain the composition of the group for the duration of the course. It takes time for groups to develop a working dynamic. Changing the groups just as members are getting famil-iar with one another leads to needless waste of time as students adjust to their new circle of collaborators. This is particularly true for shorter courses.

Group Roles $\quad$ Assigning and rotating roles within each group is an effective method of ensuring true sharing and cooperation in the work. For example, assign one member of the group to summarize, another to record the group's conclusions, and another to lead the discussion or allocate portions of the work. Then request that these roles be rotated during the duration of the course. Make the rotation frequent enough to give each member a chance at several roles, but not so frequent as to interfere with group continuity.

To some extent, the frequency of the rotation will depend on the length of the course. In a course of eight weeks or less, more than three rotations would be an unnecessary bother.

Supervision and Assessment of Groups

Although some instructors like to give groups complete privacy—from the instructor as well as from other class members—we don't advocate excluding yourself from observing the groups unless they are completely informal in nature or their work product is not intended to be assessed.

Important! *You need not participate in group activities but your supervision will encourage participation by all group members and ensure that an individual's contributions to the group are recognized.*

The question of whether groups should observe the activities of other groups when all are working on a common problem raises a different issue. We tend to feel that groups need the assurance that the instructor knows they are coming up with solutions as a result of their own efforts and will be given credit accordingly. If you provide a forum for presentation of group work to the entire class, there is no need for the class as a whole to examine earlier, prelim-inary stages of a group's efforts. However, if your course manage-ment software or other software program you are using for group work does not allow for private areas, you may have no choice but to permit everyone to view the work of other groups. In this case, the instructor's review of group work throughout the process is doubly important.

Students are often concerned either that they will expend effort not matched by others in the group or that they will be unduly hurt by uncooperative or inactive group members. An instructor who directly supervises groups can assign grades based on both the whole group's output and the work of the individual members. Combined assessment of this sort is reassuring and encouraging to well-intentioned students.

If you perceive that a student isn't holding up his or her end of the group assignments, you may want to email that student privately. Some instructors also ask group members to privately evaluate each member of the group, using a well-defined set of criteria. This provides additional input that can aid the instructor in discerning what each student has contributed to the group effort. A very simple, stripped-down rubric for final peer evaluation of group work used by one of the authors, Susan Ko, for a variety of types of classes and training courses consists of the following:

1 = *member participated at minimal levels.*
2 = *member's individual work, participation in discussion, organizing, editing, or presenting role was significant.*
3 = *member's individual work, participation in discussion, or organizational/editing/presenting role greatly influenced for the better the quality of group interaction and product.*

Jonathan Mathews had a different approach to factoring in individual contribution and group efforts. He taught an Energy and the Environment course online for Pennsylvania State University through their World Campus program. He had a very large class of 500 students formed by combining as many as fifteen sections of students enrolled in the World Campus, main campus, and other campus locations, and had support from at least two teaching assistants. Given those numbers of students, trying to discern individual contributions throughout a group project was too time consuming. Instead, he preceded the group project with an individual short research paper on one of two topics. This was then worth 3 percent of the grade. Students were then assigned to a group of four or five students based on the topic selection they chose and the quality of their two-page paper. The group project was on the same topic as the individual paper, but was a greatly enhanced study worth 13 percent. Both individual and group projects used the same interactive evaluation rubric, available online, which permitted students to calculate their own scores and get feedback as they checked to see that their papers were in the best order possible before submitting them to their instructor. Table 7.1 is a sample portion of the rubric and its corresponding feedback. The highlighted right-hand column represents how a sample student might have performed when judged by two of those criteria:

The corresponding additional automatic feedback returned by the interactive online rubric on these two categories would be as follows. Note that the feedback addresses the particular performance while it also reiterates the general principles to follow for those criteria:

Introduction: Papers require an introduction! An introduction is essential in terms of introducing the topic and background and, in general, sets the scene for the rest of your writing. The simple way to write an introduction is to introduce the importance or background of the topic, and then how you organized your writing.

Well-Developed Argument: The arguments used are weak and cannot directly support the conclusion. Outline the main findings in your paper, and then reorganize the ideas. Probably one direct way to develop strong arguments is to organize the ideas in a logical and cohesive way. Then use different transitions to strengthen the flow of ideas. Data and statistics can when used appropriately strengthen the paper. The foundation, however, is quality research; without that you have a "house of cards."

A Problem-Based Learning Approach   Pete Mikolaj used a problem-based learning approach for a group project in his Commercial Property Risk Management and Insurance course at Indiana State University. He explained to his students that problem-based learning is an instructional strategy in which "problems form the organizing focus and stimulus for learning and are the vehicle for development of problem solving skills," with he, the instructor, functioning as a facilitator or guide. The group project is intended "to provide an opportunity for application of problem solving principles to an actual commercial property situation," as Pete explained to students, and to "make it as real world a situation as possible," with the resulting report "intended as a recommended action plan to top management,"

Table 7.1 Interactive Evaluation Rubric, Sample Portion

Introduction	Paper had an introduction that addresses the title of the paper, and the introduction also raises readers' interest in reading the rest of the paper	Paper had an introduction that was both applicable and well-written	Paper had an introduction, but the introduction did not enthuse the reader or provide a clear indication of the paper's direction	Paper did NOT have an introduction
Well-Developed Argument	Paper presented well-developed arguments to support the conclusion, and showed an exceptional analysis and evaluation of material	Paper presented arguments that were supported by research and evaluation of material, and that supported the conclusion	Arguments support the conclusion partially. Paper showed some incoherent or incomplete arguments	Paper demonstrated no flow of argument. Argument is weak, unsupported and cannot directly support the conclusion

while "management looks to the report as a source of critical thinking and problem solving to support difficult corporate decisions."

With the help of instructional designer, Sharon Guan, Mikolaj devised a Project Reporting Log to provide documentation by each team of their weekly activities, both as a group and of individual contributions. A sample of the Project Reporting Log looks like Table 7.2, with each member of Team A recording none, one, or multiple entries for work accomplished in the group project for that week.

Mikolaj treated the Project Log as part of the real-life model that he was trying to convey through this assignment, telling students "it is important to keep management informed on the status and on any problems or issues that are being encountered," and that one purpose of the Project Log is to "assure management that progress is being made and to document this progress." Mikolaj also hoped through this activity to impart to students a hands-on experience with project management. The final project as well as the team itself was evaluated using the rubric in Tables 7.3 and 7.4 which reviews both the process and work product of the group.

Mikolaj provided for individual accountability through an individual contribution grade that was computed from peer evaluations from each group and a self-evaluation, with the peer evaluation counting two-thirds and the self-evaluation comprising one-third of the individual contribution grade.

A Team Marketing Communications Plan   Penny Ittner taught an undergraduate course in marketing principles at University of Maryland University College, providing an introduction to the field of marketing. Students in the class were usually business or marketing majors, but were generally neophytes on the subject of marketing. Ittner's course featured a "new product development" group assignment in which students worked in a simulated "marketing team" to develop an effective marketing communications plan for the introduction of a product. Each group picked a product to work on from those developed in an earlier activity in which each person in the class had been asked to come up with a product idea.

Ittner assigned students to groups of four or five who worked in the private "Study Groups" area of the university's learning

Table 7.2 Example of a Project Reporting Log

Name	Date	Time	Activity/Notes Attachments Can Be Added	New/Modified File Name
Whole Team	6/16–6/22	Multi Hrs.	**Problems/Next Period Plans:** Group Discussions have continued to go well by communicating through posts. Members have checked board frequently and responded in a timely manner. Parts of the report are beginning to be posted so other members can review and add their suggestions – With the multitude of threads, a small glitch in communication on a change in second hazard has been cleared up. We changed from employee theft to food contamination/spoilage – For the next period, team members will continue to work on their assigned project roles, finalizing their contribution, and communicating with members through the discussion board and collaboration chats. All material is at this time being collected by Student 5 to compile the final report and the PowerPoint slides after Janet has emailed the oral report to her	
Student 2	6/26	2.5 hrs	Searched the web for possible solutions to reduce food spoilage loss and fire hazards	
	6/29	0.5 hr	Called Student 5 to talk about her part over food spoilage and tried to get some assistance with the Cost/Benefit Analysis	
Student 3	6/23–6/27	4 hrs	Read and replied to posts. Rec'd XYZ company logo and incorporated that into the rough draft of the presentation and formatted more slides	

Student 1	6/24	2 hrs	– Did some editing and revisions to rough draft – Replaced the previous file (rough) draft with progress so far as "Business Risk Updated 6/24"	Business Risk Updated 6/24
Next week	6/29–7/2	–	– Will be doing the Weekly Team Project Logs – Continued communicating with team on group discussion board for final changes made to project and other final compiling of oral report (PowerPoint project)	
Student 4	6/29	2 hrs	– Working with Student 5 specifically for the two hazard risks of fire and food spoilage/contamination – Has posted file to file exchange for Fire Analysis Final Copy	XYZ Fire Analysis Final Copy
Student 5	6/29–7/2	3 hrs	– Continues to work with Student 4 on relative information from XYZ – Volunteered to compile the project parts into one document for the team to review before submission – Plans on submitting assignment for the team on the due date, July 2	

Table 7.3 Rubric to Evaluate Process

Process (Team Activity)	Below Avg.	Satisfactory	Excellent	Score—50 Pts. Possible
1. Team has clear vision of the problem(s)	1, 2, 3	4, 5, 6, 7	8, 9, 10	
2. Team is properly organized to complete task and cooperates well	1, 2, 3	4, 5, 6, 7	8, 9, 10	
3. Managed time wisely	1, 2, 3	4, 5, 6, 7	8, 9, 10	
4. Acquired needed knowledge base	1, 2, 3	4, 5, 6, 7	8, 9, 10	
5. Efforts communicated well within group	1, 2, 3	4, 5, 6, 7	8, 9, 10	

Table 7.4 Rubric to Evaluate Product

Product (Project Report)	Below Avg.	Satisfactory	Excellent	Score—50 Pts. Possible
Meets minimum project requirements per syllabus	1, 2, 3	4, 5, 6, 7	8, 9, 10	
Well-organized, logical sequencing	1, 2, 3	4, 5, 6, 7	8, 9, 10	
Shows creativity, solves the problem(s)	1, 2, 3	4, 5, 6, 7	8, 9, 10	
Demonstrates knowledge, conclusion(s) reached	1, 2, 3	4, 5, 6, 7	8, 9, 10	
Distinguishes between fact, opinion, and value judgments	1, 2, 3	4, 5, 6, 7	8, 9, 10	

management software. She made the assignments to groups based on a combination of factors:

> I try to put a core of the early active students together (and group the late-to-the-task students together in the same way)—this is designed to reduce frustration. But then I salt the groups as evenly as I can, sprinkling those who make the highest quality discussion postings among the groups and making sure the relatively lower performers are also evenly distributed.

Ittner explained to students that she would be "observing your group discussions, but I will not be participating in them unless you need my help." In addition to presenting the students with detailed instructions for the group project, she also drew attention to documents that were intended to assist students with their group assignment, "One is entitled Team Development and its purpose is to help you and your team work productively and with satisfaction together." The Team Development document discussed the stages of development in terms of the "forming, storming, norming and performing model." She also asked them to review the Group Project Rubric that shows the grading criteria for their assignment. The Group Project Rubric evaluated the resulting project on the basis of demonstrated knowledge of subject matter (40 percent), critical thinking and problem-solving skills (30 percent), fulfillment of assignment requirements (20 percent), and writing skills (10 percent). Finally, Ittner also had students file a peer- and self-evaluation form at the end of the project, scoring each team member and themselves on the criteria of participation in group discussions and meetings, the degree to which each contributed to helping to keep the group focused on the tasks, contribution of useful ideas, amount of work done, and quality of work accomplished. Group members were all given the same grade for their actual project, but these peer and self-evaluations, she told students, were "to assist me in assessing individual participation levels" since participation in the group project counted for 25 percent of the overall participation grade for the class.

● ● ● ● ●

Role Playing and Simulations

Role-playing activities have been used to great advantage in such subject areas as human resources, business, counseling, international relations, and economics, as well as in history and foreign languages. The same kinds of role playing can take place in an online instructional environment. The examples from Penny Ittner and Pete Mikolaj are themselves a type of role-playing exercise whereby their students take on the role of a team in marketing or insurance to practice real-world skills.

Online role-playing exercises can be carried out in small groups, with each member taking a different role. For example, in a human resources class that is studying hiring interviews, one person becomes the interviewer and the other the interviewee.

Alternatively, an exercise can be designed for teams: for example, one team playing the role of Germany in World War I and others representing Britain, the United States, and France.

A third alternative might involve an individual student making a presentation in which he or she assumes a particular role. For example, a business student might deliver a pitch for a new business while the other students serve as an audience of potential investors. A student in a history course might take on the role of a famous historical figure and respond to questions about a particular event.

Online Debates

In an online debate, students may be asked to defend their views in a public venue or to argue a point of view different from their own. Online debates can involve some of the same activities as role playing, such as preparatory research of the position the student is assigned and post-activity reflection and discussion. Yet debates can also be more pointed and more focused on a specific issue: For example, students might be asked to debate the question of whether the states should be able to tax internet commerce or whether intervention in Darfur is justified.

You can arrange students in pairs, with each student taking one side of an issue. Or you can divide students into groups, with each group doing the research and consultation necessary to represent a particular point of view. Each group would then appoint a spokesperson to debate another group's spokesperson on the issue. To encourage objectivity on sensitive issues, you might require students to sign up to represent the point of view with which they actually disagree.

If conducting the debates in asynchronous discussion forums, provide students with a carefully paced schedule for each stage of the debate. You can also create a rubric for evaluating each stage of the arguments.

As each stage of the argument is presented, you as moderator will want to stop and address some questions to the presenters or to point out fallacies in logic. For example, "Team A, your point about X seems to be in contradiction to your earlier statement saying Z," or "Team B, is there any data to support your claims?"

There are quite a few websites that feature rules for debating, sample debates, and actual debates held completely online or represented by transcripts. You can review these sites to find possible models for students to follow or to find debates on the same subject as those your students are debating—in this case, you might wait till your own debates have concluded before asking students to compare their arguments with those available on the websites, all as part of their reflection, debriefing, or summing-up activity. See the Guide to Resources for these debate websites.

In order to make the role-playing process work online, students need to be given the information or scripts necessary to play their roles, or they need to be directed to research the relevant material. In the first case, you need to make sure the preparatory materials are posted online or sent in course packets to students. In the second case, you need to provide adequate time and proper guidelines for students to research their parts.

To provide an exciting learning activity online, role playing can be combined with a simulation of a changing situation. Such simulations usually start with a scenario and evolve with planned or unplanned actions, news bulletins or other interventions supplied by the instructor. These role-playing simulations, while carried out online, are not to be compared with computerized simulations which most faculty cannot create on their own. The latter are described later in this section.

Simulations are quite popular for business and marketing classes where students benefit from coordinating their reactions to evolving situations. The availability of online data sets, developing news stories, as well as your own manufactured bulletins can be deployed to make teams respond to simulated changes. Simulations are also very effective for bringing history and political science to life, or to ask those in psychology or sociology to respond to a series of evolving case studies.

One key to the success of these types of role-playing simulations is adequate preparation by students. Students need to understand the concepts and issues of the subject matter, the roles they are playing, and the instructions and guidelines for carrying out the exercise. The instructor must not only create these guidelines, but also give a great deal of forethought to the simulated events so that they will evoke relevant and worthwhile student responses. In some cases, a relevant video from YouTube or TED Talks or news source might be introduced to kick off your exercise, adding interest and stimulating thought.

Equally important is the time spent afterward in reflecting on the role-playing experience and integrating what one has learned into an assignment. Reflection can be prompted by individual papers or by whole-class discussion. Integration can be accomplished by having students contribute their newfound understanding to a work in progress or a final project.

Computer-Based Simulations and Serious Games

"Serious games" are those games that have an element of play but also an educational or training purpose. A game may be very simple or complex but the main differences between a simulation and a game is that the latter has rules, a competitive element, awards or points or other measures of achievement, and usually, actual winners. A simulation might also form a part of a game, and those of greater complexity might include some form of incremental scaffolding to help students attain higher levels of achievement or challenges.

Games can be collaborative, involving students playing with or against each other or they can be used by individual students attempting to surpass their previous performance.

Computer-based simulations attempt to recreate an actual process or activity or, on a broader scale, model complex real-life circumstances. There are simulations that might be available through your institution's subscription to an external supplier or perhaps there is programming support at your university to create simulations for use in some of your courses. But beyond those in-house solutions, there are many free websites providing computer simulations that can be used in a class. A quick search on the internet will lead to numerous free sites that offer simulations in your subject area, for example, NASA's Jet Propulsion Laboratory at http://space.jpl.nasa.gov allows a student to look at Jupiter as seen from Earth and compare that view with Jupiter as seen from Uranus.

Animations use simple representations such as cartoons or drawings to illustrate processes, how things work, motion over time, or to offer a 3-D perspective.

PhET Interactive simulations for math and science from the University of Colorado, Boulder offers a wide variety in what is a large collection of free interactive simulations and provides teacher contributed ideas for using them at https://phet.colorado.edu/.

The SERC portal, http://serc.carleton.edu/index.html, based at Carleton College, is an excellent collection of resources for the sciences, including computerized simulations (http://serc.carleton.edu/sp/library/simulations/index.html) and simple animations. A visitor to this site can not only find links to simulations and animations but also guidelines, lesson plans, or assessments from instructors that can help provide context for the use of such multimedia objects. Similarly, the MERLOT (www.merlot.org) collection offers a number of links to simulations and animations, with commentary about how they might be used in teaching. Many MERLOT materials are accompanied by peer reviews of the resource, pointing out the special features of an item or suggesting ways in which it can be incorporated into a course activity. They will also report concerns about a site such as a high percentage of broken links. To find the gold among these resources, you will need to set aside some time to try them out on your own. However, the advantage of sites like SERC and MERLOT is that they bear the traces of other educators who have searched before you and can often give you a head start in evaluating whether they are appropriate for your own class. Keeping this in mind, we suggest that if you discover a resource and devise a way to integrate it into your course, you take advantage of the opportunity provided by MERLOT to leave your own comment for others to find.

Many publishers offer simulations and games for business and organizational management among a host of other subject areas for either a student-based or institutional fee. Some provide simulations on a low-cost subscription basis. You may want to consider these resources in the same way that you would a traditional text that you might order for your students. By integrating computer-based simulations into your readings and structuring an assignment around a simulation, you can provide a resource so that online students can participate in a hands-on activity.

Finally, if you are lucky enough to have your university create computer-based simulations or animations that you can use in your course, be mindful that it still rests with you to devise a meaningful activity to take advantage of that multimedia object. Whether it is as uncomplicated as an animation demonstrating a single chemistry process or as complex as a criminal justice crime scene game involving multiple decisions, you will still want to introduce and have students reflect or apply their experience in regard to one or more specific learning objectives. It may also be possible for you to gather data or observe how students use the simulation to pinpoint difficulties in grasping the material, diagnose problems, and provide additional instructional activities to meet those observed student needs.

The difference between computer simulations and digital "serious games" is not always a sharp demarcation, However, a simulation may be quite focused, demonstrating a simple process with only a limited range of different options and factors, or broad, representing a complex web of relationships or factors. A simulation game allows students to do more than change one or more factors. A game always involves choice or skills and strives to have some entertainment value or "play." There are additionally games that are played by one person alone or those that involve multiple players.

A free simulation game like the "Redistricting Game" from USC Annenberg Center at www.redistrictinggame.org/index.php allows students to play the roles of politicians entrusted with drawing up electoral districts, based on a variety of factors and objectives.

Jeopardy Labs allows you to create a browser-based jeopardy-style game for reviewing fact-based materials, https://jeopardy-labs.com/. Take a look at the examples there for an idea for your own.

For some examples of digital games that individual students can play on their own, competing against themselves or trying to best the scores of other players, see the language learning site, Duolingo, https://www.duolingo.com/ or any of the science games like the Blood-Typing game (www.nobelprize.org/educational/medicine/bloodtypinggame/), blending games and animated simulations. While these games may not be relevant to your own course, visiting and playing them may give you better insight into the possibilities of such games.

The Gamified wiki at http://gamifi-ed.wikispaces.com/ is operated by educators and students who contribute and invite reviews of learning games from educators and students. The reviews provide a rubric to better evaluate the game and the site is searchable by grade level and subject matter. This may be a resource for those looking for ready-made games they can use in particular categories.

You can increasingly try your hand at building your own simple games or allowing students to do so as an assignment through programs like Twine (https://twinery.org/) an open source story writing tool or a fee (or low fee premium) tool oriented toward education like ClassCraft (www.classcraft.com/).

Virtual world simulations, like those conducted in Second Life, previously described in Chapter 6, are often called immersive environments in that they contain features like 3-D, realistic graphics, or interactive elements which can help sustain the illusion and deepen involvement in a simulation. Again, in these environments, the instructor can begin with a scenario, but arrange for the role playing to take place in the virtual world environment. This form of simulation does require considerably more planning, training, and preparation on the part of both instructor and students even if the instructor is not building a new area in the virtual world. For example, if you want your students to visit a virtual Istanbul, is it for the purpose of speaking Turkish while referring to objects in the environment of that virtual city? If you are running a public health emergency simulation in a virtual world, what are the roles, objectives, rules, and other details students need to know before entering the virtual world? Once having entered a virtual world, it can be very awkward and disruptive if participants are not properly oriented to the purpose of the activity.

We are currently entering a new stage in the development of virtual reality and experiments with VR headsets (e.g., Oculus Rift) or inexpensive viewers (Google Cardboard), and a few institutions have begun to integrate these into instruction. **Augmented reality** is yet another variation, whereby one uses an app to change or provide enrichment of one's interaction in the real world. This may involve GPS, video, or a 3-D view of an existing object. Two recent examples of this for the general public were the Pokémon Go craze or the *New Yorker* magazine's use of the Uncovr app to animate the scene on their magazine's print cover. There are more and more new players emerging in the educational field for augmented reality. To get a taste of what might be possible you can purchase an inexpensive Google Cardboard and view some of the virtual field trip videos (like a rain forest in Costa Rica or a walk in Muir Woods or a spacewalk) available with an app from Discovery VR, www.discoveryvr.com/.

But the sophistication of a virtual world or specially created software is not a necessary prerequisite for instructors to create simple but effective simulations through the use of text alone or text and graphics, with the addition of documents, audio or video, and other resources available on the internet. For example, a simulation involving American history could easily draw on the wealth of materials made available through the Smithsonian's American Memory site at http://memory.loc.gov/ammem/index.html while contemporary classes in political science, economics, and the sciences might use archived news stories and videos to provide the scenarios and bulletins needed to set the stage or provide dramatic turning points within a simulation.

Digital games and simulations are becoming increasingly sophisticated and we can expect to see more of these in the future. How many will be ready-made and how many will enable instructors to design their own variations is unclear.

Games and simulations, whether low-tech or highly sophisticated can be valuable active learning strategies for the online class. To build upon these engaging activities, it is advisable to consider providing the following:

- an introduction to the simulation, setting the stage for the simulation through background information, identification of the issues or problems, readings, research, discussion as appropriate. Provide technical preparation or practice if needed when software is used in a simulation;

- an initiating scenario that "kicks off" the simulation if it is a scenario you are creating for students;

- clearly defined roles for those taking part in a role-playing simulation, with opportunities for those participants to research and prepare for their roles;

- "time out" periods if needed to discuss the activity or, at the very least, a clear indication of how to ask questions or obtain information during the simulation;

- a debriefing exercise at the end in which the results and experience of the simulation can be discussed and, if desired, a follow-up assignment. Reflection is an important element in realizing the value of most simulations.

• • • • •

Summaries, Consensus Groups

A very uncomplicated but effective online activity is to ask students, either individually or as a group, to summarize some aspect of a course's activities, discussions, or readings. This process reinforces the material and provides additional perspectives from the students themselves about the course's themes and foci. It also serves to help students synthesize the discussion and topics of study in a busy online classroom. This can be particularly important in a classroom that is highly interactive, one that has many students, or one in which students are divided up into smaller groups for a portion of their work.

When you have an online class with fifty or more students, it's usually necessary to divide it up for discussion. But students need to know what transpires in the rest of the class, as well as what they can learn from their own group activities. Having small groups of students present their summaries to the entire class forum allows students to analyze and then synthesize a wide variety of material. It permits students to feel involved in the larger class while maintaining the interaction and focus of the smaller groups.

A variation on this procedure is to ask each small group to appoint a spokesperson who not only will present a summary of findings to the entire class but also will lead a discussion. Or one person from the group can present the summary while another from the group responds to questions and comments from the rest of the class.

Yet another version of this activity is to ask small groups of students to meet and discuss an assigned topic with the goal of coming to a consensus on that issue. Each team can then be asked to present their group's findings to the whole class. Consensus groups may work particularly well when you find that students do not feel comfortable openly disagreeing with other individuals in the classroom or in conjunction with problem-based learning or the use of case studies. Consensus groups can collaborate within group areas of LMS software, in a discussion forum dedicated to a small group, by using wikis to compose their thoughts, or by means of a group blog. A consensus group might also create an audio or video to present their ideas.

● ● ● ● ●

The Experience-Based Practicum or Lab Assignment

The online class that includes a practicum or similar activity can not only provide all the advantages of traditional field-based exercises but offer some additional benefits as well.

A practicum by its nature involves the organizing and accomplishment of an individualized plan of action. Even though the practicum may rely mainly on the student's performing some activity in the real world, the online environment allows opportunities for peer review and exchanges with classmates, to help the individual reflect on his or her experience. The feedback might occur in response to obligatory weekly or monthly reports. Or students involved in a practicum could make occasional postings whenever they needed feedback from the instructor or from classmates.

In an education course, for example, a practicum or field-based exercise might involve the student's observation of a classroom situation, the creation of a lesson plan, an internship situation, or the conducting of an interview with an educator or administrator. Reports of that experience might then be shared with others in the online classroom, and classmates might be asked to critique or pose questions to the presenter.

Lab work presents unique challenges to instructors who are teaching online classes although institutions with the means to do so are increasingly using lab simulations to provide these resources to their online students. In regard to computer science studies, it is becoming increasingly easy to find reasonably priced online computer learning arrangements through subscriptions. But for those instructors who do not have access to these online lab simulations, some instructors devise lab kits that students can use to do simple science experiments at home in introductory courses. Others arrange for students to work in labs at nearby campuses or to use videoconferencing to observe lab experiments. Still others rely on a combination of these methods along with the types of computer-based simulations discussed earlier in this chapter. For some institutions whose online students reside within a well-defined geographic area or who may even be residing on campus, the blended course may be the ideal solution. Whatever the methods used to integrate lab work into the online classroom, the lab component needs to be carefully thought out and arranged well before the course begins.

● ● ● ● ●

Reflective Activities

Reflective activities such as journaling encourage thoughtful, focused consideration and critiques of a topic, and are generally carried out on an individual basis. The great thing about these activities is that they allow a student to measure his or her progress in learning over time. Sometimes, it might be helpful for the larger class to also offer feedback to the journaler, depending on the nature of the reflective exercise. Journaling already has a long history of use in online classes, especially those in teacher education. In the past, this was usually carried out through the submission of word-processed documents or written in the spaces of online workbook-like LMS areas. Sometimes this was accomplished by asking students to create personal web pages, combining text, images, and links to internet resources to create a reflective piece. Often students had to learn a bit of HMTL unless a WYSIWYG-type interface was available to them, and because it was not always convenient for students to make updates, this sort of web page journal was often limited to a single concerted effort, in the form of one assignment or project.

The arrival of blogging software made the blog one of the easiest methods to accomplish this sort of reflective journal, allowing quick and easy updates and the addition of multimedia. Many educators worldwide, from K–12 teachers to university instructors, have found the blog a good fit for students to reflect on their development throughout a course. Writing instructors in particular have found the blog to be an effective format for the showcasing and sharing of writing assignments. Students can maintain individual blogs or a class blog can be created by which all students contribute their reflections.

Les Pang taught an undergraduate course in Information Technology Foundations at University of Maryland University College, and used blogging for the purpose of what he termed "reflective learning journals." He had students use free blogging software which was external to their learning management system to create their own reflective journals. Students had three major categories of assignments related to these journals. First, students posted an introduction on their blog at the beginning of the class. Next, they were assigned a weekly blog response, addressing three questions:

- What did you learn in the preceding week—not a list of facts, but what can you take away from the lesson, what has value to you?
- How do you connect what you learned this week with your personal experience or with what you already knew?
- How could/would you apply your new knowledge?

Finally, students were assigned a reflection at the end of the course, an overall summation.

Les Pang connected all the student blogs by an index page so that students had potential access to all the journals of classmates. He was quick to point out that if your journaling activities involve more personal issues, it may be desirable to have blogs kept private, open only to the instructor's gaze. His students were free to post comments in response to their classmates' blogs, but were not required to do so. Pang added a unique element to this reflective exercise by maintaining an instructor blog. The instructor's blog affords a way to reinforce points, reassure, and sum up issues. The instructor's blog functions in some ways as an announcement section of a LMS might be utilized, but allows for more elaboration and detailed explanations than does the relatively abbreviated announcement area.

Pang noted that some of the benefits of reflective blogs to the instructor include the enhanced ability to monitor student progress, to garner continuous student feedback rather than waiting until the end of the semester, and to quickly identify challenges related to weekly class activities before serious problems set in. He conceded that it does involve increased workload for instructors to find the time to read and respond to the student blogs, but Pang found it relatively painless to keep up by using an aggregator and subscribing to each blog. This meant that he could follow all his student blogs without having to separately log in and check each one.

To make the reflective blogs a more meaningful activity, Les Pang emphasized developing a rubric for grading the blog contributions, encouraging students to find creative ways to reflect on their class lessons—whether by text, audio, video, or other means—and establishing minimum requirements as to minimum length and structure, as well as what to include or avoid (for example, avoiding blog posts or photos of a too personal nature, making impolite comments about another's blog, linking to resources that are not pertinent to the class subject matter).

Michelle Pacansky-Brock made the creation of "ArtBlogs" by students a significant form of assessment in her Art Appreciation class at Sierra College, comprising 20 percent of the final grade. But rather than simply leaving students to jot down their impressions, she assigned blog entry topics each week as homework, providing detailed instructions for each assignment. Some were open-ended "reflections" while others were more directed—for example, requiring that students visit a local museum or gallery opening. She asked that students demonstrate an understanding of course concepts and a deep reflection on what they saw. Students were also encouraged to make extra blog entries about what they observed in daily life that related to class. As Pacansky-Brock explained it to her students,

> *share your perspective about a current art controversy occurring in your community, comment about a painting you saw in a doctor's office that resembles the work of an artist you read about in your book, reflect on the form and content of a movie you saw. The ArtBlog will reflect how deeply you've internalized the concepts from our class and have begun to apply them to your own daily activities.*

Pacansky-Brock encouraged students to be creative, using color, images, and other decorative elements that reflect their aesthetic preferences and to show their own artwork as well. She further encouraged students to post comments on their classmates' blogs and even had a competition whereby she asked students to nominate an ArtBlog of a classmate that they think is worthy of being called a "masterpiece." Students who received at least three nominations could be awarded ten extra credit points.

There is a large global community of educators who use blogs to communicate their ideas about teaching and learning and many of these offer tips on the use of student blogs that may have a special relevance to your own teaching. See the Guide to Resources for a few of these.

While blogs are an obvious format to set the stage for journaling activities, Rich Cerkovnik, who taught Introduction to Physical Science to undergraduates at University of Maryland University College, used the discussion forum structure within his learning management system as a means to the same end. In weekly "concept conferences" students were asked to choose from a selection of topics on which to focus their writing and reflection. As Cerkovnik expressed it in the course syllabus, "the purpose for the concept conference is for you to personally process the information from your reading, activities, and discussions to make your current understandings visible and helpful to your classmates and me." Cerkovnik clearly laid out the requirements for the concept conference postings, with each entry comprising 50–300 words and each addressing either an occasional instructor-set topic of the week or one of the following:

- Makes Sense—discuss one thing related to this week's readings, activities, or discussions that makes sense to you. Use enough detail to convince me that you understand.

- Does Not Make Sense—discuss one thing ... that does not make sense to you. Discuss which aspects of the concept confuse you.

- My Life—discuss how a concept related to this week's readings, activities, or discussions relates to an experience from your own life.

- Change in Thinking—discuss how a concept you now understand related to this week's readings, activities, or discussions is different from what you had previously thought.

- Resource—identify a concept (i.e., gravity, inertia, balancing chemical equations, etc.) that you feel it would be of benefit to you to understand better. Identify a resource that accomplished the goal of deepening your understanding of the concept in question ... perform a search using an internet search engine and at least one University of Maryland University College database ... for resources on your selected concept ... describe your personal understanding of the concept prior to finding and using the resource and then afterwards. Report on how the resource accomplished the goal of deepening your understanding of the concept in question.

With students posting questions to another forum each week, Cerkovnik noted that these concept conference postings necessarily contained incorrect concepts that needed to be modified but that students were not assessed for correctness in these postings but for relevance and engagement. The instructor and the class, he said "can then work to modify and expand the understanding of these concepts." Students were credited up to one point for each of their weekly concept conference postings, while they could earn twice that amount for responses that provided "useful assistance to other students." Students were asked to assess their participation three times during the semester in the form of a report in which they reviewed their postings and assign a score. The instructor then either agreed or disagreed with the self-assessed score and provided feedback. The student therefore had to provide evidence and the rationale for a particular score.

In a basic science class designed for non-majors, Cerkovnik pointed out that this type of participation activity not only helped create a non-threatening environment to facilitate student reflection, but also minimized frivolous postings. Students felt they had been fairly assessed and, beyond that, there was an increased level of incentive to produce responses that assisted the learning of classmates, resulting in a "shared responsibility for learning" and a strong sense of community within the classroom.

Finally, ordinary word-processed essays still provide an effective means for quick reflective pieces. Jonathan Mathews taught Energy and the Environment online at Pennsylvania State University both through its World Campus and to resident students. For each of the course's lessons, he asked his students to write an informal reflective essay in response to a specific question. Mathews characterized these as "brain-dumps," casual pieces that compelled students to think of each topic in personal terms. For example, students studying a lesson on pollution were asked to rate their individual impact on pollution caused by their own travel. Mathews guided students with a set of simple criteria, providing some examples, and emphasized that they should spend no more than five minutes on "unrehearsed," casual responses.

• • • • •

Just Discussion

People often refer to online discussion as a given, but as suggested in Chapters 3 and 6 there are many activities beyond "just discussion" that can take place in a discussion forum—it is a logical area to base the ongoing question-and-answer sequence of a course, for demonstrations of problem solving, to provide a place for students to present their work, and many of the activities previously described such as debates, scenarios, and role playing can be carried out there as well.

But in regard to the category of "just discussion," there is still a lot of variation in what the objective might be for such an activity. As indicated in Chapter 3, this is something that should be planned during the design of your course but one should also remain open to spontaneously occurring opportunities for a discussion. In Chapter 11, we discuss how to set up and manage an asynchronous discussion. Here we want to set out a few rules for "just discussion."

1. *Coverage.* All major content areas need a corresponding forum for discussion or, at the very least, an opportunity for questions. If you are asking students to read or research a topic area, you should provide some way for them to address issues that arise with that topic. If this is not provided by discussion forum then it should be provided via a blog, wiki, or other delivery format.

2. *Objective.* Determine the level of thinking or instructional objective you are aiming for in establishing the discussion. (Bloom's Taxonomy might come in handy here.) Is it associated with both recall and identification, to make sure that students are actually reading the material? ("After reading X, what two or three major trends did you discern concerning labor in the early industrial period?") Or are you asking students to analyze the material, and perhaps question the assumptions as well? ("What were the author's underlying assumptions about X, what evidence does he cite, and are there any flaws in his logic?") Or are you asking them to share and query each other about ideas synthesized from more than one of the readings? ("Author X identifies the following as the main abuses of our globalized economy. Please share with us any results from your research that would

tend to affirm or refute author X's assertions and post at least one response, comment, or questions to a classmate whose reply differs from your own.")

3. *Spur of the moment.* While you will have likely established a regular pattern for discussions, don't be afraid to create a new topic thread when indications seem to call for it. It is impossible to anticipate every teaching situation, and the particular student mix and ensuing dynamic in our classes may change from term to term. For example, if you find on the basis of the results from the first writing assignment that many students fail to comprehend the finer points of providing evidence for their arguments, you may want to go beyond simply referring them to an external resource, and hold a discussion on the topic before they start work on the next paper. You might post a negative example of an argument and ask students to identify the missing elements in the evidence or to find the point in the reasoning when logic went awry.

Or perhaps an event in the news might spur you to create a topic thread to discuss the ramifications that event might have for one of the issues in your course. Since such news items are timely and may spur the interest of students, you might well want to take advantage of such an event that provides a teaching opportunity.

● ● ● ● ●

Scenarios and Case Studies

Scenarios present concrete situations that can be used to stimulate analysis, requiring students to imagine how they might respond to a particular set of circumstances. In an on-the-ground classroom, scenarios typically involve hands-on activities. Online, scenarios can be used to provoke responses related to matters such as procedures and planning. They can constitute a type of problem-based learning in which a specific challenge is presented and students are asked to find approaches to resolving the issues. Scenario questions can transform an abstract or theoretical discussion into one in which students demonstrate concrete problem-solving skills in a particular context. Scenarios may also stimulate debate on a variety of approaches, thus acting as a valuable tool for bringing multiple perspectives to a problem. In either individual assignments or group activities, scenarios are a particularly good vehicle for stimulating students' thoughts about step-by-step planning or the process of reaching a solution.

Scenarios have proved to be popular approaches in health and medical education, in ethics training, in teacher education, business, and criminal justice. Handling these online within an asynchronous communication environment can actually provide conditions more conducive to the success of such approaches as students are afforded more time for reflection and collaboration with others on a problem.

Case studies, similar to scenarios but typically less open-ended, are easy to transfer to the online environment. They are basically stories that present a specific situation or a set of facts, either real or hypothetical, and there is little difficulty in posting them online. Case studies call for analysis or for the application of principles learned in the class. For example, a case study in an accounting class for CPAs might describe the financial profile and statistics of a business and ask questions about its tax status. Problem-based case studies may either present a clear-cut problem or set up a situation in which students must identify both problem and solution.

In Linda Ridley's online graduate level business course in Organizational Behavior and Leadership for CUNY School of Professional Studies, she has students address case studies in small groups but also as individual assignments. She says of the use of case studies, "I believe that's one of the best ways for students to synthesize the concepts. For graduate students, there are always questions from the case that allow them to apply their knowledge." She uses the example of a case study she authored on diversity in the workplace and its impact on global business (available through the Case Centre, www.thecasecentre.org/educators/products/view?id=133460) noting,

> For instance, you'll see questions that force the students to go into the reading on symbolism, symbolic behavior, symptomatic thinking, stereotype threat, etc. In an online class, it's possible to reach deeper levels than in a face-to-face class, simply because in an online class, students are processing at their own pace, and for the most part the online environment enhances free thinking and sharing. For support materials there may be video clips that address the concepts as well as current

event stories. I spend a lot of time thinking through the student's experience—how much time will it take to absorb the reading, how much time do they have to respond to discussion prompts, and how many assignments can they do.

Case studies can easily form the basis of a written assignment, questions for a quiz, or a series of questions that you pose for a discussion forum. Like scenarios, case studies may be used for both individual assignments and group assignments. Online, case studies provide enriched opportunities over their use in face-to-face courses, with the rich variety of online resources readily accessible for research. Students can be assigned case studies as individual work, but online, the small group structure can provide increased opportunities for interaction and expanded learning through the sharing of ideas by a team.

There are many resources now available that provide examples of case studies that you might use or adapt for your own classes. For example, in the sciences there is the National Center for Case Study Teaching in Science collection by the State University of New York at Buffalo. The Center not only provides cases but also includes instructor guideline notes at http://ublib.buffalo.edu/libraries/projects/cases/ubcase.htm. For those involved in management studies, through the MIT Sloan Teaching Innovation Resources site at https://mitsloan. mit.edu/MSTIR/Pages/default. aspx, instructors can download and freely use case studies in such areas as industry evolution, sustainability, and global entrepreneurship. Public Health Games (www.publichealthgames.com) provides links to simulations and games in which scenarios such as a bioterrorism attack or a natural disaster striking a community are presented, with the participant choosing a role to play and decisions to make in response. The ChemCollective (www.chemcollective.org) hosts a variety of simulations, virtual labs, and scenario-based activities for chemistry courses.

Beyond those available on the internet, you can create scenarios and case studies on your own using simple video and slide show tools. Situations can be demonstrated through photographs, video already available online, your own staged dialogue, or narration over text and images. While purely text-based case studies and scenarios work well online, it's increasingly easy to enliven cases for your students with the use of multimedia even if you cannot create more sophisticated online applications on your own.

● ● ● ● ●

Peer Editing and Review

Peer editing, review, and evaluation are marvelous activities from the standpoint of workload management, enabling an instructor to provide students in a large class with additional opportunities for feedback. Several examples have already been provided of peer-review evaluation rubrics. These activities are also intrinsically beneficial to students, for at least two reasons. First, they require students to view the criteria for an assignment with fresh eyes. This helps them critically review their own work. Second, students get the benefit of a perspective other than the instructor's, and sometimes that can provide added insight.

Whether on the ground or online, peer-review activities are most effective when instructors provide specific questions or defined criteria to use in evaluation and editing. For example, an evaluation rubric sets the criteria for each grade designation, explaining what "100%" or "5 points" or "B+" indicates. If a student is evaluating an essay, the rubric may state that five points are to be awarded only if the essay contains certain specific elements; if two of these elements are lacking, the essay rates only three points. Similarly, a series of guideline questions, coordinated with the original guidelines for the assignment, can focus the peer reviewer's attention: "Did the paper summarize the main thesis of the article? According to the author of the paper, what evidence was given in the article that supports the conclusions of Dr. X?"

For peer review to be most effective, students should be graded as much on their work as reviewers as on their classmates' reviews of their work. Students often worry about being unfairly appraised by the inexpert eyes of their fellow students. But if they are graded on how well they review others, students will exercise more prudence and care in their reviews, and they will be assured that at least one portion of this peer assignment is receiving the attention of the instructor.

● ● ● ● ●

Student Activities Involving Guest Speakers

You can bring in a guest "speaker" for a period of several days or a week, during which time he or she will post some material and be available for questions. Or you can simply post the material from the speaker in the asynchronous class forum. The material may be plain text, or it may take the form of a PowerPoint lecture, audio or video presentation.

In some cases, a guest speaker may be available only for a live, real-time chat experience. Because chat is at best a fast-paced activity that demands quick thinking, you should make sure that students are familiar enough with the speaker's material that they can make informed comments and frame relevant questions. We recommend that you ask the guest to submit some materials in advance for you to post before the chat date. Students can then read the materials and prepare themselves for the chat. On the basis of this asynchronous posting, you may also wish to ask students to submit questions to convey to the guest prior to the chat date.

During the chat, in addition to introducing the guest speaker and setting some ground rules, you may want to act as moderator. We recommend, too, that you save and post the transcript of the chat for the benefit of students who cannot attend. Then, if it's possible for the guest to make him- or herself available later for a set period of time, students can pose their questions in the asynchronous discussion forum and have the guest reply to them there.

Livestreaming Guests   Another increasingly attractive option for a synchronous activity is to have a guest livestream a presentation. Livestreaming via Periscope (part of Twitter) or Facebook Live allows a speaker to offer commentary and even show something in their environment at the same time. So a speaker in New York might take students along on a tour of the Brooklyn Bridge or her own lab. Settings on livestreaming tools allow for some privacy, and students can also comment on the action as it is unfolding. Finally, these livestream events can also be saved so as to be accessed asynchronously by students.

Generally, then, the keys to making guest appearances serve as valuable learning experiences are:

1. providing an asynchronous channel for questions and answers, as well as for the presentation of the guest's main material;

2. budgeting adequate time for students to prepare themselves for any real-time activities.

One advantage of a guest speaker is that it provides students with another expert voice apart from their instructor. This brings fresh perspectives, and a series of speakers can add to the diversity of such views. If you teach a blended class, you can use the online environment to help students prepare for the guest speaker at the on-site meeting, or to continue the conversation online after the speaker has presented. Some guests will be available to take part online, through a guest account in your LMS that permits the guests to post materials and engage with students in the discussion area. If your guest has very limited time, at the very least you can take questions from the students and relay these to the guest. And perhaps the guest can prepare a presentation that you can provide to students. Another option is to record an audio interview with a guest speaker via online chat software. If you cannot record and save it within the program, there are free third-party software applications available that can allow you to do this (you can search for the latest of these on the internet as they change from week to week). See more about recording audio in Chapter 9.

If you do not have a guest speaker readily available to meet with your students online, with the ubiquity of YouTube videos or TED Talks or other podcasts of distinguished speakers in a variety of subject matter, you may be able to find a virtual guest speaker through the medium of video and audio resources existing on the internet. While you may not produce a live performance or customized presentation in this way, you are still providing your students with another voice and dimension to a subject. In his course Introduction to Philosophy and Critical Approaches to Literature at University of Maryland University College, Richard Schumaker found that by referring his students to podcasts on iTunesU by an eminent philosophy professor, he was introducing them to an approach in philosophy that was quite different from his own, and that this contrast in approach stimulated students to explore the reasons for that difference. While Schumaker might have achieved the same result through a series of diverse reading assignments, listening to the podcasts likely provided students with a much more immediate and lively illustration of contrasting approaches, which more closely approximates a presentation by a guest speaker.

• • • • •

Cross-Cultural Exchanges

When a course involves students from two or more countries, it can be an exciting learning opportunity. Naturally there are also many barriers to overcome.

First, assuming the countries have different languages, which language will be used to communicate? If one is chosen as the common language, will the students for whom it is not a native language be able to receive some assistance when communication is not clear? At each principal site, it is helpful to have an instructor or assistant who is bilingual and who can intervene or redirect conversation when communications become garbled or strained. Even when the language of instruction is international English, it can help promote stronger bonds between students if there is even a limited opportunity for the English native speakers to learn something of the partner institution's language.

A related issue is whether the main texts will be available in one or both languages. Even when one group of students is fairly proficient in speaking the other's language, it may be a strain for them to keep up with the pace of reading challenging texts in that language.

One barrier that needs to be dissolved before the exchange begins is that of conflicting schedules. Students in one country may be just about to embark upon vacation when students in the other country are midway through a semester. Overall terms may vary greatly in length and prolonged holiday periods may not be observed in both countries. So the cooperation may need to be confined to a particular period during which both classes are in session or it may be arranged so that certain stages of a project are carried out at some periods within one country's own group, with other stages of the project planned for times when the two countries' schedules coincide.

Another potential challenge relates to cultural patterns of learning. If students are used to an instructor-centered classroom where there is little student-initiated participation, they may need specific guidelines about when and how to volunteer their comments and questions. In some cases, students' habits of learning may not be readily apparent until the course begins. You may need to rely on your co-teacher to play the role of informant for his or her culture.

It may be best for organizers or leaders at each site to develop a set of guidelines for both instructors and students, covering communications in the classroom as well as expectations for written assignments. The latter would involve guidelines for writing as well as rules about plagiarism and originality. For example, in many Asian countries, modeling one's work on that of an authority or expert has long been a traditional study method, whereas in Western countries this might be interpreted to some degree as plagiarism. To avoid misunderstandings, you can develop mutually agreed-upon policies that are posted for students to read.

Make sure, too, that the forums for discussion are clearly established and that file-exchange methods and file formats are all made explicit. Place, time, method, and the rules of engagement should be clearly delineated in every online class or online component of a class, but these are even more crucial for classes involving two different countries.

Finally, it is a big advantage to hold real-time communications early on in the shared instructional period. It is important for students to see each other, to glimpse something of the others' environment, and such synchronous sessions, carried out through Skype or other means have proved to be of value in establishing the bonds needed for asynchronous communications.

Cross-Cultural Classes and Teams

In cross-cultural courses, one question that often arises is whether to form teams composed of a mixture of students from both countries or to have each country's students form their own team. The latter setup is easier to organize, but the former may lead to better cross-cultural exchanges and greater opportunities for new perspectives. Again, the ability to form cross-cultural teams will depend a great deal on whether or not the two countries have concurrent time periods during which collaboration will be possible.

If you choose to create teams that mix students of different countries, do prepare specific guidelines about times and frequency of communications. Remind students about the time differences. Ask your counterparts about details such as ease and frequency of internet access. Students in many countries have only limited internet access at the campus site, and internet service providers and phone connections in some countries are not stable. Find out how often students are likely to suffer broken internet connections midway through their work. If internet connections are unreliable, you would want to avoid scheduling many real-time activities, and you should probably build in more time for asynchronous activities to be coordinated. Allowing students to work in pairs may lessen the number of factors to consider in making arrangements, and it is recommended by many veterans of such experiences to allow students to mutually negotiate their channels for meeting and working.

Another potential difficulty arises when students in another country observe different religious and secular holidays than those at your site. Keep in mind that students who do not have reliable internet connections (or even computers) in their homes will be unable to communicate online during those periods.

Jon Rubin is head and founding director of the Center for Online Collaborative Learning (known as COIL) of the State University of New York (SUNY) system. The center promotes online, international learning collaborations. Recently celebrating its tenth year in existence, the COIL Center has grown in prominence and reputation, establishing a network of global partners, and offering professional development and assistance in developing courses, as well as an annual conference. Its website provides a rich repository of case studies and resources at http://coil.suny.edu/home.

Rubin himself has been teaching a Cross-Cultural Video Production course for many years, partnering with institutions and team teaching with instructors in a variety of different countries, beginning in 2002–2003 with Belarus. A detailed description of the development of this course exists on the COIL site at http://coil.suny.edu/page/cross-cultural-video-production.

Rubin emphasized the importance of getting to know the partnering instructor in some depth before beginning the teaching and learning collaboration. He suggested that partners:

> *meet face-to-face first if at all possible, at least three months before the course is to begin. Otherwise, spend some time on the phone or even better in video conference so you can establish real rapport. Your relationship will be the basis of what happens in the course.*

Other recommendations from Rubin are:

- Go over carefully all possible scheduling conflicts: academic calendars, time zone differences, university holidays, etc.
- Discuss each teacher's experience with the LMS or other software that you plan to use for collaboration. Make sure that some form of tech support is in place and that adequate technology and access is in place.
- Consider carefully the goals of the shared course. Make sure that key terms are mutually understood.
- Make each participating instructor's responsibilities clear from the outset. Teaching for some instructors may consist mainly of lecturing and such instructors may not be familiar with assuming a more facilitative role. Also, an instructor might assume that he or she will take a back-seat role, as if the course mainly belongs to the other, with himself as a participant in the grand scheme. The instructors on both sides need to commit to doing certain things such as alternating in their leading of discussion.
- When developing your syllabus, dedicate time to exploring cultural aspects of the exchange and provide time for trust to develop so that collaboration is possible. Cross-cultural courses can range from those that are more discipline-centric to those with more focus on the cross-cultural aspects.

Rubin said that collaborative exercises work well "if they are about sharing ideas rather than doing something correctly." He explained, "I think that what you learn is that what seems so evidently correct from one perspective can seem wrong or just curious from another perspective." He suggested that the tenor of questions should be oriented toward "what is your perspective on such and such?"

Rubin used an icebreaking activity involving creative writing wherein two to four students pass a story back and forth, each side adding a paragraph to the story. This served as a warm-up for his main video production activity in which duos of two students from each country collaborated on a theme to create a video. There were four scenes to be produced based on a chosen theme, with one side taking the first two weeks to make the first scene, then passing it to the second group to respond with the second scene and so on.

The Challenges and Rewards of Cross-Cultural Courses

In regard to the potential for misunderstandings, Rubin has a unique perspective on this issue. "Misunderstandings," he said,

> *were the central thread of the experience. Because students were asked to continue or respond to a video scene made in the other culture, and because their own egos were invested in their own productions, they almost always found their expectations confounded by the work of their partners. Finding a common path through this conceptual thicket was the real key to a satisfying collaborative experience.*

For example, he noted that American students often tend to be ironic or flippant in attitude and assume that others from the partnering culture will get the joke, but often that is not the case. At one point during the back and forth of creating a video on the theme of "A Day in the Life," an American student, noting the rather melancholy mood of the other side's scene, gave a teasing title, "My Life is Better than Your Life" to his video response. None of the American students took the title seriously but the partnering students were offended by this seeming deprecatory comment on their work and Rubin noted that "it then took weeks to work through the source of this misunderstanding, but this was an important learning experience for both groups." Students ended up discussing the concept of irony and what it means to be "serious."

Even seemingly trivial assignments can reveal surprising cultural differences. For example, Rubin noted that when students in a class composed of students from the United States and Mexico were asked to post "a photo that represents yourself" the American students posted frontal facial shots or somewhat humorous, very individual shots, but almost always of themselves alone. However, at least one-third of the Mexican students portrayed themselves by posting photos of them accompanied by family or girlfriends/boyfriends.

Rubin also reminds us that cross-cultural courses constitute a nexus of both cultural and personal perspectives. For example, he says that when a group views an image and tries to address the question of what is of importance in the picture, the responses will "vary by individual as well as by culture."

In Rubin's case, while the cross-cultural experience was conducted online, the context is that of a blended class, with each country's class also meeting face to face on their own. He pointed out that the question of how to share what happens in the face-to-face meetings with the other side is one that needs to be carefully considered, or there is a risk that the face-to-face sessions can become "a place for withdrawal from the interaction," with each side "talking about the other side." Rubin suggested that one way to handle this challenge is to designate a student to take notes on each face-to-face discussion to share with the other side when they again interact online. He emphasized that this approach raises the question of whether the note-taking consists merely of minutes of the meetings, with sensitive issues omitted, or whether the purpose would be to convey the essence of what was discussed, including a framing of the possibly controversial points. In any case, Rubin recommended that a template and some rules be established to ensure that the reporting follows along the lines of agreed-upon conventions. Instructors may also want to agree on an overall approach for integrating the online activity into their own face-to-face meetings.

Even though cross-cultural international courses present complex issues, the rewards can be enormous. There is an opportunity, not unlike studying in a foreign country, to encounter another culture on its own terms. There is the possibility of creating knowledge through collaborative activities that draw on the strengths of individuals as well as the diverse perspectives of different cultures. Cross-cultural collaborative assignments, noted Rubin, mean that "students have to build on others' work and also anticipate what will be workable and of interest for the other side."

Rubin noted that only a small percentage of students anywhere will ever study abroad, but "a structured interaction with a group of students in another country can really open students up to the world," while for faculty, "encountering the learning styles and new perspectives of international students is always a challenge, but one that can also be transformative, especially in a class that is focused on the value of cultural exchange."

Whether a cross-cultural course experience involves just a module and a few weeks of a course or whether it is a longer experience, one issue mentioned by a large number of speakers at a recent COIL Conference was the value of learning from and through frustration. Students working in a cross-cultural context will certainly encounter some frustrations, but learning to work through those frustrations, appreciating the complexity of cross-cultural communication, can in itself constitute a key learning outcome.

If you are interested in learning more about cross-cultural partnerships, we encourage you to explore the COIL Center resources at http://coil.suny.edu. The Center provides a level of expertise and support not easily available elsewhere.

● ● ● ● ●

Using the Internet as a Resource

One often-overlooked aspect of planning course activities is the use of the internet itself as a basis for assigned work. The frequent neglect of this option arises, in part, from the sheer vastness of the internet. To most of us, it is like an immense sea of information. There are so many documents, databases, archives, and collections to be examined that looking out at it is somewhat like standing at the edge of the ocean. It seems safer to stay within the confines of our own websites, with their more familiar course materials and tools.

But when you do limit student activities to your own course site, you and your students are totally dependent on information that you provide, and this inevitably restricts the course's breadth and scope. We hope, therefore, that you will make use of the internet's rich potential for student activities. In this section we will suggest how you can do so without allowing yourself or your students to become inundated in a sea of minutiae.

Preparing the Way

Whenever you use the internet as part of an assignment or activity, you should take care to examine the material yourself before assigning it to your class.

This point may seem obvious, but it is all too often ignored. Instructors often prefer to employ something that might be called the "treasure hunt" approach. They tell their students that somewhere out there on the internet sits a valuable nugget of information yearning to be found. They arm the students with either a list of possible sites where this precious nugget might be found or instructions for using a search engine to hunt it down. The students then spend more time than they can afford clicking through links that lead nowhere or scrolling through pages of irrelevant text until the desired information is found, copied, and bookmarked, and the requisite posting is made on the course discussion board.

It's fun to explore and rewarding to make discoveries, but the treasure-hunt approach is often both impractical and unsound. Spending an inordinate amount of time hunting and tracking through link after link can become a frustrating experience for students—one that is even more bothersome if it seems irrelevant. If the task is to examine a given piece of information, why not simply direct the students to it rather than require them to ferret it out?

There is a place for such web exploration, of course. If a student is trying to refute a given piece of information—or to affirm it—he or she may very well want to search out applicable material to make the case. Similarly, when researching an essay or a project, students often will scour the internet on their own, because they feel it is effective to do so and because they feel confident they can assess the material they find. Or if the assignment is basically one to help the student attain some level of information literacy, it may be that learning how to do a search is itself the goal.

For most situations, however—such as a homework assignment or a question on a quiz—you should probably do the hunting yourself and let the students spend their time learning instead of searching.

Evaluating Websites

What criteria should you use in choosing websites for your course? You should evaluate each site for quality, just as you would any other resource.

First, you can apply the same guidelines you would use in choosing a book or article for a reference list supplied to your students. For example,

- check the site's sponsorship;
- check the authorship of any articles or sections on the site;
- assess the relevance of the material to your topics. Does it bear only a tangential relevance to what you intend to examine or discuss, or is it closely connected?

Second, you can apply some additional scrutiny to the internet material that you probably would not need to apply to books and articles. You can ask questions like these:

- How well is the site designed?
- How difficult is the site to navigate? Will students be able to find the most relevant material without wading through extraneous details or unnecessary links?
- Is there a mobile app version available for the website or some feature of the website that would make it potentially more useful for students? For example, is there a tool or a podcast format that could be used via student smartphone?

Varieties of Useful Websites

Once you begin exploring internet resources, you'll find that articles are not the only internet materials that will prove useful for your course. Equally valuable choices are sites that provide graphic examples, documentation, or illustrations of your main topics and principles. Works of German Expressionist art from the 1920s might provide a good starting point for a discussion of the impact of World War I on Germany. Photographs found online might provide the basis for an essay. You may also base a research project on students' exploration of a website. In that case, you would want to provide some questions or pose specific problems for the students to tackle during their visits to the site. Some sites specifically categorize themselves as open educational resources (often called OER) and these can often be used within your own course. These usually carry a permissions statement that declares that the material on the website may be repurposed or copied for educational use as long as proper attribution is made. Other sites have more restricted terms of use posted that allow for educational reuse but not for distribution outside the class or repurposing or combining with other content. We discuss OERs in more depth in future chapters, but at this point, we want to make you aware of the different types of public sites that exist.

Here are some of the different types of potentially useful sites you can expect to find on the internet:

Collections and Portals Some sites on the internet offer collections of photos, speeches, essays, art, documents, articles, and recordings. These provide raw materials with which you can fashion a focused and relevant assignment or discussion. Others are portals to suggest pathways of links to find resources. Finding all of these is no more difficult than conducting a simple Google search. Some examples that demonstrate the range of these are:

- The National Geographic Map Machine (http://maps.national geographic.com/map-machine): allows one to search for maps worldwide, with street, birds-eye, satellite, and 3-D maps available. Google Maps and Google Earth can similarly allow one to interactively explore the globe and the oceans.
- Image databases of the Louvre in Paris or almost any of the major world museums offer databases of art works or at least samples of art from their collections.
- World Wide Internet TV, http://wwiTv.com, a portal featuring direct links to live online streaming from television stations worldwide, in the languages of diverse countries but also sometimes in English. Both this and various websites providing links to radio stations or podcasts worldwide provide access to material that can be used in courses on language, culture, and contemporary affairs.
- The Internet Archive, www.archive.org/index.php, is a free library resource of websites and other digital content, including archives of old radio programs and a TV news archive. This is a great source for history, political science, and other course materials related to music, the history of the internet, and other subjects.
- Free Music Archive, http://freemusicarchive.org, a curated collection of music as well as a social networking site.
- Europeana, www.europeana.eu/portal, is a portal that provides access to digital materials from different sources in Europe, including text, images, video and sound.
- UNESCO's World Digital Library, www.wdl.org, launched in 2009 and available in seven languages, offers primary-source cultural materials from all over the world—manuscripts, recordings, photographs, drawings, etc. It has a handy quick-browsing feature wherein one can browse based on a time period—so you can choose the period from 8000 BC to AD 499 and you will see a variety of artifacts ranging from an oracle bone from ancient China to rock art paintings from South Africa to various antiquities from ancient Egypt.

Online Magazines and News Online magazines and news sources include the major news sources published online in nearly every language. There are also specialized sites for those interested in finance, literature, art, photography, and science. The Public Broadcasting Service (PBS) of the United States or the British BBC, and other public broadcasters offer a wide array of multimedia resources on contemporary society. These can provide the basis of a single assignment or research project, or a continuing series of such assignments. However, not all of these sites offer open access to all sections of the site, and some charge if you want to access anything but the most recent issue. Others require registration even though they may be accessed free of charge. So, always research the access policies of online magazines and news sources if you intend to ask students to use them.

Commercial Sites Maintained by major corporations for the purpose of promoting their products and services, such sites often contain valuable information but should be carefully identified and used in conjunction with targeted objectives. The same is true for sites maintained by non-profit organizations.

Personal Sites Maintained by individuals with a particular passion for Mozart, bamboo, or World War II weapons, for example, they are often quirky (and sometimes verge on the crackpot), but can provide valuable collection points for hyperlinks, photos, and documents. Some of these sites are in the form of blogs. These sites do not always provide the necessary citations and references to evaluate their material, so their inclusion in a course should probably be supplemented with warnings or commentary from the instructor to put the material into proper perspective.

Online Classroom Materials Posted on the internet by educational institutions, materials associated with a specific course may prove worthwhile for your own class, especially if they cover topics similar to the ones you teach. But beware! These materials are notoriously ephemeral and may not last beyond next semester. If you want to use such materials, take note of the dates they were posted and contact the instructor listed to determine how long the site will remain available. More stable are the collections of open courseware made available by institutions like MIT, Yale, and the Open University UK.

Annotated Collections of Links   Some sites provide annotated collections of links to other sites in a particular field. These are often hosted by universities. For example, EcEdWeb, the Economic Education website hosted by the University of Nebraska, offers links to resources and lesson plans incorporating internet resources on economics and related topics that are geared to K–12 as well as university-level instruction (http://ecedweb. unomaha. edu/home.htm). But these may also be hosted by individual educators—Larry Ferlazzo's Websites of the Day at http://larry ferlazzo.edublogs.org is a valuable blog that is aimed at K–12 educators like himself teaching English as a second language, but his recommendations are often equally applicable for those teaching in other fields, from K–12 through university level. If you find a blog that provides worthwhile resources for your subject area, you will profit by subscribing to that blog through your RSS reader, aggregator, or email so that you can regularly review items of interest without having to schedule visits to multiple sites.

Image Collections   Beyond the many worldwide museums offering digitized views of artworks or photography, there are other sites that allow for inclusion of images in your own instructor-generated content or that can be used in conjunction with student projects. These range from amateur but often very good collections on sharing sites like Flickr (www.flickr.com) to the digital collections of texts and images from the New York Public Library (www.npl.org) or the US Library of Congress (https://www.loc. gov/). In Chapter 9 we will discuss how to find images that you or your students can use for free.

Sites Specializing in Sharing Video   The ubiquitous YouTube as well as the educator site, Teacher Tube (www.teachertube.com), permit users to upload and share video. Such sites can be valuable resources for course-related topics. YouTube presentations can be embedded (the code copied and pasted into your own classroom) so that students need not leave your learning management system to access the video. Instructions for embedding content can be found on the YouTube site handbook and if you need more directions, a simple search at YouTube for "how to embed video" will produce a large selection of instructional videos made by users on the subject of how to embed YouTube videos into blogs, Power-Point, websites, LMS, etc.

Podcast and Vodcast Collections   Educational podcasts and vodcasts (video podcasting) through iTunes have already been mentioned in this book but nearly every news source features podcasts on contemporary news and culture, including music. These have application for a wide variety of different courses whether as a single recording or a series of recordings.

Wikis on a Variety of Subject Areas   These are often most easily discovered through a simple search with Google or other search engine. Simply use the search terms for the subject matter (e.g., biology) plus "wiki."

There are some other excellent methods for finding resources in your field. You might consider joining a mailing list (listserv) newsletter or discussion forum in your discipline that shares information about internet resources or subscribe to a blog that specializes in your field. This is a great way to quickly accumulate some solid leads. Second, you might look for professional association or academic websites in your area of study that provide annotated links to internet resources. Finally, there's no substitute for visiting and evaluating sites on your own. Try to budget short periods of time a few times a year that you can use just to search the internet for resources in your field.

However you decide to use the internet, whether as a resource or as part of a group activity or exercise, think twice before making a specific site optional rather than required. Often instructors post a list of links (or resources) and encourage students to use these for valuable supplementary information. But when students learn that they aren't required to visit a site, they usually won't. This doesn't indicate a lack of intellectual curiosity on their part. Rather, it indicates that students have other priorities: jobs, families, lovers, friends, finding an apartment, fixing the plumbing, walking pets, not to mention handling a full load of coursework from other classes. So, when they see the word optional attached to a given item on their syllabus, their natural instinct is to pass it by.

Using the Internet as a Resource: Two Examples

Let's look at two examples of how internet resources can be used as the focus of an assignment.

For a course on modern China, one of the authors, Susan Ko, made use of a number of publicly available websites to give students added insights apart from the somewhat dry textbook readings and her own commentary.

For one assignment, she sent students to review original documents from the US National Security archive (http://nsarchive. gwu.edu/NSAEBB/NSAEBB66/) related to the "Shanghai Communique" of 1972 that led to the reopening of US relations with mainland China.

Students were asked to respond to questions in the discussion area:

> *Based on the NSA documents, what was most surprising to you about the way that relations between the US and China were reopened? What did you discover that you did not already know from your textbook readings and how would you characterize the discussions that took place between the two parties? Please give an example from one of the documents to illustrate your points.*

Another site used was a series of video interviews on a PBS video site, focusing on the years 1998–2001 in China, highlighting the great changes in the economy at this time (www.pbs.org/wgbh/pages/frontline/shows/red/).

The interview segments were conducted with real people and their struggles to adjust to change. This site proved very popular because the students really liked being exposed to this more personalized view of change as revealed through the video interviews.

The corresponding discussion requested that students respond to one or more of the following questions:

1. What was the situation for state-owned, state-run industries in the late 1990s? Why were workers afraid for their futures? What happened to such workers? Use examples from the video to represent the different fates workers experienced.

2. Judging from these videos, what characteristics and circumstances do you think made a person more likely to thrive or fail in the new Chinese economy and society?

● ● ● ● ●

A Grading Rubric for Every Activity?

A rubric is an assessment tool that offers a defined range and set of performance criteria for meeting learning objectives. While most instructors probably have a mental set of guidelines and criteria that they use to guide their assessment of student work, creating and posting a rubric makes this internal set of criteria more explicit, benefiting both students and instructor. The student knows what to expect and uses the rubric as a guide in carrying out assignments, while the instructor finds there are fewer questions from and challenges by students and that students are more responsive to the clearly enunciated objectives.

We have featured a number of rubrics in this chapter in conjunction with instructional activities. But it is possible to create a rubric for almost any sort of online course activity. We mentioned in Chapter 5 the importance of clearly defining your grading criteria when shaping the syllabus for an online class. In addition to including a concise description within the syllabus, you might want to consider creating a detailed grading rubric for one or more of your assignments.

An effective rubric should be detailed enough to cover all the complexity and different aspects required to complete an assignment, but simple enough that an instructor has little trouble deciding between the higher and lower parts of the grading range. We recommend keeping rubrics to no more than five or six different scoring categories. This will help ensure that you have an efficient process that avoids unnecessary hair-splitting and time-consuming deliberations.

You may overlay a late policy onto your rubric (for example, deduct one or a partial point from any score when postings are made within a specific number of days after the due date) or build your late policy into the rubric itself.

In writing rubrics for assignments in an online class, you should also address some general expectations about what constitutes quality work for undergraduate or graduate students, including coherent and largely error-free writing, adequate documentation, and your institution's policy on plagiarism. These are no less important for an online class than for one delivered face to face, and such criteria help reinforce the principle that online courses should be held to the same (or higher) standards as those delivered on campus.

Although writing a good rubric requires some initial investment of time, you may find that the process of constructing one, by requiring thoroughness and attention to each aspect of the assignment, helps produce a more carefully considered and effective assessment of student work.

A Rubric for Online Discussion

Since online participation in particular often presents a challenge to students who are trying to judge their own performance, you might find a rubric that helps set standards for online participation in discussion very useful. Here is a simple rubric for judging online participation on the discussion board that can be adapted and revised to fit a number of different circumstances:

Three Points
- Participant made at least two postings on the discussion board, one of which was a response to that of a classmate.
- Participant's comments were responsive to the discussion threads posted by the instructor.
- Participant made substantive comments or questions that significantly enhanced the discussion and served to help move the conversation forward. These included follow-up questions, examples, or new perspectives.
- Participant's comments provided evidence that the participant had read a substantial number of classmates' postings.
- Participant referred to or showed evidence of having read, viewed, or completed the relevant assignments.
- Participant's postings were constructive, and differences of opinion were expressed in a respectful manner.

Two Points
- Participant made at least two postings, but none was in response to that of a classmate.
- Participant was responsive to the greater part of the discussion threads posted by the instructor.
- Participant made comments or asked questions that contributed to the discussion and helped move the conversation forward. These included at least a few follow-up questions, examples, or new perspectives.

- Participant's comments provided evidence that the participant had read at least a few classmates' postings.
- Participant showed some evidence of having read, viewed, or completed the relevant assignments.
- Participant's postings were constructive, and differences of opinion were expressed in a respectful manner.

One Point
- Participant made at least one posting of a substantive nature.
- Participant was responsive to at least one discussion thread posted by the instructor.
- Participant's comments provided evidence that the participant had read at least a few classmates' postings or had read, viewed, or completed one of the relevant assignments.
- Participant's postings were constructive, and differences of opinion were expressed in a respectful manner.

We hope that this chapter has helped you realize that the types of instructional activities that can take place online are not only as varied and potentially engaging as those that can be achieved in the face-to-face class, but in many cases offer possibilities far beyond traditional on-campus classes. In the next two chapters we will consider how to enrich your content and opportunities for deepening the learning experience for your students.

8

●●●●●

Copyright, Intellectual Property, and Open Educational Resources

In the last chapter, we discussed the use of the internet as resource and focus of online course assignments. Instructional use of the internet has been greatly enhanced in recent years by the growth of open educational resources (OER). OERs by their very nature permit instructors to freely use, adapt, or even add to and remix their content. However, many other potential materials that you may want to include in your courses are those governed by copyright and fair use laws. Finally, instructors who create their own content may be concerned with the issue of intellectual property. This chapter deals with these three related issues of import to the online instructor. Copyright and fair use and intellectual property are but two sides of the same coin.

These three issues are treated here as follows:

1. *Copyright and fair use.* Do you have the right to use other people's materials in teaching your course?
2. *Intellectual property.* What happens to the intellectual material that you create once you've posted it online? Do you still own it? What can you do if an unauthorized person makes use of it?
3. *Open educational resources* (known as OER) are generally free materials that are available under terms of use that encourage sharing, reproduction, and, in some cases, even repurposing by educators. In most cases, while the materials are freely reusable, the user is required to attribute the resource to its original creator.

While there exist international copyright regulations, specifics in copyright law differ from country to country. Here we will discuss copyright and fair use as well as intellectual property as it relates to the United States, and touch on possible significance for other countries. We are not legal experts on these matters so our intention is merely to set out some guidelines that faculty can reasonably follow in approaching these issues. After discussing copyright, we will then discuss open educational resources, a truly international movement.

● ● ● ● ●

Copyright and Fair Use in the United States

No matter what country you are in, you need to be aware of the copyright laws where the material originates. In using materials you find on the internet, you need to know what material you can use, under what circumstances you can use it, and when you are breaking the law.

The simple answer to all of the above is that copyright law, as it is written, states that if you're using material that belongs to others without their permission and the material you're using goes beyond "fair use" and is made openly accessible (for example, on your public website), then you're probably breaking the law and thus vulnerable to a suit by the material's rightful owner.

If you are an educator, the powers that be (a consortium consisting of representatives of industry, publishing, education, and other areas in the United States convened to advise Congress on the creation of a new or amended copyright law) have made a few grudging exceptions. If you are teaching in a classroom or online, you may make use of materials that you don't own, as long as you do not make them freely available for distribution and the amount you use does not exceed certain fixed limits. These exceptions have been collected in a document known as the Fair Use Guidelines for Educational Multimedia which emerged in the mid-1990s. They are "guidelines" rather than legal code because they did not constitute a formal amendment to the basic copyright law. Nevertheless, an educator adhering to the Fair Use Guidelines is likely avoiding the risk of liability to a suit and it is likely that your institution's legal office and library services will use these guidelines in establishing rules for its faculty to follow.

So how do you determine if what you're using falls within the fair use criteria? The copyright law itself specifies four overall determining factors:

1. What is the *character* of the use? Put simply, is it for commercial or non-commercial purposes? Non-commercial use is much more permissible. If you are a teacher at an educational institution, you will have no problem satisfying this criterion. But if you are assembling courseware for distribution—say, via a DVD or public site—you may not qualify for the fair use exemption because you have copied information that does not belong to you and made it available outside the confines of your classroom.

2. What is the *nature* of the work to be used? If the work is in the public domain—that is, out of copyright or never copyrighted (created for public use or older than the copyright laws)—then, of course, you're fine. If the work is copyrighted, the "nature of the work" may include how original or creative it's considered to be. Original or creative work often requires the permission of the owner. Strictly factual material is less likely to require permission.

3. *How much* of the work will you use? Large amounts and large percentages of the original work do not qualify as fair use.

4. What effect would the use have on the *market* for the original work? Use that would significantly damage the work's market value does not qualify as fair use. This is the key provision for online educators. If you are teaching using a password-protected site, to which only students or other invited guests may gain access, you probably qualify under this part of the fair use rules. In essence, your site may be deemed the equivalent of a traditional classroom bounded by four walls. But if your class is accessible by anyone on the internet, you are, in effect, making the work available for anyone who wants it, and this presumably damages the work's market value.

To these four original factors, the consortium that developed the Fair Use Guidelines for Educational Multimedia added the following stipulations:

1. Students may incorporate portions of others' works into their multimedia creations and perform and display those creations for academic assignments.

2. Faculty may incorporate portions of others' works into their multimedia creations:

    a. to create multimedia curriculum materials;

    b. to teach remote classes where access is secured and total number of students are limited and where technology makes copying impossible.

3. Faculty may demonstrate their multimedia creations at professional symposia and retain them in their own portfolios.

4. Time limit on fair use by faculty: two years from first instructional use of the multimedia work.

5. Copies limit: Generally only two copies are allowed, but joint work creators may each have a copy. In an electronic sense, a copy is a file you have saved on your hard disk or in the cloud that is available to you.

6. Portion limits:

    a. motion media (including video and animations): up to 10 percent of the original work or three minutes, whichever is less;

    b. text: up to 10 percent of the original work or 1,000 words, whichever is less;

    c. poems: up to 250 words, but further limited to:

        i. three poems or portions of poems by one poet, or

        ii. five poems or portions of poems by different poets from a single anthology.

7. Music (including lyrics and music videos): up to 10 percent of the original work or thirty seconds, whichever is less.

8. Photos and images: up to five works from one artist or photographer; up to 10 percent or fifteen works, whichever is less, from a collection.

9. Database information: up to 10 percent or 2,500 fields or cell entries, whichever is less.

The Technology, Education, and Copyright Harmonization (TEACH) Act of 2002 is a copyright amendment that did serve to broaden the conversation to explicitly include distance education and digital creations. But the TEACH Act is complex and is not something individual instructors can be expected to interpret on their own. In some ways it has confused as much as elucidated the rules for educators and it often addresses issues that must be handled by institutions as a whole. However, if you are seeking to use text, video, or audio without paying a fee, you are probably on solid ground if you observe some of the same limits we have already noted. To sum up:

- Limit amount—do not attempt to make available an entire work (see fair use guidelines above).
- Limit time—do not make the work available for successive semesters without securing permission.
- Limit access—make available only to enrolled students in your class; use a password-protected site such as your learning management system.

Depending on your teaching situation, one or more of these three factors may be more heavily weighted or the determining factor.

Finally, whenever you use material not created by you, always provide attribution details—name, author, publisher, or other entity as the case may be, date, etc. In other words, model for your students proper documentation and credit for using resources you did not yourself create.

Is Anyone Really Watching?

Some readers may find the foregoing fair use guidelines somewhat excessive. After all, you might argue, with so much material available on the internet, who could possibly monitor it all anyway?

Think of the matter this way: It is just as easy for those who own material to find it on the internet as it was for you to secure it in the first place. Sophisticated search tools now exist, and are continually being improved upon, for tracking down pirated material. As the market for distance education grows, so do the economic incentives for people to protect any material that rightfully belongs to them.

Thus, you must be especially conscientious about materials you post on the public internet. If you aren't, the institution you work for will no doubt encourage you to revise your behavior, because it is usually the institution that bears the heaviest liability in a copyright suit. But you personally are not immune.

Finding the Rightful Owner

Ascertaining the rightful owner of copyrighted material when you need to request permission or simply want to provide a correct attribution can sometimes prove quite complex, particularly when ownership may have changed hands several times since the work was first published. It is also the case that as people increasingly remix and borrow content, they may be sloppy about providing correct attribution!

There are a number of ways to track down authorship using the internet. Services such as the Copyright Clearance Center (www.copyright.com) can help with searching out the ownership status of a given piece of material and can often give you price quotes as well. Often this is something your institution's librarians can help you accomplish so do inquire there.

What to Do If You Aren't Sure Whether You Need Permission

First, we again recommend that you consult your institution's library to see if they are able to assist you with licensing or securing permission. They will also be able to tell you what costs, if any, are associated with licensing. Such costs are not easy to calculate in advance—they can range from inexpensive electronic rights to a short article or an exorbitant price for one poem. Once you know what the costs incurred might be, you (and your institution) can make a choice about whether or not to use particular material. Your institution may have a specific form that they want you to use in applying for permission or to enable them to make that determination for you. In most cases, inquiring at your library will solve your problems. But if you do not have access to such a service and you think the work you are using does not qualify for the fair use exemption you should write the owner and ask for permission.

State who you are, what you plan to do with the material, and how long you plan to use it/when you plan to remove it from your course site. Some publishers have their own forms for permissions posted on their websites. But in other cases, you may need to write the owner directly. (See the box "A Sample Letter/Email Requesting Permission.") Keep a copy of all your correspondence, whether by letter or by email. If no one responds to your request, you can then probably use the material, relatively secure that you have made a good-faith effort to contact the author and secure his or her permission.

A Sample Letter/Email Requesting Permission

The following general template can be adapted as necessary when you need to secure permission to use someone else's work. In the paragraph where you explain your intentions, be sure to note the key features of the proposed use, such as who will have access to the site and how long the material will be made available. If the material is to be sold as part of a coursepack, you should indicate that as well.

[return address/email/phone] [Date]

[Name and address of addressee] Dear [title, name]:

I am [describe your position] at [name of institution]. I would like your permission to [explain intended use in detail—e.g., reprint, incorporate into lectures, post in online classroom, distribute via DVD] the following [insert the full citation to the original work or attach a copy of the image or graphics if needed]. The material will be made available to # students as follows [e.g., through a password protected website] for the expected period of [time period intended].

   Please indicate your approval of this permission by signing the letter where indicated below and returning it to me as soon as possible, by mail, or [by scanned image] via email. Your signing of this letter will also confirm that you own [or your company owns] the copyright to the above described material.

Thank you very much.
Sincerely,

[Your name and signature]

PERMISSION GRANTED FOR THE USE REQUESTED ABOVE

[Type name of addressee below signature line][Date]

In most cases—probably about 95 percent of the time—you will receive permission to use the material without having to pay any fee or royalty. In those rare cases in which you are not given permission free of charge, you can either pay the fee or use other material instead.

> **Important!** *If you are not sure whether or not you can use someone else's content, the rule is—when in doubt, ask.*

What about Links and Embedded Resources?

Linking to someone else's public website, whether as part of a course assignment or as an addition to a page of course notes, does not contradict the copyright strictures. You do not need to request permission to link to it. However, as a matter of courtesy, if you are teaching a course with potentially thousands of students all accessing a site at the same time, it may be advisable to let the owner of a personal site know that you are linking to it, particularly if it is a personal site housed on a hosting service that might incur additional costs if more than a prescribed number of visitors "hit" the site. Very often, when you notify the owner this way, he or she may return the favor by letting you know when the URL for the site has changed.

An increasing number of Web 2.0 sites like VoiceThread, YouTube, and TeacherTube allow for the copying and embedding of code within your learning management system, blogs, Power-Point, or web page, permitting your students to play the video or other multimedia from within your own course site. This is particularly helpful for those whose institutions have blocked access to the YouTube site or for those who do not want students to wade through all the other potentially inappropriate or distracting links surrounding a video. On the other hand, the video in question is still being hosted on the other source's external server, so the instructor does not need to worry about possible overload on a university or personal hosting server. Instructions for embedding a video and its player from YouTube are supplied at www.youtube.com/sharing. When the embed code is automatically generated by the external party as is the case with YouTube, you, the instructor, do not need to write any of your own code to embed the video, so it is a real boon to instructors who do not know how or do not have easy access to support to create code. Embedding, when it is made freely available in this manner, may be thought of as a sophisticated way of linking.

Students and Third Party Sites

An issue that has emerged in the last ten years in particular with the advent of social media and other free sites where students may share their work is to make sure that student-generated content and student privacy are both guarded.

For example, the terms of use on many free Web 2.0 and social media sites explicitly says that the company reserves the right to use content contributed there. Even when it is unlikely that the company will do so, students should be alerted to the fact that this is the policy of that site. For obvious reasons, most free social media sites promote or are configured so as to push open and public sharing of content contributed. Always find out whether a private or more restrictive sharing option is available to students who may not want to post material so that it is publicly available. Always be very cautious about providing feedback on student work that is not secured within your LMS.

●●●●●

Intellectual Property in the United States

It's one thing to borrow someone else's work to help teach your class—you know your intentions are good—but it's quite another thing if someone borrows your work. Among instructors who are leery of using the internet, one persistent fear is that their intellectual property will be stolen by some enterprising student, or worse still, by another educator.

This fear is not unfounded. Students do reproduce course notes and even sell them, often supplementing them with notes they have written themselves. This practice has been going on since long before the advent of the internet (surely no one has forgotten the dreaded copying machine). But the practice is significantly easier when lectures and other course materials are posted online, because all one needs to do is to copy the materials electronically and save them as a file.

A more sinister scenario involves other educators, or even for-profit publishers of educational material, "borrowing" your lectures and using them for their own purposes, either reworking them or reformatting them to suit their own needs. In a world in which tenured positions are becoming less commonplace and many instructors find themselves teaching for various universities at one time or another, intellectual theft of this sort may not be as rare as you suppose.

Let's look first at your legal rights and then at some practical steps you can take to protect your work.

The Legal Status of Your Work

Believe it or not, legal ownership of material you create is a very gray area at many institutions. Most faculty members are under the impression that the intellectual work they produce or publish automatically belongs to them. Not so. It is simply the accepted custom of most universities, particularly those involved in research, to cede rights to such intellectual property to their faculty members, because the administrators realize that work thus produced will bring the institution revenue in the form of grants. But institutions do not have to cede these rights. They merely choose to.

The same has been historically true for course content, including syllabi, lecture notes, and course outlines. Departments, however, often retain copies of these materials to make available to new instructors or TAs who are teaching the course for the first time. Of course, in this situation the new instructors may be expected to adapt rather than copy the original syllabus. A departing instructor is also usually free to take his or her courseware to a new institution.

Teaching online often means creating original material in the form of electronic files or web pages enriched with multimedia elements such as graphics, sound, video, and animations. Instructors who create such material may assume it belongs to them, but when a university or other institution is intent on marketing its courses and programs online, ownership of these materials may not be quite as clear-cut. From the institution's point of view, such material may not bring in revenue in the form of grants, but it can help create revenue in the form of increased tuition. Hence the institution may be less willing to cede rights to the instructor. The institution may consider what the instructor has created as work-made-for-hire, that is, work that was done in the context of fulfilling job responsibilities. Or, the institution may "unbundle" the rights, permitting themselves to continue to use the material while allowing the instructor to use all or a portion of the material at another university or in some other educational context.

At this point in the development of online courses, most universities have evolved a policy about ownership of content of online courses so this is no longer usually an issue that faculty have to puzzle out on their own. In many cases, it has become commonplace that:

■ faculty retain copyright and can reuse their own material elsewhere;
■ the institution can continue to reuse any content created for which a course development payment was made;
■ if a great deal of value-added content was created by staff other than the faculty, there is usually a contract that sets forth the copyright and reuse rules. In these cases, the institution may or may not claim copyright but will nearly always claim the right to reuse.

At some institutions, content for which a course development fee was paid to faculty will also result in those faculty being given a right of first refusal when it comes time to make revisions.

It is a good idea, therefore, to find out—in writing—your institution's policy with respect to online materials you've created to teach your course. If there is no established policy, come to some agreement with the administrators about your material. This is especially important if you're a non-tenured adjunct or lecturer and expect to use your courseware at several different institutions, either online or as part of a blended course. If you can't secure clear ownership rights to your own material, you can always copyright the material yourself before making it available to your institution or class. Although most faculty members aren't aware of this, you automatically hold the copyright of your intellectual property the moment you commit it to paper or to any fixed medium. If it came to a court case, however, you would have to prove the date you created the material. One way to do this is to send yourself a registered envelope or package with the material inside and then keep the package unopened. A second way is to submit a claim for copyright to the Library of Congress.

As online instruction becomes more lucrative for universities and private institutions alike, the question of who owns the rights to material and who benefits from revenues derived from it will become more and more important, especially since the percentage of instructors in contingent rather than secure, full-time permanent positions has also increased.

The field of copyright law and intellectual property is rife with legal experts. We do not pretend to a special expertise. What we do suggest is that you take nothing for granted when it comes to material you have created and that you make the effort to learn in advance the specific policies of the institution you are working for.

Practical Steps for Protecting Your Work

A copyright notice prominently displayed is like a scarecrow in a field. It will scare away some of the crows, but some will come pecking all the same. So it pays to be both vigilant and practical.

Various instructional materials are pilfered from ordinary classrooms every day, and the internet makes it even easier to steal material and repurpose it. With a little care, however, most instructors who post material online can avoid serious problems.

Begin with common sense. Say you have an essay you've been working on. It hasn't yet been published, but you have good reason to think it may be published. Meanwhile, you'd like your class to read it. If you're fearful that one of your students may copy it or send it to someone else, then post an abstract or description of it instead. Or, you may affix a notice that clearly cautions students that the essay is not for distribution—this is a milder approach, but surprisingly effective: most students will be respectful of this and it suggests to all that you are consciously setting up some controls on this content. In fact, there is no reason why you cannot post a notice explaining that your lectures or commentary are "not for distribution or use outside this class."

There are also some technological strategies you can use to help ward off potential thieves.

Technological Methods The first, and probably the most obvious, technological stratagem to reduce theft is to use a password-protected website. Most learning management systems possess encryption tools that prevent unwanted visitors from viewing the course. If you aren't using an LMS, tools exist that will permit your computer support personnel to password-protect your website with various computer programs. Even if you're essentially on your own, with no support, a number of easily accessible programs will allow you to password-protect your site (refer to the websites listed in the Guide to Resources).

There are also some technological methods for protecting unlawful copying or downloading of your work. Some software programs permit you to limit the way your work can be copied by others online. Take the case of a lecture you have created using Microsoft Word. If you save this document as an HTML file or post it to your website as an attachment, your students will be able to open it or download it exactly as if they had copied it from your hard disk. What you might do instead is to use a program such as Adobe Acrobat. This is the program that permits you to create the Acrobat file PDF format that you see everywhere on the internet, and it provides options that can help limit unauthorized use of your material.

For example, if you do not want your students to reprint your material or save it, Adobe Acrobat permits you to restrict how the material is used. For example, you can restrict printing out the document so that no printing out is allowed or only in low resolution. You can restrict edits or require a password to open. Similarly, assuming you are operating according to the fair use guidelines, you can copy articles or material culled from other sources and "print" them as PDF files, then limit your students' rights to repurpose them by taking advantage of the features just mentioned. (Note: Adobe Reader is a free program, but Adobe Acrobat is not. If it is not available on your computer, check to see if your institution can install it for you. Once Acrobat is installed, the PDF option should appear as one of the printing or export options available or in the "Save As" option.) It is also possible to "encrypt" your PDF on a Mac without the Adobe Acrobat program, ensuring a password is used to open it.

A determined student may be able to evade the restrictions but sending out information in this format is like building a fence around your fields. It will keep most, though not all, intruders from pillaging your crops.

Checking for Unauthorized Use

Finally, if you are worried that your intellectual property is being stolen, or even if you are just sensibly concerned, try conducting an online search every six months or so. Choose a unique sentence or phrase from one of your lectures and use a search engine to search online. If the phrase pops up, and it looks as if it was borrowed from your notes, drop the author of the offending page a warning note or query, as the case may demand. Be gracious—it may often be inadvertent on the part of the offender. Most academic sites are very quick to remedy the error when notified.

• • • • •

Open Educational Resources (OER)

Sometimes protecting your work is not your major concern—it is making it known. Perhaps you want to deposit the fruits of your research at your university on its institutional repository online. Or it may be that you want to collaborate with others or build on previous works to create a resource for other scholars or for your students. Maybe you want to create a free ebook of a new work. In that case, OER may be your best friend.

The term "open educational resources," mentioned in Chapters 3 and 7, derives from a 2002 UNESCO forum on open course-ware for developing countries. Since 2005, the OER community has grown to encompass organizations and individuals worldwide who are interested in sharing resources and creating new digital resources that can be made available to all on the internet. The definition of OER not only includes the notion that the content of OER is free for use but also that sharing of knowledge is actively encouraged. A useful handbook for OER educators is available at www.wikieducator.org/OER_Handbook/educator_version_ one—the handbook and the Wikieducator site itself are both examples of OER.

OER content ranges from small learning objects, images, quizzes, lesson plans, syllabi, or discrete modules to larger collections of modules and entire courses. OER can usually be freely reused, adapted to new uses through mixing with other content, and freely distributed in their new form. The terms of use for OER can vary but most require attribution to the original creator and are offered free for use by non-profits and educational institutions. Look for terms of use on each OER site. For example, the MIT Opencourseware site clearly sets forth its own rules as 1) non-commercial, i.e., the content can only be used by non-profit groups and educators; 2) attribution must be made to MIT and the professor whose work you are using, whether the content is used as is or mixed or repurposed; and 3) "share-alike"—anything created with their content must be offered as an OER to others. They also give explicit guidelines concerning how to affix an attribution.

There are some OER proponents who believe that only those permissions that allow for remixing of content are true OER, but we believe you do not need to subscribe to this idea to begin to adopt (or make available your own OER) and we encourage you to find the approach that is most comfortable for you and your circumstances.

You can find OER content through a number of different ways. Obviously, you can search your library databases or the internet for such resources, and while this may turn up articles on OER rather than the materials themselves, there may be links to the actual OER as well. There are some well-known sites that provide collections of OER, such as the OER Commons (http://oercommons. org), or that have more discipline-specific collections such as the previously mentioned Chemistry Collective (www.chem collective.org). (See the Guide to Resources for more collections of OER.)

By making use of appropriate OER, you are often able to enhance your course while avoiding the issues and costs associated with copyrighted material. Another approach to using OER is to incorporate or adapt the OER with your own materials. For example, you might add to your own lecture in introductory physics by using some materials from a lecture by one of the professors featured on the MIT Opencourseware site. By mixing OER with your own materials in this way, you may find that you are able to add diversity of perspectives and approaches to your own content.

● ● ● ● ●

Creative Commons License

Do consider whether or not a particular piece you have created is something you want to protect for whatever reason—e.g., it involves expected income or because you fear another educator may reuse it and claim it for their own. If you simply want acknowledgment and attribution of your work, then especially for publicly available websites, blogs, wikis, or other sites where you may share your work, the Creative Commons license (http://creative commons.org/license) may be a good approach. When you sign up for a free license with this organization, you can decide what limitations you wish to put on what you publish online—there are four basic license conditions (attribution, sharealike, non-commercial, and no derivatives) which can be combined in different ways. For example, these can range from no restrictions to no modifications or use by commercial entities; the Creative Commons site has a very helpful series of questions to take you step by step through this decision. (See https://creativecommons. org/choose/.) By affixing one of the six main Creative Commons license notices, you can let others know that you are encouraging the propagation of your ideas, but that you do want credit for originating those ideas.

Deliberately making some portion of your work available as an OER can actually benefit you in many ways—you may create a demand for your work that might not have otherwise transpired, find potential collaborators among the world of educators, and find yourself quoted, invited to present at conferences, and other unexpected benefits.

Figure 8.1 Creative Commons six different licenses. Source: By Design: Markus Büsges, leomaria designbüro, Germany - https://wikimedia. de/w/images.homepage/b/ba/Open_Content_A_Practical_Guide_to_Using_ Open_Content_Licences_web.pdf, CC BY-SA 4.0, https://commons. wikimedia.org/w/index.php?curid=36977098.

If you want to mix the use of OER materials along with some non-OER materials that are not covered under fair use, you will want to request permission from the copyright holder. The OER handbook discusses how to handle this situation and provides a sample letter requesting permission for clearance at www.wikieducator.org/OER_Handbook/educator_version_one/License/ Copyright_clearance.

As the cost of textbooks and journals has risen, more and more educators have been actively promoting the use of OERs. This has become particularly attractive to those in the community colleges. One of the crucial aspects of using OERs in place of textbooks is to selectively curate and knit together materials.

There are a growing number of peer-reviewed sites for OER materials like MERLOT (www.merlot.org), College Open Textbooks (www.collegeopentextbooks.org/), the Open Textbook Library (http://open.umn.edu/opentextbooks/), and OpenStax (https://openstax.org/higher-ed).

● ● ● ● ●

Special Issues Related to Free but Commercial Web 2.0 Sites

Many of the free Web 2.0 sites mentioned in this book and the many others not explicitly mentioned here may invoke terms of use that, while granting that what you blog, record, or otherwise create using their tools and hosting service remains your intellectual property, may yet contain provisions that entitle them to display and reveal your content as part of their publicity, demonstrations, or other possible uses. This is especially true for any content that you choose to make public, but may also potentially include your "private" areas. While you should not overreact to this sort of policy (which, in effect, is part of the bargain, like advertisements, in exchange for free use and seldom exercised), it is a reminder that you should hesitate to post anything or create content—such as something incorporating private contact info, personal details, photos, etc.—that you would feel uncomfortable having revealed to the world. As noted earlier in this chapter, it is a good idea to make your students aware of the terms of use for the sites and encourage them to use similar discretion outside your learning management system. There is also the fact that a Web 2.0 site may be hosted on a server in a country that does not hold to the same privacy provisions as those of your own country, so that is yet another reason to carefully read the terms of use and privacy policy posted on a site.

Having looked at the subject of content ownership, in the next chapter we shine a light on the ways in which lively content for online courses can be created, assembled, or enriched by those with limited technical skills as well as those who are more technically proficient.

9

• • • • •

Creating Courseware: Selecting "Web 2.0" Tools and Other Resources

If you are lucky enough to have access to instructional techno-logy staff who can create your every wished-for simulation, beautifully displayed web pages, and videos with high production values, then you may not care much about creating course content beyond the usual text-based materials on your own. But even the most fortunately equipped and staffed institutions may have some limitations as to time that can be expended on just your course. So if the course you are teaching is not already fully supplied with superb multimedia and beautifully crafted modules, you will want to think about how to enhance your courseware through the use of multimedia, additional resources, and tools that add interest and enhance interaction in your class. By the term "courseware" we mean all the software tools, digital materials, and resources used as course materials to deliver an online class. Courseware thus includes both text-based and multimedia-enriched materials. We also include applications and tools that are inseparable from the communication of course content.

This book has always promoted the use of low-threshold, low-barrier types of software solutions for instructors to create course materials. The term, "low threshold application" was originally coined by Steve Gilbert of the TLT group to describe those easy-to-learn, reliable, and low-cost technology tools for educators. Low-threshold, low-barrier means those technologies that are easily learned by you (and perhaps by your students) and that can be used to easily accomplish your instructional objectives. While the term "Web 2.0" is waning in use, it hasn't really been replaced by any term (not even the ubiquitous "ed tech tools" that includes all those characteristics implied by that Web 2.0 category).

"Interactive" and "collaborative" are two elements of these tools but the easy-to-learn and easy-to-use aspects are not encompassed by any other term. When considering what constitutes the category of Web 2.0 tools for this book, our definition includes "easy to learn and easy to use" tools that have built-in sharing and collaboration features.

Because of the increasing use of "apps" on mobile devices, apps are another source to look for courseware that can enhance the teaching and learning experience. Some of the tools described in this chapter are available in mobile form but others are not. Because the availability of these tools is constantly changing, we will not attempt to exhaustively catalog these here. There are some tools that are designed only for mobile devices, while in other cases it may be that the mobile app version does not possess all the features of the web-based one. So if you are looking for tools that are available in mobile app format, you will need to carefully review the mobile app capabilities for that tool before deciding to adopt it. And unless your students are all standardized on one type of platform, you will want to select apps that can be used on both Apple iOS and Android devices.

For most online instructors, the learning management system or virtual learning environment software still serves as their main stage. Within your LMS, it may be that you can already create HTML pages via WYSIWYG ("what you see is what you get") editors, and perhaps even generate audio clips, PowerPoint slides, videos, and images within this system. If you have an LMS, it makes sense to fully exploit the capabilities that reside within it to create enriched content. So find out what the capabilities are in your LMS and experiment with the various document formats available to you. Beyond that, you can easily link out to open educational resources, internet resources that incorporate media, and perhaps connect to textbook-publisher-supplied multimedia.

But what if you have no LMS, or want to consider some options not available in your LMS? In the past, if you wanted to go beyond enlivening your course with just a few relevant graphics or charts to creating a narrated slide show with the sound of your voice synchronized to the display of images or a video lecture, there was a substantial learning curve to accomplish these things. Some technical staff and instructional designers might have told you that this was beyond your reach, that creating "really good" learning objects required knowledge of complex software programs in order to make really cool web pages, the ones with text flying around like swarms of locusts and colors undulating like the northern lights, or to make videos that have that professional studio look.

But the great news about software is that every year it becomes easier and easier to use. The obstacles that formerly impeded instructors have been removed. In fact, there are a number of low-tech tools that cost very little, or even nothing at all, that are easy to learn, easy to use, and easy to remember when you use them again a month or so down the road. Better still, much of what you may need to do can be accomplished using software that is menu-driven, freely available (or low cost) to use, and that requires no programming ability at all. Web 2.0 tools in particular may not even require a download of software but may instead allow you to accomplish everything you need to do through your browser or mobile app.

To fully appreciate the possibilities that come with using Web 2.0 tools to create multimedia, just look at some of the educators' blogs available on the internet. A great way to start is by viewing some of the blogs by educators nominated or awarded by Edublogs (http://edublogawards.com), which not only recognizes educators' blogs but also class blogs by students, best educational use of social networking sites like Twitter, and best ed tech resource-sharing blogs. While these are focused on the K–12 world, the use of multimedia on these blogs, especially through the use of Web 2.0 tools, is instructive for those in higher education as well, and can open your eyes to the possibilities now available to ordinary instructors.

Let's look at some of the options for creating courseware and the use of Web 2.0 tools, beginning with the simplest means.

●●●●●

Creating Text for Course Pages

To write text for your course pages, you can generally avoid having to learn HTML at all. In most cases, there will be a WYSIWYG editor incorporated into your LMS or you can create pages outside that LMS using the built-in blog or wiki or free website software of your choice—all of these contain WYSIWYG editors as well as design templates. If you still need to create a web page on your own, we recommend using a free web page WYSIWYG editor.

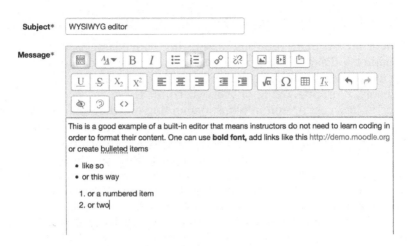

Figure 9.1 Built-in WYSIWYG Editor within Moodle. Source: http://demo.moodle.org.

Creating Web Pages in a Web Editor

If you really have the need to create web pages outside your LMS editor, or the blog or other software you are using, whether it is for separate use or to upload to your LMS, a reliable way to produce a web page is to work directly in an HTML-editing program. One of the most popular commercial editors is Dreamweaver and your institution may well have a license for it or a similar program. However, this may be way beyond what you need and there are some free, cross-platform (for Windows, Mac, and Linux) editors like KompoZer (www. kompozer.net) or SeaMonkey Composer (www.seamonkey-project.org/) that will do the job for you—because these vary so much in features and frequently change, try searching for "open source WYSIWYG editors" to find one most suitable for your needs. Most internet editors work the same way and are not unlike standard word processors. Functions such as boldfacing and centering a line of text are invoked by clicking on an image or icon. Once you save a page created in a WYSIWYG editor, it is automatically saved as a web page complete with all the requisite code.

Creating Class Website Outside an LMS

There are so many options for hosting your class, as noted in Chapter 6. Easy to use, menu and template-based designs, with drag and drop features are characteristic of the aforementioned Weebly, Wordpress.com, or Wix (wix.com). These are available in free or low-cost premium plans, depending on what features you need. They may include their own royalty-free images, or their own audio and video players (e.g., Weebly for Education). Their availability to be accessed by students via mobile apps or seamless connections to social media make these an increasingly sophisticated and rich alternative to those hosting classes outside an institutional LMS. Take the time to explore before selecting one of these, based on your needs. Some questions to ask yourself are:

- What are the limitations of the free version if any for creating the site, features offered, limitations as to size or security, commercial free or not?

- Does the free version offer or present limitations on what your students can do—for example, can you set up blogs for your students, or only for yourself?

- If this site is not only for you to host content but is also going to be the locus for all or a majority of your student activity, do the structure and features match up with the kinds of instructional activities you are planning?

Designing Web Pages for Instruction: A Few Tips

Keep the background simple. The fact that you can add a background color or design doesn't mean you ought to. Your students are visiting your page in order to get information they need. What's important to them is seeing the information clearly. So, if you must use a background, make it very light so that dark text will contrast with it.

When choosing fonts, don't overdo it. Too many fonts, sizes, or colors confuse the eye rather than guide it. Look at any published book and notice the relative simplicity of the layout. One size of font (generally between 10- and 12-point type) defines the body text. It is usually a font with serifs—the fine strokes at the top and bottom of letters—because serifs help make a visual connection between one letter and the next. Headings tend to be printed in either bold or a sans serif (that is, non-serif) font. Sans serif fonts tend to look stolid and important—or so our brains have been trained to think. So use a font like Helvetica.

Never use light text against a light background, such as yellow text against a white background. It's usually unreadable. Always use very light against dark, or very dark against white.

Don't force your readers to scroll down the page to follow the main text. Reading on a screen isn't the same as reading a printed page. Many people don't like to read too much text from the screen, because of eye fatigue. On the other hand, it isn't particularly enjoyable to follow links from one short page to another short page. Usually the best compromise is to create one long page and then provide some way, other than tedious scrolling, for your reader to navigate through it. This means creating a table of contents somewhere (usually at the top of the page) with links to "anchors" you set up on the page. This also complies with universal design rules.

Pay attention to basic universal design/accessibility rules. Don't use text boxes. Use style headings. Provide alt-text descriptions for all non-decorative images and captions for all videos. Some of the website building sites have provided good support for accessibility but don't take it for granted. Consult a list of guidelines before you begin.

Don't overload your page with web links. Your students are visiting your page; they should be able to see or get to the information they want to find immediately. Provide descriptions of links rather than just saying "click here." Try to make it easy for students by listing the main topics on the front or main page, with links to related pages. On the related pages, make sure you provide them with a way to get back to the main page. That way, your students can move back and forth with ease.

The How and Why of Images

Images include everything from drawings, charts, and maps to photographs, fine art, and cartoons. Building on the examples noted earlier, here are some of the ways that images can enrich your course:

■ To illustrate an abstract or unfamiliar concept, object, or phenomenon. For example, a Japanese woodblock print from the late nineteenth century showing the Meiji emperor dressed in a western suit and viewing cherry blossoms might reinforce a lesson on the concept of modernization of Japan. Photos or artworks of the trenches of World War I might remain in the mind of students long after a text description has faded from memory.

■ To provide more vivid detail than possible with text alone—for example, maps documenting the changes over time in the course of the Mississippi River, a drawing or photo showing the past practice in China of foot binding for women, or a diagram clearly marking the parts of an animal or the stages of digestion in a biology lesson will provide more information than from the student's reading alone.

■ To enliven and emphasize points in a lesson—for example, photos and artwork capturing major historical events, portraits of an author or politician, street scenes depicted in paintings and watercolors may help make your points in a lecture.

■ As the basis for an assignment—for example, students can be asked to take photos to document activities outside the classroom, to create graphs or tables to demonstrate their work, or to find examples in the real world of the topics studied in class.

Finding Images

There has never been such a wealth of images available on the internet as exists today, especially photographs, now that digital cameras are ubiquitously embedded in our smartphones and photo-sharing sites like Instagram and Flickr have encouraged everyone to post and make public their photos. You can save almost any image you find on the internet by clicking on it once, and then (if you're on a PC) right-clicking your mouse or (if you use a Mac) just holding the mouse button down. The dialog box will pop up and permit you to save the image to your hard disk. After that, you can easily upload it to a web page, into your LMS, or edit and change it for these and other uses. And of course, instructors can easily create their own photos for their courses using those same smartphones.

Two issues are connected with finding and using images—terms of use (that is, are the photos freely usable or not within your own course or can you simply link to them?) and finding images that are relevant and appropriate for your class.

You can find royalty-free or reusable images through the Creative Commons page at https://search.creativecommons.org/ which serves as a gateway to search services. Wikipedia Commons, Google Images, Flickr, Open Clip Art are just a few of the sources available through this page.

Note that going directly to Google Images search allows you to insert a keyword to find a great variety of images related to your topic, but it is not always obvious which of these are royalty free. A sample search for the image of T. S. Eliot, even though further refined to look for only medium-size photos of the face, results in 4,300 images! When you click on each image, the standard Google language declares, "Image may be subject to copyright." To determine copyright, you must then go to the original site and see if there are any notations on the status of the photo. You can see that this might get very time-consuming so a better option might be to use the Google Advanced search option under "usage rights" to filter out those images that are royalty free from those that are not. By choosing the criteria "any size," "photo" in "JPEG" format, and specifying that the usage rights should be those "free to use or share" or "free to use, share, or modify," the results are much more manageable—under 200, of which only about a dozen actually include images of T. S. Eliot.

Flickr allows one to search for photos that are offered under the terms of the Creative Commons. If I would like to find a photo of a pine tree, I can use the Advanced Search to "Only search within Creative Commons-licensed content" and I can further refine it to those images that I can modify, adapt, or build upon in case I want to alter the images. Such a search results in over 11,000 different photos of pine trees.

Another site to try is PicFindr (www.picfindr.com) which allows you to search multiple sites for royalty-free or inexpensive stock photography, a search further organized by the type of usage (educational, free but give attribution, etc.) or license you are looking for. A search for pine trees here produces a large number of photos, most of which are royalty free with a few others offered at a small price.

Pics4Learning (www.pics4learning.com/) is a site for educators that features a collection of free images. You can search by topical collections ("food," "history," "science") or by advanced key word search.

Clipart　There are several collections of clipart illustrations. For example, Clipart ETC (http://etc.usf.edu/clipart) is a collection sponsored by Florida's Educational Technology Clearinghouse, containing tens of thousands of pieces of clipart suitable for students and teachers, offered free for educational use of up to fifty

Find images with...

To do this in the search box

all these words:	T.S. Eliot		Type the important words: `winter hoarfrost`
this exact word or phrase:			Put exact words in quotes: `"frost flower"`
any of these words:			Type OR between all the words you want: `trees OR weeds OR grasses`
none of these words:			Put a minus sign just before words you don't want: `-windows`

Then narrow your results by...

image size:	any size ▸	Find images in any size you need.
aspect ratio:	any aspect ratio ▸	Specify the shape of images.
colors in image:	● any color ○ full color ○ black & white ○ transparent ○ this color: ■	Find images in your preferred colors.
type of image:	Photo ▸	Limit the kind of images you find.
region:	any region ▸	Find images published in a particular region.
site or domain:		Search one site (like `sfmoma.org`) or limit your results to a domain like `.edu`, `.org` or `.gov`
SafeSearch:	Show most relevant results ▸	Tell SafeSearch whether to filter sexually explicit content.
file type:	JPG files ▸	Find images in the format you prefer.
usage rights:	free to use or share ▸	Find images you are free to use yourself.

Advanced Search

Figure 9.2 Advanced Google Images search to find royalty-free images. Source: www.google.com.

items without permission. (No T. S. Eliot here when we searched, but several of George Eliot as well as illustrations of other notable writers.)

Openclipart   (https://openclipart.org/) is a collection of clipart provided for the public domain by the contributing artists.

Computer Screen Grabs/Screen Capture   Sometimes all that's needed is a screen grab/screen shot of a portion of the computer screen. Perhaps you want to show a portion of a web page or the way that a form should be completed. Whatever the reason, if it resides on your device, you can snap a picture of it. Computer "print screen" keys can provide capture of an entire page, but when you only want the menu on the left hand side of the screen, you need to use screen grab software for that purpose. There are a number of free or inexpensive tools that can do this and screen capture is also included in image editors like Adobe Photoshop—check first to see if your institution has a license for such software. Also check to see if you already have this type of software on your computer. For example, Mac OS X owners can take screen shots of any portion of their screen using the existing keyboard shortcuts like Command+Shift+4. Windows devices may offer a Snipping Tool that can take similar screen shots. It is usually possible to take a screen shot of something on your smartphone as well simply by holding down a requisite pair of buttons. (Keep in mind that depending on what images you capture and how you intend to use them, you may need permission to use those screen shots. See Chapter 8.)

If you do not have suitable software for screen grabs, there is the popular and very easy to use Snagit (https://www.techsmith. com/snagit.html) available for a free trial. Snagit can also be used for short screencast videos. There is educator pricing for a low-cost purchase. For other current recommended software, see Jane Hart's C4LPT site for a listing of those programs in this category.

Scanning Images   Scanning means converting printed material (whether graphic or text) into a digital format that a computer can read. No matter how many images you can find searching on the internet, you can't find everything. If the images you want reside in a book or magazine, you will have to scan the image into a digital format that you can then further manipulate through editing. Your institution is likely to have scanners available through the library, your department office, or through a unit that handles instructional technology, but as is increasingly the case, many inexpensive home printers contain scanning capabilities. Such printer-scanners contain their own software which allows you to save the image in the format and to the folder on your hard drive that you select—the built-in menus and steps to make a simple scan are generally easy to follow.

Editing Images Some found or scanned images need a little help. Some look dark and dreary, and others, such as those gleaned from magazines or newspapers, seem tinted, grayish, or full of dots. More common still, the image you scanned is upside down or tilted. Or the photos and images you saved from the internet may be too big or need cropping to cut out unwanted portions of the picture.

It's fun to fix up these images, but to do so you're going to need some sort of image-editing software. There are many programs available. The venerable monarch of all image-editing programs is Adobe Photoshop. This is the program you would want to use if your goal were to show a politician standing next to a beautiful young woman he had actually never met. In other words, it's pretty sophisticated but also expensive. In our view, for most faculty members such a program amounts to software overkill. It has so many features and special effects that remembering them after two weeks or so is a considerable feat. GIMP (www.gimp.org) is a free program of similar complexity to Adobe Photoshop and is available for multiple languages on multiple platforms.

But the lesser-known and often free or low-cost image-editing programs are often a better choice for educators. They are also easier to use and to learn and will let you do almost all of the things you need to do to fix up your images.

Canva (https://photo-editor.canva.com/) offers a free online photo editor that does not require you to download a software program. You can simply upload your image to the site and use a few simple tools to crop, resize, etc.

Google Photos, successor to the Picasa program, is offered free to edit and manage collections of photos, and is available for both PC and Mac. If you have a Mac or other Apple device, you can also use the iPhoto editing software that comes installed on your machine or its successor, OS X Photos.

If you have Microsoft Office suite for either Windows or Mac, prior to Office 2013, you may find it includes Picture Manager, an image editor. Or you may have Paint, which is a very simple program with some standard editing tools. Finally, you may not realize that you can make simple edits to pictures in MS Word— just click on your picture within your document, then use the Format tab to select the tools you want, such as cropping the photo or adding a border.

For most instructors, experimenting with one of the above programs will be sufficient to meet their needs.

Now that you've fixed up your image, the last thing you must do is to save it in a format you can use on the internet. Fortunately, there are only a few common choices for this purpose.

If your image is an artist's illustration or a piece of line art, then the file format you should use is GIF. It was developed many years ago as a way to send or display graphics on the internet. GIF remains an excellent choice for an image with relatively few colors. It can also support animation.

If, however, the image you are saving is a photograph, GIF is not an appropriate format. You should save a photograph as a JPEG file, a format developed specifically for this purpose. The acronym stands for Joint Photographic Experts Group. JPEGs aren't so good, though, for simple line art with just a few colors; with that type of art, the JPEG format often smudges lines or makes them look ragged.

A third type of image file is—PNG—or Portable Network Graphics. PNG files are often smaller than their GIF counterparts but usually larger than JPEGs. PNG is good at preserving clarity and image quality. You are unlikely to save images you create in this format unless you have specialized graphics. However, if an image you are capturing is in this format there is usually no problem using it in your image editor, learning management or other programs.

If converting an image from one format to another, check the colors, clarity and file size in the converted version, and also make sure that it is an appropriate format for the program in which you intend to use it.

The How and Why of Audio

How about sound? Sound is a much-overlooked element in courses. But it can do a lot. You can search for sound files on the internet and perhaps discover a radio show or speech that is relevant to your class. Or you can record an interview with a colleague in your field, make the recording available on your web page or in your learning management site, and then ask your students to comment on what your colleague said. Here are reasons and ways (apart from the use in language and speech classes previously discussed) to use audio:

- Introduce yourself to the class in a personalized manner.
  Even without a visual element, the voice conveys a sense of who you are and your attitude toward teaching the course. An initial short video is a way to begin to construct a sense of your presence in the classroom. Encourage students to do the same but make it optional.

- Use audio for feedback on assignments—this can range from comments on papers to projects to insertion in online gradebooks. It is especially helpful for delivering sensitive criticism—your voice can easily soften what might seem like hard criticism in text.

- Record your lectures in a natural manner—the idea is to record lectures and commentary prepared specially for your online students rather than trying to capture something recorded from your delivery in a face-to-face class. For best effect, keep your lectures and commentary short. It is tedious to listen to long audio clips—we recommend you keep such clips to no more than 5–10 minutes. If you have the equivalent of an hour-long lecture, it is best to split this up into shorter segments. That way, students can more easily play back just that topic or topics that they need to review. If you decide to do this on a regular basis, consider using a podcast format to which students can subscribe.

- Allow students to create presentations that include audio.
  Some students are best at expressing themselves through the spoken word while others may excel in writing or video. Role playing, debates, and interviews are all examples of assignments in which audio may play an appropriate part.

- As discussed in Chapter 7, use audio to bring interviews and guest speakers to your class.

It used to be that if you wanted to play a sound file (usually in the WAV or AIFF format) that you found on the internet, you had to download it first. That was often a tedious process. A sound file one minute in length might take ten minutes to download. If the file was particularly important (such as a clip from President Kennedy's inauguration speech), you might have accepted the inconvenience. But for anything else ... well, you had to think about it.

Then, with the advent of streaming media technologies you no longer had to wait for the entire file to download in order to hear it. Instead it began playing, and continued to play, within fifteen seconds or so of your making the request. That's what the term "streaming media" means: information is fed in a continuous stream, rather than in one huge hunk, to your computer.

The second major development that affected the availability and practicality of using audio for instructional purposes was the MP3 audio format. This is a compressed file—meaning that it produces a file many times smaller than the earlier formats and has thus enabled the explosion of downloadable music and music players such as the iPod and mobile devices of all sorts—that has been taken up as the leading format for listening to and sharing music. While it does not have the same audio quality as the earlier formats, it has proved good enough for most listeners, and in any case, if you are creating instructional material such as lectures or interviews and not a symphony, we don't think you or your students will find it lacking.

These days, you can capture digital audio through a microphone onto your computer, or record via your smartphone or other device. Again, it has become easier than ever for a rank amateur to do this. Let's look at a few programs and website services that offer you some different approaches to recording audio for your classes. Which you choose will depend on the purpose of the audio as well as some other factors. Before discussing any of these, we recommend that if you plan to do more than produce snippets recorded by smartphone or tablet, you should consider purchasing a headset microphone with a boom mike that automatically positions itself to the side of your mouth. This need not be an expensive one—$30–$60 is sufficient to obtain a decent quality headset with microphone. In addition, we recommend that you choose a headset microphone that connects via USB (assuming your computer still has a USB connection or a connector that can attach to USB) because these generally offer the most flexibility for different types of use and the best sound. Using handheld microphones or those that are built in to your computer do not always work well for recording or real-time conversations as they are apt to create muffled sounds, lack of clarity, and background noise. You invariably move the mike about and it's difficult to place the microphone at just the right distance. Generally the microphones built into web cams or into your computer or other device are not the highest quality and you will still have to deal with background noise. However, these are greatly improved in recent laptops and mobile devices, so don't hesitate to test out the capabilities of your "built-ins" before looking elsewhere.

Companies such as Logitech, Sennheiser, and Plantronics sell decent inexpensive headset models that have USB connections, but they and others include higher-end versions that include more noise-canceling features or more comfortable padding on the headset. There are also wireless microphone headsets that are convenient for mobile connections but these are more expensive than the USB plug versions.

What Kind of Microphone Do You Need?

Purchasing a headset (or earpiece) with a microphone boom (one that you can situate at the side of your mouth) along with a USB connection is recommended for the best sound quality in recording audio and for communicating via real-time synchronous tools.

Embedding Audio for Feedback in PDFs and Word

To use audio for quick feedback on student papers, try out Adobe Acrobat Pro—follow the help instructions to quickly insert and record short audio clips after converting student Word documents to PDF. All you need are the Adobe Acrobat program and a microphone. The virtue of this is that the audio clip is directly inserted at the relevant spot in the paper and the student needs only the free Adobe PDF Reader to listen to the clip.

You can embed an audio file in a Word document in two ways—you can record it using the Insert>Object>Create New menu path, or you can import a prerecorded file using the Insert>Object>Create from File path.

The main drawback to embedding audio in PDFs or Word is that the resulting file size may balloon to an unwieldy size. Depending on how you plan to transmit the new file, this might be an obstacle. For example, if your LMS class site has file size restrictions, either by individual file size or the overall quota for files, this would be something to consider before choosing this solution. Best to test and check the resulting file size of a representative document before deciding on this approach for your class.

Audio Recording and Sharing for Multiple Purposes

A free recording and editing program called Audacity (http://audacity.sourceforge.net) will also allow you to simply and quickly record an audio file and encode it in MP3 so that you can upload to your course management software, website, or blog. We have used Audacity over many years with great numbers of faculty who were complete neophytes and yet able to produce good audio to suit their instructional objectives. It must be downloaded to your computer and is available for Windows, Mac, or Linux. It will allow you to create several types of audio files and to import and convert files as well.

A very simple and free, browser or app-based audio sharing site that requires no downloads or even registration (although you have fewer options without registration) is CLYP (https://clyp.it/).

Figure 9.3 Recording on Audacity. Source: http://audacityteam.org/about/images/recording.png.

You can upload a recording but also record directly to their site. It will provide you with a URL and embed code to share your audio clip. It is also available for mobile apps. That makes it a great option for classes in which you want your students to practice speaking, like foreign language or speech courses.

Many people use Skype (www.skype.com) for making phone calls over the internet, and this is a tool that can be used for providing feedback and consultations with students or to permit students who are collaborating on a project to communicate. There are a number of low to reasonably priced (Pamela Basic, Call Recorder for SKYPE, TalkHelper) or free (Vodburner, Amolto) third-party plug-ins that allow you to create recordings of audio or video interviews. Some of these plug-ins are for PC only, others for Mac; some allow for a free trial so you can see how you like the product features before purchasing.

Podcasting Services

Some of the online hosting services that are used for podcasting may also be used to create standalone audio files. But true podcasting is generally used to make a series of recordings, publish those recordings to a website, and to enable others to subscribe to those podcasts. The ability to subscribe to a podcast is what really differentiates it from just a collection of recordings. Your own institution may facilitate your setting up podcasts. There are many types of podcasting software that allow you to not only record and edit your audio file but also to publish it to the internet, using wizards to create the RSS feed code and tags that will allow others to find and subscribe to your podcast. There are also podcasting services that will take your MP3 recordings and do all the coding and hosting for you.

Podomatic (http://podomatic.com) is a hosting service that allows you to create podcasts for free. It also features Web 2.0 types of sharing on the site. There are limits on monthly bandwidth data transfer for free users—in other words, the free service would not accommodate large files and large numbers of students accessing his or her podcasts. Take a look at the Education category here to see some examples of podcasts in higher education.

Two other online browser-based podcast creation and hosting services at the time of this writing are Buzzsprout (https://www.buzzsprout.com/ and Chirbit (https://www.chirbit.com/) which have limited free versions and low-cost expanded plans.

Narrated Slide Shows

So now you see that for minimal or no cost at all, you have the ability to make web pages, insert graphics (which you've scanned and fixed up), and create audio that you've made yourself. Though we don't want this to sound like a sales pitch for miracle kitchen devices, there is more, much more.

A narrated slide show can be a very useful tool for any instructor. With it, you can take a series of slides—say, for a biology instructor, pictures of a cell dividing—and create an illustrated lecture in which you talk to your students directly, explaining the significance of the images they are seeing.

There are a number of ways to create narrated slide shows. Probably the simplest way is to use PowerPoint's own "record narration" option—all you need is your slides and a microphone. Follow directions to set your voice volume level and to choose other options. Once you have saved the presentation, you have the option to re-record one or more slides to correct or revise as you like.

However, your resulting file may be quite large. For this reason, many educators like to use other programs that can reduce the size of the narrated PowerPoint slide so that it is more convenient to post online. However, beginning with PowerPoint 2010 it is possible to use the "Compress" feature to reduce the size of your document containing audio and video.

Your campus might have access to other sophisticated programs like Captivate or Articulate which can incorporate slides and other content into a presentation—these are otherwise too expensive for the average instructor to afford on his or her own, and are likely much more than you need. Generally the simplest tool that will do the job is your best bet because you are more likely to become skilled at and actually use a tool with a smaller learning curve.

Perhaps the best solution for those who want to use a lot of narrated presentations is create a screen-cast version of your slide show. See the section on Screencasting Video in this chapter.

Non-Narrated Slide Show Presentations

Prezi (Prezi.com) is an alternative to the basic slide show approach—it is good for those who use a lot of images and a minimum of text in their presentations. You can easily insert visual material although multimedia like video must be inserted via a link to a site like YouTube hosting the video. The screen changes in Prezi presentations provide a lot of movement and variety by animation, zooming, and panning. They offer a free basic educational account and a low-cost EduPro account with many more features (includes a free trial). It's easy to share online and embed the presentations on different devices and platforms. Prezi also offers a lot of helpful tutorials on its support site.

Slideshare (www.slideshare.net) is a popular hosting site that allows users to upload and share PowerPoint slides (before narration has been added) and other types of presentation files or PDF. It's free and one can create files as large as 300 MB, tag and share your presentation, and make it public or private. However, this is not a good choice for narrated slides and you cannot directly upload video but must link to a site like YouTube. Slideshare is best for creating a "document" version of slides that you want to share.

Scripted Versus Unscripted Narrations and Presentations

There are two ways to do a narration or audio/video presentation: scripted and unscripted. Scripting—that is, writing out exactly what you want to say in advance, word for word—is effective for those instructors who are dealing with complex or detailed material and don't want to make a mistake. Unscripted narrations and presentations, with the instructor speaking to the students from notes or even from memory or off the cuff, replicate more of the face-to-face classroom experience.

With the advent of YouTube and iTunes, students may be becoming more accustomed to hearing casual presentations and there seems to be a movement away from overly formal presentations. The ad-libbed quality of unscripted presentations, even with an occasional hesitation or error, creates a sense of intimacy between instructor and student. On the other hand, the ad-libbed presentation may ramble on too long.

If you have software that allows you to easily edit audio, video, or narrated slide shows, you may opt for the more unscripted production since you can still clean up any major gaffes or shorten long-winded passages and need not re-record. But whether you work from a script or not, do remember to add captions to your final video before making it available to your class!

The How and Why of Video

The how of video is the easy part nowadays—nearly everyone, whether sitting in front of a laptop or desktop webcam at work or home or walking around with a camera or smartphone or tablet now has the ability to take short videos of a quality that is surprisingly clear and sharp, and then to do some minor editing and upload or share these videos via their favorite social media site or simply transfer the files to a home or work computer via the cloud or a USB drive. While these devices we use may not have the features and versatility of more expensive professional video cameras, they do make it convenient to create on-the-fly videos, are unobtrusive because of their size, and easy to use. With the steep learning curve gone, often easy to use translates into "more likely to use" as well.

Larry Ragan, currently co-director of Penn State's Center for Online Innovation in Learning, previously talked to us for an earlier edition of this book in his role as director of faculty development for Penn State World Campus. What he had to say about some of the creative opportunities this greater ease of use presents to instructors was summed up in a few examples that have retained their currency and validity:

- Making a personal introduction video to form a personal connection with your students. Ragan advised instructors to do what is comfortable and true for them—that means you can just as easily film yourself sitting at ease at your desk or petting your dog or presenting a more formal pose.

- Creating transitional bridges between segments or at the end of a course. By displaying a video clip at the end of a lesson to reflect and summarize, "I've watched the dialogue around these discussions this week. Now let's talk about next week, when we will be moving into topic X..."

- Enriching course content by adding the voices of other individuals in the community or profession, through interviews on the fly. Using small devices to capture video makes interviewing a more casual and seemingly less intrusive activity, "What you said is interesting," Ragan typically found himself saying in approaching a potential interview subject, "may I just capture that?"

- Asking students to use video to do similar interviews in the community and in their workplace. For example, Ragan suggested, a student in health policy might do an interview with a public health administrator or even interview other students about what they think about a concept. Ragan noted that this in effect helps moderate the responsibility of the instructor for having to generate all course content and puts some responsibility for learning into the hands of the students themselves.

- Taking a virtual field trip. The instructor might go out in the real world and show a sample of something for the benefit of the students who can't be there in reality. For example, an agronomist can demonstrate local soil samples for the benefit of his online students who cannot be there with him. Or the students may be sent out on their own discovery quests. For example, Michelle Pacansky-Brock, in teaching Art Appreciation, encouraged her students to create their own video or find video on the internet that pertains to art in everyday life and to share it with their fellow students through easy uploading to their class online social network.

Richard Schumaker's deployment of videos in his classes can serve as an encouragement to those instructors who hesitate to create informal or relatively unpolished videos or who imagine that making videos is a necessarily time-intensive activity involving many hours of training and practice before one can produce something "class-worthy."

His use of video in his online courses, Intro to Philosophy for University of Maryland University College and Writing at Work for CUNY School of Professional Studies, has evolved over time, steadily trending toward adoption of the easiest techniques and increasingly varied in the ways in which it is applied.

He comments on his current methods,

> *Even though I have access to a sophisticated media lab and the support of highly qualified, experienced technicians, experience has taught me that the following process works best—I put my smartphone on a small, very inexpensive tripod and place it in an interesting environment—my home study with maps and cultural photos in the background, my book-lined professional office, or sometimes a more informal place, like a museum, library, or something of that sort—for variety and to give the online students a feel for the cultural and academic richness of where I live, in Metropolitan Washington, DC.*

I simply turn on the "video" function in my iPhone and create a short video. Once I stop the video, I upload it to my YouTube account, and then load it to our learning management system.

I do not script my presentations and keep my talks to ten minutes. I have experimented a great deal with "to script or not to script" and the overwhelming majority of students seem to prefer a somewhat improvised presentation. I speak slowly, warmly, and naturally and deliver my 5–10 minute talk. Sometimes I do multiple individual "takes" of videos but generally I can get a lot into one clip that is under ten minutes.

Among the various uses for which Schumaker creates videos are:

- Administrative and course management—at the beginning of the course and then the beginning and end of each week, he posts a five-minute video focusing on the primary tasks for the week, or provides a recap of that week or highlights the tasks still remaining to complete the week's work.
- Content summary and overview—in very concise video clips, he summarizes the key content for the week.
- Deeper dives into the content—in somewhat longer video clips, he discusses the importance or implications of course content.
- Research and assignment issues—presenting his expectations and tips about the major research projects in his classes. One of his goals is to motivate the students, communicating how important and interesting these projects are.

Sites and Tools for Hosting and Sharing Video

The YouTube and TeacherTube sites mentioned previously, or others like Vimeo (www.vimeo.com), have some features in common. They allow you to share videos publicly or with groups, to "tag"—categorize your video to make it searchable by topic— and often facilitate embedding by providing code you can insert into your own website or learning management class site.

Livestreaming Video   As mentioned in Chapter 7, livestreaming video programs like Periscope or Facebook Live permit instructors, students, and guest speakers to create live videos. These programs are available as mobile apps, allowing for greater flexibility in regard to time and place. (Although you may want to experiment with using a tripod with your smartphone for greater stability.) They do offer privacy options so that you need not make the livestream public. For greater privacy on Periscope, location information can be turned off, and you can limit the viewers to whom the stream is available. You can also separate Periscope from other parts of Twitter so that people follow you only on Periscope and no tweets are sent out when you start to livestream. Viewers can comment in real-time chat on what is happening in the video and this feature can be limited to those following on Periscope. The resulting videos from Periscope or Facebook Live can also be saved for later asynchronous access and review. Livestreaming can be used instructionally:

- to provide a means for virtual field trips, affording students or faculty the ability to narrate and demonstrate something in the real world outside the class;
- to facilitate interviews to provide content or as a way for students to fulfill an assignment;
- students can use livestream videos to deliver presentations— this could be very helpful for any class in which speaking and presentation skills play an important role, whether in business, public speaking, foreign language or other courses;
- to see some of the work being done on Periscope, try searching for Periscope and teachers or Periscope and education— many teachers have made public broadcasts and there are lots of examples that are worth watching before you try it on your own.

Screen-Capture/Screencasting Video Software

These programs do not only capture the still shots or screen grabs of something on your computer screen but actually record a short video (say, 5–10 minutes) of your movements onscreen as you click and scroll or otherwise manipulate the software you have on the screen. For example, if you want to demonstrate to students how to use an online library electronic database in order to find a full text article, how to use an Excel spreadsheet, or how to use an online chemical experiment simulator, you can capture the entire process, along with your narration (if you have a microphone), by using screen-capture video software.

Three easy-to-use and, at the time of this writing, two major programs available in free versions are Screencast-o-Matic (www. screencast-o-matic.com) and Jing (www.jingproject.com).

Screencast-o-Matic allows you to make and host your video right on its website without even having to download anything. (Be aware that makes your video public.) The free version has a limit of fifteen minutes. Or you can go for the premium but low-cost Pro version that provides more options, privacy, and more powerful editing features. You can provide a link for your students to their site to view the video or embed it in your own site or upload directly to your YouTube channel. Or you may want to export its files in a number of different available versions to your own computer—for example, as an AVI file (for Windows Movie Maker, for example), a QuickTime file (MOV), or Flash (SWF) file, then edit and finally upload it to your own site. Your LMS or one of the video hosting sites we have mentioned make uploading a matter of following a series of menu-driven directions.

The free Jing allows you to take screen grabs as well as screen-cast videos and the latter are limited to five minutes. Jing does require a download but can be used with either Windows or Mac. There is no longer a Pro version of Jing but Snagit, a sister product from TechSmith mentioned earlier allows for longer screencast videos as well as screen grabs and is available in educational single user pricing for about $30.

Step-by-step tutorials on the respective websites provide helpful instructions on how to use these programs and you might want to search for additional video tutorials on YouTube. For most instructors, any of the above free or low-cost programs will be sufficient for your needs.

For those who want more sophisticated or longer screen-casts, and who are prepared to invest a little time in learning how to fully exploit the program, we recommend Camtasia Studio. Your institution may already have a license for this program which is available for both Windows and Mac. One of the authors of this book, Steve Rossen, was an early adopter of Camtasia and taught his first multimedia classes over a decade ago using Camtasia videos to demonstrate software while also instructing his students how to use Camtasia for their own work. Camtasia offers a free trial of its software for thirty days, which can be ideal for student use. There is also individual educator pricing for Camtasia, which reduces the price to under $200.

Creating Interactive Video Lessons

Two programs that allow you to edit, annotate, and interpolate videos with your own slides and interactive quizzes are EDpuzzle (www.edpuzzle.com) and PlayPosit (www.playposit.com, formerly known as eduCanon). These programs are menu driven and oriented toward educational use of videos. All have free versions. Expanded tools and privacy options may be offered through the premium versions. Videos are pulled through via sites like YouTube or other streaming sites. Analytic data on student viewing and their interaction with quizzes and other elements you add are also made available to the instructor. Integration with learning management systems varies by program.

There are endless uses for such interactive video lessons. For example, foreign language learners may benefit from quizzes that test students on their comprehension at key points in a video conversation or instructors may interpolate key passages from readings with illustrative video segments.

Animation and Whiteboard Animation

Video animations use cartoon-like animations, writing on a whiteboard and voiceover among other effects to deliver a lesson. The resulting videos can be shared in various ways, including uploading to YouTube. Khan Academy popularized this narrated "animated pencil" approach for illustrating the procedures to solve math problems.

PowToon (www.powtoon.com/edu-home/), GoAnimate (https://goanimate4schools.com/public_index), and VideoScribe (www.videoscribe.co/education) are three programs that have been used by educators to deliver short but stimulating animated presentations. They feature easy-to-use libraries of templates, images, and effects, allowing for voiceover narration. These are often more stimulating than simply watching and listening to narrated slides or a video of the instructor. PowToon has a free version but also low-cost educational pricing while GoAnimate and VideoScribe offer educator plans and pricing along with free trials. Both offer a whiteboard and animated "writing pen" style presentation which is particularly well suited for demonstrating problems and explaining concepts. VideoScribe must be downloaded to your devices, while PowToon and GoAnimate are hosted services.

Whiteboard/Screencast Capture

A simpler sort of whiteboard app for tablets and other mobile devices allows the instructor (or student) to capture writing on a whiteboard, narrate what is being created, and record, then share the resulting video. This is a great tool for demonstrating math or other lessons that benefit from step by step explanations and can also be used to create presentations. Some of the most popular with educators are ShowMe (www.showme.com/) and Screen-Chomp for the iPad (https://www.techsmith.com/screenchomp. html) and Doceri (doceri.com) or ExplainEverything (http:// explaineverything.com/) for both iPad and Android devices. These are all either free or relatively low cost. They are all relatively easy to use for both instructor and students. We recommend that you test out the free ones or experiment with trial versions to find the right fit for your needs.

Social Curation/Bulletin Boards

In Chapter 3, we introduced some social bookmarking tools. These were largely those that involved selection and sharing with annotation. You may be familiar with popular visual social curation tools like Pinterest that permit people to collect, "pin" and share objects of interest. Padlet (https://padlet.com/) provides an educational version of such tools. Offered in both free and educator versions (the latter providing many more control options and privacy levels than the free version), Padlet allows instructors to create a class "wall" on which students can pin items of interest, such as images, links to videos, comments, etc. The instructor can arrange and control the degree of student participation by moderating contributions. By embedding the code to the Padlet into an LMS, instructors can allow students to participate without leaving their LMS. A tool like Padlet can be used for brainstorming sessions, self-introductions at the start of a class, as well as collection and annotation of resources.

Student-Generated Content

Let's take a moment to further consider how encouraging your students to create content as part of their course work is now a feasible and attractive approach to teaching and learning. The Web 2.0 tools we highlight in this chapter and that we have mentioned in previous chapters are often those that can be wielded by students. So why should you think about trying this approach to course work?

■ Students learn by doing.

Hands-on projects, when properly planned, compel students to research, experiment, and discover their strong points, as well as reveal the areas of difficulty they may encounter. The instructor can then give feedback and provide guidance to resolve these areas of difficulty and help the student move forward.

■ Students add diverse perspectives and approaches.

Students all have different learning preferences and see issues from diverse vantage points. By allowing students to make these differences more evident through creating content, the instructor can mediate, discuss, or help students learn to evaluate or critique ideas. By allowing students to express their ideas or solve problems through the means of diverse media, individual student learning may be better facilitated while new perspectives may also be brought to bear on an issue.

■ Students learn by sharing and collaborating.

By working together or sharing ideas, students are often led to reflect on their own ideas, to learn to work as a team, to negotiate different approaches, and to learn how to communicate their ideas in an effective manner.

■ Student interest is sparked by choice of format.

While some students will prefer to simply write a paper on a given topic, others will find their interest stimulated by a creative project that involves finding or creating multimedia resources or collaboration and sharing online. While the instructor must decide what the relevant options are for a particular assignment, giving students some measure of choice in how to accomplish the assignment may increase the student's involvement and interest in the task.

Bradley Gardener has recently selected a new and free tool, ESRI's Story Maps, to enhance what was already a rather creative approach to a key assignment in his Geography course, "International Migration & Ethnicity" for CUNY School of Professional Studies. He explains,

> In the migration course, there is a landscape assignment for which students are asked to visit Harlem after reading about the Great Migration and reflect on some of the themes related to migration and settlement patterns. The most important reading here is Isabel Wilkerson's The Warmth of Other Suns. This book, written in the last ten years, provides ethnographic accounts of the Great Migration from folks in their eighties and nineties. Students visit Harlem, record what they see, and reflect on the legacy of the Great Migration, making some comments about gentrification.
>
> In the past I have encouraged them to take pictures of what they see and describe their journey—how they felt—to make it geographic. I also have encouraged them to include music videos of artists who are from Harlem or use Harlem prominently in their songs.
>
> I am hoping to roll out a new version of this based on ESRI's Story Maps application. I had experimented with Story Maps for a face-to-face geography class I taught at Middlebury and I think it is a wonderful tool to present qualitative spatial data— exactly the kind my students will be collecting on their trip.
>
> In Story Maps students in the migration class will start with a base-map of Harlem and then can plot journey points (they basically annotate it)—each point on the map is a new slide or perspective focused on the exact geographic location they visited. Here they can include a picture (or some other form of media) and describe what they saw in this place and make some reflection on what they experienced at that point.

Gardener is committed to further learning the ins and outs of the tool before asking his online students to use it, and because they will be using it on their own rather than in a supervised lab setting, to provide them with adequate tutorials and step-by-step instructions.

He notes,

> *I will probably want to try it with a small group first as I want to see what kinds of pitfalls there might be. And in the assignment prompt I'll need to ask them to be careful to record geographic location. Although students don't have to take pictures on their own (they can search for existing ones via the Story Map application), I think it would be really useful for them to do so.*

In encouraging student-generated content, there are just a few issues to keep in mind.

First, find out if your institution has any regulations about the use of sites external to the university. In regard to considerations of student privacy—before recommending a particular site or tool, investigate the privacy options. Some sites have special provisions for educational use and some do not. Some services maintain the right to use content created on their site in connection with publicizing their service. Second, if there are materials that will become publicly accessible online, suggest that students do not use their full names (you and their classmates can still know who they are), that they are familiar with any opt-in privacy options, and caution against divulging any private identifying information.

There may be times when you want students to have the option to share information with others publicly or to join a site where they can contribute to the building of knowledge. We have known instructors who had students contribute to Wikipedia as part of their assignment while others may select sites where there is a more narrowly defined community for those in their discipline. One important reason to let students engage in the online public sphere is to teach students about how to create and manage their public image, how to decipher the "terms of use" of a site, how to share responsibly, and how to use the features of a site to opt in to different degrees of privacy.

● ● ● ● ●

Other Tools

Polls and Surveys

Polling or surveying your students on a frequent basis is a quick method to track how your students are faring in the class. It is an easy way to conduct formative assessment. For example, you can ask students whether or not they are finding a particular assignment difficult, or having a problem working through a solution, and depending on the response, you can provide some additional explanations. While you may have already invited students to post their questions or note any problems in the asynchronous discussion forum, many students hesitate to raise questions until they are really in a muddle—a poll can make the matter seem less weighty and students are more likely to indicate problems are afoot. Some learning management systems have built in polling and surveying instruments. But if you do not have access to these, for polling, Polldaddy and Poll Everywhere are two easy-to-use programs that offer free versions of their software to create polls or surveys for your courses. Polldaddy (polldaddy.com) provides a variety of features even in its free version, such as the ability to add media or images to questions, offers mobile collection of responses and offers integration with WordPress via WordPress.com. Poll Everywhere (polleverywhere.com) is designed for real-time response so it is particularly useful for synchronous online sessions or for blended classes. With Poll Everywhere, students can respond to the polls using text messaging or from a web browser as they sit at a computer or via a smartphone. You can create the poll or survey on their site, using your browser, but you can also provide access to the poll in your own online learning management software or other course site so that students do not have to leave the precincts of your class. Poll Everywhere has educator plans that provide many different options even in the free version.

Polls can be used to provide real-time feedback in the manner of clickers used in a lecture hall—this can be a vital tool for those conducting synchronous sessions to gather quick feedback on whether a point is clear or not, whether a demonstration has resolved all questions, or to stimulate interest by relating the lesson content to the opinions and real-world knowledge of students. By polling at the beginning and end of a real-time session, or at the beginning and end of an asynchronous online unit, polling can serve to measure progress in learning, or to provide a point of reflection. Or they may help resolve more practical matters in a timely fashion.

For example, an instructor might ask students to rate the class readings—"Which of this week's readings has proved most helpful to you in understanding the X concept?"—or to get a quick count of how many students want to sign up for virtual office hours in a particular week. In an asynchronous online class, the instructor will want to be sure to budget sufficient time for even answers requiring some immediacy. Polls may be announced via multiple channels of communication when timely response is required.

Surveys   Survey tools permit you to pose multiple questions and responses are usually available in a variety of types such as multiple choice, ratings on a Likert scale, or open-ended questions. A popular online survey creation tool is Survey Monkey (www.surveymonkey.com). The free version allows one to survey up to a hundred people with up to ten questions per survey. They also offer discounted educator plans that provide more features and options.

An easy-to-use menu-driven survey format is also available in Polldaddy.

Real-Time Quizzes

Please see the Chapter 6 discussion of quizmakers for those programs that provide a means to offer quizzes and tests in online and blended classes. We will simply note here that some free versions of quizmakers allow for the inclusion of multimedia, embedding the quizzes into your own website, and tagging and sharing. Because the features of these programs change so rapidly, you will want to scrutinize their free and paid plans to see what options are available, and test the software before deploying it for your class.

However, we do want to mention as part of our discussion of Web 2.0 types of programs, a game-based quizzing program called Kahoot (https://getkahoot.com/). Used in the context of a real-time online activity that can be deployed during the F2F session of a blended class or perhaps online during a synchronous session like Google Hangouts or through other real-time conferences, this

Poll Question

FOLDER

Which format made for the most engaging assignment in unit 3?

Media   My Content

☑ Make poll public

✛ textbook   Media   ✖ Delete

✛ video   Media   ✖ Delete

✛ PowerPoint slides   Media   ✖ Delete

✛ audio commentary   Media   ✖ Delete

⊕ Add New Answer

☐ Allow multiple selections   ☐ Randomize answer order   ☐ Allow users to enter their own answer

Figure 9.4 Creating a poll for formative assessment using Polldaddy.com.

browser-based and mobile program provides a timed rapid-fire contest as students compete to be the first to respond to questions and earn points for their answers. Kahoot was designed to be used with K–12 students and it is very easy for instructors to use and students to participate. The Kahoot website offers lots of guidance and assistance. Kahoot is a free program, designed expressly for educators, and students participating do not even have to have an account to play since you can simply provide them with a pin number to join one of your kahoots.

Videos, music or other audio, diagrams, and images can be included. In the spirit of a friendly competition, such quizzes can be used as an icebreaker or low-stakes exercise, a way to review a lesson or prepare students for a test, or to explore what students already know about a topic before introducing a new lesson. A non-competitive Survey mode is also available and Discussion mode allows one to pose a single question with some possible answers and have everyone weigh in on the response, providing an introduction to a real debate on a topic. Kahoots (as those quizzes made with Kahoot are called) can be kept private or made public and shared on its website. Students can play in "ghost mode" to try and beat the score of past players. You can even ask your students to make their own Kahoot quizzes.

Another tool targeted for educators which facilitates real-time quizzing is Socrative (www.socrative.com). Socrative is free and students do not need an account to participate in quizzes you create. Instructors can add a game element by dividing the class into competitive teams. Reports of quiz results based on individuals or aggregate results can be emailed to the instructor for later review.

Like the earlier generation of "clickers" in the F2F classroom, real-time quizzing tools can provide an important source of formative feedback for instructors to gauge how well students are grasping recent lessons and can provide follow-up to online activities during the F2F session of a blended class.

Mind-Mapping

Either you, as instructor, or your students might want to create a mind-map (also known as concept maps) to illustrate relationships between various categories of things, to present an outline of an upcoming project, to brainstorm, or for any other number of creative purposes. A browser-based program that allows you and your students to do this is Mindomo (www.mindomo.com). You create the mind-map online and can either link to it on the Mindomo site or embed it on your web page. Users can delegate permission to edit to other users so a group of students could work on a mind-map together. The mind-map can also be exported to a text-based outline format. Another with a free but limited (three mind-maps) option that has been much used in classrooms is Bubble.us (https://bubbl.us/). Mindomo offers a paid education version and Bubble.us provides education discounts for their premium versions.

Another program of this sort that offers a limited but free version is Coggle (https://coggle.it/). There are a number of other programs in this genre, some geared to business users, some that require downloads of software. In looking at free versions, in some cases, you must register, or it may be that what you make with the free version becomes public, so be sure to check if these are concerns for you or your students. Additionally, some are for an individual's use while others allow for collaboration from multiple users—an excellent source to find continually updated reviews of mind-mapping software (or any of the other categories of tools for learn-ing) may be found at Jane Hart's Top Learning Tools site, http://c4lpt.co.uk/top100tools/ or the previously mentioned blog of Larry Ferlazzo. See the Guide to Resources for other sites that review and constantly update information on the latest Web 2.0 tools.

Word Clouds

There are many word cloud generators, two simple and free sites being Wordle (www.wordle.net/) and TagCrowd (http://tagcrowd.com/).

By feeding text into a word cloud generator, you can produce an image that shows the relative frequency of particular words in that text, with those words appearing more often in the text assuming a large font or prominence in the word cloud. Some word cloud gen-erators offer different shapes (triangle, heart, etc.) of the resulting word cloud.

How can these be used for instructional purposes? First, a word cloud can provide a visual way of summing up a presentation, pointing out the main themes after a class discussion, or con-stitute a kind of overview when introducing an assigned reading.

You can ask students to create word clouds from their own essays or to analyze the relative importance of certain terminology in a reading with the help of a word cloud.

For those teaching elementary school classes, the ABCYA word cloud generator is colorful and particularly easy to use (www.abcya.com/word_clouds.htm).

Tricklar (http://tricklar.com/) is an international news site that can be sorted by country or topic to produce word clouds that reflect a current news story. You can select the topic and country and generate a cloud (with options for different shapes and colors), download it as a PDF, all free without registering on the site, and then explore to find the sources or share on social media. This is a great resource to get students engaged in contemporary issues.

Infographics

An infographic is a way of depicting or rendering dense textual material or complex ideas via visual images. Using infographics, reports, data, and other information can be more easily grasped or be provided with an overview or summary in visual form.

Students might be asked to generate infographics as part of their research, presentation of data, or as an alternative way to show their understanding of assigned readings. Infographics can be used by instructors as a way to break up otherwise dense texts and information when they create course content.

Two popular and relatively easy to use infographic programs are Piktochart (http://piktochart.com/) available in both a free and paid education version, and Canva (www.canva.com), which is a graphics design site with both free and premium options, that also offers templates for creating infographics.

These infographic programs provide a variety of templates along with a bank of images, making it easy for those with no graphics talent whatsoever to create surprisingly good quality visual representations. You can upload your own images or choose from the collection of free images they provide.

Timelines

Timeline creation software is an updated version of those time-lines kids used to create out of a long roll of paper, ruler, and pencil. By providing a visual representation of events over time, timeline software allows one to chart the course of historical events or to show the development of a process. There are many timeline software tools—some of the free ones are housed on sites with advertisements, some are very basic while others allow for the inclusion of multimedia, maps, or other web resources. Again, it is important to try out a few of these tools to find the one that is most appropriate for the needs of you and your students. Some allow for varying degrees of collaborative building of the timeline or allow some interaction by the viewer. Dipity (www.dipity.com/) timelines can be created by one or more people, working collaboratively. There are free and premium versions. Timeline JS (http://timeline.knightlab.com/#fileformat) is a free tool and it allows one to start building a timeline from a simple Google spreadsheet template. HSTRY (www.hstry.co) is specifically geared toward the education sector—even the free version allows one to create a "class," embed interactive quiz questions, share with students, and permits generous student participation in timeline creation of their own. In selecting timeline tools, beyond checking to see what is included in the free version and whether what you create can be made private for your class or must be shared on their website, you will want to note that these providers also vary by:

- whether multimedia and what types of multimedia (video, audio, images) can be included;
- what kind of collaboration or interactivity is provided for a timeline;
- whether the timeline is displayed as a succession of event images or is one in which the chronological structure is emphasized.

Interactive Maps

Maps can be used in conjunction with mark-ups, historical facts, images, and other media to provide a visual image of a place or a place in time. Google Maps, Earth, and Street View all provide some raw material that can be used as the basis for a map-making activity. (See http://maps.google.com/help/maps/education/ for some ideas and manuals for use.)

National Geographic's Mapmaker Interactive (http://mapmaker.nationalgeographic.org/), Scribblemaps (www.scribblemaps.com/),

Animaps (works with Google Maps, www.animaps.com/), and the previously mentioned Esri Story Maps (https://storymaps.arcgis.com) all provide different tools, options, and formats for creating interactive maps and displaying maps. Before adopting one for your class, make sure you note terms of use, file saving formats available, and ease of use.

Avatar Generators

An avatar is a pictorial stand-in for a person. The term is sometimes used to mean any image (unicorn, clown, cartoon version of yourself, peace symbol, flag) that replaces your real image, but it can also denote a small stamp-sized version of your real photo that appears when you post or send communications. The use of an avatar of the first sort may be an option for students who are shy about introducing themselves through photos, or who might want to speak through an avatar presenter. Some instructors use them to inject a note of whimsy. To create an avatar it is not necessary for students to enter a virtual world. Programs like Voki (www.voki.com) make it very easy to create a 3-D avatar and then record a short (limited to sixty seconds for free version) introduction or short presentation of opinions. The recordings can be made using telephone, microphone, or uploading a prerecorded audio file. (If you don't want to use your own voice, it is even possible to type in text and have it rendered by Voki into audio.) Voki is focused on avatars for education.

Beyond such "talking" avatars, other free sites that allow one to create avatar images that can be easily downloaded for use in a class site are DoppelMe (http://doppelme.com/) for a very simple, cartoon-like avatar with face and body. You do not even need to log in or save your image on the site—couldn't be easier. Try Faceyourmanga (www.faceyourmanga.com/) for a manga-style avatar face that offers a wide selection of options for customizing facial features. There are many such sites—if selecting for your students, be aware that some require registration, may be littered with ads, or may be inappropriate for educational purposes.

Finally, there are a number of cartoon creation sites that allow you to select cartoon variants of yourself or others and to insert a narrative over a few panels. Two examples of this sort of site are WittyComics (www.wittycomics.com/) and Makebeliefs Comix

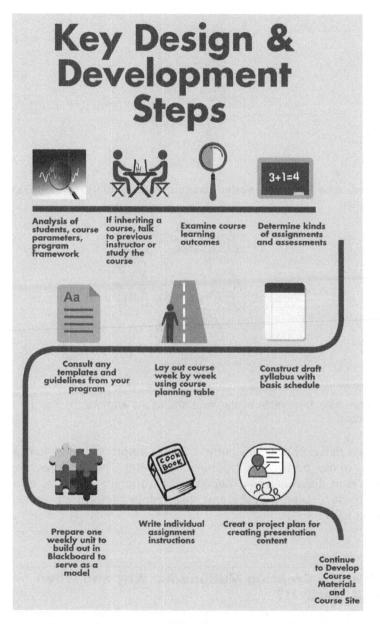

Figure 9.5 Infographic made using Piktochart. Source: illustration from CUNY SPS Course Design tutorial at https://spscoursedesign.commons. gc.cuny.edu/.

Figure 9.6a DoppelMe avatar versions of the authors. Source: Doppel Me.com.

Figure 9.6b DoppelMe avatar versions of the authors. Source: Doppel Me.com.

(www.makebeliefscomix.com/). These simple sites are free and easy to use, and you do not need to register. The cartoons can be saved in different ways, depending on the site (you can always save via a screen grab) and inserted in appropriate areas of your LMS.

● ● ● ● ●

Using or Creating Multimedia: Why and When Is It Worth It?

Okay, now some of you may be asking, is it really worthwhile for me to create audio or video, search for appropriate existing multimedia, or even ask my students to create multimedia? Many of you will have neither the time nor the desire to make your own audio, video, or narrated slide shows even as you recognize how much easier this is to do than ever before. If you decide it is not worth your time, you should be aware that a lot of material is already available on the internet, as noted in Chapter 7. One place to start for curated collections of open educational resources is the OER Commons at https://www.oercommons.org/curated-collections. You can search by type of material, subject, grade level, etc. The great variety of resources are evident from just a few examples: sites like C-Span video library maintain a continually updated collection recording contemporary public events in government and politics at www.c-span.org/about/videoLibrary/, TEDEd (http://ed.ted.com/) features lessons built around videos on a great variety of different subjects, SERC features resources for the sciences and engineering (http://serc.carleton.edu/highered/index.html), while Curriki (www.curriki.org/) has curated collections of resources geared to K–12 educators.

If you teach art history, then using graphics of an artist's work will seem a self-evident reason for employing multimedia. But if you teach mathematics or philosophy, the need to enhance your pages with graphics, sound, or video may not seem quite so obvious. Such subjects are traditionally taught with nothing more than plain old text or at most some graphs or tables thrown in. So why would an instructor choose to spend the extra time and effort to create or integrate existing multimedia?

To summarize and build upon what we have discussed in this chapter, here are some possible reasons:

1. *To illustrate the mechanics of how things work or to guide students through procedures.* Often, instructors in seemingly abstract subject areas are called upon to describe the process of how things work. An economics instructor may need to illustrate how demand affects cost, or an electrical engineer may want to demonstrate how digital information flows through logic gates. These needs call for multimedia. Sometimes the process in question can be illustrated with a graph or a series of illustrations. At other times, an animation showing the process in motion is preferable.

2. *To clarify or emphasize abstract concepts or highlight points of analysis.* Complex abstract concepts are often difficult for students to sort out or remember. Often, graphics can serve as

memory jogs for students who are attempting to keep a host of such concepts straight. For example, a history professor teaching the Spanish Civil War might want her students to visit a website in Spain exhibiting posters and paintings from the period as a way of keeping track of the seemingly bewildering array of acronyms for the anarchists, trade unionists, socialists, Falangists, and other political groups of the period. A comparison of word clouds created from two opinion pieces on the same topic might help students have a more fruitful discussion as they analyze the differences in approach and emphasis by two authors.

3. *To provide another approach or perspective to learning.* Sometimes what is learned through more than one medium is more effectively retained by the student. Listening to a narration of slides may reinforce the content on the screen, and watching a video may be more enlightening than simply reading a text description of a place, culture, or event.

4. *To enliven or illustrate unfamiliar material.* Whether you're dealing with historical or geographical contexts (poverty in nineteenth-century London, the ecology of Central American rainforests), the identification of organisms or structures (spirochetes, postmodern architecture), or the way things function (human ambulation, a four-cycle engine), the use of graphics and animation can greatly enhance your students' comprehension. A major value of textbooks is the profusion of illustrations, graphs, and tables they provide. The internet provides a vehicle by which individual instructors, using comparatively inexpensive tools, can "publish" their own textbook-quality material and make it available to their students.

5. *As the basis for an assignment.* Illustrations and videos can be powerful and fascinating stimuli for an assignment. Newspaper articles, advertisements, photographs, even articles found on the internet or scanned and displayed (following copyright prescriptions), can provide the basis for an assignment requiring students to critically evaluate the material and post their analyses.

Students can also be asked to capture something in the real world on audio or video and present it online as part of an assignment. Allowing students to use multimedia to fulfill an assignment may be the most compelling reason of all. Such options are becoming more feasible through the wider availability of digital devices and free Web 2.0 software tools.

● ● ● ● ●

When to Avoid Multimedia and Web 2.0 Tools

Putting together a site enhanced by graphics, animation, or video poses an immediate problem: How much is too much when it comes to the time and effort involved in creating and assembling these multimedia elements?

For those fortunate enough to work at an institution that provides ample financial, administrative, and staff support, this question may be moot. However, for the majority of instructors, the burden of putting together such materials falls squarely on their shoulders. How can you gauge in advance whether creating a graphic or an animation is worth the time you will need to produce it? And when might you be simply overwhelming your students? Here are some factors to consider.

1. *Institutional support and your own priorities.* Some institutions encourage innovative teaching by rewarding faculty members with either merit promotions or release time. Other institutions provide support through labs, media centers, or paid student assistants. In such situations, taking time to enhance your course with multimedia makes sense.

   If, on the other hand, your university will regard your extra work with indifference, putting in the extra effort becomes strictly a question of how much experimentation with new forms of expression means to you personally. It does take time to learn even a simple menu-driven program or tool let alone devise the lesson plan underpinning its use. Even an advanced user needs a few hours to put together a presentation, for example, or to find or search for multimedia objects. If the effort cuts into your ability to do your own research and if your institution offers no compensation for your endeavors, then obviously you will want to use discretion before embarking on anything too ambitious. But many instructors have found that simple multimedia elements have the power to greatly enhance their teaching and their students' learning, sometimes resulting in less work for them and better outcomes for students after that initial investment of time to create or find resources. If that Web 2.0 tool or multimedia resource helps you to do your work more effectively and saves you time in creating lecture material, explaining processes, or grading students, this itself will likely be a compelling reason to pursue it.

2. *Relevance of the material.* It may seem that using an animation or video will encourage your students to dig into the material you are presenting. All too often, however, instructors sacrifice relevance to convenience, using a graphic that almost, but not quite, expresses the concept or the subject they are trying to illustrate. In these cases, students are often more confused by the material than aided by it. In such situations, it would be better not to produce the material at all.

3. *Availability of the material elsewhere.* Before you create a multimedia presentation, make sure that the material doesn't exist on another publicly accessible website. Spend some time searching online. If you find what you're looking for, create a link from your web page to the site, thus saving yourself the considerable time and effort to create the material from scratch.

4. *Accessibility or ease of use of the material or tool and conditions for use.* Before embarking on the production of a complex multimedia element, consider whether your students will be able to view it or use it easily, as the case may be. Readers of this book range from those whose students will have no problem at all accessing content to those whose students have severely limited computer equipment and even more limited internet access. Always test out your content under the real conditions in which it will be used. If you're linking to another site that has videos or animations, make sure you tell your students if there are particular types of software or plug-ins that they will need to access it. If you are asking students to register and contribute on a hosted site using the tools furnished there, make sure you read the "terms of use" first and do your best to understand and communicate these to students so that they are making an informed choice. In the end, for content you create you must ask yourself:

   ■ Is the material you're planning to produce so complex that viewing it online may be more tedious than helpful?

■ Does it necessitate the downloading of software or accompanied by other conditions that would make it not worth the time expended for students to access it? Is it accessible to students with disabilities, and if it is not in an accessible format, can you easily render it accessible (by adding captions, transcripts, image tags, or other means)?

5. *What does it add to enhance the course experience and learning objectives?* Multimedia and Web 2.0 tools should add something to the learning experience that might otherwise be unavailable or less readily available. These considerations can be very practical in nature or more complex to discern. For example, screen grabs and text or a screen-capture video program may allow you to more easily demonstrate step-by-step instructions than would be possible with just directions in text. Less tangible but equally important is the increased interest students might register in the course content and activities having been stimulated by the multiple perspectives on the subject available through external and multimedia resources, or through their direct participation by creating and sharing content with their classmates. Finally, many instructors have found that multimedia elements and Web 2.0 tools provide a refreshing and stimulating element to their teaching. Enthusiasm on the part of the instructor is certainly communicated to students and may in itself be a valid reason to embark on this activity. And while you may decide that your presentations do not gain much with the addition of multimedia, allowing your students to fulfill an assignment using multimedia might be a true enhancement to the learning process.

Evaluating Web 2.0 and Other Ed Tech Tools

Focusing on Web 2.0 tools, Bethany Bovard produced a succinct and focused checklist for selecting appropriate tools, available at her TekTrek blog, http://tektrek.wordpress.com/2009/03/02/web-20-selection-criteria. We featured this in the third edition of our book, and the criteria remain valid. Her selection criteria were Access, Usability, Privacy and Intellectual Property, Workload and Time Management, and Fun Factor. Michelle Pacansky-Brock in the first edition of her book, *Best Practices for Teaching with Emerging Technologies* built upon these to create eight factors that include Accessibility, Learning Curve, Cost, Authentication (e.g., must create an account to use, LMS integration options), End Product (e.g., kinds of files produced, hosting options), Sharing Options, Intellectual Property, and Privacy. You may find it useful to create your own checklist that includes some or all of these factors, but that is more tailored to your own specific needs. For example, is privacy a major concern or are you willing to use a site that does not allow for anything but public and searchable versions of what you create with a free tool? Is it important for your students to be able to access via a mobile device? Is single sign-on to your LMS to access all tools essential or are you and your students willing to undergo the nuisance of logging in to multiple sites?

● ● ● ● ●

Pulling It All Together

As the possible resources and tools dramatically increase in number, so does the responsibility for the instructor who must exercise his or her discretion in selecting what to use and how to use it. Some concerns have been voiced about the use of Web 2.0 sites that pull students out of the LMS environment and into other websites where educational purpose is invariably mingled with non-educational and non-student content. To some extent, as we have noted at many points, instructors can avoid much of that by choosing services catering to educators or with special environments for educators, by embedding content from external sources within the classroom software. In other cases, instructors will simply need to scout out where they send their students in order to issue appropriate warnings or for the purpose of giving better directions to finding the sought-after objects.

But the greater responsibility is to devise a plan for your course that will integrate all the elements you have chosen, and to provide a rationale and purpose that will be clear to you and your students. If integration of tools and resources is lacking, the course will simply seem a bothersome or diverting but often irrelevant collection of content and activities to your students. We recommend that you always maintain a focal or gathering point for your students, a sort of virtual "homeroom"—whether that is a home page or blog, the learning management system classroom, or, in the case of blended courses, an actual face-to-face meeting place.

Finally, a reminder about the changing and sometimes ephemeral nature of Web 2.0 tools:

Important! **Free sites in particular may not provide you with advance warning of their demise or major changes. Always keep a copy of your presentation documents and multimedia files and advise students to do the same for material they create. In regard to discussion, comments or chat, you will want to capture and save any content and transcripts that may be necessary for you to use in evaluating students.**

III

Teaching in the Online Classroom

10

●●●●●

Preparing Students for Online Learning

Learning online can be as exasperating for the student as for the instructor, particularly for those taking an online course for the first time. Suddenly thrust into a world in which independent or collaborative learning is heavily stressed, students accustomed to traditional classroom procedures—taking notes during a lecture, answering the occasional question, attending discussion sections—must make unexpected and often jolting adjustments to their study habits.

In addition to these pedagogical concerns, students must contend with varying website formats requiring special equipment or software. Indeed, it isn't unusual for students at the same university to encounter two or sometimes three different learning management software systems or different sets of tools during a single semester. Add to that the tendency of faculty to set up online class sites according to their own design, resulting in students encountering variations in layout and navigation scheme with potentially each different course. With sometimes outdated equipment and busy schedules, perhaps unsure whether they should communicate by email or by posting queries on discussion boards, students often feel frustrated, abandoned, or confused.

Students' problems fast become those of the instructor as well. Instead of teaching their course, posting information, and responding to legitimate queries on the discussion board, instructors often find themselves trying to troubleshoot technical queries for which they have minimal expertise. Tussling with why a student using a particular browser can't see part of a given web page or why another is unable to install a program on her home computer, instructors expend too much time and energy providing support and maintenance while struggling to keep up with the normal duties of teaching a course. Ideally, every institution should have 24/7 tech support to which every student can turn for help or a mandatory student orientation that ensures each student has mastered the basics of software and processes before accessing online classes. But we realize that some readers do not teach under those conditions.

This chapter will address these and related issues concerning preparation of students for the online learning environment. The key is to identify and be forewarned about potential problems and to learn some effective methods for handling them.

Problems That Students Typically Encounter

A student logging on to a course website for the first time has a lot to contend with. To begin with, there's the terminology. Those neat rows of icons or links, either along the side or across the top or bottom of the screen, meant to guide students to the course material often bear names, captions, or titles the users have never seen before. For example, a button or link might say "Course Notes," "My Course," "Course Information," or "Main Page," all of which generally mean the same thing. The icons under which such captions appear may look like an open notepad, an owl reading a book, or a blackboard.

Similarly, an area set aside for students to post information about themselves, including a small digital photograph, might say "Course Information," "Student Home Pages," or "Biographies." Most variable of all is the button or caption leading to the discussion area. In some learning management systems it is called the "Threaded Discussion," while elsewhere it might be called "Conference Board," or "Discussion Forum." Tests are sometimes called quizzes, sometimes assessments, and the areas where students collaborate on projects may bear names like "Group Pages" and "Student Presentations." When students submit an assignment, does an icon or message appear to them to signify that it has been correctly submitted or do they see nothing in particular?

Often these mysteries of nomenclature and icons are just the beginning of the puzzles a student must solve. There are also technical problems and communication difficulties.

We have also observed over the years that while students strongly prefer consistency in the layout of all their online courses, faculty like to depart from any templates to put their own stamp on the design and even navigation of the site. This can create further problems for the student in the first days of a course unless the instructor has made a point of explaining that course site layout and navigation to students. Thus our strong recommendation that the very first announcement in an online course briefly orient students as to where everything is and how to get started.

Technical Problems

When they begin a course, students may find themselves unable to view the web pages properly, either because the browser they're using is too old (for one reason or another they haven't updated it), or because they haven't installed the necessary plug-ins. Or perhaps the instructor has not tested out the mobile app version of her course that many students are using and so there's a disconnect between what some students see and what instructor and students using the desktop browser can view. Far less common these days as MS Office products are more readily available and Google documents ubiquitous, is not being able to share word-processed documents, but there may be occasional problems. Even if students are using the same software program, those with earlier releases may not be able to read documents created by classmates or instructors with more current versions without the help of a plug-in.

Problems Related to Learning Style and Online Communication

Far more significant, perhaps, is the variance in learning styles required of those learning online. Students used to instructor-directed learning may feel somewhat lost in an environment that relies heavily on individual initiative and independent learning or even more dismayed to hear that collaboration with peers is an expected element of the class.

Even though the requirements of the course are clearly outlined in the syllabus and in the class announcements, the effect isn't the same as seeing an instructor glare severely at the class and announce that the essays are due the following week, without fail.

Assignments are completed at home, often in solitude, and sub-mitted through the click of a button, without that warm feeling students sometimes get when they pass in their exam papers or hand their essays over to their teacher in person. Indeed, without the discipline and structure imposed by the requirement of phys-ically sitting in a classroom, students often feel cast adrift.

The complicated mechanisms of human expression—facial expressions, voice intonation, body language, eye contact—are also no longer available. In their place are the contextual and stylistic conventions of the written word, a mode of communication that favors verbal over visual or kinesthetic learners, thus leaving some students curiously unsatisfied. Learning how to modulate their own speech is also a concern for online students. Most of us rely on body language to deflect the impact of what we say; we convey our true intentions through gestures and vocal intonation. The absence of these conventions sometimes causes students real distress. Or students accustomed to communicating daily via messaging apps, Facebook, Instagram, or Twitter may have difficulty adjusting to the norms of communication in the academic environment.

The asynchronous nature of much online communication adds a further dimension to this problem. We are all used to instant feedback: Susan says something, and Steve responds. Online, in an asynchronous format, Susan may still say something to which Steve responds—but the reply may come a day later. This spas-modic flow of communication takes some adjustment.

None of these problems is beyond the reach of a dedicated instructor. Now that there are so many ways to easily incorporate audio and video into classes, we encourage instructors to think about selecting opportunities to add these personalizing elements to the classroom, both in the form of their own short recordings as well as permitting students to do the same in their projects. Knowing when a particular student might be in need of a real-time communication, whether by phone, in person, or via online mes-saging, is crucial for retaining students who might otherwise be at risk of dropping the course. Dealing with these problems effectively can save both the student and the instructor valuable time, redu-cing some of the tensions inherent in learning something new. The key is to understand the need to prepare students adequately for what they are about to encounter and to provide them with the necessary tools to get through the course. These efforts will com-plement the work you put into designing your course and syllabus.

• • • • •

Preparing Your Students

To address the kinds of problems we've been describing, the most successful online programs offer student orientations as well as continuing technical support and resources. They may also offer study-skills courses that include a strong focus on the issues particularly relevant to online learning. But instructors who are left mostly to their own devices can also find effective ways to meet their students' needs. In the following pages, we suggest approaches for both the individual instructor and the institution as a whole.

Readiness Programs

Many institutions have short online quizzes or lists that allow students to judge their readiness for online classes. Some of the areas they seek to gauge are:

■ whether students are proactive, self-disciplined, and well-organized;

■ whether students are comfortable communicating entirely online without face-to-face meetings (for fully online courses);

■ whether students are comfortable with learning new technology, have access to adequate computer equipment and software, and if not, whether they are willing to update their equipment.

Two examples of different types of readiness quizzes online are:

■ Penn State University, https://pennstate.qualtrics.com/jfe/form/SV_7QCNUPsyH9f012B;

■ Washington Online, www.waol.org/prospective_students/isonlineForMe.aspx.

There is a whole collection of these self-assessments on MERLOT at https://www.merlot.org/merlot/viewPortfolio.htm?id=731796.

While you may not be creating your own quiz for students, you may find these serve as good reminders about behaviors of successful online learners that you will want to promote among students in your own class.

In recent years, the emphasis at many institutions has switched from having prospective students self-assess to providing more detailed explanations and illustrations of how online learning works. Videos capture the navigation of an online class and interviews with online students set forth the expectations for online learners. We recommend that you familiarize yourself with these initial views of online learning to which your new students will have been exposed.

Orientation Programs

Ideally, your institution should devise a student-orientation program that will take care of major issues such as these:

- any equipment or browser requirements;
- a general introduction to the learning management or other software used for instruction and its major features;
- instructions and links for downloading necessary software;
- information about issues that arise in an online class—perhaps in the form of a checklist about what one can expect as an online student;
- issues concerning the importance of student time management in an online class.

Lists of frequently asked questions (FAQs), referral email addresses, and toll-free numbers for reaching support staff (advising, student services, tutoring) and accessing library services are other useful features often included. Some orientation programs also use this as an opportunity to inform students about academic integrity policies at the institution.

Many institutions or their hosting and delivery partners have created such orientation programs. Most are simply self-paced series of web pages or videos, some interactive and some not. Many incorporate self-assessment surveys that seek to help students identify whether they are suited for online learning. Others test knowledge about computers, the institution's procedures, and so forth. At some institutions, student orientation is an actual experience that takes place within the learning management system in which courses will be conducted, providing a preview of what students can expect. This may be a self-paced orientation or one conducted with a cohort of new students and a facilitator prior to a semester start.

Once students have enrolled with their cohort, such orientation programs contain an element of human supervision and feedback, so that students must complete a few tasks in order to "pass" the orientation and be admitted to the classroom. These requirements are particularly effective in ensuring that students have the minimum skills, resources, and knowledge for an online course.

Having well-prepared students will mean that you as the instructor can concentrate on teaching rather than on resolving extraneous problems. There's enough for you to do once your online course has begun without having to divert attention to these preparation issues. Effective student orientation is also beneficial to the institution, because it makes a significant difference in the retention rates in online programs. Students who start off with a good orientation are more likely to have a positive experience and to return for further courses.

Preparing Your Own Orientation Program

What if your institution hasn't yet made arrangements for an adequate student orientation? What should you do?

Two methods will resolve your dilemma. First, you can devise a simple orientation of your own, one that will satisfy at least the minimum requirements. Second, as noted in Chapter 5, you can give clear directions in your syllabus for dealing with documents, as well as explicit explanations of how and where you will handle material and activities in the classroom. If you are teaching a blended class, we suggest using the first class meeting as a chance to take the students step by step through an orientation to the software used in your class and to answer any questions students may have. For those teaching a fully online class, creating a brief screencast video may also help students quickly get up to speed on use of a new technology tool or how to access a resource.

Before you begin creating your own orientation, you may want to take a look at some of the information and orientation pages that other institutions and their LMS partners have set up. The following offer useful examples:

■ Arizona State University, http://online-student-welcome.asu. edu/

This orientation is delivered mostly through video.

- Xavier University, www.xavier.edu/online/Student-Orientation. cfm

This orientation is in Canvas, but is viewable by the public.

Elements of an Orientation

If you create your own student orientation, there are several elements you should consider, as outlined below. If you find that your institution covers some elements but not others, you might focus your attention on the latter.

1. General introduction, including our expectations for online students
A general introduction can be made available to students even before they enroll in your course. Michelle Pacansky-Brock created such an introduction for her students at Sierra College, combining a short video, "Preparing for Your Online Class," with a text introduction, all linked from the distance learning web page at her institution so that students could view this as early as when they were shopping for classes. She told students in the video,

> *I created this website in an effort to increase the success of your learning by providing you with some very important information about my classes before the semester begins.... This page is important for all my online students but especially for those of you who are about to embark upon your very first online learning experience ... You're going to find, as you embark upon your journey with me that I really love teaching online and I work very, very hard to make your experience exciting and relevant.*

Pacansky-Brock discussed the attributes of successful online students and referred students to her institution's online student-readiness quiz and a video of a Student Success workshop she had created, "Are You Ready for an Online Class?"

In the video, she explained how communications worked in her class,

> *This may sound a bit odd to hear from your instructor but communication is the foundation for any successful relationship ...*

yep, that's right. I expect you to fully communicate with me throughout your semester learning experience. You'll have plenty of opportunities to interact with me in our discussions and activities but if you, at any point, need further help to successfully meet a specific learning objective in our class, it is your responsibility to reach out to me and let me know.

She commented on this,

I try to explain what my class consists of ahead of time so I can be more assuring of having prepared students enrolled on day one. I know there are students who do NOT want such a technologically enriched learning environment, and they have the right to be informed about the components of my class before they enroll so that they can find another class that suits their preferences.

2. Requirements for computer equipment and software (other than the platform being used)

State these as simply as possible. Realize that many people don't actually know the "numbers" for their computers, such as how large the hard drive is. In most cases, computers and many mobile devices will be adequate for online learning although you may have a few students on older, inadequate equipment. Based on your learning management system, you will want to specify if they require a particular browser or browser version or if there is any function that they cannot use via mobile devices. You can also devise your own "tests" of certain requirements. For example, if students need to be able to access audio in your course, give them a sample to test— either on your own site or elsewhere on the internet.

Many institutions can make a common word-processing program available to your students, or they have site licenses for other software. But if your students don't have access to a common program supplied by your institution—and this is often the case for continuing-education students—you will need to stipulate how documents will be shared. You might ask students to save all documents in a particular format or to use word-processing and spreadsheet or other software freely accessed through a service like Google Drive. Or you might want students to paste their documents into text boxes provided in your learning management software.

Gather information about the software possibilities ahead of time, and let students know whom they can contact for technical support or to obtain software. Include links on the internet where students can download any free programs, such as Adobe Acrobat Reader, that you intend to use in the classroom or indicate if there is a mobile app version. In regard to technical resources, don't overload new online students with many different references; instead, choose a few carefully evaluated resource links that will meet the students' needs.

Pacansky-Brock addressed the issue of technical requirements humorously in a section of her introductory materials called, "Your Transportation to Class":

> *"What?! Why do I need transportation for an online class?!"* *Well, you wouldn't enroll in an on-campus class if you didn't have a reliable way to get there, right? So, you shouldn't enroll in an online class unless you have regular and reliable access to the internet. This class requires high-speed internet access … due to the large, multimedia files you'll regularly be accessing…. Reliable "transportation" is paramount to your success in this online class.*

3. Computer skills needed

Most students taking online classes these days generally do have the basic computer skills needed and the institution will sometimes say that is an assumption for students registering for an online class. Depending on your student audience and the course materials, you may want to suggest a computer skill set necessary for taking your course only if it goes beyond the basic knowledge of email, attachments, downloading, and uploading. There are video tutorials on YouTube that cover just about every computer-related skill or program you can imagine. In some cases, you may be able to refer students to on-campus workshops as well. In an online language or speech class, you will need to discuss any software that you will be using to facilitate audio communication.

4. Introduction to the learning management software or other programs you will use to teach the class

Some learning management software companies have already put together a general introduction, student manual, or classroom demo for their software. Whenever possible, refer students to such pre-made resources. You may also be able to find examples of software introductions at the sites of other institutions that use the same software version your institution does.

Michelle Pacansky-Brock added information about the technology and programs students could expect to use in the class and how she planned to use that technology in a section entitled, "How Much Technology Does This Class Require?"

> *As you may have heard from other students, my online classes employ many forms of emerging technologies as learning tools. This is a topic I'm passionate about, folks, and I assure you I have carefully evaluated each technological tool before integrating it into my class and requiring you to use it.*

She continues,

> *Podcasts (Art 10 and Art 1E)—Both of my online classes offer options to my students. Lectures are offered in printed PDF form and in podcast form so you can select between reading or listening, based upon your own reading preferences. Interestingly, nearly 40 percent of my students have shared that they read and listen to my lectures because it enforces their learning. The other wonderful option that podcasts provide is mobile learning...*
>
> *VoiceThread (Art 10 and Art 1E)—If you enroll in either of my online classes, you will also be engaging in weekly discussions and activities using an online tool called VoiceThread. VoiceThread allows you to leave your comments in text or voice, it enhances our class community and enforces visual learning through image-based, interactive discussions ... If you're interested in using the voice commenting feature of VoiceThread, you are encouraged to consider purchasing a USB microphone for your computer or you have the option to purchase one hour of phone commenting through VoiceThread for $10. The phone commenting option allows you to leave comments through your telephone, just like leaving a voicemail (pretty cool!). Voice comments are encouraged but not required...*

5. If not otherwise available as links in your class site, provide contact information for such essential resources as library services for online students, writing or math assistance, or student advising. These can be critical for ensuring the success of online students.

6. A first assignment that requires students to demonstrate some familiarity with the software being used

This might be combined with one of the icebreaking activities described in Chapter 7. Typical of such assignments (depending on the software features available) would be these:

- Write a short self-introduction and post it in the discussion forum.

- Take an orientation quiz using the online testing program that will be used throughout the course.

- Fill in the template of a basic web page or blog with some biographical data and an optional photo of yourself. Add a video clip or audio recording if you like.

A Final Note

We recommend that you avoid beginning any orientation with material that consists *only* of a streaming video or animation that requires the downloading of a plug-in. Although many institutions are relying on video to deliver all orientation information, it can intimidate students who are already nervous about their ability to take an online course or who may wrongly assume that most of their online course will be delivered via video. Make sure there are captions for any video, and if possible, provide students with some summary material in downloadable format so that they can easily refer back to this information as needed once the course has begun. End the orientation on an upbeat note. This might include an assignment or a self-assessment quiz that provides feedback and encouragement and reinforces students' sense of readiness to begin their online course.

Providing FAQs

Take a good, hard look at your syllabus and ask yourself if anything you're requiring your students to do will require special additional skills or equipment. For example, if you've devised an exercise that entails uploading or downloading software, using a plug-in, or accessing a useful but difficult to navigate site, go through the steps yourself and jot down any parts of the exercise that may not be obvious. You may think that all of the operations involved are commonly known, but you'll be surprised to discover how many students don't understand them. If you don't provide some way for students to readily find out, you may spend an inordinate amount of class time filling in the blanks.

One approach is to gather all these possible sticking points into one FAQ file. You can compose it using a word-processing program, or create it as a web page. In this FAQ you should list each procedure your students may encounter and provide a short explanation of what they need to know to complete it. The internet convention for composing such FAQ pages is to list all the possible questions at the top of the page and then create a link to each one with a bookmark (in Word) or an anchor (in HTML), thus permitting your students to find the question they want answered without having to search the entire document.

● ● ● ● ●

Introductory Techniques

Your initial postings in the discussion forum, your first messages sent to all by email, or the greeting you post on your course home page will do much to set the tone and expectations for your course. These "first words" can also provide models of appropriate online communication for your students.

Your introductory remarks should reinforce what is contained in your syllabus, your orientation, and other documents students will encounter as they commence their online class. Note some of the examples we have already given of instructor remarks that set a tone and reinforce expectations.

The last thing we would like you to remember is that you must establish a presence and rapport in your classroom that are evident to students as soon as they walk through the online classroom door. Even though this would seem to be a matter of an instructor's own preparation, it is also an important part of what you can do to foster your students' readiness to begin the learning process.

Here are a few tips for establishing your presence:

• Convey a sense of enthusiasm about teaching the class.

For example, you might say:

> *Welcome to our course! I look at teaching Intro to Biology as a chance to share my enthusiasm about this subject with all of you, whether you are taking this class to fulfill a general requirement, have a personal interest in biology, or because you are exploring whether or not to major in this area. If you are one of those who feel some trepidation about science classes in general, I hope that you will soon realize that biology is all about the life around us and I look forward to helping you discover the underlying principles of this subject.*

■ Personalize and provide some touchstones about yourself and encourage students to do the same.

A biology instructor might share the following information about himself:

> *I first became interested in biology as an undergraduate, changing my major from business. My particular interest is in the biology of marine animals and I have spent many summers at a research center in California. Here's a photo of me chatting up the sea lions…*

or,

> *I have been teaching biology for twenty years here at State College. In my private life, I am a member of the chamber music group here in Smithtown and play the violin.*

Or you might present the same information in a brief, informal video made with webcam or on your smartphone, then uploaded. If you include both a text and video version, students will select the format with which they feel most comfortable. They may watch the video to get a sense of your personality while scanning your text for the actual information.

Or an instructor might share her enthusiasm about online education,

> *I began teaching online two years ago and found that it has opened up a new world for me, broadening the range of*

students with whom I come in contact to include those from many different places in the world and diverse backgrounds. Please tell me and your classmates a bit about yourself and what you hope to learn in this class.

■ Indicate your availability for questions and communications, the protocol to follow, and reassure students that they are not stranded on their own when it comes to online learning.

For example, you might say:

If at any time you have a question, please post it in the Q&A discussion area after checking the class FAQ. If it is something relevant only to yourself, please send me an email. I log in each day and should respond to you within twenty-four hours. Sometimes your classmates will come to your assistance, but please don't wait to contact me if you are encountering a serious issue. If you have a technical problem, contact the 24/7 help desk as soon as you can rather than endure frustration and delay trying to figure out the problem on your own.

A well-organized course, with signs that you have anticipated the students' problems, plus a welcoming attitude apparent in your first communication, conveys your appreciation of student concerns. Your initial efforts set the tone, and when these are followed by a responsiveness to students throughout the course, they will go a long way toward instilling student confidence in the online learning process.

11

• • • • •

Classroom Management and Facilitation

Classroom management, as we use the term, includes all the organizational and procedural measures that keep a class moving along. Like any class on the ground, an online class can get out of hand if you don't manage it properly. Facilitation is defined as the way in which an instructor interacts within the online classroom to set things in motion and to respond to students, creating successively greater opportunities for engagement with the course. In this chapter, we'll look at record keeping, class communications and participation, facilitation of both asynchronous and synchronous discussion, different approaches to facilitating discussion, providing feedback, and arrangements for team teaching. Chapter 12 will deal with special issues, such as student behavior problems.

Your classroom software, whether a full-scale learning management program or simply a set of web pages, Web 2.0 tools, and discussion boards, will have an impact on your classroom management and facilitation alternatives. We urge you again, therefore, to become familiar with your software in advance, so that you can exploit its capabilities and compensate for its shortcomings.

• • • • •

Record Keeping and File Management

Teaching online can be a nightmare for record keeping. By the end of a course, there may be thousands of postings and emails from students. Where and how will you save this information? How will you organize it?

Begin by finding out what the rules are for the server on which your course is housed. Will material be left on the server after the course is over or archived in a way accessible to you? Even if you're lucky enough to have such an arrangement, it's a good idea to prepare a system for saving material on your own computer. Moreover, if you intend to save any discussion materials, it's important to do so at intervals during the course rather than trying to sort through them all at the end.

If you are using Web 2.0 applications and technology tools outside your institution's control, you will want to be even more assiduous about developing a system to capture the content you create and you should encourage your students to do the same for their own content.

Tips for Record Keeping

Here are some suggestions for setting up your record-keeping system:

1. When you compose major pieces of information, do so first in your word-processing program or your HTML composer software rather than directly in your online classroom. If you are writing online and your connection is interrupted, you may lose all or part of your material. Also, if you start out in your word-processing program—and save your work there—you will already have created an instant "archive" of your material. This is not necessary for brief or off-the-cuff communications, but it is a good idea for your major content pieces.

2. On your computer's hard drive, storage you maintain in the cloud, or on a flash drive, create a series of folders that parallel the divisions of your course. For example, if your course is organized by week, create a folder on your computer for each week and then subfolders for "Discussion," "Lecture," "Exercises," and whatever other components you may have.

3. Create folders for student work on your computer and make sure that you've set up folders for student assignments in your email program if assignments are not all being submitted via your learning management system. If possible, don't leave students' assignments in your email program only, but download and store them along with the other classroom folders. Some

instructors like to house all Assignment #1 papers from students in the same folder, while others keep all assignments from an individual student in a sort of portfolio set aside for him or her alone.

You may also find it useful to take notes on the contributions of individual students while you read postings in the discussion forum, particularly in a large or active class. This can be done with simple paper and pen, in your word-processing program, or even by copying and pasting representative snippets of a student's postings into a folder for that student. Some learning management systems make it easy to assemble and store or print discussion threads. Any measures that help you build up a profile of individual students will assist you in following their progress and evaluating their work.

4. Make sure that all student email is sorted automatically or manually by you as it arrives at your email address. One of the greatest organizational perils is email from students that becomes commingled with email from other sources. This results in misplaced assignments and late responses to communications. It helps when you set protocols for emails sent to you (course name and assignment number, for example) and if students comply with those subject line conventions.

If you're working from a business account or a personal email account, you may want to consider establishing a separate email address for your class communications. There are many free email services available on the internet but be certain to ask about the limitations for size of individual attachments and total storage capability. If your students send you multimedia files, those may exceed the service limits.

In regard to IM or text messaging, you will need to sort out the ephemeral from the potentially worth saving communications from students. You may simply want to keep a log of questions asked and answered via these means. If you use Skype or phone communications with students, it's best to either record a quick summary of the conversation or for more complicated or sensitive discussions, to follow up the communication with an email summarizing your talk with the student.

5. As noted earlier, make sure you specify how students should use the subject line in email communications with you. For example, you may want to specify that the subject line consist

of *student's first name + last initial + number of assignment*. Gently remind class members if there are lapses (and there will be) during the progress of the course.

Extend this system to students' attachments as well, whether text or multimedia: make sure that students put their name and assignment number in the body of the attached text itself.

Often, attachments are downloaded and saved separately from the emails that delivered them or the learning management system assignment folders where they were submitted. In this case, if students remember to affix their names and assignment numbers, you will be able to print out assignments, if you wish, without having to guess who authored each paper!

Relabel assignments and emails if necessary before saving them to folders. Keeping the nomenclature uniform will enable you to sort quickly through your students' contributions. This is a valuable time saver.

For multimedia files uploaded to a third-party site—put the onus on students to maintain their own copies in the event of a third-party host incurring disruptions or even going out of business. With the ephemeral nature of many of the new Web 2.0 sites, such a loss of service is not an idle notion. Or, if you prefer to view such files offline and want your own copies, clearly express that wish to your students as part of the rules for creating these types of assignments.

6. If you are using external websites outside your institution's control—for example, a blog or other Web 2.0 tool—be sure to create a system for handling student communications and student-generated content housed there. These sites can change or even disappear with little or no opportunity for you to recapture content. Even as you caution students to keep a copy of their work, few students would think of preserving their discussion postings. Your review and record keeping (or downloading as the case may be) of student activity at these sites is essential as an ongoing procedure. You would be wise to keep tabs on communications on at least a weekly basis. Depending on the nature of the content, this might mean anything from copying and pasting everything into a word-processed document or simply taking notes on student contributions and copying and pasting only graded assignments.

Electronic Files versus Hard Copy

In contemplating the multitude of online activities and student assignments, you may be wondering how much you need to read online and how much you should download and print out. This is really a personal choice. However, don't feel somehow less "cyber-expert" if you want to print out and read most assignments or even some discussion offline. It can be very hard on the eyes to read a great deal online. Some instructors print out and read all assignments offline, preferring to make their notes in the paper margins while on the train, at the coffee shop, or lying in bed. Others read the papers offline but make their notes in word-processed documents, which they then copy and paste into their emailed correspondence with their students. Still others may create PDF versions of documents to read on their mobile devices and take screen shots of assignments posted on third-party sites. *What works best is the system that you are most likely to follow regularly and consistently.*

The same issues apply to record keeping. If you want to keep paper records as well as electronic ones, that's fine. In any case, always keep a backup copy—either on a flash drive, in the cloud, computer hard drive, or on paper—of your gradebook and any other important class records. You may want to have a paper chart that you use while online, to tick off credits for student participation as you read. This may save you the time and bother of having to toggle back and forth between the classroom and your word-processing program. You may also want to keep a paper journal of events in your class. Perhaps your learning management system gradebook can be saved as an electronic spreadsheet—if so, plan to download it on a regular basis so that you have your own record of the class as it proceeds.

You may have to experiment to find out which system works best for you. The factors to balance here are flexibility, economy of time, security of records, and how much time you want to spend online. But do devise a system of your own and follow through with that system.

● ● ● ● ●

Managing Communications

Not surprisingly, many online classroom management issues involve communication—between you and your students and among the students themselves. Designing an effective communication system and monitoring it are key steps in teaching online.

Creating a Uniform Announcement Area and the Use of Announcements

You need some area within your course where students know they can receive the latest updates and corrections. If you cannot easily update a web page announcement area linked to the course's home page, consider using a mailing list to email students your updates. If you have a discussion board, you can also choose that as your venue: let students know from the first day of class that each time they log in, they should check a particular area for the latest announcements. Depending on your preferences and those of your students you can also send SMS text messages to students that repeat online announcements or simply remind students to log in to view those announcements. Some faculty have experimented with using Twitter for this purpose. Twitter has an advantage in that its communications can be followed on mobile devices as well as via the internet. If you send a weekly message via email or some other format, make sure these are identical to any announcements in your online classroom—one way to do this is by starting an email with words to that effect—"This message is a duplicate of one posted in the classroom." Since Twitter messages are very limited in length (140 characters) you may need to remind students to visit the classroom to see the remainder of the announcement. For example, you might send out a "tweet" that says "Reminder essay assignment due Fri, see classroom for details or to ask questions."

If your LMS has an announcement feature that has an email delivery option and especially if your LMS has a mobile version that can be accessed by students from the app, such a feature is an ideal tool for managing announcements.

It's a good habit to make regular announcements on a weekly or biweekly basis—to keep students on task, and get them in the habit of checking in, even if there are no special changes or updates to announce. Simply give an overview of the week ahead or of upcoming due dates for assignments and exams. Here are a few examples of the types of information that might appear in announcements:

1. Reminding students about upcoming due dates and stages of the course:

   As we start Week 5, all of you should now have chosen your topics for the final essay. It's a good idea to start outlining your ideas now for the rough draft that will be due at the end of Week 6.

2. Offering a preview or overview of the week's activities to reinforce the students' attention to tasks:

   This week we will be focusing on the romantic poets. Be sure to visit at least one or two of the recommended websites for additional background information before taking part in the discussion about the readings.

3. Taking stock of progress and encouraging students:

   We are now entering the seventh week of the course. I am pleased that so many of you are participating in the weekly discussion forums and that the quality of those conversations is so evident. Nearly all of you have turned in your journal entries for Week 6. You can expect to receive your grades and comments from me during the next week. Feel free to email me if you have any questions about how I determined your grade.

4. Noting problems in computer access:

   Our server experienced a shutdown this morning from 8:00 a.m. to 9:00 a.m. EST. If you tried to access the classroom at that time, you would have received an error message.

5. Updating, clarifying, or changing the syllabus or schedule:

   Please note the following change in the reading for this week: pages 10–25 in White (not 110–125 as recorded on the syllabus). Quiz #2 will be postponed until after the holidays—therefore, it has not yet been posted. Also, there will be no on-campus meeting this week, due to the holidays. However, I will be holding live online chats throughout this week, by prior email appointment only. Student groups who hoped to meet on campus are encouraged to use the live chat as well.

6. Reminding students about special events or introducing speakers:

   This week we are fortunate to have as our guest Dr. Basstone. I have posted Dr. Basstone's lecture in Unit Three. He will be available on Tuesday and Thursday of this week only to answer your questions in Discussion Forum Three.

7. Maintaining your presence: Bring in the outside world when relevant to demonstrate your own active interest in the class topics and to involve your students:

   Don't know if any of you have seen the news today about the economic stimulus plan, but it highlights the importance of our current discussion concerning that issue. I was very struck by the fact that the New York Times editorial challenges the findings that have hitherto been accepted by nearly everyone, including me, on this issue. Take a look for yourself at the following URL and post a response to my message on the discussion board...

That All Important First Announcement

Perhaps the most important announcement of all is the first one that students see when they enter the online class site during the initial days of the course. This initial announcement does much to get the class off to a strong start. It can include a link to a class site video tour or a short individual intro by the instructor, and it need not be long but it should include at least the following elements:

■ A welcome tone and something to show the instructor's enthusiasm about the ensuing course.

■ A brief explanation of the course site layout, where to find the syllabus and other important information.

■ If a blended class, a statement defining the blended nature of the class. Be sure to write the announcement from the point of view of students reading it while already logged into the online portion of the class.

■ Directions for how to get started in the first days and week.

Using Video for Announcements

All of the uses of announcements described above may also be delivered via short videos posted by the instructor.

An example transcript from Richard Schumaker of his use of an announcement video during the first days of his online philosophy course provides an overview of the structure of the class,

> *Welcome to Philosophy 100. Our class will last fifteen weeks and every single week will have a similar structure.*
>
> *The purpose of this video is not to get into the details, but to communicate to you that there are four things that will happen each week and that the same structure will occur from week to week.*
>
> *First, the "Monday Missive,"—pretty close to 10 a.m., you will get an email from me that will be identical to what is posted in the announcement area of our course … telling you what we will be doing during that particular week … this can serve you as the simple checklist for the whole week…*
>
> *On Friday, you will get a recapitulation message that has two things in it. First, it will have what we have accomplished during the week, and second, it will also indicate what you should be doing over the weekend…*
>
> *The third part of our weekly lesson is Sunday office hours. I will be online between 6–9 p.m. almost every Sunday … Sometimes we will have optional chats … sometimes I will just be there if you need me … I am also happy to give you a call during that time frame during most weeks…*
>
> *The fourth component of each week will be the weekend philosophical quest. During the week you will be basically reading the assignments … and then discussing them in the discussion area of the course. Over the weekend you will have a single, relatively brief, very practical philosophical question … it will take the form of your going out into the community and*

asking questions or probing people you know ... sometimes will have you go to a shopping area of the mall, sometimes go into a restaurant, sometimes will have you talk to your friends or family ... there are many possibilities.

What you have to do is apply what you have learned during the week to a lived real world situation ... That is what philosophy is all about ... it has to do with relationships and give and take between people ... That's what Socrates and Plato meant by the dialectic ... Each one of these philosophical quests will be very short ... you will have to write something about your quest and most of the written assignments will be under 500 words ... in which you recount what you said or what you did ... not meant to be onerous but to apply what you have learned to your experience ... these are all due on Monday morning.

That's it, each week has four parts ... and so you will get another video on Friday at 10 a.m. and it will be similar, focusing on what you really need to know for the week.

Another example from Schumaker's writing course, provided here in transcript, demonstrates how he uses a short video to provide some more detailed guidelines for a challenging assignment,

Good morning everyone. We are starting Week 3 of our course. I hope everyone had a really rewarding weekend. Thank you very much for submitting your papers on time ... I am in the process of reading them now and will have them returned within roughly twenty-four hours.

As everyone knows we are moving into a new part of this class ... in this new module, new segment we will be working on what we are calling an "innovation report" ... the guidelines and models and tips are in the classroom site ... those are very detailed and precise, but ... this video is to emphasize two important parts of this report.

The first has to do with the focus or scope of the paper—there is a don't and a do here. The don't is don't make it excessively general ... What I want you to do please is to focus on a very precise region ... What do we mean by region? This is where you have some choices to make. At the most broad, I would do something like the New York metro region or metro Paris. That is certainly all right. But I think these reports work better when they focus on a neighborhood ... focusing on a region that you know really very well. They can be limited to a very small area.

A question I get often is do I need background? The answer is very strongly, no. Keep it to just a few sentences of background framing, if any. As you can read in the instructions, you are assuming a very knowledgeable audience so ... the reader of the report ... will know ... the background.

The second thing I want to bring out—make sure that your research focuses on that area. Don't spend time doing general research ... and once again, assume a very knowledgeable reader who is just looking for the key thing, the innovation.

So make sure that your papers have a regional focus and that your research integrates into that regional focus ... okay, so I hope that helps and be sure to contact me as needed.

In both of these examples, not only has Schumaker used video to deliver vital information to clarify matters for students, he has also provided a reassuring message, speaking in a casual delivery mode, making him seem approachable and anticipating student concerns.

Setting Rules and Establishing a Protocol for All Communications

One key to handling the email problem—the potential deluge of email you may receive—is to divert individual email, as much as possible, into the common classroom space. This prevents your having to make the same response over and over again, and it also has the positive effect of promoting students' consciousness of the online classroom as a shared space, not simply an assemblage of web pages or sites. If you make your presence felt primarily in the online classroom and only secondarily in the private email realm, your students will look for you in that common space. When you receive an emailed question or comment that isn't really private in nature, praise the student and encourage her or him by requesting that the student post the item in the classroom—or offer to do so yourself. A common protocol is to ask students to first post a question in the appropriate discussion forum or a separate Q&A area and wait twenty-four hours for a reply before attempting to email the instructor.

The more tools and avenues of communication that are available to students, the more important it becomes to establish a protocol for communications. A protocol for communications makes it clear how and in what order students should communicate in different situations and for different purposes. For example, if you are using blogging or other Web 2.0 communication tools you will need to add those to your mix in thinking about where and when and what students should communicate in each type of venue. For example, a logical rule might be that blog comments are only for postings directly related to the blog content, while all general questions are to be asked in the learning management system discussion area.

Among younger students, you may find that the email influx is diminished by the tendency of these students to favor text messaging or instant messaging for their communications. With synchronous communication tools—whether text messaging, chat, instant messaging, audio messages, and the other options in Web 2.0 tools that we have discussed in this book—you will need to set rules for your own response times (or perhaps you don't want to be available via text message or instant message at all) and for your students in regard to using these tools for course-related work and assignments. For example, if you allow students to do their group work using synchronous tools, do you want them to save a transcript or create a group log for you to review? If you do communicate with your students via instant message or text message, how will you keep a record of your communications so that misunderstandings are avoided?

These modes of behavior and protocols will not evolve among students on their own—you must set the rules and procedures early in your course and carefully consider how to structure the channels of communication.

Important! **With the increasingly diverse channels of communications that might be available to you and your students, it is necessary to establish rules, procedures, and expectations for all chosen forms of communication.**

● ● ● ● ●

Encouraging Participation and Managing Your Workload

Most instructors would like to promote as much interaction as possible in an online class—not only between instructor and students, but student to student as well. Instructors who run large, lecture hall, on-campus courses with an online component would perhaps like to use the online environment not only to replace some of the lecture time, but also to give students additional opportunities for discussion, presentation of projects to their classmates, and other forms of participation that are difficult to manage in a large classroom meeting. In previous chapters, we discussed the variety of activities you can set in motion to engage students. Here we want to take a look at how you can promote participation in these activities. At the same time, we will examine how the choice and design of activities may affect your workload.

Two factors determine the level and quality of participation and interaction in a class—your course design and student dynamics. The second part of this formula, student dynamics, is really not wildly different online than it is in the on-campus classroom or discussion seminar. Students will bring their own expectations and work habits to your online classroom. To some degree, you will be able to shape and influence their behavior, but in other respects it's the luck of the draw. Experienced instructors can fairly quickly identify the core group of students who are active participants (perhaps including obnoxious students as well as the most delightful), and these can be enlisted to get the classroom dynamics moving. Here, though, the factor of course design comes into play as well: instructors need to design the course so that other students are drawn into the orbit of the core group and begin to participate, even if in different ways and to a lesser degree. The trick is to get enough of the reluctant or shy students to be active in the classroom, at least occasionally, to make the class more diverse and interesting for all.

The Effect of Class Size

The way you use classroom design and organization to promote student participation will probably depend on the class size. As in the handling of email, your own workload can become an important factor in your decisions. Let's look at the issues involved in an online classroom or online component for classes of various sizes.

Classes of 10–30 Students If you have a class of only ten students, your major problem will be how to encourage participation and student-to-student interaction. Given that, in a class of ten, perhaps only three to five students will have a tendency to be very active, while the others will be nearly inactive or only moderately active, that group of three to five may become discouraged, fatigued, or bored if it spends most of the course carrying the load for the entire class. While you can give each of your students more individual attention than in a larger class, you presumably would like to avoid having the course become a de facto independent study class. So you have a real incentive to encourage student-to-student participation.

With a class of twenty, you may have several active coteries of students, and if even half of the students are active in discussions, they can potentially generate hundreds of messages for you to read—not to mention homework or exercises. You need to achieve a balance of energy between relating to students as individuals and relating to groups of students. This means not only getting students to talk to one another, but also apportioning your assignments and activities so that at least a few are group efforts or involve peer contributions.

In a class of thirty, your potential problems are your workload and the risk that students will disappear into the corners of cyberspace. In a class of thirty on the ground, you can see the rows of students and generally keep track of them visually. Online, you really do have to remember the names and check your records and notes to keep track of all of them. At this level, group work and presentations become a necessary part of your course design. You'll want to create smaller groups for the purposes of at least some discussion topics and projects. This arrangement will give shy students a more comfortable environment for airing their views and asking questions. It will also allow students to form social connections with other students and build up a sense of camaraderie. In any class of more than thirty students, you will probably also want to use some type of self-assessment or an automatic assessment vehicle such as online testing.

Classes of 40–100 Students (or More)   Beyond thirty or so students, you will find it difficult to operate without the assistance of a teaching assistant (TA) unless you dramatically redesign the class. There are two approaches you can take if you do not have a TA—first, the implementation of group strategies, and second, replacement of some instructor-student interaction with built-in interactivity of content. The latter can be accomplished by an individual instructor investing a good deal of time in creating modules, but it is more commonly done by a course development team.

Group Strategies and Interactivity of Content

In a class of forty or more students, even with a TA, and the addition of rich content and exercise modules, you must interact more with groups of students than with individuals. In such classes, if possible, you should use online testing with automatic grading for at least one-third to one-half of your assessments, and you should have students working in groups and making presentations to the entire class.

In such a large class, discussion forums can be established for groups of 10–15 students. You (and your TA or team teacher if you have one) can then observe the groups, noting the interaction and responding when necessary. You can think of this as the party-host model. You and your colleague circulate among the various groups of guests, joining in on conversations at times and making sure there are no wallflowers sitting by themselves.

In order for students to benefit from ideas and questions that arise in groups other than their own, you should set up dual levels of the classroom—one for the entire class and the other for the group level of organization. Establish a forum where students can ask general questions about the course; this will prevent your having to answer these questions in each group. But also establish discussion areas where student representatives from each group can address the topics of discussion with the entire class.

For example, in Week 3, if students are discussing the chapter reading assigned on the French Revolution, you might have students meet first in their groups to discuss and summarize the main ideas of the chapter on Robespierre or to reach some conclusions about the dominant causes of the Revolution. You would set a time limit for these group discussions to conclude. Then you would post the same discussion question or assignment in the discussion forum for the entire class, asking the student spokes-person for each of the various groups to exchange and discuss their groups' ideas.

When there are individual assignments for a large class, you can choose examples that typify the responses and the problems encountered, then post these anonymously (without the student's name attached) for all students to view. In this way you can create a lesson by means of your comments. This method works best for courses with much factual or objective material—computer science, math, and so forth. For courses that involve more sub-jective responses, you can spotlight those you think are full or good responses. Some instructors do this by creating presentation pages, while others use the discussion forum areas for this purpose. To comment on problems the students may be encoun-tering, you can derive principles and illustrations from the poorer student work without actually posting individual examples.

Christine Appel of Universitat Oberta de Catalunya (Open Uni-versity of Catalonia) in Spain and Jonathan Matthews from Penn-sylvania State University were previously highlighted in Chapter 7 as those who taught large online classes and rely on group strat-egies and interactive content to manage their teaching load. Both of these instructors were able to avail themselves of strong instruc-tional design or course development and technology units on campus to provide interactive content.

Christine Appel noted that the Modern English 1 course she taught to fifty students consisted of five major types of assessment tasks. "Some are self-correcting, like reading exercises for which students can check their answers after a certain date," she noted. There are three tasks involving writing and/or speaking for which students received individual feedback from the instructor, while another two projects were based on group work, with the instruc-tor offering feedback to the group midway through the project, "intervening in the process, highlighting changes that need to be made." The final versions of the group projects in this highly standardized course were set up so that the instructors gave feed-back to the groups but could use their own discretion to decide whether or not to give additional individual feedback as well. Mat-thews and his TAs similarly used computerized quizzes, inter-active modules for content, rubrics, and group projects to deliver feedback and assess their students. Such a strategy of providing a mix of different assignments in which feedback may be given to individual students, to small groups of students, and through automatic computer programmed or pre-written feedback, allows for effective assessment of students in a large online class.

If you find yourself in a situation where you alone teach and provide nearly all course content for a class of forty or more students, a good solution is to find appropriate Web 2.0 tools that enhance the small-group capabilities that might exist in your LMS and to seek out relevant enriched content available on the internet. At the same time, seriously rethink the objectives of your assignments and assessments so as to target a smaller number of assignments for individualized feedback. If you formerly gave individualized feedback on five separate assignments, you might replace a few of these with rubric-guided grading, designate one as a group assignment, or consolidate closely related assignments into one larger project. Depending on the sophistication and course level of your students, you may also be able to designate students to help with some of the discussion facilitation, or to employ peer review for at least one assignment.

Changing Class Sizes

Perhaps the hardest thing for instructors to adapt to is a sudden change in their class size—one gets used to teaching within a particular design and context and to suddenly be confronted with an increase of even 25 percent—say, from twenty-five students to thirty—can be a challenge. If you are faced with this situation, what you need to do is think about redesigning, not merely adapting, your syllabus and manner of interacting with students.

There is really no one ideal class size for an online class—the quality of teaching and learning hangs on understanding the model, purposeful design, and the instructor's skill in managing the class. A poorly organized and haphazardly designed course for twenty is not going to promote better learning than a richly enhanced and carefully designed course for forty students. As an instructor, you may prefer teaching under one model rather than another just as those who teach face to face may prefer small seminars to large lecture hall classes. But if you do find yourself facing a change in the model to which you are accustomed, (especially if it is not in the nature of a radical change), you may find it comforting to realize that by implementing a few changes in design of activities and content, you can attain the same level of effectiveness in your teaching and perhaps find equal enjoyment in the teaching experience as well.

Here are a few tips for adjusting class design to a larger class:

- Trim the number of topics in the main discussion forum to a manageable number of items or create a new forum to handle additional topics. When the discussion area is overcrowded with large numbers of topic threads and postings, it becomes difficult for students (and you) to follow the discussion.

- Consider reducing the minimum number of postings you require of students each week and weigh the participation grade more heavily on the quality of the responses, guiding students by means of a clear but detailed participation rubric.

- If appropriate, replace at least one individual assignment with a small group project. Have groups present their projects in a common discussion area. Consider having students use a peer-review rubric to evaluate themselves and other group members.

- Use detailed rubrics to give guidelines and to supply general feedback on assignments. Save your more detailed individual feedback for key assignments—at least one of these should be on an assignment given early in the course so that the student receives the necessary feedback that will enable him or her to improve.

- Revisit the class schedule, consolidating assignments if possible, and revising due dates or expected feedback times for assignments if necessary—don't set up unreasonable deadlines for yourself in regard to returning long assignments.

- Maintain a pattern of frequent visits to the classroom to avoid feeling overwhelmed by a backlog of postings you must read. Frequent visits will also help promote a sense of your presence in the classroom.

- Do not attempt to respond to many individual discussion postings each week. Try to read all, answer any that pose an actual question or that impart incorrect information to others, and then make comments that address or summarize or highlight the overall themes and issues noted by students during that week.

- Prepare a list of resources to which you can easily refer students who may need assistance in writing, the use of the library, or computer skills. You may also want to prepare a FAQ of questions and answers about assignments based on your past experience teaching the class. While both these ideas constitute a helpful approach for any class, they are even more effective for a larger class in which your feedback time is at a premium.

Finally, find comfort in meeting the challenge of a larger class with the knowledge that the diverse backgrounds and potential for greater interaction among students may actually make the course more stimulating than one of a smaller size. Keeping yourself organized is the key to maintaining your enthusiasm and energy for teaching, and transmitting that enthusiasm and energy to your students.

While some of the above tips may be relevant even for such super-size online classes like MOOCs (Massive Online Open Courses), we specifically address the challenges of teaching in the latter in Chapter 14.

The Debate about Class Size

Class size of totally online courses has been an issue since the inception of online education. With the advent of MOOCs, the conversation has expanded, like the class size, to encompass thousands or even tens of thousands of students. Often overlooked in this controversy are the underlying assumptions about the online instructor's role in the classroom, the nature of the course, and the design considerations that are appropriate for the course.

We can state one point quite emphatically here: You can't have a high level of instructor-facilitated interaction with individual students in an online class of forty or more students. Having said that, a course design based on small-group strategies, highly interactive content, and targeting of key assignments for individual feedback may adequately compensate for this overall lower level of individual instructor–student interaction.

Some institutions have applied the same rules to their online courses as to their on-site versions—for example, assigning one TA for every 20–25 students if a class exceeds thirty or forty students. Applying such equations is a good start. However, the cut-off point for the "average" class served by one instructor should be lower for the completely online class than for an on-campus version, assuming that the same level of instructor-student interaction is desired. From the experience of those who have taught in both formats, it appears that one instructor in an on-campus class can comfortably handle a class of 30–50 by herself, whereas the equivalent online is closer to 15–30 students, with the latter number dependent on the level of instructor–student interaction desired in the class.

Some instructors who have taught online would put the number even lower—say, 15–20 students for one instructor. Although this estimate may come from a heartfelt reaction based on their experience, it cannot necessarily be applied to all cases. Our observation is that many who teach online automatically fall into a pattern of very intense instructor-generated activity and a great deal of one-on-one interaction. In fact, the workload issue is usually the number one complaint of first-time online instructors, whether they have fifteen students or twenty-five.

The very seductiveness of the online environment, with its seemingly endless avenues of communication, can cause an instructor to become far more interactive online than he or she would be in a traditional on-campus class. Student expectations also play a role here: online students tend to be more demanding and to need more affirmation and attention than their on-campus counterparts. Further, the fact that one can see and review one's interactions with students may make an instructor more acutely self-conscious and eager to respond more often and more elaborately than in an on-campus class.

While this high level of instructor responsiveness may be a desirable thing in itself, it may not be practical for some programs to have classes small enough to make it feasible. More importantly, it is not necessarily true that actual student learning outcomes are higher in small-scale models. Programs should ideally base their decisions as to class size on the type of course, design of course, resources available, and workload that may be expected of instructors. And institutions need to prepare instructors to teach under the resulting new model rather than assume that instructors will simply continue to teach the same way for forty as for fifteen students!

● ● ● ● ●

Finding a Balance between Student-Centered and Instructor-Centered Activities

No matter what the class size, most students appreciate a balance between student-centered activities and those that focus on the instructor. In other words, they want the instructor to contribute something unique, something they can't "get from the book," but they also respond well to an environment that asks them to be active participants in their own learning. While there is strong consensus that the online instructor needs to emphasize facilitation of student learning, we believe that it is a mistake to think that students have ceased to seek inspiration and the imparting of experience or the sharing of expertise from their online instructors.

In a class of fifteen, you might wish to do away with the formal lecture mode and simply provide a segmented lecture as described in Chapter 3: a running commentary of short paragraphs that offers the initial material—the thread topics—on which students can base their discussion. But in a larger class, you will want to provide a more structured presentation of instructor-generated materials. Students would quickly lose their way if they had to find the tidbits of lecture material hidden among hundreds of discussion topics or anecdotal comments.

Your ideal mix of instructor-generated and student-based activity depends on the number of students, the length of the course (for instance, whether there is enough time for several projects and how long students will have to get organized for group efforts), the number of TAs you have (if any), and any matters related to the level or type of course you teach. We recommend that you include some calculations for your ideal mix in the planning stage for your course.

We also encourage you to take advantage of the increasing ease of use of Web 2.0 tools to allow students more opportunities to generate content whenever this choice seems appropriate and relevant as a learning activity.

Some General Guidelines for Student Participation

One of the most effective ways to promote student participation in an online class is to make it required and graded. As explained in Chapter 5, this should be clearly stated in your syllabus, and the criteria must be defined.

Participation online ranges from "attendance"—defined as logging on and (presumably) reading in the online classroom—to actually posting messages in discussion forums and taking part in small-group activities. It is not possible to gauge pure attendance unless you have tracking features in your software that monitor the opening of files or time spent in a particular portion of the classroom. These tracking capabilities can help give you a clearer picture of a student's activities, but they are generally not sufficient for assessment purposes. For example, they may tell you that a student opened up a particular document and kept it open for a period of time, but not whether the student actually read the document. So it's best to think of the information you gain from these features, if you're lucky enough to have them, as merely a small piece in the puzzle. They are chiefly valuable for alerting you to a negative—i.e., telling you that a student has never accessed a portion of the class. Therefore, it's best for those in blended classes to limit consideration of "attendance" to the face-to-face portion of a course and focus only on participation and submission of assignments for the online portion.

To be an effective goad to activity, participation grades for a completely online class or true blended class should constitute somewhere between 10 and 40 percent of the student's overall grade. If you include a separate category for contribution to small-group activities, you might end up with 50 percent of the grade in the "participation" category. For an online component in a mainly face-to-face course, we recommend that at least 10 percent of the total grade for the course be reserved for online participation.

You may want to establish criteria for both quantity and quality of participation. For instance, one-third of the participation grade might be based on the student meeting a minimum quantity level (say, posting a comment or question in the discussion forum once a week), with the remaining two-thirds based on the quality of participation. Or, if your course involves lots of teamwork, you might divide the participation grade between individual accomplishments and contributions to the group.

Depending on your course objectives, presentations—either group or individual—may be an essential part of student participation. You might define participation to mean completing all weekly classroom exercises, taking part in discussions, and presenting a project to the class. The use of presentations, whether group or individual, fosters interaction among students, but it is most effective if you emphasize that student comments and questions about their classmates' presentations are counted in participation grades or are separately graded.

Important! *However you choose to define "participation," make sure that a significant part of the grade depends on what the student does in the shared classroom, not simply on the completion of assignments submitted to you alone.*

So think about how you can structure opportunities for student-to-student interaction—it's not something that will necessarily happen without your deliberate effort.

Asynchronous or Synchronous Discussion?

Some instructors are firm believers in synchronous communication for fostering a sense of online community while others find it difficult and exhausting to facilitate synchronous sessions with a large group. Both asynchronous and synchronous communication have their advantages as well as disadvantages. Asynchronous discussion allows time for reflection and encourages more careful consideration but often lacks spontaneity and it may take longer to arrive at a conclusion or for a group to reach a decision. Synchronous communication provides a sense of immediacy and cultivates a feeling of responsiveness among participants while allowing for quicker problem solving, but at the same time the greater speed and short-hand expression can lead to misunderstandings, superficial interaction, and poorly considered decisions. Many of the shortcomings of synchronous discussion can be alleviated by software that provides a means for archiving or replaying as well as by careful preparation leading up to a synchronous session. The disadvantages of asynchronous discussion are downplayed when the discussion prompts and questions are well-constructed and stimulating, the facilitating instructor has some skill in tending discussion, and there is a clear beginning and ending schedule for the asynchronous discussion, with students willing to post throughout the week rather than all jumping in during the last two days of a week.

Tips for Fostering Asynchronous Discussion

In Chapter 6, we discussed the impact that a particular discussion software structure may have on the way you organize your discussions. However, no matter how your software may be organized, there are techniques you can use to foster greater participation and clarity among your students.

1. *Start the major topic threads yourself.* It's a good idea for the instructor to start all major topic threads unless you have designated a forum for student presentation or have designated students to act as the moderator. If you wish to (and your software permits), you can allow students to contribute additional threads anywhere as they feel the need. This arrangement should be considered with great care, however, because students often tend to create new topics without real necessity, and your discussion area may soon be overwhelmed with too many threads on duplicate topics. Generally better to create specific forums where students can initiate threads.

2. *Narrow down topics.* A good discussion needs pruning and shaping. An overly broad topic thread—say, "The French Revolution: What Do You Think of It?"—will often result in very fragmented discussion. This is especially true in an introductory class, in which most students know little about the subject. If you divide up broad topics into logical subtopics— say, "Economic Conditions on the Eve of the Revolution" or "The Execution of the Royal Family"—you can prevent the discussion from going off in too many directions. In an introductory class, you may want to provide even more guidance. For example, a discussion based on specific readings in the textbook, on a focused website visit, or on assigned exercises, coupled with your guideline questions, will likely be more productive than simply pointing students to the forum and expecting them to find their own direction.

   A short series of closely related questions can allow students to jump in on any one of the points and still find themselves "on topic." In our example of the French Revolution, a topic thread might contain several questions about the economic conditions and invite students to choose one to which to respond:

Please address at least one of the following, "What were the landholding patterns? How important was foreign trade? Had the average well-being of the citizens improved or worsened in the years leading up to the Revolution? Give a rationale and provide support for your response."

The shaping of discussions takes some genuine forethought. You might think of this task as similar to creating chapters in a book or long article you are writing. Threads will stay of manageable length if you keep topics specific and allow a place such as a lounge or question-and-answer forum for off-topic conversations.

Sometimes, of course, a thread goes off on a digression that is so valuable and interesting in itself that you don't want to curb it. The pruning and organization of threads is for the purpose of sustaining discussion, not stifling it. Allow students to digress, but if you think that the new direction in the conversation calls for an entirely new thread, you might create one or suggest that a student begin a new topic message to explore the subject further.

3. *Organize forums and threads to reflect the class chronology or topical sequence and suggest a pattern for posting.* The organization of discussion forums should complement the class structure but also provide some reminders of the course chronology and sequence. For example, creating one forum for each week or unit of the course helps students know at a glance where they should be looking for that week's activity. Even if you don't have a forum structure, you can designate all the threads for a particular week under the rubric "Week 1" or "Unit 1."

Suggest a schedule for posting that is appropriate to the topic, assignment, and your student audience—for example, if you want students to comment on other students' postings, you might suggest that everyone post their first responses to your question by midweek and to classmates during the remainder of the week. You may even set up your system of credit for the discussion participation rubric to reflect that. (If you have many working students who must do the greater portion of their schoolwork on the weekends, and you are able to do so, you may want the class week to run from Tuesday through Monday rather than Monday through Sunday.)

If you have a general forum area for ongoing questions about the course, you might want to divide this up by week so that students can more easily find questions that pertain to a particular week's activities.

4. *Address students by name and encourage students to signal topics and clarify responses.* Mention the student's name in responding to their message: "Joan, your point certainly reflects on the issue of the previous chapter." Change the subject line to reflect the topic of your response ("Response to Joan," or "Joan and the previous chapter's issue," etc.) and encourage students to do the same. Clarify the portion of the message to which you are responding through copying of the statement before your own reply, quotation marks, or whatever means your discussion software features most readily allow and remind your students to do the same. (While some discussion software automatically repeats the entire message to which one replies, you may need to pinpoint the relevant portion.)

5. *Key the thread topics to appropriate and relevant activities.* Keying thread topics to the assignments, readings, projects, and exercises for a particular week will help keep students on topic in their discussions and also provide an obvious place to discuss anything that occurs in the course during that week. While you may have some key topics in mind, do allow students to ask related questions that you may not have anticipated. Adding a prompt at the end of the discussion question such as "If you have another question based on this week's reading, feel free to post it in reply/post it in a new thread." Or you may create a thread each week that is a placeholder for "other questions about this week's readings and activities."

6. *Establish a pattern of frequent response.* Students tend to follow instructor expectations for online participation, and these expectations are communicated not only by the declarations of the syllabus but also by the instructor's behavior. During the first week or so, if your class size allows (this would be in a class of no more than thirty students), greet all students individually in the classroom as they arrive and engage as many as possible in discussion. Thereafter make an effort to respond to a diverse group of students each week—not just to the same one or two individuals. If you have a large class, you will find

yourself rotating your time among all the small groups, as well as tending to any all-class forums to share what their groups have accomplished.

In large classes, rather than engaging in long, concentrated visits to your classroom, it is best to establish a predictable pattern of short but frequent activity. When students see you "poke your head into" the classroom (that is, see your postings), it makes them feel that you are truly present and actively responding to the class. In contrast, when students see that an instructor rarely engages with them, they are discouraged from posing questions and comments aimed even indirectly at the instructor, and they may also conclude that the instructor will be unaware of what is going on in the classroom.

Think in terms of three to five short periods of logging on each week, rather than the one or two sessions you may be used to in your on-campus courses. If you have only four hours to devote to the classroom in one week, spend an hour for each of four days in the classroom, rather than two hours twice a week. This will allow you to keep up with the flow of student discussions and will also reinforce the impression that you are responsive and on the scene.

If you are teaching a primarily on-campus course that meets once a week and also has an online component, you will have to decide how important student discussion online will be in your class. If you really want students to make use of this venue, then you too must actively attend to it. The discussion forum is a great place for you to continue conversations you started in class or for the TA to extend the weekly discussion section. Initiate topics on a weekly basis and require some weekly participation from students in the online forum. This is also the best place to update the class on changes and errors, to pose and answer questions, and to help students review material. Again, unless you are actively "showing the flag" in this area, students will quickly learn that they can ignore it with impunity.

7. *Facilitate and build on participation.* While the instructor needs to be seen as engaged, don't try to respond to every posting in the classroom. Even in a class of twenty, this will quickly overwhelm you and can actually put a damper on student discussion. The quality of your postings is as important

as frequency. And you want to encourage students to interact with each other, not only with you. So make comments that address a whole train of thought—responding, for example, to five or six related messages in the thread rather than to each of the five individually. In this way you will do your part to encourage participation as well as interaction among students. Think about jumping in or tending to the conversational fires at critical junctures, working as a facilitator to help move the discussion forward and keep the fire going.

Don't merely post friendly expressions of affirmation. You should also contribute comments that summarize what students have posted, as well as follow-up questions that stimulate further discussion. In some cases, it might be appropriate to invite students' responses to their classmates' ideas: "Anyone else want to comment on Tom's observation?" "Did anyone reach a different conclusion about this issue?"

If a class is fairly quiet, it may seem that it's a good idea to jump in and reply as soon as someone finally posts something. The truth is, instructors feel uncomfortable when nobody's talking. Resist the temptation to jump in too quickly and risk squelching student voices with an excess of chatter or by answering the question you have posed to them. There are also times when there will be a lull in conversations because students are working on a major assignment. Some instructors may even schedule a "quiet time," such as a few days during which students are encouraged to devote most of their time to a project.

8. *Provide feedback that stimulates higher-level thinking.* Look for student postings that imply unspoken assumptions or suggest a line of other questioning. Provide follow-up responses that ask for more information or deeper consideration, from the student posting and/or the other students in the class. For example, ask students questions like, "What are the implications of your statement?" "What evidence is there to support your point of view?" "Does anyone want to add to/dispute/ verify that?"

Equally important is to confirm when students are on the right path but then help guide them to the next step: "What Joe has said about X theory is sound, but when we look at it operating in the area of Y rules, how would we go about testing that theory? Anyone want to tackle this?" It may also be appropriate to ask students to apply issues to real-world situations— "Several of you have posted comments on the economic price of environmental protection. Can anyone think of a current example in which economic development has been negatively impacted by environmental degradation and explain how?"

9. *Be aware of cultural patterns as well as differences in personal styles in discussion.* If you have a classroom that includes students from another country, be alert and request information from informants (rather than making assumptions) about the best way to ask questions. For example, a group of students from a particular culture may not respond very well to questions and topics that call for volunteered responses. In this case, a question like "Anyone want to comment on this?" is better altered to "I would like to hear what you think about this. Please post your response to this question by Wednesday afternoon."

   Be aware, too, that not all students respond well to the same approaches to discussion. For example, some students respond poorly to a question that asks them to share personal experiences, while others are not at all shy about divulging information about their background and preferences. We think it's important to respect these differences and not make students feel boxed in by the way you frame a question. A way around this problem can be to split the question in such a way as to offer an alternative: "Can you relate this to your own experience or one you have heard or read about?"

10. *Prepare a strategy for potentially controversial discussions.* It is even more important to have a strategy for approaching potentially controversial subjects online than in a face-to-face class since it is more likely you will see a wider range of students posting online than might have been willing to venture an opinion on-campus. If you have a code of conduct or netiquette stated up front, that will help matters as you gently remind the class as a whole when people tend to stray from the rules. When strong opinions are expressed that seem irrelevant to the subject matter, you may redirect as needed. When relevant but unsupported opinions arise, don't hesitate to ask for facts to back up assertions or to ask for clarification. Avoid irony or heavy-handed phrasing—remember that as the

instructor, what you say automatically carries a lot of weight and without vocal cues, students may easily misinterpret irony. If you know that the subject matter is inherently controversial, you may want to ask students to debate an issue and either assign them randomly to a particular viewpoint or ask them to take the side most opposed to their own personal view. Having to research and defend a position with logic often helps students discuss highly charged subjects.

A Study in Workload Management

A community college instructor, Fred is assigned to teach an online course in American history. He finds that he has been asked to teach a class of fifty students, the same number as in his on-campus course. He has always prided himself on promoting active discussion in his courses and wants to continue to do so in his online course, so he requires that all students contribute to the discussion on a weekly basis in order to receive participation credit.

Two weeks into the course, Fred is overwhelmed by the time it takes him to read through and respond to the student discussion postings. Instead of the dozen students who usually dominate the class discussion, a much larger percentage of his class freely express themselves on the discussion board, to his surprise and delight. However, most students seem to respond directly to his postings and seldom to other students. This means a substantial amount of his time is needed to read and respond to students.

Also, the sheer number of postings on the discussion board each week makes it hard for him to follow the conversations. Students often arbitrarily start new threads instead of replying to a thread, making it hard to follow the continuity of a discussion.

Following the advice of a colleague, an experienced online instructor, Fred divides the class into five smaller groups of ten students each for the purposes of discussion. He refines his participation credit so that students must respond to at least one other classmate each week rather than only to the instructor's initial discussion threads. He asks students to remember to reply to a message rather than start new threads for a response and to save new threads for new topics or clearly divergent subtopics.

Fred finds that he is able to circulate among the five discussion groups, addressing his remarks to each group as a whole as much as to individuals. Discussions are easier to follow, and as an added benefit, students begin to provide more follow-up questions and comments to their classmates, raising the overall quality of the discussion.

● ● ● ● ●

Managing Student-Led Discussion

Perhaps you have a TA who will help lead discussion and help you manage a large class. But what about the students themselves? How feasible is it for students to facilitate discussion? Facilitating a discussion is sufficiently challenging for even an experienced online instructor but there may be times when there are pedagogical reasons for you to allow students to take the lead. Generally speaking, it is difficult for students in lower level undergraduate courses to facilitate discussion, because they may have neither the subject matter knowledge nor the experience in the online instructional setting to undertake the task, but it may be a suitable approach and more tractable situation when it involves students in upper level undergraduate or graduate program courses. Nonetheless, it is wise to provide some guidelines to students for effective facilitation of discussion and to incorporate particular objectives you may have for the exercise. This holds true for both facilitation of small group discussion as well as students taking the lead in discussion activities involving the entire class.

Linda Ridley, who teaches an online graduate level business course in Organizational Behavior and Leadership for CUNY School of Professional Studies, has quite appropriately developed an approach to student facilitated discussion that emphasizes the exercise of leadership. In her syllabus, she explains the leadership of the discussion board, saying, "The leader should generate discussion, monitor the discussion, stimulate the discussion with responsive commentary and questions, and then, at the end of the week, summarize themes that emerged." Linda also provides guidelines for leading the discussion in the form of a rubric (based on a rubric from Rubistar (http://rubistar.4teachers.org/index.php?screen=ShowRubric&rubric_id=1779750&/) that demonstrates how students will be graded on their facilitation skills, emphasizing stimulation of discussion through initial prompts as well as moderation of discussion that serves to advance the quality and focus the direction of the discussion.

In addition to providing rubrics for discussion leaders, it is best to provide some examples of good facilitation and in some cases, depending on level of sophistication or if it is early in the course, it might be wise to ask student discussion leaders to submit their discussion prompts to the instructor first for approval and feed-back before posting.

• • • • •

Tips for Establishing Effective Instructor-Facilitated Synchronous Communication

The most common form of synchronous communication available to instructors is text-based chat. However, voice-enhanced and video-enhanced chat and presentations have become more widely available.

You should carefully consider any requirement that students participate in chat as a graded assignment. When students live on campus, chat arrangements are not a difficult problem, but if your group includes working adults or students from a mix of time zones, chat can be a real impediment to their full participation in the class. In such cases, you will have to be very flexible about scheduling times for chat. It is best to offer some variety in the choice of times. If possible, too, you should copy the chat to post asynchronously (if archiving is not automatically generated by the chat) for the benefit of those who cannot attend. If you are super-vising group work, request that groups post their chat transcripts in a group asynchronous area or email it to all the group's members and to you.

Here are some tips for organizing an instructor-led chat or other synchronous session with more than one student:

1. Try to limit group chats in which students are all expected to fully participate to four or five participants. However, if the point of the synchronous session is mainly for you or others to present information, and not everyone is expected to engage in the conversation or ask questions, then an entire class participating in a session may not be a problem.

2. If you have a group of more than five students, establish a system for granting turns to speak. If your chat software includes a crowd-control function (the equivalent of raising hands to be recognized), then you should definitely make use of it. If your software doesn't have such a built-in system, you can design one: for instance, a question mark, asterisk,

or some other sign that, when typed, will appear next to the student's name, allowing you to recognize him or her to speak.

3. Allow some time at either the beginning or the end of the chat for students to ask off-topic questions and to socialize. Announce this before the chat or at the opening of the session. Budget an extra two minutes as well for greetings and goodbyes.

4. For synchronous presentation formats like Adobe Connect, Blackboard Collaborate and other such software, make sure participants test out their equipment ahead of time to ensure that browsers, microphones, etc., are all available. As presenter, have a backup plan in place for those who encounter problems speaking or hearing the presentation. When presenting, it can be helpful to have an assistant to help handle technical issues. If this is not possible, make sure you practice before the presentation under realistic conditions.

5. Chat may be used to bring in a guest speaker. This is best done in conjunction with an assigned paper or lecture by the guest, and it may follow the guest's participation in an asynchronous discussion for a period of a few days. This technique is most effective when you adequately prepare students for the guest chat and when you have provided some advance time for the guest to do a practice "run-through" with the real-time software before the event.

   You can time the chat event to coordinate with associated activities and give students an interval to formulate questions they can pose to the guest. If the guest is not available for a particular time, consider a one-on-one interview which can be replayed for students—you can even gather the questions ahead of time from students and ask the guest on their behalf.

6. Limit each session to approximately one hour or less and announce the time limit before the chat. An hour period allows for the social niceties that smooth the way, as well as some spontaneity, but also provides a substantial period of time during which all can focus on the pre-announced topics.

7. Prepare students for the chat by posting the topics or agenda, assigning readings or activities, or giving them questions to consider before the chat. Ask them to keep these questions or

notes at their side while chatting. Have ready your own notes or outline so that you can keep track of all the items on the agenda. In some chat software, students entering late can't read anything that was said before their entrance. In such cases, strongly emphasize in advance that students should appear on time. You won't have time to keep recapitulating the "plot."

8. Whenever possible, preface your response with the name of the student to whom you are replying, or include bits of the question or comment to which you are responding. Using student names is particularly effective when you answer two students in one reply:

> *Joe, I think reading the book before seeing the film would be best. No, Elsa, Exercise 1 is not due until the day after tomorrow.*

Including bits of the question also helps pinpoint the object of your response. This is often necessary when several comments have been made in rapid succession.

> *Joe, book before film is best, but, as Linda reminds us, there are some films that are merely loose adaptations of books.*

9. If the software you use does not indicate when someone is in the midst of typing your students will not know (without a video cam of your actions) when you are thinking or entering a response. Students are often impatient in chat, trying to keep alert and anticipating your answers. So, in a fast-paced chat with a group of students, break up any long responses into two or three parts each ending in a word that indicates the thought is incomplete. This will let students know you're actually formulating a reply, not ignoring what they've said:

> FIRST RESPONSE: Joe, book before film is best, but,
> SECOND RESPONSE: as Linda reminds us, there are some films that are merely loose adaptations of books, while
> THIRD RESPONSE: at the same time it is true that some books are created after the fact, to capitalize on interest in a movie.

This technique can also help you set the pace of the chat. Students automatically slow down, knowing that you're still sending your response. A similar slowdown tactic is to type just the student's name with a comma and send that, and then send the rest of the message in your next segment. As students see "Joe," they will await the remaining phrase, "book before film is best."

10. Have a backup plan in place, in the event that you or some of the students encounter a computer crash, lose the internet connection (in countries where connections are unstable), or experience a dropping out of the audio or delays between responses of the participants (still common, unfortunately). For example, note all participants as they come in, so that you can email everyone in the event of a break. Remind students that they can use the text chat if unable to use their microphones. If you have twenty-four-hour technical support, make sure the phone number is available ahead of the session.

Chat and Other Synchronous Communications: Benefits versus Drawbacks

Let's be honest about the shortcomings of chat and other synchronous communication. Real-time communication is often productive of disjointed or widely digressing conversations, sloppy or impressionistic responses, bad spelling, poor grammar, and flippant attitudes.

The lines of communication are often out of sync. While you're creating your response, the other participants may already have moved on to other questions. An instructor-led chat with more than five people can quickly become difficult to follow. In fact, real-time chat is probably the most exhausting intensive activity an online instructor will ever encounter. Your attention must be attuned to rapid-fire comments and questions from several students; you must respond quickly, and, if your typing on the keyboard (or thumb-typing on your mobile device) isn't the most skillful, you may struggle to keep up with more nimble-fingered students. Worst of all, while your students may allow themselves less than complete sentences and partially formed ideas, they are still likely to take everything you write as official pronouncement.

Given all these shortcomings, why use chat or other synchronous communications at all?

And when is it most appropriate or effective? Here are some answers:

1. One use of chat is to provide reinforcement and immediate feedback for students. When there are no face-to-face meetings in the course, chat can provide a forum for such communication.
2. Virtual office hours and personal consultation can be provided by chat (and instant messaging). Such real-time communication can serve in lieu of an email or phone conversation, or provide clarification for communications by those methods. For example, you may have a student who writes cryptic emails with key information missing. You may be able to clarify his questions via a real-time chat. If a whiteboard feature is available as well, you might be able to assist a student with a problem that requires more hands-on demonstration. You might also want to schedule individual chats with students for the purpose of asking follow-up questions about their work.
3. The social aspect of chat and IM may be one of the most important uses, especially now that video is often included in the features. Students may appreciate the opportunity to use chat and IM among themselves without its being an official class activity. It can help students form bonds with others in the classroom. Casual group chats may add to the sense of cohesion among group members collaborating on a project. Some students miss the spontaneous interaction common to on-campus classes, and chat may provide a suitable outlet for humorous exchanges, social chatter, and team-building conversations.
4. Chat may be used in conjunction with asynchronous group areas for group project meetings and discussions. Typical reasons for holding a chat are brainstorming and finalizing unresolved issues.
5. Chat may be used to bring in a guest speaker. This is best done in conjunction with an assigned paper, lecture, or even asynchronous discussion with the guest. To be most effective, you should carefully prepare students for the guest chat. You should time the chat to coordinate with associated activities and give students an interval to formulate questions they can later pose to the guest during the chat.

●●●●●

Team Teaching Online

Team teaching, whether online or on the ground, presents some unique challenges as well as opportunities. Students can derive the benefit of the multiple perspectives and teaching styles brought by two instructors, while instructors may appreciate the intellectual stimulation of the collaboration as well as the prospect of sharing some of their duties and workload. However, instructors who have experience of team teaching know that being half of a two-member team doesn't necessarily mean doing only half the work. Moreover, the difficulties involved in coordination can be legion.

Important! **Team teaching online requires even more advance planning than its on-the-ground counterpart.**

Even though you and your colleague aren't together in a physical classroom setting, you are very much occupying the same online classroom space, and you can easily trip over each other there as well! Once teaching begins, differences in teaching style and approaches will invariably appear, so it's best to discuss your pedagogical approach as well as practical procedures before the course begins.

Avoid team teaching a course with fewer than fifteen students. Such a small group of students will tend to feel overwhelmed by two instructors seemingly vying for their attention.

There are three basic models you can adopt in team teaching: shared responsibility, division of labor, and primary-secondary. Let's look at each of them in turn.

The Shared Responsibility Model

In the shared responsibility model, both instructors do everything; that is, each of you shares the responsibility for all activities in the class. Online, this means that both of you read and respond to all discussions and assignments. Students will know which instructor is which in the discussion forum, because your name will appear next to your comments.

Assignments can be graded by consensus (very time consuming if you're communicating with each other only online) or by averaging. However, unless you have an online gradebook in which to enter grades, one of you will have to take charge of notifying students of grades and passing along the corresponding comments by email. If you wish, you can sign both names to the grade and add comments.

One risk in this form of team teaching is that students may not know whom to address a particular question. Students may also become confused by the two instructors' different teaching styles and approaches. No matter how much we instructors like to imagine that we have a student-centered classroom and an anti-authoritarian style, students do tend to adjust themselves to the prevailing classroom mode that we set.

This model of team teaching also presents some of the same problems encountered by two parents. You want to be two individuals, offering different opinions, but you don't want to contradict or undermine each other. You must also avoid being played off, one against the other, by students.

A further risk of this model is that neither of the instructors may have the course firmly in focus. Areas of the course can become relatively neglected if no one takes responsibility for them. Finally, this model can be exhausting for instructors because not only are they responsible for teaching the entire class, but they also must spend additional time coordinating with the other member of the team.

Nevertheless, in some situations you may decide that the shared responsibility model is the best approach for you. If so, here are some tips on making this "everything" model work:

1. Ask students to send any emailed queries to both instructors.

2. Each instructor must assiduously read all discussion threads in the class. If one instructor has more comments than the other on a particular topic, that's fine, but the other should make at least a few responses to the same topic.

3. In your syllabus or introductory messages, clearly state the procedures for students to contact you and to submit assignments.

4. For grading and evaluating student work and participation, work out a procedure that you can easily follow. If you're meeting with your co-teacher online, you'll need a way to smoothly exchange any emailed assignments and to maintain record keeping as well.

The Division of Labor Model

The division of labor model involves just what the name suggests: the two instructors divide their responsibilities according to a pre-arranged plan. Like the shared responsibility model, division of labor also requires a great deal of planning and coordination, but it is generally easier to implement.

The division of labor may be arranged by weeks (Joe for Week 1, Mary for Week 2); by topics (which may overlap with weeks); by types of class activities (Mary handles the research project, and Joe supervises all group reports); or by a combination of these factors (Joe takes on the research project and Weeks 2, 4, and 6 of the discussion, while Mary handles all individual presentations and Weeks 1, 3, and 5 of the discussion). You may also want to have some activities handled separately by each of the two instructors, while other activities are a joint effort.

The biggest risk in this model is that one instructor may lose track of the classroom while the other instructor is taking his or her turn. Here are some tips for making the division of labor model most effective and least frustrating:

1. Make sure each instructor contributes something to the overall effort. This contribution should start with the selection of texts and planning of class activities.
2. Decide how you wish to divide up the classroom responsibilities, and state the arrangement in your syllabus so that students know who has the primary responsibility for any particular activity.
3. Make sure that your introductions during the first week of class, or your comments during the first topic of discussion, are carried out jointly with your co-teacher.
4. Ask students to copy (cc) the other instructor on any queries sent to one instructor. This will ensure that each instructor is kept "in the loop."
5. Even if you divide up the discussion responsibilities by week, make sure that the instructor not assigned to that duty in a particular week reads through the discussion. The "off-duty" instructor might want to make a comment as well, and he or she can best do so after the other instructor and the students have had their say.

6. Divide up grading of assignments as evenly as possible but in alternating cycles so that neither instructor loses track of students. In other words, Joe grades assignments 1 and 3, while Mary does 2 and 4. Each instructor should cc the other on any emailed evaluation comments to a student. Each instructor should have copies of all grades and comments. If there is no central gradebook online, the two instructors need to keep identical records. This may mean that after each grading turn is taken, the instructor who did the grading emails a list of grades to the other. If there is a central gradebook, make sure that both instructors consistently make use of it.

The Primary-Secondary Model

In the primary-secondary model, one instructor assumes the primary or dominant role in managing the class. This approach is necessary when one instructor cannot participate in the class to the same extent as the other, yet is still making an active contribution. For example, one instructor may have less internet access or more workload issues than the other, or one instructor may feel less expert in certain areas of course content.

Tips for making the primary-secondary model work include the following:

1. Make sure that each person is fully aware of the responsibilities he or she has agreed to take on. Work this out by going over the week-by-week activities of the course.
2. Try to balance the workload to each person's satisfaction. If one instructor cannot participate online as much as the other, for instance, let him or her take on more of the record-keeping duties or slightly more of the grading of assignments.
3. Clearly indicate to students the respective responsibilities for each instructor, but ask students to cc each instructor on any email correspondence sent to the other.
4. If one instructor does not have as much uninterrupted internet access as the other (this would be particularly true for partners who have no home access or when one partner resides in an area where access is spotty), set up a system so that the partner with good access does the posting. For example, if you need to post a message but lack ready access to the web page or

discussion forum, you can email or IM to send the material to your partner, who can then post it for you. In this case, your name, as the instructor who wrote the actual message, should be typed at the top of the message itself (because the posting will automatically bear the name of the person who puts it online). Students need to be reminded about this practice to avoid confusion about the two instructors' contributions.

12

• • • • •

Classroom Management: Special Issues

In addition to the issues discussed in Chapter 11, several other problems may arise in conjunction with managing your online classroom. Some, such as student behavior problems, aren't unlike those that may occur in an on-the-ground classroom, except that the online environment may introduce further complications. Other issues, such as privacy concerns and the difficulty of confirming student identity, are unique to the online environment.

• • • • •

Privacy Issues

It's hard to argue that anything on the internet is truly private: computers automatically make records, students may share their passwords, and so on. Password access to classrooms and discussion forums brings us some measure of privacy, but short of encryption and identification by eyeball, voice, or fingerprint, it is hard to ensure complete privacy or security. Perhaps, however, we can speak of "more or less private."

In previous chapters, we have mentioned the new privacy issues raised by the use of Web 2.0 and social media for communications taking place on sites and servers external to your institution. It is worth reading the "terms of use" for each such site and giving your students fair warning or the option to use an alias on public sites if you are not able to or do not choose to create a private group area.

Beyond the security measures afforded by our software and hardware, there are other things we can do to protect privacy.

For example, we must be careful about distributing student work, discussion transcripts, and email outside the classroom without permission. It's surprising how many otherwise discreet and caring instructors will think nothing of posting student materials, complete with names, on an open website for the entire world to access without permission or even notification.

> **Important!** *What is said in the classroom is origin-ally said in a defined context. Those later reading these words outside the classroom may not understand that context.*

Similar privacy concerns affect your own contributions. You can expect that students will copy and download your words for the purpose of learning. Do give some thought to what you wish to disclose about your private life and opinions in the classroom dis-cussion. If you're concerned about students distributing your material, then make sure you state upfront that words and mater-ials are for class use only, not for distribution. With social media networking sites like Facebook, Twitter, and Instagram, many instructors would do well to separate their private profiles and accounts from an academic one. And it doesn't hurt to remind students who are networking with their classmates about the many privacy options available in Facebook that can help them control what information they want to release to classmates as well as the instructor.

We recommend that instructors teaching completely online classes never give out their personal phone numbers to students unless absolutely forced to by the program. If your institution requires some phone "office" hours each week, use either your campus phone or your work phone or consider a Google voice account, selecting a new number so that it serves as a proxy for your real phone number, but setting it to ring the phone you use. This will shield your real number from the caller and preserve your privacy.

It is also sometimes possible to work out an arrangement by which students who want to contact you by phone call your department, which relays the request to you via phone or email. You can then return the student's call. The prevalence of Skype as a communication medium provides another option—you may create a Skype account just for the purpose of communicating with your students.

Most issues can be resolved in the online classroom or by private email. This has the advantage of giving you a record of the communication with the student. It also means that the student has to think a bit about his or her question and perhaps has a greater opportunity to reflect on your answer as well.

● ● ● ● ●

Identity Issues

How do you know the real identity of the person you encounter online? The truth is, sometimes you don't. If students are registered with the university, we can assume with some degree of certainty that they are indeed the people they say they are. Presumably, they had to show an ID at some point. Yet in the continuing-education classroom—and especially for students who live far away from campus—this authentication may not occur. Generally, institutions are more concerned about identity confirmation when a student is enrolled in a state certification or degree program. In those cases, students may be required to take at least one live, proctored exam or to prove their identity when applying for and exiting the program.

In terms of our daily interactions with students online, we cannot always detect gender, ethnicity, age, and other characteristics that are often more easily detectable in a live classroom. This type of identity might be thought of as social identity as opposed to the authentication of those enrolled. Some institutions may give you a roster with no more than name and ID number and address, while at others you will have access to computer databases holding extensive information, but most instructors are unlikely to have ready access to more than the most limited details about students.

Although there may be clues—for example, a name that sounds Italian or references to foods and customs belonging to a particular culture—these are all merely guesses unless the student confirms our conjectures. Approximate age is sometimes easier to detect but also prone to error. Are those references to television shows of the 1950s or music of the 1960s the product of firsthand experience or a love of retro fashions?

We are particularly prone to mistakes about female students, because their surnames are often not those they grew up with, but instead represent new identities taken on through marriage.

Immigrants may also take on new names that they think are appropriate to their new country. Students with names such as Pat, Dale, Sasha, Kim, and Ming may be male or female. Or your student's name may be in a language so unfamiliar to you that you have no way of knowing whether the syllables signify a particular gender. Finally, these days there is more recognition of gender fluidity—there may be students who are transitioning to a different gender or who are not fixed in one gender at all.

You may ask for voluntary submission of photos, but even photos, short of the student's official ID photo, can be less than revealing of the truth. Is that your student in a photo taken ten years ago, or is that your student's handsome friend?

There's no point in trying to stop ourselves from imagining our students (and them from imagining us); our minds can't help trying to categorize. But be alert to the possibility that you may be dead wrong about the identity of your students. Avoid making statements and assumptions that aren't based on information actually provided by the student. The best policy is to allow students to self-identify. Unless you think fraud may be involved (for example, one person masquerading as another to take a test or complete an assignment), we would advise you not to worry too much about such identity issues. Just keep an open mind and watch for clues.

The use of virtual worlds and the creation of avatar identities can present unique identity problems. Instructors in courses in which students are using avatars for course activities will want to immediately create and publish a "cast of characters" so that all participating students know who's who in the virtual world. Some instructors request that students incorporate their real first names when choosing a first name for the avatar to aid in this process of class identification.

In Chapter 3 we discussed student behavior issues related to cheating, plagiarism, and other departures from academic integrity and how to guard against these through our assignment design, clearly posted expectations for students, and use of anti-plagiarism software. But when cheating involves identity issues such as suspicions that there is someone other than the enrolled student completing the assignment or taking the exam or even taking the whole course, this is a situation that you as instructor should not try to handle on your own. Notify your department head of your concerns—most institutions have a student code and disciplinary procedures in place that cover such matters as "fake IDs" and related types of cheating, whether in online or on-campus classes, and staff who are prepared to review and manage these sensitive issues.

● ● ● ● ●
Managing Student Behavior Online

When it comes to the topic of handling "difficult students," we think that most problems can be averted by the skillful management of student expectations such as we have outlined in earlier chapters—the comprehensive syllabus, clearly written assignment instructions, protocols for communications, codes of conduct, and clearly stated policies and criteria for grading, as well as instructor responsiveness, are all ways to ensure that students understand how to do their best in your online course. Some students are being "difficult" because they are having problems handling the conventions and habits of learning online (or the complexities combining online and face-to-face classes). Such students can benefit from a quick explanation, some patience, and possible referrals to appropriate resources. A phone call or Skype or communication through another real-time meeting medium may do much to help clear up problems and establish rapport.

But there is another important point to keep in mind: sometimes the "difficulty" actually resides with the instructor, not the student! So, before jumping to the conclusion that you have a "difficult" or intractable student, do a quick self-review to make sure that you have not been ambiguous or lacking in clarity about your expectations and instructions for students.

In the online asynchronous discussion forum, the blog, the wiki, or chat room, the range of student types remains pretty much the same as in the on-the-ground classroom. There are the quiet ones, the nurturers, the take-charge types, the class clowns, the disruptive ones, and the imaginative procrastinators. There are a few aspects of the online environment, however, that create new opportunities for the "usual suspects" to manifest their trademark styles.

Noisy Students

A noisy student in an online classroom, much like his or her traditional counterpart, spends much energy raising issues that are only tangentially related to the topics under discussion. One way this occurs in online discussion is that the student will begin new topic threads even when the comments he or she has to contribute actually fit in with pre-existing threads. Such students often avoid replying to anything but the instructor's comments. And when they do join in the discussion, they generally ignore the direction of the conversation and simply pepper the thread with inane comments.

This type of student is actually easier to handle online, in asynchronous discussion, than in the regular classroom. There is more space and time in an online classroom for such students to perform without seriously affecting others. When they start a new thread on what is already an ongoing topic, most other students will simply ignore this detour in favor of continuing the more active and peopled conversation. In the interest of housekeeping and to prevent the area from over-blooming with threads, you may want to drop this individual an email note. Ask him or her to please reply to an existing thread if the aim is to participate in a conversation rather than to break out a true new topic. Or, treat the problem as a technical one. Remind the student of the difference between replying to a subject and starting a new one. Many students are actually confused by the differences in discussion software response methods.

When the student peppers the existing conversation with inane comments, this isn't really as disruptive an influence as it would be in an on-the-ground setting. Classmates will read this student's inane comments but simply not respond to them and move on to the next message in the thread. Other than the moment required to read the inane comment, nothing is really lost. The noisy student hasn't forestalled the comments of others because the clock isn't ticking away in the asynchronous classroom, and no "air time" has been consumed.

As more video commenting options have become available, a particular type of noisy student has emerged—one who uses video the way others may use text messages—constantly bombarding everyone with inconsequential video clips. Like the student who continually posts inane comments, the video version of noise is usually equally subject to being ignored by classmates.

A good way to deal with the noisy student is to give him or her some personal attention in the form of a personal email. Sometimes a noisy student is just feeling a bit lost and anonymous, and wants some individual attention. Suggest that the student share some of his or her ideas with others in a lounge forum. In the public discussion area, acknowledge the student, but then steer him or her back on track: "What you say about X is interesting, Joe, but how would you respond to Ian's comment about Y?" or "This is an interesting point. We may be able to take this up later, in Week 5."

In the synchronous chat room, a noisy student can take up precious "real time," so setting rules and procedures for chat will make a major difference. Some forms of chat software will actually allow you to eject a student who isn't following the rules. While that is an extreme measure, it may be necessary if the noisy student crosses the line to become disruptive. Other software permits you to call on students, supplying the equivalent of the raised hand. However, even if you don't have such software, simply requiring students to type an asterisk, exclamation mark, or question mark to be recognized before speaking will have the same regulating effect. The noisy student will have to wait his or her turn along with everyone else.

There are ways to deal effectively with the noisy student. Be gentle and remember that the noisy student may prove to be your salvation when the classroom discussion hits the doldrums and you desperately need someone to respond to your prodding!

Quiet Students

Quiet students can present even more of a problem online than in the traditional classroom situation, because you can't see them nodding their heads in assent or shaking their heads in disagreement. If the quiet student doesn't post anything, whether by text or audio comment, you can't readily tell if he or she is even in the room, occupying a virtual seat.

Two strategies can come into play here:

1. If tracking is available through your software, you can follow the quiet students to see if they are present, how often, and what they are reading.
2. By requiring a minimum level of participation by posting, you can probably coax a few contributions out of them.

You can also use private email to gently urge quiet students back into the classroom discussion space. Send a message saying that you've noticed that the student has been accessing the classroom but not actually posting and that you wonder if he or she is having any technical problems. Or say that you wonder how the course is going for the student—does he or she have any special questions about procedures? Offer to talk with the student by phone or Skype (or in person, for those in blended courses) to discuss matters.

Often you can find a way to bring the student into the classroom discussion by virtue of his or her special talents or background—information you've gleaned from the biographical introduction. Sharon Packer, a psychiatrist who, for many years, taught online courses in psychology and religion for the New School, suggests that asking questions in the introduction phase, such as "What do you want to get out of this class?" (rather than the usual "Why are you taking this class?"), often elicits information that the instructor can later use to motivate students to participate. For example, in a comparative religion class, if Joe has mentioned that he lived half his life in Japan, you might address a question to him directly during the discussion of popular religious practices: "Joe, is there anything you can recall from your experience in Japan that relates to this type of folk practice?"

Some students may actually be "learning while lurking," but if participation constitutes a major portion of the grade, they must be reminded that a lack of active participation will have consequences. Look to their written assignments to gauge whether learning is indeed occurring. Also, once the student has completed an individual assignment, see if there is something worthy of note in it that you might ask him or her to share with the class. If the quiet student happens to send you an email or reply to an inquiry of yours, grasp that opportunity to say that his or her presence is missed in the classroom. Emphasize that a good question is as valuable for discussion purposes as a brilliant comment, and that he or she should feel free to contribute in a casual tone to the conversation. Some quiet students are really just overly self-conscious about writing and posting their thoughts, imagining that anything seemingly "published" to the world in this manner ought to be perfectly expressed and articulated.

In audio- and video-assisted communication modes, quiet students may shy away from using voice and appearing on a web cam—if the class is not one that requires audio (for example, a language or speech class), consider allowing such students to choose the text option that is usually available.

Disruptive Students

The disruptive student will attempt to take over your class by commandeering the discussion and questioning the major thrust of your course or some essential aspect of it in the public forum. He or she may answer questions addressed to you, contradict you, and in some cases become abusive. This is one of the worst situations an instructor has to face online. Few students will stage such behavior face to face, but more feel emboldened to do so online. The situation is considerably worsened by the fact that the comments will sit there for days, to be read by all. Increasingly, we have seen students using video for these purposes, with the video format bringing out the worst impulses in bombastic and self-absorbed personalities.

At the extreme, when a student uses foul language or is abusive or threatening, you should immediately notify your administrator. Copy and save all posted or emailed communications with that individual. Although you may be moved to delete (or ask your administrator to delete) outright four-letter words and the like, knowing how to handle comments that don't sink to that level may be more difficult.

Some instructors post their own classroom codes of conduct at the beginning of the class to help set boundaries for students. Sharon Packer, whose online classes concerned the psychology of religion, history of psychiatry, and approaches to dreams, was particularly sensitive to discussions that might elicit personal or controversial topics. She recommends that instructors keep objective criteria in mind when formulating a code of conduct. These criteria often must be keyed directly to the type of course being taught. For example, in her courses she often included such guidelines as "There will be no discussion of personal use of illegal drugs" and "This isn't the place to discuss personal psychiatric history." She also urged that students maintain a cordial atmosphere and use tact in expressing differences of opinion.

Many instructors provide a link to, or an excerpt from, the text of their institution's honor code and emphasize that the code applies in the online classroom as well. Often, such codes are not specifically related to online education situations and may not be sufficient to provide all necessary guidance for your students. Nonetheless, in terms of issues such as plagiarism, cheating, and so forth, these may provide useful material. Other institutions have been more forthright in addressing these issues as they pertain to online. Sometimes these are called a code of conduct for online students or referred to as "netiquette." For example, Kansas State University has published guidelines concerning student behavior online (see www.k-state.edu/provost/ policies/student-conduct.htm) to augment its regular student conduct rules, drawing a distinction between dealing with non-threatening disruptions as well as those of a threatening nature.

University of Central Florida combines general netiquette, some samples of online protocols and references to applicable student code on their Rules of Student Conduct & Online Expectations at https://online.ucf.edu/learn-online/online-course-protocols/, reminding students that instructors will generally post the specific protocols or guidelines for their classes in their syllabi or start-up materials.

Your institution's code of conduct for online may simply be included as a section in the general student handbook. Whether the institutional policies exist as a separate document or not, it is a good idea to familiarize yourself with all institutional or departmental codes that address student behavior in online instruction and online communications.

Dealing with Disruptive Students

In dealing with disruptive students in particular, it's important to achieve a balance between asserting your authority in the classroom and overreacting to a student provocation. However, you must act quickly to prevent disruptive students from escalating tensions in the classroom, and you must take the lead in informing your department if students cross the line.

Following are some examples of different types of disruptive behavior and instructor responses, based on real situations we've observed or heard described. Please note that these are composite examples, not actual case histories.

Example 1: The Know-It-All Midway through a course, one of the students, Janet, who had some real-world experience in the subject, began to answer questions that were addressed to the instructor in the asynchronous forum. At first this seemed fine, because Janet was contributing some good tips to the student questioners. The instructor simply acknowledged Janet's comments and then added her own remarks.

At some point, however, Janet began contradicting the instructor's information. Janet even offered her own website information and suggested that students use it as their guide. The instructor checked her facts. She wasn't wrong, so she simply reaffirmed the information to the other students (and, by implication, to Janet as well) without responding directly to Janet's contradictory message. Her message was polite and generous, beginning with:

> *Although there may be some disagreement by scholars in the field on the details, the general principle I enunciated remains sound and is the one I would like you to use in this course.*

Janet wasn't directly mentioned, and she was able to save face; yet the instructor reasserted the primacy of her authority and refocused students on the objectives of the course.

Example 2: The Mutineer   Professor X's approach to the subject matter wasn't interesting to one of her students, Jerry. Jerry was a bright student and knew quite a bit about the subject. Therefore, he had already formed his own ideas about the way to approach it.

Jerry began to sound somewhat critical and condescending toward the instructor in the class discussions. But his first direct attack came in response to the instructor's comments on Jerry's public presentation. The instructor's comments were dry and very brief. Jerry commented in the classroom forum to the effect that the instructor had "not given me any constructive comments at all." Note that, at this point, the instructor had not responded in turn.

A few days later, in a private email to the instructor, Jerry blasted the instructor's teaching methods and complained about the poor quality of the class. The instructor got angry, but instead of answering Jerry's more abusive private email, she posted a public reply to his less strident public note:

> *I believe I have given you constructive comments, and I don't appreciate your tone here or the way you expressed yourself in your recent email.*

This set Jerry off, and he began to post angry messages in the classroom, trying to enlist students to his way of thinking:

> *I'm sure a lot of you feel the same way I do—this course is a gigantic waste of my time and money. I think we should ask the department for our money back.*

A few students actually posted affirmative replies, such as these:

> *I agree—am not satisfied with Professor X's responses.*

> *I feel that I was misled by the way this course was advertised.*

Professor X was well on her way to losing control of this classroom. Jerry's original public posting about not getting constructive comments was sharp and somewhat rude but hadn't yet overstepped the bounds of decency. In responding publicly, the instructor would have been better advised to hold her criticism in check, merely noting the sharpness of Jerry's public message by implication.

> *Jerry, I have been rather brief due to the constraints of time, and perhaps you did not get the full import of my comments.*
> *Any time students feel they need more feedback, I hope they will let me know via private email. I will send you a private email within a day or so that I hope will provide you with the additional details you have requested.*

This response by Professor X would have had the effect of noting Jerry's complaint while ignoring the hostility behind it and addressing what she as a teacher could do to respond to the student's needs. She would also have succeeded in moving the conversation to the private sphere.

As for Jerry's private email, she should have responded to it privately and firmly.

> *Jerry, I'm glad that you have expressed these thoughts with me via private email. I'm sorry that you don't find my approach one that is helpful to your study of the subject. Because it is too late to withdraw from the class, I suggest that you do the best you can with the material and activities. You have many good*

ideas, and I welcome your airing of alternative approaches in the classroom, as long as this is done in an objective manner and in the appropriate forums.

The subtext here is this:

I did not appreciate the personal comment you made in the classroom; you should have withdrawn from the course when you could, but I will not penalize you for your opinions even though I do expect you to follow my syllabus. I appreciate that you are bright, and I will give you some opportunity to display your knowledge, but don't make any more personal comments in the classroom.

Note that even if an instructor doesn't normally express herself in a formal manner in the classroom, this is a situation that calls for a certain degree of formality. Formality in online forums signifies seriousness, clarity, and firmness to students. It is particularly effective when it contrasts with an otherwise casual instructor tone.

Example 3: The Belligerent Student Who Hasn't Kept Up   Andy barely participated during the first part of Professor B's course, but he seemed suddenly to reappear, apparently angry that he was finding it hard to catch up with the class. He posted angry messages in the public classroom that reflected his very real frustration arising from his lack of understanding of what was going on in the class.

What's this supposed to be about? I don't get it. What's the point of this assignment?

In a case like this, Professor B should ignore the emotion in Andy's comments in the classroom forum. The professor should post objective, concrete suggestions in reply:

This concerns Lesson 5. You might find pages 10–25 the most useful.
*   Andy, as I mentioned in my previous lecture, this assignment asks you to focus your attention on Problem 2. See the guidelines for Assignment #1 in the syllabus. All students: If you have any specific questions on this assignment, please feel free to post your questions here.*

Professor B needs to back this up by emailing this student and being supportive, while still calling him to account.

> *Andy, I have noted your expressions of frustration in the classroom and have responded. Since you were somewhat late getting started in the class, you may need to go back and review Lessons 1 and 2 and the guidelines. If you need further help, just email me and I will try to assist you.*

The subtext of this is:

> *I can see that you're frustrated, and that may be due to the fact that you didn't keep up with the work. I think you can do it—go back and try again. Read the relevant material, read the guidelines. You aren't the only one who may have questions. If you really don't understand after making a decent effort, I'm here to help.*

Example 4: The Belligerent Student on the Attack   Professor Y teaches an online course in contemporary American politics, in which students are encouraged to explore their assumptions about American political parties and hot topics of the day. Professor Y does have a code for students to follow in expressing their opinions; however, she likes to keep the classroom as open and free as possible.

During a particularly heated argument about school vouchers, Tom attacks another student, Linda, saying, "You're a right-wing bigot!" Professor Y cannot track the readership of individual messages, but she assumes that many students have read this one, because it has been posted for two days and the record shows that many students have logged on during that time.

She carefully copies and saves a record of the online exchange. She then posts a response, without naming Tom:

> *I would like to remind everyone to base your arguments on the issues. Please observe the code of conduct posted for this class, which asks students to refrain from personal attacks and labeling of other students.*

At the same time, she writes a private email to Tom:

Tom, perhaps this was not your intent, but your remark to Linda seemed inappropriate and insulting. I hope you will apologize by private email to her and then delete your comment.

But then Tom attacks Professor Y in the classroom forum:

Who are you, the pope?! We should be able to say whatever we want to say.

At this point, Professor Y telephones an urgent request that her department head deal with this student and, if necessary, officially remove him from the class. She follows up with an email that makes the same request but also includes a copy of all the online and email communications. She sends a brief private email to Tom, letting him know that she has referred his case to the department and warning him to refrain from any more personal comments; she forwards this to the department as well. She continues to monitor the situation and all classroom communications carefully until the matter is resolved.

There are a few particular things to note about this situation:

- Professor Y felt that she had to post a public response, but she wanted to avoid targeting Tom in public, so she posted a general reminder to all in the class about the code of behavior expected. She emailed Tom privately to give him an opportunity to make things right. If Professor Y had simply responded to Tom in the classroom forum with an equally personal remark, the situation would have rapidly degenerated.
- Even though Professor Y had the ability within the software functions to delete Tom's note, she felt that it was better to ask Tom to delete it himself and apologize to his classmates. Had Tom's note been even more blatantly derogatory, or had he used profanity, Professor Y may have chosen to delete the note immediately upon discovering it, after carefully copying and preserving a record. She then should have followed up this deletion by notifying the department and Tom that she had felt compelled to take this action.
- When Tom escalated the situation by posting a direct attack on her, Professor Y decided to let the department handle the

matter. As a last resort, she was prepared to delete any more comments by Tom.

■ Professor Y needed to back up her story and protect herself by forwarding a copy of the communications to the department. Otherwise, the department head might not have reacted quickly enough.

At this time, more and more institutions have guidelines in place for student conduct online, but where online education is new, guidelines may be lacking and there may be few administrators who have firsthand familiarity with online classroom management. Although you should keep your department or other relevant institutional authorities in the loop whenever special issues arise—and protect yourself by keeping scrupulous records—you may find that you, as an online instructor, are often out there on your own. You must be proactive and quick-witted when dicey situations arise.

Other Behavior Problems

In addition to students who are unusually noisy, quiet, or disruptive, there are other behavior problems that may create problems in the online classroom. We'll comment on a few of them here.

The Controller   Sharon Packer notes that a student who emails you before the class begins, to request all assignments in advance, may not be the conscientious eager beaver you assume, but one who actually wants to control the class. By getting a head start on everyone else, this student can be the first to post responses to the discussion questions. Perhaps this student will post in such extensive detail that the entire discussion is squashed. Or perhaps this student wants to seem in control of the material because he or she actually lacks sufficient background for the class.

Naturally, there are students who request assignments in advance for valid reasons. Maybe they will be traveling during the first week of class, or they may have a disability that could slow their assimilation of the reading material. Some students just want to see the reading list to find out what they're getting into before committing to the class. These valid concerns can be discovered by simply asking the student his or her reasons for requesting all assignments in advance.

The Staller   Packer also suggests that students who delay logging on to the class (barring actual technical problems) may be unmotivated or stalling. These students may not want to become part of the group process and may fail to create bonds with others in the class. Some students of this sort simply like to work alone, and they may eventually access the class, absorb the material, and do all the necessary work; many more, however, are likely never to finish the course.

Another possibility is that such students are deeply insecure about their abilities or intimidated by the unfamiliar online environment, even when they've gone through an orientation. The strangeness of the online environment can make those who are normally competent and professional in their chosen fields fearful that they will look foolish or somehow lose control. An email reminder to such students, to encourage their participation, can sometimes be the personal touch needed to bring them into the classroom. Technical problems are a wonderful face-saver: even if they aren't the real issue, asking a student whether he or she has delayed logging on because of technical problems may elicit the actual reasons or at least cause the student to realize that he or she shouldn't delay any longer.

If you can use your tracking features and observation to keep track of student progress in the classroom, you may be able to intervene to encourage students who delay or stall. It's also important to keep a record of student "attendance"—how often and when the student was in the classroom—because being able to document a student's participation may be necessary in the event that a student challenges you about a grade. If attendance reports aren't available from your software, you should keep a manual record. Unfortunately, a small percentage of students imagine that they can more easily get away with a lack of participation in an online course than in a traditional classroom.

The "Must-Have-an-A" Student   Although the student who tells you early in the course that she or he "has to get an A in this course" is a familiar phenomenon, these students may be particularly drawn to distance learning and online courses. Some find it easier to assume a pose of invincibility and grandeur when they know they won't meet you in person; this type of adult student may even claim honors and credentials he or she doesn't really possess. Some students may simply find it easier to harass you about their grades by email than they would by coming to your office.

In any case, those words, "have to get an A in this course," should definitely raise your antennae. Meet such declarations with firm, objective statements about your grading criteria and standards, combined with a mild rebuff:

> *Thank you for your note. It is good to see that students are motivated, but there can be no guarantees that any particular student will receive an A in this class. This online course is a challenging one, no less rigorous than its on-campus version. See my grading criteria listed below. Students will receive further instructions about the requirements for assignments as the course proceeds. To do your best in my class, follow the guidelines and schedule in the syllabus and pay attention to the rubrics for all assignments.*

Keep every scrap of correspondence with this student and be cautious in your email to him or her. Be aware that this student will likely keep a record of everything you say.

A Special Word about Social Media

Social media and other third-party sites that are used as part of your course instruction should be governed by the same rules of conduct you apply to the rest of your instructional environment. However, when students make you aware of others using social media outside the class but in connection with your course and the conduct seems questionable—violating academic integrity, publishing private information about other students, or even issues like bullying or threats concerning you or other students, you may want to bring this to the attention of your department head. Many institutions now have policies governing student and instructor use of social media, so it is worthwhile to know any rules governing this, to the extent they may exist for your campus.

In other cases, students may simply be using social media to grouse in the same way they used to gossip and complain in hallways outside the lecture hall. It may be interesting or perhaps annoying to know about it, but if it falls within the realm of free expression, it probably doesn't require any action on your part.

● ● ● ● ●

A Final Word

The foregoing examples are offered to help you recognize and deal with potential problems. Naturally, each student presents a unique profile and must be responded to as an individual. Avoid jumping to conclusions, and don't hesitate to rely on those gut feelings derived from long experience in the traditional classroom to help you sort out one situation from another. Sometimes a phone call or Skype conversation will allow you to better evaluate the student through the aid of voice and tone (and perhaps the web cam video as well), but keep in mind the need to keep a record of such communications and follow up with an email that summarizes the conversation.

When in doubt, err on the side of softening your language in emails and postings. A "might" or "perhaps" in your advisory or disciplinary message can often provide the face-saving gesture needed to defuse a tense situation. Finally, don't allow yourself to become overly reactive or distracted by difficult students. Remember that there are other students who also deserve your attention, and don't get too caught up in one student's drama.

13
• • • • •

Teaching Web-Enhanced and Blended Classes

Although we've discussed issues as they pertain to "blended" classes throughout the book—classes that combine online and face-to-face activities—this chapter focuses specifically on them as well as those in which online elements play a merely supplemental role to the face-to-face class. You may find that material that was discussed in the context of the chapters in which it occurred is here summarized or treated in greater depth.

Today, the use of the internet by instructors is broad and varied. Some universities maintain their own "channels" on YouTube and their faculty use it to host video course introductions or to stream video versions of some of their on-campus lectures to the internet, while other instructors schedule just a few online discussions throughout the semester and post their lecture notes, while still others teach classes that regularly meet online one week and on campus the next. How can you best integrate the online and face-to-face elements of a class? What factors should you think about? Are there any pitfalls to avoid? To answer such questions, we'll try to offer helpful tips for blended classes as well as for integrating online tools for a primarily face-to-face class.

Let's look for a moment at those instructors who make minimal use of online. Perhaps they teach a traditional on-campus course but maintain some sort of online presence for the course. Typically, such websites, blogs, or site in their institution's LMS contain a course syllabus, a schedule of required readings and assignments, a listing of the course office hours, and some hyperlinks to relevant websites in the instructor's particular subject area. They may also include a link to a discussion board which may be entirely an optional area, with students deciding whether to use or not use the site. In these cases in which students seldom look at the website, the situation suggests that the instructor isn't using online resources and tools to maximum advantage. If asked to provide a reason why their online sites are so lightly utilized, instructors might cite their students' lack of reliable access to the internet from off campus (a typical complaint for developing countries), or even a lack of interest on the part of students who are having their instructional and social needs met on campus. Instructors may also say that because of their own workloads, they don't want to spend more time creating material to post online or moderating instructional activities or communications there. They may even express the fear that if they use online resources more extensively, their students will no longer have a reason to come to class. In other words, instructors are asking why they should work more for the same pay, doing something that perhaps threatens their livelihood. The ultimate answers to this question are beyond the purview of this book. Academic senates and other faculty organizations, institutional administrators, and union representatives must work them out. But we don't believe that using the internet and online tools effectively requires you to labor twice as long for the same pay. We do think that it can improve the way you teach your traditional course. To that end, this chapter will also provide some practical suggestions for this skeptical audience.

As previously noted in this book, the Online Learning Consortium (formerly Sloan Consortium) definitions of Web Facilitated (what we call "enhanced" here), Blended/Hybrid, and Online are based on the amount of content delivered online. They term "Web Facilitated" as those courses with 1–29 percent of content delivered online; "Blended" courses as those in which 30–79 percent of the content is delivered online but still require some face-to-face meetings; and true "Online" as containing 80 percent or more online content with few or no face-to-face meetings. But another way to approach this is to look at the types of instructional activities carried out online and whether or not they are required or the degree to which they replace face-to-face time. (Still persistently termed "seat time" by many.) For the purposes of this chapter, we will use the following definitions:

■ *Web-enhanced.* A broad category of courses with associated websites, mobile apps or online tools, or learning management system class sites that contain materials relevant to the course (perhaps a syllabus, a list of web-based resources, a course calendar, a reading list, lecture notes or video lectures, discussion board, and/or real-time online meeting functions and chat). Actual online activities may be required or optional.

■ *Blended.* Courses in which both online and face-to-face instructional elements are required and complementary. A sizeable percentage of content is delivered online, there are required online student activities, and a significant portion of the student's grade is based on online activity.

● ● ● ● ●

Tips for Teaching Web-Enhanced Courses

While we want to focus first on those teaching web-enhanced courses, readers who are mainly interested in true blended courses may find that many of the following tips are also relevant to their needs.

Posting Lectures Online

The matter of online lectures is probably the biggest bugaboo teachers face when considering whether to use the internet. Why should students bother to come to class if they can simply read (or view video versions of) the lectures online?

Most lectures consist of a body of core material, factual or introductory in nature, followed by a discussion of more complex issues, proofs, or processes. The core material constitutes the main dish of the lecture. It's usually this material that students are expected to know. The other material serves as side dishes, which help differentiate the A students from the B and C students. If the core material were posted online, enriched by graphics and charts (perhaps with a few links to other relevant material available online), students would be relieved of the chore of reproducing this material word for word in their notes. That would allow them to concentrate on the finer points of the lecture. In other words, posting the lectures online frees the students to concentrate on what is being said.

Yet that argument still raises the question: Why should most students bother to come to class?

The answer may have something to do with preferred learning styles. Some students learn better or are more readily engaged by listening and taking notes. Others do better by reading rather than by listening to lectures, and a third group seems to benefit by doing specific assignments based on the material covered. In that sense, posting lecture notes online helps some, but not all, students.

But the answer goes deeper still. It involves the basic approach to lecturing. Perhaps you need to rethink how you use your face-to-face time with students.

A Revised Approach to Lecturing

Admittedly, an instructor who posts lecture notes and reads them aloud in class may be in danger of putting students to sleep. But if the lecturer alters what he or she does in class, relying on the fact that the material is freely available online, then the experience of attending class may have a different meaning. This approach is often referred to as "**flipping**" the class and it is a model that may be implemented as part of a web-enhanced or a blended course. This means to free up class time by moving more of the instructor's lecturing and presentation online, and to replace that face-to-face class time with student activities, peer-to-peer interaction, and individualized attention from the instructor.

Say that the assignment for the week is to read the core notes posted online, along with whatever textual material supports it. In that case, instead of spending the first twenty minutes or so reviewing the core or introductory material, the instructor can concentrate on a particularly knotty issue or complex concept, examining it, elucidating it, debating it in class. Those students who have read the material beforehand will gain a deeper insight into the concept. (Of course, those who have not read the material will have considerable difficulty following what's going on. One hopes they will get the message and come to the next session better prepared.)

Online lectures offer other advantages as well. For the instructor, posting lectures can be an aid in reevaluating older and possibly out-of-date course materials, improving organization, coherence, and comprehension. For the students, having the core portion of the lecture online provides an opportunity to review the material in its original form (rather than using their scribbled notes) or to catch up on material they may have missed because of illness or absence. Putting the lectures and lessons online also means that students can more easily work through the material at their own pace, then come to class prepared to delve into the issues at greater depth or to translate their newly gained information into hands-on activities.

Important! **The point here is that posting your lectures online is neither a panacea nor a threat. It depends entirely on how effectively the online material is integrated into the class and what you do with the freed up face-to-face time.**

How to Post Your Content Online

Posting your lecture notes or other content online does add to your initial workload, particularly if you've never prepared your course this way before. But once you've done it, you'll find it comparatively easy to update your notes the next time you teach the course. There are more and more choices available to accomplish this, which were discussed in Chapters 6 and 9 in some detail. You may post your lectures by uploading PowerPoint, by creating a PDF version of your word-processed documents, by writing directly into your learning management system content area, or use one of the free sites mentioned in earlier chapters to create course web pages or a weekly blog posting. You may also use one of the many Web 2.0 programs already mentioned in this book to create narrated slides or an audio or video lecture. You may want to experiment with these diverse ways of offering lectures before deciding on one that is easiest for you to create and for your students to access. If your institution provides for lecture capture, you may opt to post the video of your lectures originally delivered in the classroom. However, the latter is probably the least motivating in terms of persuading students to come to the live lecture although it may serve to help students review the material.

Give your students a reason to come to the face-to-face class—either use the face-to-face time to do more than lecture or use the face-to-face lecture time to provide more depth or focus to your lecture, and leave the background information or broad overview, additional examples, resources, etc. to be accessed via the online class site. Then tell your students what the plan is—what to do online before coming to class, and what to do afterwards.

Using a Discussion Board

Most classes, particularly smaller, seminar-style classes, involve discussions of some sort. Ordinarily, students prepare for the discussions through readings. In some graduate classes, students prepare "position" papers, which are then circulated to other students for their consideration before coming to class. Using the internet in conjunction with the work done in class can enhance any of these techniques. Take the case of the seminar. In order to present the topic properly, the instructor will generally introduce it with either a short lecture or an impromptu talk. The students will then offer initial reactions to the discussion topic, setting the stage for the eventual discussion. A half-hour or so may have elapsed before the discussion is really joined.

An alternative approach is to have the students post their initial reactions to a discussion topic online and read the postings on each topic before coming to class. Although this would require more work from the students, it would not increase the instructor's workload except insofar as he or she had to read the work posted to the website. What it would require of the students is perhaps a more carefully considered appreciation of the discussion topic and a greater awareness of where they stand in relation to other students in the seminar. Presumably this would make for a livelier and more informed discussion, and it would elicit remarks from all the members of the class rather than merely the most vocal.

A discussion board can be of use in large, lecture-style classes as well. For most students, "attending" such a class means finding a seat somewhere in an auditorium, staring at the back of someone's head, and listening to the instructor intone the lecture from a stage. Discussion in such a setting is usually fairly haphazard. The instructor pauses to solicit input from the assembled students. The more intrepid dare to raise their hands, while the rest sit quietly.

The internet can humanize such a class and permit students far more interaction with their colleagues and instructors than might otherwise be possible. An instructor can divide up the class into groups of twenty or so, depending on the number of TAs or assistants available. The instructor with a large class and no assistance might even devise a system of rotating student moderators who take turns facilitating their groups. Students using the discussion board will thus have a work group composed of class members whom they might not ordinarily get to know, a considerable advantage in schools where a majority of students don't live on campus, or in large universities where most students know only their dorm-mates.

Instructors and students can use these virtual study groups for a number of purposes. Students can post and discuss questions related to the material covered in class. Or, having delivered a lecture in class, an instructor might post a follow-up question, requiring the students to formulate an appropriate response as part of their grade. These responses might then become the basis of a future class discussion or lecture. They might also serve as an archived resource for students reviewing the material.

An instructor can monitor the comments posted in the discussion groups and use them as the basis of a frequently asked questions (FAQ) page containing general answers to the students' more noteworthy queries and concerns. This will save the instructor the extra time of having to respond to the same question over and over again, either by email or in one-to-one advising sessions. Finally, if the instructor creates some relevant and focused initial discussion prompts, the discussion group postings can provide the instructor with valuable insight into how effectively the material in lectures has been conveyed.

Enlisting Technology in Your Favor

Much has been made of the ubiquity of laptops, tablets, and smartphones (some of which are as large as tablets) and the distraction these pose to students in the on-campus classroom, taking attention away from the lecture or other activity that the instructor has so carefully prepared. Rather than fight it, try to enlist technology in your favor. This goes beyond the "clicker" personal response systems many universities have introduced on campuses whereby instructors can poll students or ask them to contribute questions. Why not make something on the internet the object of your attention (for example, a photograph representing a current event, or a video) and ask students to log in and take five minutes to post their quick responses in a chat. Then display the chat and its results and discuss the issues. (For those students who may not bring an electronic device to class, you might provide the option of logging on after class to an asynchronous forum you have established to add their responses to those of their classmates.)

Similarly, there are ways to take advantage of the popularity of social networking sites like Facebook. However, be careful to allow students to preserve the boundaries between social interaction and "official" class participation. You can create a special Facebook group to communicate with students, or ask students to create a limited class profile with appropriate privacy settings for participating in your class.

However, start by deliberating what you would like to accomplish and then try out those activities of interest to you within Facebook to judge for yourself whether it would be easier to use a learning management system or one of the other sites mentioned in previous chapters rather than Facebook for your purposes. It may be that you decide to use Facebook primarily for community-building activities for the class or as a way to update students on the class activities.

If your subject matter involves current events, you might want to highlight topical exchanges on Twitter to discuss in class or assign students to search for relevant subjects. Because students do not need to register on Twitter to read what is being tweeted, this can be a great way to widen the classroom conversation. Beyond that, you have many options, depending on whether you or your students register on Twitter and how comfortable you are using Twitter for instructional purposes. For example, you can create a hashtag (#) for your class, and encourage students who want to tweet their comments (during or after lectures, for example) to do so using that hashtag. If you prefer more privacy, you can make your own tweets protected so that only those you accept as followers (your students) can see them (this does mean that students must sign up on Twitter). You can display Twitter on a screen in your classroom and ask students to use their mobile devices to take part in a short real-time exchange "chat" on a topic. All these are possible ways to leverage technology to enrich your classroom time.

Using Online Quizmaking Tools

If your course is enhanced or blended, you presumably can conduct your high-stakes testing in a proctored on-campus environment. But online quizmaking tools can provide valuable assistance by permitting you to construct self-grading quizzes online. Most learning management systems contain this feature. They permit you to construct a quiz consisting of true/false statements, multiple-choice questions, one-word answers, multiple answers, matching answers, ordered answers, or short or long essay questions. Even if your institution offers no access to learning management systems, you can make use of the numerous free quizmaker tools available online. (See Chapters 6 and 9 for more detailed discussion of this.)

Students taking these tests can receive immediate feedback. This feedback can consist of a simple "correct" or "incorrect" message, or a statement explaining in detail why the student got the answer right or wrong. Questions can include embedded graphics. Depending on the software, they can even include sound or video files you've made, or links to such files that you found elsewhere on the internet. Another use of such online quizzes is to provide sample practice exams for students to use to prepare for midterm or final exams. Using one of the quiz generators, the instructor can provide answers as well as focused feedback, so that those taking the practice exams can learn from their mistakes. As with the preparation of lecture notes, creating quizzes can be time-consuming at first and then save you a great deal of trouble the second time around. One caveat, however: be sure to save the questions and answers in a word-processing file of your own. Sometimes institutions change their learning management systems, and it isn't always possible to import a set of questions in one software system into another.

Providing Advice and Support

Providing counseling, advice, mentoring, and support is part of the job of teaching. Instructors list their office hours in their syllabi and, once or twice a week, sit dutifully behind their desks waiting for someone to knock on their door. All too often, nobody comes, leaving the instructor to wonder about the utility of sitting in an office for two hours a week. For some, the meager trickle of students is an opportunity to catch up on paperwork. Some may see it as a testament to their pedagogical skills—a sign that students aren't having any difficulties. To others, however, the lack of office visitors is a warning signal that something may be wrong—either the allotted time isn't convenient or the students don't feel they are getting what they want from the course. Using two of the online tools readily available to most instructors—email and instant messaging—can improve the flow of communication markedly. Instant messaging applications have become so sophisticated that it is possible for you to have something closely akin to an office hour conversation. Depending on what tools you and your students have, and your own preferences, you can use Skype, FaceTime (with Apple iOS users), Facebook Messenger, What's App, or other popular free messaging tools to talk with individual students via text, voice, or video. To preserve your own privacy, use a service that allows you to set up a separate account that you can use just for teaching, or ask your institution if it is possible to create an institutional account.

Conferring with Students Online

With email and instant messaging, instructors can respond to student inquiries at a time and place of their choosing, leaving them freer to structure their activities during the day. Students can submit their inquiries as the need arises—for example, in their dorm room late at night when they're studying.

But shifting the counseling load to online has its obvious downside as well: it can significantly increase the instructor's workload if it isn't kept in check. To control your workload, we suggest the following guidelines, some of which we've recommended in earlier chapters as part of establishing a protocol for communications.

- Set strict parameters for responding to emails and other online messages and make these clear to your students in both your syllabus and your class. For instance, make sure your students understand that although you will accept emails from them, you will not necessarily respond to each one immediately and that you may provide responses to a question in the classroom if you see it is one that has been repeatedly posed. (A good reason to create a Q&A discussion forum online.)

- Specify which kinds of problems you will respond to: for example, personal problems, requests, or issues; or difficulties comprehending the subject matter. Steer clear altogether of administrative issues, such as dates for upcoming tests or questions about homework. Such information is either available in the syllabus or more properly discussed in an online or on-the-ground discussion session. State that you will respond most quickly to emails whose chief issue is clearly identified in the subject line of the communication. This will save you the trouble of having to read through the entire email to discover the problem at hand. It will also allow you to forward a student email to a TA or assistant when appropriate.

■ Respond to a problem you perceive as being potentially a question for all by sending one email to your entire class, or by posting an announcement in the online classroom or by compiling a FAQ page with your answers and post it on your website. Finally, depending on the complexity or private nature of the issues to be discussed, know when to move the conversation to a face-to-face meeting or an online real-time communication. If you are teaching a blended or web-enhanced course, there is likely to be a time that you can arrange to meet with the student. Then follow up the face-to-face or online real-time meeting with an email in which you summarize the conclusions of the conversation. Doing this will provide a record of your advice or decisions made during that conversation.

Establishing Virtual Office Hours

Whether you establish contact with individual students via one of the messaging apps already mentioned or use an online chat program that is designed for use with a group or individuals, by conducting virtual office hours you can, for instance, lighten your advisory load, or at least make it less onerous, if you use it in a focused way. Say, for example, that you tell your students that you will be available for consultations for an hour or two on certain days. If you're in your office, or even your home, you can open a chat session, leaving the chat window visible on your screen. As you wait for students to check in, you can do other work, glancing at the screen now and then to see if anyone has arrived.

Once a student has arrived, your conversation (depending on the tool you're using) can usually be logged; that is, a record of your conversation is automatically saved to a text file. This permits you to edit the text file at some later date, extracting material for your FAQ page. Check the capabilities of your chosen tool for saving a record of the interaction.

Some chat software tools include a whiteboard function. The whiteboard, as you may recall, is a communal area where an instructor can draw or type. The students in the chat session can then discuss the instructor's display or present material of their own as part of the online give and take. Such software tools permit you to display in the whiteboard area any document on your hard disk (such as a PowerPoint presentation or an Excel spreadsheet) or any web page you have bookmarked; you can do this simultaneously while chatting with your students. More impressive still, the students can do the same thing. Thus you and your students can see the same documents, web pages, or applications at the same time that you are discussing them.

Today's instructor now has a broad array of communication tools with which to conduct advisory or small-seminar sessions with a class whether or not their institution provides such tools. See some of the tools described in Chapters 6 and 9 if you need to select one for your class. It's best to try out these tools well in advance and make sure you are comfortable with their operation. If you have a real-time communication tool that is bundled in with your LMS and students are accustomed to using it, this might be the best solution. However, the very best solution is the one that is easiest and most likely to be put into use!

Assigning Group Projects

One feature commonly available in most learning management software is the ability to divide large classes into small student groups, affording them a private area online in which to collaborate on the production and publication of group projects.

In these private areas the students have access to the full panoply of online tools—message boards, chat rooms, and whiteboards. They can create information, format it, and share these newly created items with each other, unseen by the rest of the class. This gives them a virtual workspace, permitting them to work together on a schedule convenient to them—a particular advantage to students with busy schedules or difficult commutes. It also permits you as the instructor to assign group collaborative projects with the assurance that they won't overwhelm the students' time or capabilities. Many institutions and learning management systems also provide wiki software for such group collaboration purposes.

In a small private college, using a discussion board or other tools to promote online group work may seem superfluous. But in a large urban school, where students commute long distances, have jobs, or are raising families, the opportunity to work online overcomes a number of logistical obstacles while at the same time affording a level of intercommunication that wouldn't otherwise be possible. It also helps students learn how to collaborate with one another, a communication skill highly valued in the workplace.

Access to online group collaboration tools may permit you to assign more complex research projects than you might have before. By dividing the workload, students can tackle problems of much greater complexity than might have been possible if the assignment were for one student alone. With adequate preparation and planning, students from different institutions, cities, and even countries can connect online and may be able to work together collaboratively using the same set of group tools. Finally, the group projects can be released for viewing to the whole class and form the basis of a vigorous face-to-face or online discussion. To explore this subject further, see Chapters 6 and 7 for discussion of some of the specific options available for group activities.

Online as a Student Presentation Medium

The online environment is a powerful presentation medium, and it can be used in both web-enhanced and blended classes to display work created by students as course projects, either individually or in groups. Some instructors understandably prefer the more traditional means of expression, such as the research paper or the PowerPoint slide show delivered in front of the class. Frequently, however, an inordinate amount of classroom time is required to present such projects to the class. How much more efficient it can be to have students present their work online instead.

Using the online medium to present such reports permits students to use a wider range of media to make their points. Students can create videos, narrated slides, blogs, and web pages replete with graphics, sounds, animations, and links. Students can be asked to create an ePortfolio of their best work from the semester. Even without such multimedia embellishments, student work artifacts posted online can be viewed and evaluated by all the students before or after they come to class, leaving more face-to-face class time for discussion, analyses, and critiques.

Assembling such projects should no longer be considered a hardship for students. In most cases, it is a skill they can master easily, and one they ought to learn. Using simple, menu-based Web 2.0 type tools described in earlier chapters, they should be able to assemble relatively sophisticated presentations with ease.

Web-Based Exercises

The internet is so rich in potential learning materials that traditional instructors would be depriving their students of valuable educational resources if they ignored it altogether. No matter what subject you teach, be it molecular biology or cultural anthropology, a multitude of sites can provide you and your students with information, simulations, or resources to consider, critique, analyze, or discuss. A list of some very useful sites on the internet to search for such resources is provided in the Guide to Resources at the end of this book.

Aside from visiting informational websites, students can participate in global science experiments, perform experiments in online labs, collaborate and communicate with students from another school, state, or nation, analyze and critique articles published online and post reactions to them in a discussion board, and meet and discuss relevant issues with a "guest host" in a discussion board or chat room.

Here are some pointers for incorporating internet resources into your face-to-face on-site class:

■ Identify each site you want your students to visit by its URL, both on your website and in the syllabus. Revisit the site just before you begin teaching the class to make sure it's still live (sometimes sites are moved to different URLs or simply no longer work).

■ Be very clear when defining what you want your students to see or do when visiting a site. Be respectful of the time they must spend online to accomplish the assigned task. Generally, you'll want to avoid the treasure-hunt approach—that is, having your students hunt for information before they can critique it.

■ Avoid wasting time displaying websites in the on-site class unless it is for the purpose of discussing a specific assignment focused around that web page or it otherwise requires some explanation that can't be duplicated online. If your internet connection in the classroom is not stable, you may want to prepare screen shots of a website being used for this purpose.

Team Teaching

Just as students can collaborate easily online, so can teachers. Team teaching a large, lecture-style course requires a great deal of advance planning and preparation. Traditionally, this is done in face-to-face meetings, but using the collaborative tools available on the internet can ameliorate the process, speeding up the production of course materials and easing the task of approving them once they are done.

Once a course is under way, using the internet has its advantages as well. Instructors can spell each other at certain tasks, with one instructor handling lectures in the classroom while the other publishes backup materials on the internet and replies to student inquiries on discussion boards.

In less common cases, instructors may be situated too far apart to commute easily to the physical class. Using the internet is an obvious alternative, permitting the use of "experts" to prepare online lectures, but leaving the discussions to the instructor in the on-site class.

A Final Thought on Web Enhancement

In this discussion of ways the internet can be integrated in an on-the-ground class, one key thought underlies our comments.

Important! **Making the use of the internet optional rather than incorporating it into the curriculum dooms it to failure.**

When you make the internet an integral part of the coursework, you automatically make it more relevant and valuable to your students and yourself alike. Treating the website, online tools, or LMS site merely as a repository for chance comments or random postings reduces it to the level of a technological appendage and squanders its considerable potential to enrich what you are doing on the ground.

● ● ● ● ●

Tips for Teaching Blended Courses

While many institutions new to online education have surmised that the road to online teaching is made easier by first exposing instructors to blended teaching, there is little or no research that bears this out. In fact, many people who are experienced online teachers might tell you that blended courses can actually be more difficult to teach than fully online ones. Why is this? It is chiefly due to the challenge of integrating the two modalities of teaching in a way that makes both equally meaningful and effective.

Two of the biggest errors made by those attempting blended courses are:

- overloading students with a great deal more work than they would have in either a completely face-to-face or fully online course;
- not giving clear directions about what will be accomplished in each mode and how to coordinate the two.

The first issue has been termed the "course and one-half syndrome." The second is best handled along the same lines as fully online courses—with a comprehensive syllabus and schedule that clarifies how the class will operate, and with timely reminders about the sequencing and due dates for tasks.

The tips offered here in some cases reiterate principles already stated in this book and previously illustrated by examples, while in other cases, tips supply some additional information specially tailored for the blended format.

Preparing for the Blended Course

- Take advantage of any training or training resource materials offered on campus (or off- or online) if you are new to online teaching and blended learning. Look for training that not only focuses on how to use online software from the technical point of view, but also offers some insights into approaches to teaching and learning and design for a blended course. See Chapter 15 for some suggested training opportunities for blended teaching.

■ Review the face-to-face version of the course if that's what you have been teaching. Consider what is best reserved for face-to-face delivery and be able to explain your rationale. Find the weakest points in the teaching experience as you see them and consider how these may be improved with the addition of online activities and resources.

■ Review the schedule for your blended class. Are the face-to-face meeting dates already determined or can you determine the pattern yourself? The first class should ideally meet face to face so that students can be fully prepared for the blended format. On many campuses, students are accustomed to thinking about the first class day as provisional, a waste of time, or not a "real" class meeting. For this reason, it is a good idea to email your students ahead of time to stress the importance of not missing this first class date. If this would seem to be a losing battle on your campus, strongly consider making both the first and second class meetings face to face.

■ Generally speaking, in putting together your syllabus schedule, it's a good idea to plan discussions of the most complex materials for a face-to-face meeting. This doesn't mean that complex issues cannot be handled just as well in a fully online class, only that you may find that it will be relatively quicker for you to clear up misunderstandings if you have the opportunity for a face-to-face session. Many instructors have found that scheduling the first small-group meeting for a face-to-face meeting week greatly facilitates the rate at which groups form and establish cooperation. Some instructors also recommend that groups be scheduled to meet face to face at other critical moments in a group project. Again, this doesn't mean that the same objective cannot be reached purely online, but if you have the opportunity to convene groups face to face, you may find that it simply accelerates the process of forming groups or reaching consensus on key aspects of the project.

■ Be prepared to offer an orientation to students on your learning management system or other software if this is not supplied to students elsewhere.

■ Define how your blended class operates in the introductory area of your syllabus and what expectations are for students in regard to participation in online and face-to-face activities. Clarify whether the online activities are in real time or asynchronous or both. Explain how the weeks will work in tandem as a fully integrated course. Make sure your syllabus schedule clearly delineates in a graphic manner (through use of bold font or other means) those weeks in which the class meets face to face and what online activities, if any, are expected for those same weeks. (See Chapter 5 for more details about how to do this.)

Design Issues for the Blended Course

■ Pay careful attention to the transition between face-to-face and online activities. Ideally these two modes are not completely separate—*therefore, always have some online activity, no matter how minor or brief, within the week in which the class meets face to face.* For example, you might ask students to go online to the discussion board within forty-eight hours after a face-to-face meeting to continue to reflect on the topics broached at that meeting. This gives students who may be reticent about speaking in the on-campus class a chance to weigh in and it also provides an interval for all students to reflect on the preceding face-to-face discussion. It also signals to the students that what happens in these two modalities is not disconnected, but interrelated. The online work following directly upon the face-to-face meeting helps bridge the topics and activities of the two successive weeks, and can serve as preparation for the entirely online week. The opposite is also true—a carefully planned activity in the online-only week may be designed to provide essential background for the upcoming face-to-face meeting.

■ Consider the pacing and time needed to complete each week's activities, both online and face to face—calculate the total time expected for students to be on task—whether that means reading, researching, discussing, or completing other "homework." The total time should be comparable to that expected for a purely face-to-face class. This avoids the problem of "a class and one-half."

■ Don't confuse attendance and participation. Generally speaking, attendance is for face-to-face meetings or real-time online ones in which you are able to track the arrival and departure of students. In devising a participation grade, be sure to define what participation means in the context of a face-to-face class meeting and an online discussion. Keep in mind that there generally isn't time for every student to participate in the average one-, two-, or three-hour face-to-face classroom meeting. You may want to give students an opportunity within a face-to-face meeting week for participating in either format. In other words, if you give ten points for participation, you can stipulate that the ten points can be distributed over both the face-to-face and online meetings or confined to just the online. Or you can set up separate criteria or a rubric for each modality. Perhaps there are a certain number of points for participating in three of the fifteen face-to-face discussions with another total number of points for online participation in a face-to-face meeting week and yet another collection of points for those weeks in which the class is only online.

■ Carefully incorporate internet resources into your course content and instructional activities to provide more diverse pathways to learning and supply guidelines to help students devise a more critical approach to reviewing information.

■ Avoid scheduling all your face-to-face meeting time for lecturing! The on-campus meeting affords valuable time to explore ideas and gauge understanding by engaging students in active discussion and debate, case studies, or other active learning strategies.

■ Unless required to do so by your institution, do not design the new blended course so that online activity is limited only to an hour or two each week of real-time, synchronous meeting. We have seen conversions of face-to-face classes which resulted in 1.5 hours of a Monday lecture in an on-campus classroom followed by 1.5 hours of a Wednesday in a real-time, online session. Then nothing until the following Monday. While this may replace some "seat time," a more profound opportunity for teaching and learning is lost when instructors use all their precious face-to-face time just to deliver a lecture, or when students cannot use the remainder of the week to complete work, review content, or communicate online in an asynchronous mode. So the idea here is to develop a plan to use the entire week. Do not make students wait an entire week or even half the week to have a question answered. Provide a means for students to do some of their "homework" online.

Teaching the Blended Course

■ Post your syllabus online but depending on your student audience and expectations for the on-campus meeting, you may want to bring hard-copy printouts to the first class meeting (if that is indeed face to face) as well. At some campuses, students can be emailed in advance and instructed to read and bring the syllabus to the first class (on their laptops or in hard copy).

■ At the first and perhaps second class meeting, you will want to review the syllabus for the course. Additionally, here is when you may need to lead that orientation to the learning management software for students. At the very least, you will want to clarify how and when and where to carry out online activities, as well as to point to your syllabus schedule to emphasize the face-to-face meeting dates and the required online activities.

■ Provide weekly announcements in the online classroom every week to highlight the week's activities ahead and guide the "handoff" from the face-to-face meeting week to the purely online ones and vice versa.

■ Send weekly emails to students to remind students of continuing online activities during weeks in which the class does not meet face to face. Sometimes students in a blended class tend to think of the weeks in which they do not meet on campus as "weeks off." Here is where your syllabus schedule comes into play—you should clearly indicate what is happening in each mode. (See Chapter 5.)

■ Send a personal email to provide a friendly reminder to students who at any time are not participating in the online portion of the class or the opposite—to encourage students to come to face-to-face meetings.

■ Use an online gradebook to allow students to follow their progress in the class. By grading students on their online activities on a weekly or biweekly basis, it is easier for you to keep track of student learning and for the students themselves to be reminded of an ongoing class in which they may seldom meet face to face. Make sure the percentage of the grade accorded to online activities reflects the importance of the online portion of the blended class.

■ Strive to interact with students online every week in some manner. This may range from active facilitation of online discussion to announcements or posted commentary that help illuminate the readings and assignments under way. Let students know that you will be monitoring their online activity. Show your presence by strategic and meaningful postings.

■ In addition to any student course evaluations your institution may administer at the end of a course, consider asking students some of your own questions tailored to the blended course design you devised. For example, you may ask students questions such as, "Which assignments provided the best learning experience for you this term and why?" "Was it clear to you what needed to be done in weeks in which the class did not meet face to face?" or "Rate the following internet-based activities from our class…"

Finally, after teaching your first blended class, carefully review it and don't be shy about enlisting the extra pair of eyes that a trusted colleague can provide. It's difficult to get the blended course "recipe" exactly right the very first time, but your effectiveness will improve with feedback from students and colleagues along with reflection and practice.

14

●●●●●

Teaching and Learning in a MOOC

Now that the initial hype over MOOCs (Massive Open Online Courses)—referred to by some as "MOOC Mania"—has subsided, we have the benefit of research studies and accounts of first-hand experience to provide us with a clearer sense of what MOOCs are all about in regard to teaching and learning. However, so often have MOOCs and online education in general been conflated, that some have begun to refer to the instructor-facilitated online course for 10–50 students as a "traditional online course." This chapter will forego lengthy treatments on the history of MOOCs and the attendant controversies, referring you to some excellent curated resources on these subjects (see Guide to Resources, Online Education, Research on MOOCs section), and focus on a few aspects of teaching and learning in MOOCs in regard to the instructor's role, pedagogy, student learning and participation, and the design issues that may affect teaching and learning. Let's assume that your institution has asked you to teach or help develop a MOOC or that you are contemplating one yourself. Or perhaps you have already participated in some way in the design or implementation of a MOOC course and you are not completely satisfied by what you have experienced in regard to teaching and learning.

The advice we give here builds on what those in the online education field already know about effective online teaching and learning, on the major research already conducted on MOOCs, and on the issues previously discussed in this book concerning scale and pedagogical approaches for large online courses. While we previously talked about thirty or a hundred students, with the MOOC one has to consider potentially thousands or tens of thousands.

In addition to the above, we include our experience as online instructors experiencing MOOCs first-hand as participants. We enrolled and participated or lurked over the period of four years in more than two dozen different MOOC courses, representing a variety of different platforms (Coursera, EdEx, Canvas, Course-Sites, and even other ad-hoc non-platform formats) and sponsored by universities of the United States, Canada, the UK, Europe, Hong Kong, and Scandinavia. We have interviewed faculty and instructional designers and others connected with MOOCs, but our role as lurker or participant in MOOC courses and our interviews with instructors and instructional designers remains a salient feature of our observations here. In some cases we enrolled in successive versions of particular courses so as to better observe the evolution of a course in its subsequent iterations.

Our treatment of MOOCs in this chapter is also based on the underlying values of this book. We do value models of online learning in which interaction among students and the relationship between instructor and student is pivotal. So the idea that the instructor matters, that interaction between student and instructor and student with his or her peers is of great importance, will inform the treatment of MOOCs here.

Defining MOOCs and the Role of the Teacher

The first O in MOOC, *open*, means a number of different things to different people—open as in free of tuition, open as in freedom to participate a little or a lot, or open as in using only free, open educational resources. The first two "opens"—free to access and free to participate a lot or a little are the two that I want to consider here first.

MOOCs that have no barriers to registration and participation have meant that many, if not a majority of registrants, will be passive participants—onlookers (or "lurkers" in the old parlance of traditional online education)—or those who participate for a short time in the beginning, or only intermittently. So if you are teaching or designing a course for such a group, it might be helpful for you to consider this something akin to planning a course in which 30–50 percent of your students could, at any point, change their status to auditors or just be undeclared withdrawals from the course.

If you peruse any history of MOOCs, you will doubtless learn about the cMOOC and xMOOC distinction. The c in cMOOC stands for Connectivist, stemming from the first MOOCs delivered by Downes and Siemans in 2008, and the x refers to the large-scale platform design of those staged on platforms like Coursera, EdX, and Udacity which would seem to have been built on the model of the traditional large lecture hall. The cMOOC features a design of decentralized but connected personal networks in which participants create and share their own constructed sites of learning from blogs or websites or social media accounts or combinations of these. The xMOOCs are a more centralized, deliberately enclosed learning environment—from a design standpoint, much closer to an LMS.

Having participated in both types of designed learning environments, we feel that each had some benefits and some limitations. In the cMOOC, it was sometimes confusing to follow the course, especially for those who were not active social media users. Having to hop about to access each participant's contribution housed on wildly different platforms, one could easily become exhausted as each participant was encouraged to create his or her own locus of learning—be it blog, web page, or some other base. In the xMOOC, the design efforts seemed to support self-paced learning at the expense of interaction, sharing, and the creation of knowledge. In both of these the teaching aspect is often minimized or the role narrowly drawn—in the cMOOC resulting in self-directed learning and in the xMOOC as self-paced learning. The majority of MOOCs are xMOOCs and we will focus on these in this chapter. For a detailed history and analysis of the design of cMOOCs and xMOOCs, we recommend Tony Bates' chapter 5.3 from *Teaching in a Digital Age* (see Guide to Resources, Online Education: Theory and Practice section).

Bayne & Ross in a 2014 study, "The pedagogy of the Massive Open Online Course: the UK view" nicely encapsulate the situation described in which the teaching role is poorly defined, saying "the complexities of teaching on MOOCs have been largely absent from the debate, which typically describe only three forms of teacher—the distant 'rock star' or 'academic celebrity lecturer,' the co-participants or facilitator within a network, and the automated processes which serve as proxy tutor and assessor." (See Guide, Online Education, Research on MOOCs section.)

Putting aside the arguments for cMOOCs vs. xMOOCs, this book takes the position that teaching still has an important role to play in massive courses, albeit one that must adapt to the challenges of interacting with and providing for the acknowledged vast numbers of students. On the other hand, we echo cMOOC's emphasis on the value of student-created artifacts and student-constructed contributions to their own learning and to that of their peers in the class.

Because of the massive numbers in a MOOC, the ability of an instructor to provide guidance, suggest paths, to encourage and stimulate interest, are all valuable contributions to the learning environment even while one has to accept that it is impossible to individually assess and interact with even a substantial proportion of the enrolled students.

Teaching presence as defined by the Community of Inquiry theory is the guiding and facilitating hand that faculty exert both before and during a course—planning and designing the course activities with the learning outcomes in mind, facilitating the social and learning activities that occur during the course.

What are some of the ways that instructors can demonstrate teaching presence?

Actually, through just about every aspect of the MOOC!

Instructor Presentation of Content and Instructor Presence

While there are doubtless some students who are content to simply watch videos of lectures, MOOC-derived learning analytics have tended to confirm what had already been the gospel about video length—after about ten minutes there is a great fall-off in student attention. Many MOOCs consist of narrated slide presentations, with or without talking heads, or the Khan Academy style in which the narration follows as a moving hand writes and doodles across the whiteboard. Some MOOC videos have very high production values, with scenes filmed inside museums or in front of famous landmarks. The China X MOOC series of courses from Harvard X featured a variety of methods of presenting content—in addition to readings, there were short videos that varied from conversations between two faculty or a faculty member and students, to interviews with well-known scholars. Most MOOCs display simultaneous transcripts or captions which aid accessibility but also provide another mode of learning that enhances the overall presentation.

In organizing the online classroom, many xMOOCs in the early years of their appearance initially failed to follow a commonly accepted piece of wisdom from "traditional" online courses—the necessity of telling students where and how to find everything in the site. A map to the site, what to do each week (in the case of courses with different categories of content modules or those with many optional choices), and in which recommended order, are all necessary for the MOOC. Some MOOCs wisely provide a screen-cast course video tour—again, a technique familiar from "traditional" online courses.

Videos have become a preferred way to provide content, but too many are still of the long-winded, talking head variety. Despite their featuring real professors on camera, too many do not really create a sense of instructor presence, even as many have very high production values.

There are a few cases in which audio may even be a better choice than video. For example, if you teach a MOOC on a subject that attracts students from areas where internet access may be limited, narrated slides via screencast or simple MP3 files may be more readily accessed by students. Ira Gooding is Manager of the Open Education Lab at the Johns Hopkins Bloomberg School of Public Health, assisting faculty in designing MOOC courses that are delivered via the Coursera platform. Its public health courses are popular with an international audience, including those from developing countries. Many of its courses rely on voice-over-PowerPoint narration to deliver major content. On this point, Gooding noted,

> We have found that eschewing video does not negatively affect learning outcomes and that using speaker video introduces a number of negative effects that we prefer to avoid. Presenter video is more time-consuming to edit, it is more costly and difficult to revise and update over time, it is less accessible for students in developing countries, and it offers students less playback flexibility.

Al Filreis, a renowned professor from University of Pennsylvania who has been teaching the Modern and Contemporary American Poetry (known as ModPo) MOOC class on the Coursera platform for several years, has managed to provide a strong sense of teaching presence despite the great number of students in what has proven to be a very popular MOOC.

He has not made his presence known through video lectures in which he is the star—rather his videos are actually dialogues with his students in a seminar format on camera. Students in the MOOC can easily envision themselves in the role of the students in the video and it provides a model for how to approach the analysis of poetry.

Filreis as a teaching presence is strongly felt in these videos as he gently directs the conversation, asks follow-up questions, proposes a deeper analysis of a question, or summarizes key aspects of the conversation. Filreis seems thoroughly at ease in conducting these video seminars—the fact that he has never been enamored of the traditional classroom lecture has probably made it easier for him to arrive at this approach when he planned his MOOC,

> *I have not lectured since around 1990. I wasn't going to start lecturing now! Too many people assume that the MOOC mode requires video recordings of lectures. I don't think so. We record open-ended discussions—collective, collaborative close readings of difficult modern and contemporary poems, one poem at a time. The students tell us again and again that watching these videos offers them a model for the act of interpreting—and then they of course are invited to try it along with us and others in the course (in the discussions, during the webcasts, in study groups and meet-ups).*

Here are some recommendations for video content, drawn from our observations and research:

- High production values are not as important as creating the illusion that the narrator or person(s) on video are addressing or including the student viewer.
- Keep videos short—divide up into 5–10 minute segments—and always include captions.
- Variety is an asset—vary lectures and commentary as much as possible—for example, between narrated slides, videos of single speakers, interviews, marking up a whiteboard, etc. and when including conversations between the instructor and students or guests, try to include among those students or speakers those of different genders, ages, ethnic background whenever feasible.

Richard Edwards from Ball State, teaching a MOOC on film noir, had a dynamic approach to presentation and one that responded to feedback from students,

> *I really wanted my sense of presence to come alive in the lectures. While each week I had previously recorded video lectures, I created a second lecture each week using Storify and built that lecture around questions that the students emailed or tweeted me. That way, the course could be tailored to the concerns that the students were raising, were interested in, and it allowed the course to have a liveliness of discussion that I don't think operates as well around pre-produced lectures.*

Creativity in designing the MOOC can extend to the way of presenting content, as described by Richard Edwards,

> *In terms of presenting my main course content for my MOOC, I wanted to have a "hook" that would organize all the material. I ended up deciding to embrace the metaphor of "investigation"— investigations, like a private detective's investigation, looks for clues, attempts to deduce some kind of underlying chronology and content for ideas and events, and does not go in a strictly linear direction. Investigations can go off on tangents, both productive and non-productive. That is why I called the course "Investigating Film Noir." And it didn't hurt that many film noir narratives themselves follow the action of an investigator—so I found that made a nice homology between my pedagogical goals and the course content.*
>
> *Once I knew that I was building around the pedagogical metaphor of investigation, I used many different tropes that help structure the learning environment—I used the metaphor of an "evidence board" and used Pinterest to "pin" ideas to a shared evidence board. I used Storify to contextualize "tweets" to see how different learners in the MOOC were going down different paths in their investigations of noir. I build my six-part lecture around a structure of investigation—and arranged my lectures around a basic set of questions: Who had the means, the motives, and the opportunities to create films noir in the 1940s and 1950s? That is the basic way a private eye would have approached it if assigned to the "Case of Film Noir."*

● ● ● ● ●

Designing for a Disparate Student Audience

There is consensus that the student audience for a MOOC will necessarily vary greatly in regard to both the reasons for enrollment and the intended degree of participation. Those enrolling are not of one mind in regard to expectations, nor in what they hope to gain from the course nor do they necessarily bring the same level of knowledge to the learning experience. Some are there merely to observe or sample a bit of the content, others want to absorb all the content and perhaps listen in on a few of the discussions, while a smaller subset of enrollees are fully committed to completing the course, perhaps signing up to earn a certificate or some other sort of credit if those options are available.

Richard Edwards, having recognized this, has transformed what to many is a stumbling block into a positive aspect of his design—providing for "personalized learning paths." He views the various types of content or software tools for his course (whether these are the Canvas LMS, podcasts, videos external to the LMS, or the use of Twitter) as part of a "learning ecosystem." He thinks of each different software platform or tool as "a separate community with different protocols and community rules, different types of engagement and experts, and different metrics of success."

A student who feels comfortable using Twitter to issue a rapid series of brief comments might not have the same profile as the student who seeks to engage only in the LMS discussion board, responding at length to instructor prompts.

Edwards suggests that the greater the number of students you have in a MOOC, the more you should consider personalized learning paths. Rather than expecting all students to participate in all activities of your course, you might want to think about designing to accommodate such variations in the learning experience as when the student joins the course (beginning, midway, near the end), whether they want a great deal of structure or just an opportunity to explore, the pre-existing knowledge they bring to the course, and a desire to participate in one or more formats (discussion board in LMS, Twitter, etc.)

Edwards then emphasizes the importance of explaining to students why the course is designed the way it is, "revealing some of your teaching and learning intentions … when we do something different in a course, it is a good idea to let the learner know that so they can calibrate their expectations, too."

For example, one of Edwards' first messages to students in his "Into the Darkness: Investigating Film Noir" course offered in 2015 through Ball State University in conjunction with a film noir summer festival by Turner Classic Movies (TCM), explained the various elements of the course,

> *If you are new to the course, the best place to start is on the Canvas homepage and click on the "Getting Started" link. "Getting Started" is the first module of this nine-week course and is filled with useful information (such as the syllabus, a punchlist for tasks to complete, a Film Noir Viewing Guide, and a Film Noir Quick Start Guide). The first module is your best guide for what this course is about and how it will work as a vibrant and communal online learning experience ... There are three online sites we are using to facilitate engagement, to provide additional context and curation on the films, and to support learning in this course. We have the Canvas course, Twitter, and the TCM Message Board. Use the Canvas course to get the lectures and learning materials and to take your weekly quizzes. Use Twitter to connect with other students, share your thoughts about the films, and engage with the learning materials. Use the TCM Message Board for more in-depth analysis and discussion about the films and the Daily Dose of Darkness. Instructions and help guides to all of this can be found in Module 1.*

Another aspect of design he has explored is how to increase student engagement and encourage persistence. As one of his strategies, he evolved a series of email communications that he called the "daily dose," which Edwards defined in this way:

> ### What is the Daily Dose of Darkness?
> *Every student ... will get four Daily Doses of Darkness a week. They are sent Monday through Thursday, one a day. If you miss one of the Daily Doses, they are all archived under the "Announcements" link on the left-hand navigation bar in Canvas. The Daily Dose will be a curated four-minute film clip and learning lesson on a film ... The best part of the Daily Dose is that they allow us to communally share our observations on*

these great films. Important tip: The Daily Dose only takes five minutes a day. It is a great way to get involved in our discussions of film noir since every enrolled student receives the same Daily Doses!

How do I post my comments on the Daily Dose of Darkness?
We have set up special topic threads for the Daily Dose over at the TCM Message Boards. Each week the new Daily Dose topics will be pinned at the top of the message board.

Each one of his "daily dose" messages contained a number of different ways to approach learning about the film(s) in question. It offered some insights into the film, provided a video clip of the film, and suggested some questions for reflection and discussion. It also served to stimulate interest and tie together the various venues or parts of his "course ecosystem" in which course activities took place, implicitly encouraging each student to engage with the course in a way that was best suited to that learner.

Here's an example of a portion of a daily dose message from the fourth week of the course,

The theme of the fourth week is "Film Noir and the Studios." These Daily Doses will supplement the material in video lecture #3 ... and provide further evidence and examples of points made during the lecture about the studio system and its influence on the development of film noir. You can start watching video lecture #3 by starting Module 4 ... now available on the Canvas course site ... in our first Daily Dose this week, we will watch a key early scene from Out of the Past *... a quintessential film noir, made at RKO, that influenced many films noir that came after it ... After watching the clip, please go to Twitter or the TCM Message Board to continue your reflections on this clip ... Here are a few discussion starters...*

Facilitation of Discussion

Due to the large numbers of participants in some MOOCs, it is often left to teaching assistants to help facilitate the discussion, oddly emulating that old lecture hall/TA discussion section model. In some MOOCs, those student participants who have excelled in previous courses are sometimes invited to help facilitate among their peers in follow-on courses. Nonetheless, many MOOC instructors realize the importance of following and participating to some degree in the discussion as well.

Al Filreis and his teaching assistants provide a presence and actively facilitate the threaded class discussions—an aspect of MOOCs that is often perceived as one of the most difficult to manage. In regard to the structure of threaded discussions he notes,

> *In ModPo's forums, we organize threads for each poem. So a reticent participant can look for the one poem about which they seek discussion, can find the thread, and participate only in that thread—and not be overwhelmed. We also provide lots of guidance about managing the forums...*

He also shares a few specific tips for facilitating discussion and offering feedback

1. Respond succinctly and strategically. Maximize the time you have to respond. Choose a question or comment for response that is an example of many other similar questions participants have posted.
2. In the second offering of the course, recruit "community TAs" who are willing to spend time answering questions that the faculty instructor doesn't need to be answering.
3. Create "office hours" so that everyone in the course knows you will be fully responsive for that hour.

Filreis doesn't remain aloof from the discussions,

> *A MOOC will be successful if the instructor is involved in the discussion—sees it, understands what students are saying and how they are responding, and knows how to adjust the course according to what students are saying. It's that simple.*

Some other methods to effectively manage facilitation of discussion in MOOCs, drawn from our observations, interviews, and research, are:

■ Providing a forum for each week or topic of the course, with at least one instructor-initiated discussion prompt.

- Providing a forum or thread for each week for Q&A related to that week.

- Dividing the areas between free form sections where students can create new topics and those which follow the weekly topics and whose initial prompts are provided by the instructor and teaching assistants.

- Providing notice of time-based participation by the instructor in a particular discussion—for example, that the instructor will be present on these particular days to take questions and respond about this topic.

- Visually marking the instructor or TA postings clearly to distinguish them from those of students—students can then more easily find those first or after reading those postings from classmates, as the case may be.

- Allowing and encouraging students to rate or "up-vote" those discussion postings they found to be of greatest value. This not only encourages higher-quality postings but also helps students locate postings found to be of assistance to their peers.

- In MOOCs which have large numbers of international or multi-state US participants, providing an option for students from a certain geographic area to communicate about the course. This can be purely social or a combination of social along with topics keyed to course content.

- Highlighting questions from the discussions each week via a week's end video presentation (used in the China X MOOC with great effectiveness), a recorded synchronous session or some other means. Because there can be such an overwhelming number of discussion postings in a large, active MOOC, focusing in greater depth on a few crucial questions from the week can be a way to provide students with a satisfactory sense of lessons well learned from the week's activity.

In our experience, the discussions that are easiest to follow are those that are clearly marked by week or module of the course and topic or subtopic. This highlights the importance of creating an adequate number of areas for each module, week, or unit of the course, helping to avoid a situation where students post willy-nilly in any forum or thread they can find.

Grading and Feedback

Automated quizzes with feedback are perhaps the most common form of assessment in MOOCs, whether graded or ungraded. These may be more useful in some courses than others. For example, in courses in which there is a lot of factual information to absorb, multiple tries and practice afforded by ungraded or low-stakes quizzes each week can provide a good foundation for higher level assessment activities. As adaptive learning software becomes available in a particular subject, the value of these automated quizzing methods may increase.

Interactive videos with quizzes delivered through some of the tools mentioned in Chapter 9 are another way to provide more context and focus to review and assessment.

Many MOOCs have relied on peer-graded essays and papers to relieve some of the crush of grading so many submissions, with varying degrees of success. This topic is the focus of a good deal of MOOC research, some references for which you might want to explore in the Guide to Resources.

Some approaches to peer grading exercises are:

■ Those that not only provide clear and sufficiently comprehensive grading rubrics, but provide some training to students in how to use those rubrics, illustrating by way of grading and explanation of some sample submissions. This could be in the form of a video discussion in which a few students participate in a "norming" exercise, discussing a sample assignment.

■ Those in which students are paired or in peer groups in which at least one member is of a similar or higher level of skill. A large-scale research study of peer grading in MOOCs demonstrated that peer-grading bias is lowest when the performance of peers in the course is not widely divergent. In other words, the best students tend to grade the lower more harshly while the worst students inflate the better performers. (See Guide, Research on MOOCs, Piech et al., 2013.)

■ Finding peers who are on a similar level is not always easily accomplished in MOOCs but can sometimes evolve after a few weeks in the course after seeing the results of quiz scores or other student work. A simpler way to ensure more reliability is to have more than one peer grader assigned to rate each person's submission. Research on this topic suggests that at least three or three to five graders will add to reliability of scores. (See Guide, Research on MOOCS, Luo et al., 2014.)

■ Providing opportunities to revise graded assignments *after* peer review may be a good option in some courses.

■ According a portion of the grade to the assessor for the quality of the peer assessment of another. This is an old tried and true technique from peer-review methods in traditional courses, and tends to focus the attention of the assessor on understanding and applying the rubric.

A common feature in MOOCs from Johns Hopkins Bloomberg School of Public Health is the use of peer assessment. In talking about the evolution of this feature of its courses, Gooding reflected,

> *The most significant challenges were in the area of rubric design. This is an area in which some of our instructors had little experience. Planning a rubric that students would be able to fairly and effectively apply was a real challenge, and we have found that students take the task of grading their peers very seriously. Our first two attempts at peer assessment were very messy because we made the stakes too high and the rubrics too detailed. We also found that the students were ill-prepared for the task. In courses with peer assessment, our current approach is to offer at least two peer-assessed activities. The first has relatively low stakes in terms of their final grade; this gives students the opportunity to learn the processes of submission and evaluation and allows them to benefit from both reading some of their classmates' work and absorbing the feedback on their own. The second peer assessment is generally a higher-stakes opportunity to demonstrate what they have learned and also apply the feedback they received during the first round.*

Finding the right mix of assessments and feedback for a MOOC require a good deal of deliberate thought, attention to detail, and a willingness to revise based on results. Gooding noted that in working with faculty to develop a MOOC, "I always try to stress the high volume of planning and effort required to develop an online course, particularly the assessment components. Instructors frequently short-change the amount of time that they devote to the latter."

The Social Element

In a MOOC, providing opportunities for social interaction can be highly motivating to students who might otherwise feel lost in the crowd. We know that social interaction is vital in traditional online courses. While some MOOC participants are simply there for self-directed learning, many participants feel isolated and bored among the very large numbers in MOOCs without some social "glue" to maintain their interest. Some ways we have seen to add more social interaction are:

- Encourage students to form "meet-up" or in-person study groups in their own local geographic areas and give them a place to organize in the discussion area.
- Encourage students to blog, either informally, or as a journaling assignment to chart their progress in the course, and to comment on others' blogs—allow students a choice from among several tools—traditional blogging programs, Tumblr or Instagram, or any micro video platform.
- Encourage students to introduce themselves via a brief video or using some of the tools mentioned in Chapter 9 and provide a space to collect these introductions.
- Provide a dedicated socially oriented discussion forum, or optional synchronous sessions.
- Offer options for small group assignments that involve collaboration.

● ● ● ● ●

Issues to Consider before Teaching a MOOC

Creating an effective and engaging MOOC course requires a substantial investment of time and skill. Before agreeing to teach a MOOC, it is wise to inquire about the following (in addition to asking about release time, payment, intellectual property, or other customary contractual issues):

- What is the enrollment cap on your MOOC course? If open to non-credit participants, what is the cap on for-credit participants (these will require extra workload)?

■ Who will be available during the design and building phase to assist you? From your own institution? From the hosting platform?

■ What is the lead time being provided for development of the course? Are there separate schedules for creating the multimedia elements of the course?

■ What support will you have during the teaching of the MOOC to facilitate as well as create feedback videos or other content not created beforehand? How are you expected to handle feedback and interaction for those taking the MOOC for credit vs. those who are not?

■ What preparation and expectations will students have for your MOOC? Are there any orientation materials being provided or will you need to develop these for your course?

■ Follow the same design principles enunciated in earlier chapters of this book—know your platform and tools thoroughly before embarking on design and development of your course, think about your learning goals and objectives and work backward to design teaching and learning activities, providing adequate feedback loops and scaffolded assignments, and pay attention to the pacing of all activities, decide on a clear and coherent navigation and layout for the course site, carefully select the tools you and students will use, devise clear course communication protocols that will work for a large number of students, provide guidance to students in regard to expectations they should have of the instructor and TAs.

Al Filreis offers encouragement to those who, having taught "traditional" online classes, feel somewhat intimidated by the prospect of teaching a MOOC,

> *I have been teaching online, partially and/or wholly, for twenty years—in as many combinations and modes as you can imagine. The MOOC was an easy and natural next step. Nothing I'm doing with the MOOC is surprising or unanticipated as a matter of format or pedagogy...*
>
> *The key is to teach a massive open course as if it's a small group of people. It's not, but the feel of the experience for the student should be similar. No participant in such a large group*

expects lots of individual attention, but a teacher can respond to individuals' questions in a way that serves as a model response.

Here are some other tips from Richard Edwards for those embarking upon teaching of their first MOOC:

1. *Manage your time wisely. I worked on my MOOC for six months before I taught it (esp. preparing for my video lectures and designing a course template in a new LMS), and for the six weeks of the course, I was extremely busy handling the social media aspects of the course. So make sure you have a strong production strategy to have all your MOOC materials prepared, and be aware that once the course goes live, it can be very time consuming, if you are seeking to participate in social media activities.*

2. *Keep experimenting. The Humanities are underrepresented in MOOCs because some of our most effective teaching strategies (such as being an effective seminar instructor) have difficulty scaling up from a classroom with eighteen students into the hundreds and thousands. Therefore, we need to explore new avenues of engagement and discussion that can operate at scale…*

3. *Embrace participatory learning. Regardless of how one teaches a Humanities MOOC, I would still urge that the focus be upon active rather than passive learning. A MOOC shouldn't be a series of TED talks with multiple-choice questions. The internet as a learning environment is just too terrifically social and dynamic to create an online course that is based on a "sage on the stage" model. Think about how to be a "guide on the side" and be a participant yourself in the course. And consider ways, especially in a Humanities course, to tap into your students' imagination and creativity. You won't get there with just multiple-choice questions. The Humanities, for me, are about critical and creative thinking.*

Edwards shared this further reflection on his experience teaching MOOCs,

Ultimately, I find the final "C" in MOOC a bit of a misnomer— my Investigating Film Noir MOOC was a "course," but it really

operated most successfully as a "community." That strikes me as the potential here—that we are in the very early stages of a potentially evolutionary shift in the breadth and depth of learning environments, and we likely have only tapped the surface of what a powerful, persistent, and global community of learners can accomplish together—the shared knowledge they can and will build—in the twenty-first century.

Whether you are just beginning to consider whether to take the plunge into teaching in a MOOC, or have the grand ambition to contribute to new ways of learning, it's important to remember that the best online teaching and learning experiences still depend on the creativity and skillful guidance of instructors who want to contribute to the learning experience of their students through such actions as course design, sharing of knowledge, feedback, and facilitation. If you decide to teach a MOOC, don't be a mere "subject matter expert" but immerse yourself in the action.

As Al Filreis so succinctly expressed it,

MOOCs will succeed if the instructor is involved. They will not, if not.

15

●●●●●

Taking Advantage of New Opportunities

Because online education is a relatively new enterprise, you have an opportunity to make a positive contribution to this growing field. To take full advantage of this new opportunity, you would do well to keep yourself informed of the latest trends and issues and to continually improve your skills and knowledge. Each time you teach online, you have the chance to acquire insights and experience that can be used as the basis for further exploration. In this chapter, we hope to point out some of the possibilities for your development as an online educator.

●●●●●

New Career Directions

The field of online education has become the preoccupation not only of most institutions of higher education but also of software producers, media conglomerates and publishing houses, and education-delivery companies. The so-called Ed Tech industry, an omnibus term to describe companies in which technology and its affordances for teaching and learning are the focus, has become the target for investors hoping to latch onto the next big thing.

Many of these players are beginning to appreciate the need to employ people with solid academic credentials, experience in the classroom, and, of course, an understanding of how teaching and learning can be effectively handled and enhanced in an online environment.

Because online education ranges from self-paced independent study modules to fully instructor-led courses, career prospects cover a similarly wide range. For instance, you can find new opportunities in areas like these:

- creation of courseware for your own courses;
- design and creation of courseware to be used by other instructors;
- curriculum development for both non-profit and profit-making entities;
- course development or instructional design and instructional technology services;
- student services (advising, financial aid, disability services, tutoring, library services) provided mostly online to support online learners;
- administrative positions at all levels directing online and blended education programs;
- specialists in learning analytics, assessment, or accreditation compliance as these pertain to online education;
- training and support positions in technology and faculty development training programs.

Academic and staff jobs related to online education are growing in number and even a cursory look at some of the online job-listing sites demonstrates the range of non-academia-based jobs for which educators with online expertise might qualify. As technology races ahead of content, those with the intellectual capital to create courseware and shape curriculum will be increasingly in demand.

Already, online teaching has revitalized the careers of many longtime instructors, allowing them to experiment with new approaches to teaching and to create courses for an expanded audience of learners. Many have assumed new positions of leadership within their own institutions. For others, online experience has provided an opportunity to start a new career outside academia, to bring their needed expertise and perspectives to associations and companies engaged in education-related businesses.

Moreover, instructors who are ready to retire may consider extending their teaching lives with online courses. As part of regular online programs as well as continuing education, online teaching offers new opportunities to retired professionals who have much to offer students in the way of expertise and experience.

● ● ● ● ●

What to Do after You've Read This Book

Although this book strives to provide you with a comprehensive guide to online teaching, we hope that it will also inspire you to explore some additional pathways for your continued development as an online educator. Here we'll suggest a few of them.

Further Training

This book was developed as a practical guide for instructors who wish to teach online, but it wasn't meant to replace a formal training program completely. In fact, although a good training program would include at least some of the information provided by this book, a training program should also include the experience of teaching and learning online.

Important! **Whenever possible, opt for a program that emphasizes online training, not just on-site training.**

Most of us are used to learning in a workshop or lab arrangement, with an instructor hovering over us or directing from the front of the room as we struggle with a software program. Such personalized attention can be very helpful; the face-to-face interchange and the ability to ask questions "on the fly," gaining immediate feedback and support, can be quite valuable.

But trying to learn to use a specific learning management system in a workshop environment can have its disadvantages as well. For one thing, some learning management software programs are too complicated to master within a manageable amount of real time (three hours, for instance, which is about as much time as the average instructor has to spare in a single afternoon). This isn't because the software itself is especially difficult to use, but because it contains too many individual parts and functions to cover adequately in the space of a few hours. Learning how to operate the basic functions in software is one thing, but knowing what to do with them is quite another. In a workshop devoted to a learning management system, most instructors, especially novices, find the information too plentiful to digest in one sitting. Without repetition over time, much of the experience is lost. Or—and this is probably just as harmful—instructors may leave the workshop thinking they know pretty much all they need to know.

Coupling an on-site workshop with further work online is often the best solution for those eager to learn enough to proceed confidently on their own. Until you've become a student, there's no way you can properly appreciate, or even identify, the problems and pitfalls of learning online. Sitting in a classroom with other instructors is a totally different experience from sitting at home and communicating with your instructor and fellow students online. Using the actual online tools to complete an exercise or post a comment on a discussion board is entirely different from experimenting with the tools in an on-site workshop.

An added advantage to learning online, rather than in a workshop, is that students can progress at a speed that suits them. Thus the novice can afford to proceed at a slow pace without worrying that he or she may be holding back the rest of the class, while more advanced users can proceed quickly to get to the material they need to learn.

You can learn some fairly complex and technical material online. For example, in a course we taught about how to make effective use of multimedia, instructors learned how to make animations, short videos, and narrated slide shows on their own, submitting their completed work to a website. Most of these instructors had never used the various software tools before taking the class, yet none of them complained that they could not learn without a live instructor standing by. These instructors were not "techies"; they ranged from English professors to instructors of machine-shop technology in a trade high school. The instructional material supplied—narrated slide shows and screencast video demonstrations—guided them through the various exercises, and the online discussion board provided a forum in which they could voice their problems and concerns.

Training Outside Your Own Institution   If you have a good training program at your institution, we strongly recommend that you sign up for one of its offerings. Your institution's center for teaching and learning, instructional technology or academic technology units, may all provide one or more types of training. What should you do, however, if your institution isn't offering faculty development training in online teaching?

First of all, you can enroll as a student in an online course of your own choosing. There are many online courses being offered now by institutions all over the world. You might base your choice on any number of criteria:

■ a subject you've always wanted to study;

■ a course that is in your field or similar to your own course;

■ a course that uses the same software platform your own institution is considering;

■ a course that simply suits your schedule and budget.

Even though such courses won't show you specifically how to teach online, they will give you vital experience as a learner in the online classroom.

In terms of specific training for teaching online, there are now a number of national and vendor-operated programs, including the following types:

■ short online courses and tutorials in particular software platforms, offered by the providers of those platforms or their partners;

■ short, site-based training courses and workshops for particular software platforms and tools, often available at conferences focused on the use of technology in education;

■ full-scale, comprehensive programs covering teaching methods, curriculum development, and tools that aren't specific to any software platform.

Many of these programs are available completely online, thus eliminating the constraints of geography. Online training is particularly advantageous in that it doesn't involve removing an instructor from the classroom in order to be trained, and it is particularly economical in that it doesn't require the travel and lodging expenses necessary for an off-site workshop.

You may be able to work on an interdepartmental, districtwide, or consortium basis to arrange discounted tuition for yourself and other faculty members. You can also investigate whether any regional or statewide opportunities are available. For example, the Illinois Online Network has developed a program of instruction in online teaching for all of its interested instructors and external partnering institutions and even a program for online education administrators. Pennsylvania State University similarly offers various forms of online teaching training to faculty from all their campuses. Instructors in the California Community college network can take advantage of the online instructor training offered by @One (www.onefortraining.org/about). City University of New York faculty can join the online Preparation for Teaching Online workshop (https://cunyonline.commons.gc.cuny.edu/) offered throughout the year to faculty teaching for any of their campuses.

● ● ● ● ●

Opportunities for Further Training Outside Your Own Institution

For those who do not have access to an institutional program or regional consortium, or who are interested in programs offering a certificate or graduate-level degree that are open to the public, there are such programs as the Online Learning Consortium's Online Teaching Certificate Program and its separate Blended Teaching Certificate. The California State University, East Bay similarly offers a Certificate in Online Teaching, while the University of Wisconsin provides a certificate program in Distance Education.

For those interested in a deeper commitment represented by a graduate program, there are such programs as California State University, East Bay's Master of Science in Education, with an Option in Online Teaching and Learning (MS-OTL). Athabasca University in Canada offers a masters and doctorate in distance education as well as degrees in instructional design. The University of Colorado, Denver, offers both a Masters in eLearning Design and Implementation and one in Information and Learning Technologies. All these programs differ in regard to time involved, focus of study and career path, qualifications, and cost but they are mentioned here because all are delivered online and all have reputations for quality.

It can also be advantageous to have several instructors from your single institution take an online teacher-training course together. You can point out to the administration that training several people at once will provide a seed crop of informed faculty who will go on to share their new insights with other faculty members. Faculty collaboration and sharing will often stimulate others to continue learning. But whether or not your institution is willing to offer financial support for you and your colleagues, taking a course together will provide a mutual support network for all of you.

General Characteristics to Seek in a Training Program   What characteristics should you look for in a training program? First, as we suggested earlier, it is essential that the core of the development program be conducted online.

The ideal training program should also have a flexible schedule, emphasizing asynchronous (not real-time) communication, although there should be a start and stop date to prevent participants from losing focus and motivation. Lessons and activities should be arranged so that faculty can work on them on a weekly basis, rather than on a specific day. Faculty should participate three to five times a week, for short intervals, in the discussion forums, rather than once a week for longer periods of time. This replicates the ideal online teaching experience.

Ideally, the program should be a minimum of about six weeks in length if it is aimed at neophyte online instructors and if it is to include some time for actual course design and development. This sort of time frame will allow a week for general introduction to concepts and time to get accustomed to the software. This would be the minimum to ensure that you and your fellow participants have adequate time to get up to speed with the software, interact in the online environment, and begin to build your own courses. However, a program may also consist of a shorter series of focused modules, or separate workshops, each only a week or two in length. In investigating the different training options, you will need to determine whether the course is comprehensive or organized into shorter courses on discrete areas like LMS tools, course design, facilitation, etc.

It is advantageous if the person leading or designing the training is someone who has experience in both teaching and learning online, has taught in a face-to-face or blended class as well as online, and has a working knowledge of course design. Perhaps you will find that the training is done by a pair or team in which one of the members is an instructional technologist or instructional designer. That's fine, as long as at least one of the trainers can share the perspective of teaching in a live classroom. Such a person is better able to comprehend the sensitive nature of transferring years of experience in the face-to-face classroom to an online setting.

Content to Seek in a Training Program What content and topics should you look for in a training program? We think there are five important categories of training content: software training, facilitative or methods training, course design, personal consultation, and supervised start-up.

1. *Software/technology training.* Naturally, software training is important. In an online teaching program that isn't platform specific, you will learn the software being used for the program and perhaps be introduced to several different platforms. As in the process of learning a foreign language, you will find that learning one platform and analyzing others will improve your facility in learning further platforms. Sometimes these programs will ask you to produce a demo in your own chosen platform. If your program has been specifically designed for your institution, then the software training may include having each participant build a basic shell for a model classroom.

   Training in HTML code used to be automatically included in training programs. However, with the rise of built-in HTML editing through WYSIWYG tools, this is most often an unnecessary expenditure of time. Other vital technology training may include specialized topics on multimedia production, whiteboard, and synchronous conferencing systems or mobile learning. Good programs combine observation and analysis of how tools are used with opportunities for hands-on experience.

   Overall, how much do you need to learn about the software and technology tools you'll be using? Naturally this will depend on how much help you can expect to receive from support staff. But even if you have technical support, including instructional designers or instructional technologists to assist you and do a good deal of the work for you, we suggest that you learn as much as you can so that you can provide direction and make informed decisions. In the end, because decisions about design and organization affect curriculum, a wise online instructor will seek to be fully involved.

2. *Facilitative or methods training.* The next layer of training is what may be called "facilitative" or "methods, approaches, and techniques." A good training program will give you the chance to explore the differences and similarities between live and online classrooms. For example, it will help you confront the sometimes-troubling issue of the instructor's "voice" and style in the classroom. In large part, a sense of your own online voice will develop as you engage in online communication with others. The trainer as well as other colleagues can help you achieve this vision of yourself through interaction and positive reinforcement. It's difficult to achieve this sense of ease about oneself in a one- or two-week training program; that's one reason why we recommend a longer course or a succession of shorter ones.

   Any comprehensive training program should also include classroom management, course preparation, methods of handling student participation and interaction, the use of internet resources, and other areas explored in this book. Moreover, we believe that a substantial portion of the training should involve analysis of case studies in online teaching and learning. You'll want a chance to observe real online courses, at your own institution or even elsewhere if the latter is possible. The program should offer guided discussions of the diverse teaching methods and styles present in online courses. Especially in a short-term program, we believe you will find analysis of teaching models as they are actually used in a real course to be more valuable than instructional design theory in the abstract.

3. *Course design.* This need not involve extensive exposure to traditional instructional design training, but it should involve real, hands-on practice under authentic conditions and it should cover the basics of planning a course, writing instructions for assignments, and other issues related to design and development. The training course itself should provide a model for good course design, and there should be opportunities to observe and analyze examples of actual online classrooms. Some training programs use the Quality Matters™ rubric

(see Chapter 3) or other such formulations as their framework for exposing instructors to online course design.

4. *Personal consultation.* In either the final portion of your training or as a follow-up to the training, some personal consultation is desirable. Ideally, training instructors or other staff should be available to work with you on a one-to-one basis or to provide individualized feedback in the context of the training course to arrive at a model that will satisfy your particular goals and objectives. Finding a good fit for your own preferred teaching methods and style is paramount here.

5. *Supervised start-up or mentoring.* Finally, in an ideal training program, the last stage should involve a supervised start-up of your actual course. If this isn't available to you, we recommend that you ask another instructor with experience teaching online to critique your online classroom setup. At CUNY School of Professional Studies, new online instructors are provided with a peer mentor who is an experienced online instructor. For the period of one semester, the peer mentor helps the novice online teacher bridge the gap between completion of training and confronting that new online classroom on one's own. The advantage of having the assistance of a faculty peer mentor is that the instructor is often less self-conscious about and more likely to request help from a peer than a supervisor like a chair or department head, and a peer mentor will ideally welcome the new online faculty into the community of practitioners at that institution. This can be vitally important when the new faculty is an adjunct online faculty who may not otherwise have contact with a community of colleagues.

Focused Workshop Training

Again, if you have access to regional programs, distance education associations, or faculty development offerings from your own institution or consortium, take advantage of these free programs. For those wanting to explore the emerging new technologies, organizations like the Online Learning Consortium offer focused, short, completely online workshops. The topics are varied, with new ones introduced on a regular basis. Best of all, you will find yourself in the company of a worldwide audience of other instructors who are eager to share their experience and discover new approaches. Conferences by organizations like the Online Learning Consortium, NUTN, WCET, AACE, CATE, the Teaching Professor, University of Wisconsin's Conference on Distance Teaching and Learning, ISTE, ICDE, EDEN, and countless other groups typically offer short, pre-conference workshops geared toward acquisition of a particular skill or area of knowledge related to blended and online teaching.

Learning from Your Own Experience

No matter how good your preparation for teaching online, there's still more to be learned when you actually begin teaching your class. It takes time to feel entirely comfortable teaching online. It's quite common for instructors to feel anxious, lost, confused, or disoriented by the new teaching situation.

The following profile of an online instructor describes some of the stages you may go through as you embark on your first experience in teaching online.

Profile of an Online Instructor

Joanne is a new online instructor assigned to teach a marketing course. Before planning her class, she conscientiously completed the short training and orientation course offered at her institution, and she took advantage of opportunities to consult with support staff. Besides asking for technical assistance, she sought advice about her syllabus and course activities.

After putting together an electronic "pack" of articles for her course, she submitted it to the program office at her institution, which promised to arrange with library services to secure copyright permissions and post the material in the online classroom. She worked out her syllabus on a weekly basis, making sure she had thought out the activities and readings students would pursue, as well as specific discussion questions she would pose in her discussion board threads. She also thought carefully about the procedures for students to deliver assignments to her and about whether she would schedule virtual office hours via real-time chat. She decided that she would offer real-time chat office hours only by prior appointment (arranged by email), because it was difficult for her to carve out a specific time in her schedule when she would be available each week.

Joanne did have some trouble deciding how to convert one of her favorite assignments to the online setting. She was accustomed to giving students a twenty-minute "quick writing" assignment each week, requiring them to brainstorm rapidly and formulate a basic marketing plan. How would she handle "quick writing" in an asynchronous class? What, she asked herself, was the equivalent of twenty minutes in the asynchronous mode? Or should she use the real-time chat room instead, having each student meet with her there for a twenty-minute period? With twenty-five students, the latter option didn't seem feasible. She finally settled on a two-day window for each "quick writing" topic; that is, from the time she posted a topic in the online classroom, students would have two days to upload their responses to the online classroom's assignment submission area. She would then post the best examples online. The entire sequence of procedures would be explained to her students in the syllabus.

Joanne was surprised at the amount of time she ended up devoting to the preparation of her online class. She had created new courses before, and that always took an enormous effort; but because this wasn't an entirely new course, she didn't imagine that it would require so much preparation. For example, although she had some lectures already written out in full, most of her lectures existed simply in outline form. Over the years she had been able to speak at length on the basis of the outlines. She hadn't calculated that it would take so many hours to put her previously spoken words into print, and then upload or copy and paste these documents into the course presentation areas. After all that work, she wondered if, after all, she should simply have created a series of audio recordings along with text summaries, but by the time she thought of that solution, she had already invested too much time in creating text lectures and decided to leave that option for the exploration of another day.

Joanne also discovered that, despite her extensive preparation, issues that she hadn't anticipated arose during the course. Students required more clarification of assignments than she had supposed they would. The activities and assignments turned out to be too closely scheduled. She unexpectedly encountered problems getting internet access while attending an international conference and subsequently missed logging in over a period of three days right during the middle of the course.

It was a very active class, with hundreds of postings from the twenty-five students. As the course progressed, she felt it was successful overall, but she was a bit overwhelmed by the intensity of the experience. She was online nearly every day, and she found herself logging on at odd times, as though she might otherwise be missing something. She was always a little surprised to see how many new postings there were. The little signs indicating new, unread postings began to trigger feelings of anxiety in her. She also found that she was sometimes overlooking a message, or that she had read it quickly and forgotten to respond.

During one particularly difficult and busy week, she discovered that she had made a mistake in announcing the due date for an assignment. She worried that students would lose confidence in her. At this point, she emailed a colleague, who had been teaching online for a few semesters, to express her feelings of anxiety. The colleague wrote back with what proved to be an important piece of advice: "Anxiety is normal at this stage. Don't be afraid to make a mistake. If you make a mistake, just tell the students as quickly as you can of the corrections needed."

By the fourth week of the eight-week course, she was beginning to feel less anxious. She also started to feel confident that she could take a less interventionist role in her class. She realized that she could pose questions in such a way that students would begin to address each other rather than her. She recognized, too, that she need not answer every single posting. The large number of initial questions on technical issues could be greatly reduced by creating a short FAQ to precede each unit of the course. She implemented these changes for the remainder of the course.

By the sixth week, Joanne was already scrutinizing her class with an eye to improving it next time around. She also contacted a few colleagues with whom she had trained, to find out what had worked or not worked for them in their own online courses. After this review of her course and some useful anecdotal evidence from her colleagues, which seemed to confirm her own conclusions, she decided that she needed a better mix of individual and group activities to reduce the number of individual students' postings on each topic. She also resolved to replace the large number of different assignments with an incremental series of assignments, each building on the preceding one. This change would mean that students could choose a single topic, research it, and structure each successive assignment around it. She felt this approach would save time and provide a more focused, in-depth learning experience.

Joanne enjoyed the remaining portion of the course and felt optimistic about teaching online in the future. She realized that her preparation time had been a wise initial investment and that, despite the revisions she planned for the next go-round, she wouldn't have to totally recreate the course. She resolved to stay in touch with others involved in online teaching at her institution and to spend some time before every term exploring tools in her LMS that she had not previously used, taking advantage of possible relevant training opportunities offered by her campus, and in keeping herself informed about new trends and tools in online education.

A few things stand out in Joanne's case history. First, Joanne took good advantage of training opportunities to prepare herself for teaching online. Second, her planning was comprehensive—not only for the overall arrangements, such as distributing reading material and establishing virtual office hours, but also for the week-by-week online classroom activities. Nonetheless, the preparation time involved was more than she had expected. Moreover, despite all her preparation, she went through a period of adjustment in the first weeks of the course, during which she felt great anxiety about her ability to manage the classroom.

She responded to her worries by taking action. Midway through the course, she made certain adjustments that were immediately feasible, and she began to note aspects of the course that could be improved the next time it was offered. By talking with others who were teaching online, she was able to get practical suggestions that confirmed her own best observations.

We imagine that your own experience will be similar to Joanne's. Although you'll do your best to prepare yourself, you'll still have adjustments to make as the course progresses, and you'll find ways to refine it in the future. It's important that you take the time to reflect on and fine-tune your course each time it runs. As we mentioned earlier, the online course, with its recording of student–instructor interaction, permits a higher degree of scrutiny of our teaching methods than a face-to-face classroom.

A good student evaluation designed for the online classroom can provide valuable feedback. If members of your institution's instructional design staff or support staff have observed your course, they may also be able to provide insights about improving it. Of course, this can be a delicate issue, and you may feel uncomfortable with the heightened scrutiny. What we have in mind here is a review for the purpose of improving your online instruction, not for judging or criticizing your performance as an instructor. We want to encourage you to see this process in a positive light. Greater appreciation of what you do will also become possible, and, we hope, greater rewards for excellence in teaching may one day result from this climate of openness.

You may find that you need additional professional development to maximize your potential as an online instructor. You can avail yourself of opportunities for further formal training in online teaching. You may take on the challenge of learning more about your course software so that you can use some of the higher-end tools. Or you may want to explore some entirely different software programs to attain skills in the creation of multimedia.

Where Do We Go from Here?

The Importance of Lifelong Learning   Online education is an evolving field. In years to come, it will feel the impact of many technological improvements.

Unfortunately, it is quite common for faculty members to learn one approach and one type of software and convince themselves that these are the answers now and forever. After all, few people relish putting in extra time to learn new programs or retrain themselves. Nonetheless, faculty who want to teach online need to adopt the same attitude they often prescribe for their students—that lifelong learning is for everyone.

Keeping Up with New Ideas and Technologies   This book is based on our knowledge of the teaching approaches, technology, and software currently available to instructors teaching online. Because it is intended as a practical guide, it has focused on the types of tools you are most likely to encounter and find useful and the best pedagogical approaches to take advantage of these tools.

We are currently in the midst of another sea change in online education technologies wherein student access by smartphone or other mobile device has become much more common, and there is a greater ease and variety of new tools for creating content and communicating typified by the Web 2.0 phenomenon, the ubiquity of social media, and mobile apps. It is becoming more plausible to rely less on the written word and to instead see your students on camera and talk to them via a microphone. Small, mobile smart devices allow us to be untethered from the desktop computer. "Cloud computing," i.e., browser-based software, has made it easier to do our work from anywhere we can deploy a browser. Mobile apps optimize software and tools for smartphone and allow us to more easily use the LMS, video, and audio for communication. The effect of this change on the way classes are conceived and administered is just beginning to be felt. Therefore, we expect that many more instructors will be likely to make the switch from the face-to-face classroom only to online, whether to blended or fully online.

Consider the dynamism of education today. Education is now a "commodity" that is much in demand. Without it, many people can't secure decent jobs or advance in their careers. The previously termed "non-traditional" college student—i.e., working, living off campus, perhaps first in his or her family to attend university—is now in the majority. Online learning doesn't necessarily save money. In fact, because it requires so much training and support, it can be quite labor and staff intensive. But as the tools for delivering it become more effective and easier to use, and if the costs for its delivery have diminished, how many more students might then opt for it rather than for the more expensive traditional courses of study, particularly when online learning allows them to hold a job and support a family while getting a degree?

It would be nice if we could tell you just what is going to change, and when. But we aren't soothsayers. For us to try to predict what the world of online learning will look like five years—or even one year—into the future would be at best an entertaining diversion, and at worst a complete waste of time. At conferences you can find gurus galore delivering keynote speeches with smug aplomb, peering into the future with laser-like eyes. Now the world of technology so dominates our lives that it's hard to remember when there was no "online." For many instructors it isn't just "publish or perish" anymore. It's "keep up with new developments or risk missing the boat."

Finding information about online learning and educational technology is fairly easy. Leading periodicals and newspapers, many of which are available online, cover technology, and distance education in particular, in considerable depth. A teacher seeking to keep up with general trends need look no further than the *Chronicle of Higher Education* or *Inside Higher Ed*, among US periodicals for news and spotlighted hot topics in the field. For the latest research in the field, there are publications that reflect the new worldwide reach of online education, with topical articles ranging from program administration to teaching methods to emerging technologies. Just to illustrate this point, such journals range from the Online Learning Consortium's *Online Learning Journal* (formerly *JALN*, http://onlinelearningconsortium.org/read/online-learning-journal/), Athabasca University's *International Review of Research in Open and Distance Learning* (www.

irrodl. org), to Anadolu University's *Turkish Online Journal of Distance Education* (http://tojde.anadolu.edu.tr) to the *European Journal of Open, Distance and E-Learning* (www.eurodl.org) and the *Australasian Journal of Educational Technology* (http://ajet. org.au/index.php/AJET).

Then there are the blogs and wikis, often written by individuals in the field of online and distance education, that highlight new tools and innovations or cast a spotlight on case studies of online teaching practice. These include blogs already mentioned in this book, as well as countless others that are extremely diverse in their interests, focus, and content—from Larry Ferlazzo's Websites of the Day (http://larryferlazzo.edublogs. org), to Tony Bates' Elearning and Distance Education Resources (www.tonybates.ca) or Ray Schroeder's Online Learning Update Blog (http://people.uis.edu/rschr1/onlinelearning/), or Jane Hart's E-Learning Pick of the Day (http://c4lpt.co.uk/pick/).

For some other sources of innovative thinking about educational technology and online education, sample Audrey Watters at Hack Education (http://hackeducation.com/), George Siemens' elearnspace blog (www.elearnspace.org/blog/), or subscribe to the newsletter OLDaily from Stephen Downes (www.downes.ca/). These sources may provide you with fresh ideas about where you stand in relation to teaching and technology.

We highly recommend that you choose such blogs based on your own interests and situation, select the best of these blogs, subscribe, and then review regularly via your preferred mode of accessing these resources, whether via email, an aggregator like Feedly, or Flipboard.

Finally, not to be overlooked is Twitter. There are many educators and educational technology people active on Twitter. You can find ongoing conversations and scheduled "chats" by searching for hashtags like #edtech, #elearning, #onlinelearning. Even if you don't use Twitter for instruction, these are often worth following for news and discussion, providing links and references of interest.

• • • • •

Networking with Others Involved in Online Education

At some institutions there are certain faculty members who have succeeded in promoting themselves as chief watchdogs and opponents of online education. They may express the idea that online education has nothing to offer pedagogically and that it will undermine face-to-face interaction between student and instructor. Oddly enough, some of them have little or no experience in an online classroom, as either student or teacher. In this sense they resemble the anthropologist of Bali who undertakes all his field research without leaving his apartment in Manhattan.

It's useful, then, to remember that ignorance can be found even in the most erudite academic circles. Don't allow the naysayers to dissuade you from becoming experienced and knowledgeable in the area of online teaching. There are many more of your colleagues in higher education who are excited by the new possibilities afforded by online education and who are anxious to share their enthusiasm and learning. There are likely to be at least a few such colleagues at your own institution, but if there are none on your own campus, they can be readily found through online discussion forums or at conferences such as WCET, the Online Learning Consortium's various conferences, at EDEN, or Ed-Media. The people you meet online or at such conferences can provide a wonderful support network for you. Conferences also provide opportunities to hone your skills in a focused workshop setting.

Such online communities or regional and discipline-related groups of online educators provide instructors a venue in which to talk with those of similar interests but perhaps divergent amounts of professional experience. Therefore it is almost always possible to learn something from someone who is just the right number of steps ahead of you for you to benefit from his or her experience and advice.

• • • • •

Student Expectations

Steal a look over the shoulder of any student today, and you will probably see him or her chatting or texting with friends. Or you may see students updating their Facebook pages, taking selfies and uploading photos to Instagram, or tweeting their latest observations. Or perhaps they are bringing up a music playlist as they sport the ubiquitous earphones marking the use of a smartphone which houses their music. While the student clicks out a response to a text message, he or she may be working on an essay for a class or taking notes on the professor's lecture. Maybe the student is viewing the latest video of interest on YouTube, and not necessarily a video produced by his professors.

This rather stereotypical portrait may in fact be telling us where we as online educators may be headed. While we should not assume that all students expect the classroom to resemble a social networking site, it is wise for instructors to keep up with the latest communication and content-creation trends and to judiciously choose those that seem to harbor a promise of enhancing their instructional strategies. Doing so will make life more interesting for your students and for you!

Learning management systems have also changed. While there has been greater consolidation in the field of integrated systems, there are a constantly evolving set of tools being developed outside these major companies. Therefore, learning management systems have had to become more open to incorporating such applications. But beyond any LMS, the ubiquity of free Web 2.0 tools and mobile apps has encouraged instructors to try out new technologies without having to depend on prior large-scale institutional commitment.

Now, using readily available and inexpensive software tools such as those described in Chapter 9, an instructor can create some relatively sophisticated courseware products customized to the needs of his or her students. These can be narrated lectures or digital videos demonstrating in real time how to use a software program, or a series of audio interviews. The content depends on the individual instructor's needs. Instructors can do it; departments can do it; whole schools can do it, all without having to secure a grant or solicit a generous donation from a rich alumnus. What is more, it can all be done with simple tools on basic machines with a bit of ingenuity and no small amount of determination. And many of your students will expect to be allowed to try their hand at alternatives to writing a paper or taking an exam when it comes to assessment.

● ● ● ● ●

The Educational Marketplace

Academics have traditionally lived in a world in which, for the most part, they control their own fate. Academic bodies convene and vote to make changes; administrators sit on committees and devise policies; and trustees meet to set tuition schedules. The pace is often unhurried, especially when academics must wait for legislatures to allocate tax monies to fund expansive plans. Yet the leisurely pace with which academic change takes place may no longer meet the needs of those living outside academia. As the workplace evolves and becomes more dynamic, as adults find they must upgrade their skills and knowledge every three to five years, as older citizens hunger to return to school, as corporations search for employees with cutting-edge skills, as young students desperate for a decent education find they can no longer afford the cost of residential colleges, people may increasingly turn to online learning, with its improved tools and easier access, as not just a viable alternative but a more desirable one.

Already there are signals that this process is under way. Large institutions and small ones have established a presence online, sometimes far out of proportion to the size of their physical plants. Public and private non-profit entities embarking on online programs have at last begun to dominate over the earlier for-profit online entities.

What leads students to choose one institution over the other may have to do with cost, or it may be the cachet of a famous name. No doubt a significant part of their choice, however, will be based on the quality of the education provided by the institution, and that quality can be provided only by well-trained, well-supported, and well-motivated faculty using tools equivalent to their energy and skills. We're used to thinking that change in the academic world takes place from within, through a vote by the academic senate, a decree from a "visionary" chancellor, or a policy set down by a governor that can control the shape and rate of social change. But it may well be that in the case of online learning the "marketplace" itself will dictate the pace of change. While many educators shudder at the very idea of an educational "marketplace," what we are really talking about is meeting students' needs. If educators are unwilling to step up and take an active role in directing online education, it will indeed be left to others to assume control. We hope that this book has provided some valuable techniques to help you take advantage of new opportunities in this changing world of education and to perhaps play a role in helping to shape the future of education. Who knows? In a few years, in order to polish up our skills, we may find ourselves in an online course taught by you.

Glossary ●●●●●

adaptive learning Lesson content is programmed so as to respond to a student's progress. For example, additional support or help may be provided or a lower or higher level of difficulty in content may be presented to students in response to work completed.

adaptive release A forced sequencing of content whereby students must complete or master content at a certain level before the next unit is released.

application service provider Also known as an ASP, it is a private business set up to host the latest course management software on its own servers and provide technical support as well.

application sharing Using real-time software that allows the instructor or student to give access to the computer desktop of the other party and provide assistance in real time.

apps Mobile apps are application software that are downloaded to a tablet or smartphone and designed to perform specific functions. These functions may duplicate those that can be performed in the web browser version of a program but are generally optimized to operate in the mobile environment.

asynchronous Occurring at different times; for example, discussion boards are said to be an asynchronous form of communication because messages are typically posted at one time and read at another and the participants do not have to be online at the same time to communicate.

augmented reality When computer applications are overlaid on reality to modify experiences and perceptions of the real world, or provide additional information as with GPS, video, 3-D images, etc.

avatar Graphic representation of a person to interact in a virtual world or in chat or other online format. Avatars can take the form of icons, animals, cartoon-like characters, or images more closely based on a person's own appearance.

biometric Verification of physical characteristics of an individual to provide authentication of a student such as login via eye scan or fingerprint.

blended course (also known as hybrid) A course which includes both face-to-face meetings and online components as required elements. Definitions of blended courses vary from one institution to another. The Online Learning Consortium has defined a blended or hybrid course as one in which 30–79 percent of the content is delivered online.

blog Short for "web log," it is a website on which a person (could be more than one) posts commentary, and can allow others to respond. The blog is usually arranged in reverse chronological order, providing a journal-like series of frequent entries. The blog does not require knowledge of HTML to create, and blogging software usually provides a variety of templates that can be used without having to design a site. Visitors can choose to subscribe to the blog so that they are notified via email when a new entry or response has been made.

Bloom's Taxonomy A hierarchical system of classifying different levels of thinking that can be helpful in designing assignments.

bookmarklet Sits in the bookmark toolbar in the browser and is a small application that can perform a specific function with a simple click. Unlike a plugin, they are not specific to any one browser and do not require installation.

chat Online communication that occurs synchronously, that is, in real time. Usually chat conversations are conducted with typed text, but some employ audio or video. A chat room is the online area where a chat is held. Typically, it consists of a window where messages are displayed, as well as a message box where each individual can type in a response.

cloud-based services/cloud computing Software utilized through a browser and the internet rather than downloaded or installed on one's own computer.

competencies/competency-based education (CBE) Usually more general than learning outcomes, competencies describe the desired skills, behaviors, or knowledge to be attained in a course or program.

discussion board Also known as discussion forum, electronic bulletin board, conference area. An asynchronous software program that allows one to post messages and permits others to reply to your messages. Generally messages are posted in text, but many allow for the attachment of images or sound files, and there are also versions that allow audio or video postings.

distance education Any form of learning that does not involve the traditional classroom setting in which student and instructor are in the same location at the same time. Examples range from correspondence courses to videoconferencing to online classes.

download To retrieve a file from a remote computer and save it on your own computer.

ebooks Electronic books accessed either online or downloaded to special reading devices (such as Kindle or iPad), or to other mobile devices like smartphones and PDAs.

eLearning (electronic learning) Another name for online learning, often the preferred term used in connection with corporate training.

embedding Taking code automatically generated by an external site and inserting it into your own course management software, web page, blog, or other site. This allows your students to access the site without leaving your classroom pages while the embedded object is actually playing on the external site's server.

emoji Originating in Japan, the term is a combination of emotion with character/word) and means something like "word pictures." As a successor to emoticons, they consist of pictures rendered by computer code. So one can simply insert a smiley face without having to type out an approximation, and sets of emojis have been widely adopted for use on smartphones, in messaging and other online communications to add indicators of emotions.

emoticon A text-based or graphic symbol used in online communications to express emotions that might otherwise be misunderstood when relying only on text. The word comes from combining emotion with icon. Text-based emoticons are formed from keyboard characters, like the smiley face :), and are usually designed to be read from left to right in Western cultures, but may be created to be read vertically (^_^) in Asian cultures.

fair use The allowable use or reproduction of material without specific permission from the owner. Although copyright law itself outlines the extent of fair use, various rules and guidelines have extended the definition for educators.

FAQ Acronym for "frequently asked questions"; typically an online list of common questions and their answers.

flipped class An instructional model for either a web-enhanced or blended class in which face-to-face class time is freed up for activities other than instructor lecture. The term was popularized by Colorado high school science teachers Bergmann and Sams in 2007 and indicates an inverted or reversal of the usual sequence of instruction.

forum A unit of discussion board software. Plural is *fora* or *forums*.

GIF Graphics Interchange Format, a compression format useful for graphics files with a limited number of colors. An animated gif is one that appears to move, like a sparkling star or a pulsing heart.

hotspot An access point by which wireless devices can connect to the internet.

hybrid See *blended course.*

hyperlink An element on a web page (typically an image, icon, or highlighted word or phrase) that makes something happen when you "click" on it with the mouse. Typically, it takes you to another web page, but it can also cause a digital movie or audio file to play. Also known simply as a link or web link.

instant messaging (IM)   A form of chat that is most often between two people, although it is increasingly possible to IM multiple users. The distinctions between chat and IM are gradually blurring, but for the purposes of this book, you can think of chat as taking place in an online classroom site to which one or multiple users are invited or able to enter, while IM involves summoning another who is online to chat privately.

ISP   Internet service provider; that is, an organization that provides the user with access to the internet.

JPEG file   A format developed specifically for the purpose of digitizing photographs. The acronym stands for Joint Photographic Experts Group.

learning analytics   The ability to collect and analyze data on student activity in an online course so as support more effective student learning

learning management system (LMS)   A learning platform and online delivery system also known as **course management software (CMS)** or a **virtual learning environment (VLE)**. A software program that contains a number of integrated instructional functions. Instructors can post lectures or graphics, moderate discussions, invoke chat sessions, and give quizzes, all within the confines of the same software system. Not only can instructors and students "manage" the flow of information and communications, but the instructor can both assess and keep track of the performance of the students, monitoring their progress and assigning grades. Typical examples of an LMS are those produced by Blackboard and Canvas, or adopted from "open-source" products such as Moodle or Sakai.

link   See *hyperlink*.

listserv   See *mailing list*.

local area network (LAN)   A network made up of interconnected computers in a relatively small geographic area, ranging from a single office or lab to a campus.

LTI (Learning Tools Interoperability)   A software specification that allows connection of otherwise separate software tools with an LMS, allowing for smoother integration and use, often allowing for a single access login rather than having to separately authenticate again for each tool.

mailing list (listserv)   An online discussion group, administered by a software program, in which each message is sent to a common email address, which then forwards the message to all members of the list.

mind-map or concept map A representation through diagram or flow chart of the interrelationships between ideas, words, or other items.

MP3 audio format A compressed file, meaning that it produces a file many times smaller than other types of audio formats and has thus enabled the explosion of downloadable music and music players such as the iPod and cell phones. It has become the leading format for listening to and sharing music.

multimedia A combination of two or more different communication media, such as text, graphics, audio, animation, and video.

open educational resources Resources available on the internet that allow for free educational use. These open educational resources (referred to as OERs) range from courseware made available by such universities as MIT to open textbooks available for free reuse, to freely shared podcasts from an individual biology instructor at a community college.

open source software Software in which the underlying source code is made known, collaboration in its development is encouraged, and which is distributed with the ability for others to use and modify. Linux is an example of an open source operating system, while Moodle, Sakai, and Open EdX are examples of open source learning management software.

operating system The software that controls a computer and allows it to perform its most basic functions.

PDF Portable Document Format, an electronic file format designed to be readable by different operating systems. A PDF document can be created with Adobe Acrobat software and viewed with the free Adobe Acrobat Reader.

plug-in An application that supplements a web browser, downloaded and then automatically activates itself when it is needed. Sometimes called an "extension."

podcasting Series of audio recordings that can be subscribed to and downloaded by listeners on demand. The term "vodcasting" is sometimes used for the video recording version of these.

post To contribute a message to discussion board; more generally, to place any message or document on a website.

RSS (Really Simple Syndication) feed readers Also known as aggregators. These permit you to subscribe to a blog, podcast, or other resource site so that you can receive the latest news or installment from that site without having to actually visit it each time.

scaffold To incrementally arrange the tasks (or a series of assignments) so as to allow students to gradually build on their knowledge and skills and to provide the necessary support resources at each stage.

screencasting   Software that records the entire sequence or an edited version of what you display on a computer screen as you click and scroll or otherwise manipulate software. Also known as screen-capture video.

streaming media   Audio or video files that are sent in a continuous stream from a source computer (usually via a website) to a receiving computer. Using a "player" software program, the recipient can hear or view the content in real time.

smartphone   Phone with features that allow one to do such things as access the internet, chat or IM, send text messages, utilize global positioning systems (GPS), and play music.

SMS (short message service)   Commonly known as text messaging, generally limited to 160 characters and commonly accessed via cell phones and other mobile devices.

social bookmarking   A method by which users can easily annotate, tag, search, and share bookmarks to internet resources with others, either the public or limited to small groups or individuals. Delicious and Diigo are examples of programs that offer social bookmarking tools.

storyboard   A series of sketches, slides, or pages on which the sequence for a video, website, or other product may be mocked up and planned. Storyboards are a way to organize and plan a dynamic design.

synchronous   Occurring simultaneously and in real time. For instance, a synchronous online discussion is one in which users can communicate immediately in real time; examples include online chats and internet telephone calls.

tag   Give a searchable term or topic label to a bit of information.

text messaging   See *SMS*.

thread   An ordered row of online comments on a particular topic; a number of threads in a single discussion board forum constitute a threaded discussion.

upload   To transfer a file from your computer to a remote computer; the reverse of download.

URL   Short for Uniform Resource Locator, the address for a site on the internet. An address such as www.ucla.edu is an URL.

virtual classroom   Also known as online classroom or virtual learning environment (VLE). Any online area in which instructors and students "meet," via their computer connections, for course activities. This term is sometimes applied to environments in which communication is asynchronous (people do not have to be online at the same time to communicate) but sometimes indicates a synchronous (in real-time) environment or a combination of both.

virtual worlds Online 3-D immersive environments that simulate reality and in which participants interact by using avatars. A well-known virtual world is Second Life.

VOIP Short for Voice over Internet Protocol which allows one to transmit voice calls via the internet. One of the best known examples is Skype.

Web See *World Wide Web*.

Web 2.0 Those tools and sites which allow for easy interaction and creation of content (from text to multimedia) on the internet without special technical skills, and whose structure and features foster collaboration and sharing among users. Most of these tools are available for free use. Blogs, wikis, YouTube, and social networking sites like Facebook are among the better-known Web 2.0 tools and sites available.

web browser A software program that permits you to view and interact with material on the internet. The most popular browsers are Internet Explorer, Firefox, Chrome, and Safari.

webcam A small digital camera attached to the computer with software which can capture and save or allow one to transmit live images and video over the internet. Over time, webcams that are built into the computer or device rather than separately attached hardware have become the norm.

web-enhanced A broad category of courses with supplementary associated websites or learning management system classrooms that contain materials relevant to the course. Actual online activities may be required or optional.

web link See *hyperlink*.

webmaster Person who administers and maintains a web server; usually a programmer.

web server Software that "serves" out, or disseminates, web pages across the internet; also may refer to the computer on which this software has been installed.

website The "place" on the internet where online teaching and learning generally take place. A site typically includes a series of pages (a "page" is equal to a screenful of information) containing text, images, and hyperlinks to other web pages.

whiteboard An online version of the traditional blackboard that allows an instructor or student to draw or write on the whiteboard in real time (and in some cases to use math and science symbols as well) while students can type in their questions using the chat function. Participants might be able to use video or audio to communicate and screen-sharing may be available as well.

wiki Software which allows for the collaborative creation and editing of content in web page format without knowledge of programming code.

Various built-in controls allow for the setting of different authoring permissions and the tracking of each contribution and different versions over time. The online encyclopedia, Wikipedia, is a prominent example of the wiki format.

wireless Also known as wifi for wireless fidelity. A wireless-enabled device can access the internet without cables or wires, through radio-wave connection with a wireless network.

World Wide Web A vast network of internet locations that share common protocols, allowing displays of text and multimedia as well as hyperlinks between one site and another.

WYSIWYG An acronym for "what you see is what you get," referring to screen displays that match the appearance of the eventual product. WYSIWYG web page editors look much like word-processing software and allow you to format text within an LMS or other program or create a web page without using the actual HTML coded tags.

Guide to Resources ●●●●●

In this section we have gathered together most of the various resources mentioned throughout the text, organized them into a few simple categories, and added a number of other references. Our intent is not to be exhaustive, but rather to concentrate on sources that are useful and practical, noting those that are free or targeted toward education. Most of the sites and texts listed here include their own hyperlinks or references to other resources.

FUNDAMENTALS

HowStuffWorks, Computer   http://computer.howstuffworks.com
> This site has articles with clear graphics and video tutorials on the internet basics but also covers subjects for the not-so-newbies on topics like "How RSS Works," "How Podcasting Works," social networking, wifi and mobile technologies, and much more. Another nice feature is that the site includes options for printable versions of the articles.

Lynda.com   www.lynda.com
> Short self-paced and hands-on courses on tech topics, free trial offered, then subscription.

ONLINE EDUCATION: SELECTED RESEARCH

Books

Garrison, D. Randy (2011). *E-Learning in the 21st Century: A Framework for Research and Practice* (2nd Ed.). New York: Routledge.

Means, B. (2014). *Learning Online: What Research Tells Us About Whether, When and How.* New York: Routledge.

Miller, M. D. (2014). *Minds Online: Teaching Effectively with Technology.* Cambridge: Harvard University Press.

Picciano, A., Dzuiban, C., & Graham, C. (2013). *Blended Learning: Research Perspectives (Vol. 2).* New York: Routledge.

Siemens, G., Gasevic, D., & Dawson, S. (Eds.) (2015). Preparing for
the digital university: a review of the history and current state of
distance, blended, and online learning. MOOC Research Initiative. http://linkresearchlab.org/PreparingDigitalUniversity.pdf
Book length publication, includes some valuable sections on
MOOCs and MOOC research.

Research on MOOCs

Bayne, S., & Ross, J. (2014). The pedagogy of the Massive
Open Online Course: the UK view. The Higher Education
Academy, 1–76. https://www.heacademy.ac.uk/sites/default/
files/hea_edinburgh_mooc_web_240314_1.pdf
EdX Research and Pedagogy, https://www.edx.org/about/
research-pedagogy, and http://blog.edx.org/mooc-research/
Collection and blog about of research on MOOCs from EdX
partner institutions
IRRODL Special issue on OERs and MOOCs, Vol. 16, No. 5 (2015),
www.irrodl.org/index.php/irrodl/issue/view/71
IRRODL Special Issue on Research into Massive Open Online
Courses, Vol. 15, No. 5 (2014), www.irrodl.org/index.php/irrodl/
issue/view/64
Luo, H., Robinson, A. C., & Park, J. Y. (2014). Peer grading in a
MOOC: reliability, validity, and perceived effects. *Journal
of Asynchronous Learning Networks*, Vol. 18, No. 2, n2. http://
olj.onlinelearningconsortium.org/index.php/olj/article/view/
429
Milligan, C., Littlejohn, A., & Margaryan, A. (2013). Patterns of
engagement in connectivist MOOCs. *MERLOT Journal of Online
Learning and Teaching*, Vol. 9, No. 2, 149–159. http://jolt.merlot.
org/vol. 9no2/milligan_0613.pdf
Piech, C., Huang, J., Chen, Z., Do, C., Ng, A., & Koller, D. (2013).
Tuned models of peer assessment in MOOCs. Retrieved from
www.stanford.edu/~cpiech/bio/papers/tuningPeerGrading.
pdf

ONLINE EDUCATION: THEORY AND PRACTICE

For those who are interested in learning about theories underlying
distance education and online teaching and learning practice, we
suggest the following short list, all available online:

Community of Inquiry https://coi.athabascau.ca/

Can read and review information about the COI model, publications and discussion on the influential community of inquiry approach promoted by Randy Garrison and others—the concepts of social, cognitive, and teaching presence.

Teaching in a Digital Age, by Tony Bates, published in 2015 is available for free at https://opentextbc.ca/teachinginadigitalage/.

A far-ranging book about the changing nature of education, it addresses a host of topics related to online and technology-enhanced teaching and learning. Chapter 2 provides a very engaging treatment of learning theories and ways of viewing knowledge. Chapter 5 provides a good overview of MOOCs. Chapter 7 analyzes the pedagogical differences between different forms of educational media.

Tips for Teaching Adult Students Online, http://wp.wpi.edu/atc-ttl/2012/09/28/tips-for-teaching-adult-students-online/

A concise explanation of adult learning principles and examples of how to incorporate these into online course design. From Worcester Polytechnic Institute.

The Theory and Practice of Online Learning, edited by Terry Anderson, the second edition of this popular book, published in 2008, available for free download www.aupress.ca/index.php/books/120146, click on Free PDF tab for free download.

Recommend reading the first two chapters, "Foundations of Educational Theory for Online Education" by Mohamed Ally and "Toward a Theory of Online Learning" by Anderson.

ONLINE EDUCATION: TRENDS AND DATA

Educause Library https://library.educause.edu/topics

Search the topic areas under Teaching and Learning for resources and reports from a number of Educause publications and research, as well as presentations.

Grade Level: Tracking Online Education in the United States www.onlinelearningsurvey.com/reports/gradelevel.pdf

The Babson Survey Research Group, from February 2015, with data from the College Board and the National Center for

Education Statistics' Integrated Postsecondary Education Data System (IPEDS).

Horizon Report   www.nmc.org/publication-type/horizon-report/
The yearly Horizon Report for Higher Education is one of the best ways to read critical insights about technology in education trends on the short-, mid-, and long-term horizon. This site also includes links to Horizon Reports for K–12, libraries, and other special reports, also available in a variety of different languages.

National Center for Education Statistics   https://nces.ed.gov/fastfacts/display.asp?id=80
Fast Facts page on distance learning participation in US. See also U.S. Department of Education, National Center for Education Statistics. (2016). Digest of Education Statistics, 2014

Online Learning Consortium (formerly Sloan Consortium) Survey Reports   www.onlinelearningconsortium.org/read/survey-reports
A great resource page to keep updated on the latest OLC Survey reports.

COURSE DESIGN AND DEVELOPMENT

Creating a Syllabus

Accessible Syllabus Template and Syllabus Checklist   http://fdc.fullerton.edu/teaching/basics.php
From California State University, Fullerton, College of Education.

Online Course Sample Syllabus & Online and Blended Course Development Guide   www.bgsu.edu/center-for-faculty-excellence/resources/forms.html
From The Center for Online and Blended Learning at Bowling Green State University.

Online Syllabus Templates   http://tlinnovations.cikeys.com/online-learning/online-syllabus-templates/
From the Teaching and Learning Innovations group at California State University Channel Islands.

Sample Online Syllabus   http://dl.bristol.mass.edu/wiki/images/7/78/SampleOnlineSyllabus.pdf
From the distance learning program at Bristol Community College, Massachusetts.

Sample Syllabus Format—Online and Hybrid Courses www.mtsu. edu/university-college/faculty/docs/faculty_syllabus.pdf
From Middle Tennessee State University.

Online Syllabus Template, University of Wisconsin-La Crosse https://sites.google.com/a/uwlax.edu/course-syllabi/templates

Bloom's Taxonomy

"Bloom's Taxonomy" https://cft.vanderbilt.edu/guides-sub-pages/blooms-taxonomy/
From Vanderbilt University Center for Teaching, provides short summary and history of Bloom's Taxonomy.

Bloom's Taxonomy http://edorigami.wikispaces.com/#Bloom's_Taxonomy

Using Bloom's Taxonomy https://tips.uark.edu/using-blooms-taxonomy/
From University of Arkansas, tips and clear explanation of how Bloom's can be used in course design and in writing of learning objectives.

Instructional Design

Adult Learners https://www.rit.edu/academicaffairs/tls/course-design/instructional-design/adult-learners
From Rochester Institute of Technology, a succinct explanation of adult learner characteristics and teaching strategies best adapted to them.

Blended Learning Toolkit https://blended.online.ucf.edu/
Multifaceted resource from University of Central Florida and American Association of State Colleges and Universities to assist those developing blended courses. See also their Blended Learning Toolkit at https://blended.online.ucf.edu/blendkit-course-diy-project-tasks/

Flipped Classroom https://www.rit.edu/academicaffairs/tls/course-design/flipped-classroom
From Rochester Institute of Technology, a useful resource page for designing and teaching using the flipped classroom model. Explains difference between flipped and regular blended model.

Instructional Design   https://www.uwlax.edu/catl/instructional-design/

University of Wisconsin instructional design page, Guides and Tutorials has links to some useful design and planning documents, including Online course and module level planning document, Alignment of course outcomes and assessment guide and planning document, and their online course evaluation rubric and checklist, www.uwlax.edu/uploadedFiles/Academics/online/guidelines.pdf

Instructional Design Models   www.instructionaldesigncentral.com/instructionaldesignmodels

Instructional Design Center website provides a clear explanation of the basic models of instructional design. Also see its section on Adult Learning Theory, www.instructionaldesign central.com/adult-learning-theory

Instructional Design for Online Resources   www.ion.uillinois.edu/resources/tutorials/id/index.asp

From the Illinois Online Network, links to short topics related to instructional design and development of online courses. The information is presented in clear and easy-to-read fashion for non-specialists.

Planning Tools   https://www.rit.edu/academicaffairs/tls/course-design/instructional-design/design-tools

From Rochester Institute of Technology, a collection of planning templates, organizers, and checklists to help with the planning stage of course development.

SPS Course Design & Development Tutorial   http://spscourse design.commons.gc.cuny.edu/

Modules covering broad array of topics in online course design, including use of multimedia, accessibility, assignment instructions, along with some templates, from the Office of Faculty Development and Instructional Technology at CUNY School of Professional Studies.

Open Learning Initiative's Creating Effective Online and Blended Course   https://lagunita.stanford.edu/courses/StanfordOnline/O.P.E.N./CourseDesign/about

A free, self-paced course in the step-by-step process of planning and creating an online or blended course.

Time on Task https://www.rit.edu/academicaffairs/tls/sites/rit. edu.academicaffairs.tls/files/docs/RIT_Time%20on%20Task%20 In%20Online%20Courses_v2.0.pdf

From Rochester Institute of Technology, for those converting from an F2F course to online, tips for thinking about time needed by students and instructors to perform tasks in the course.

Wiggins, G., & McTighe, J. (1998). What is backward design? In *Understanding by Design* (Chapter 1), https://www.fitnyc.edu/ files/pdfs/Backward_design.pdf

Accessibility Issues/Universal Design

Accessibility and Universal Design in Learning https://spsfaculty. commons.gc.cuny.edu/accessibility/

A collection of how-to guides and resources for making online course elements accessible from Office of Faculty Development and Instructional Technology at CUNY School of Professional Studies.

Universal Design for Learning Activity Center http://ctfd.sfsu. edu/udl

Offers case stories in video format concerning faculty's use of Universal Design in their classes.

National Center for Universal Design for Learning www.udl-center.org

Guidelines, many of which pertain to online courses, for making learning more accessible to all. "Learn the Basics" section offers a good introduction.

Multimedia Design

Clark, R. C., & Mayer, R. E. (2016). *E-Learning and the Science of Instruction: Proven Guidelines for Consumers and Designers of Multimedia Learning* (4th Ed.). San Francisco, CA: Wiley. The updated classic on multimedia design.

7 Things You Should Know About Microlectures https://net.edu-cause.edu/ir/library/pdf/ELI7090.pdf

Tips on creating short audio or video lectures.

Effective Educational Videos https://cft.vanderbilt.edu/guides-sub-pages/effective-educational-videos/
From C. J. Brame at Vanderbilt University Center for Teaching, summarizes research on instructional multimedia and provides some good recommendations.

Readability and Learning Styles

Edit Central Style and Diction Tools www.editcentral. com/gwt1/EditCentral.html
Has demo of six different readability indexes.

Index of Learning Styles www4.ncsu.edu/unity/lockers/users/f/felder/public/ILSpage.html
An online instrument to determine one's learning preferences, developed by Richard Felder and Barbara Solomon.

Tests Document Readability And Improve It www.online-utility.org/english/readability test_and_improve.jsp
Readability index tool uses four different systems to calculate readability of text.

Quality Online Course Design Rubrics and Standards

Distance Education Certificate Program, Quality Principles http://depd.wisc.edu/html/quality3.htm
Reviewed selection of works on guidelines and quality standards for distance and online education.

Illinois Quality Online Course Initiative rubric www.ion.uillinois.edu/initiatives/qoci/categories.asp
Online course evaluation rubric and checklist.
www.uwlax.edu/uploadedFiles/Academics/online/guidelines.pdf from University of Wisconsin-La Crosse.

Open SUNY Course Quality Review (OSCQR) rubric http://oscqr.com
From Open SUNY, can be freely used.

Quality Matters http://qminstitute.org/home/Public%20Library/About%20QM/RubricStandards2008–2010.pdf

Rubric for Online Instruction www.csuchico.edu/celt/roi
From California State University, Chico, can be freely used.

ASSESSMENT RUBRICS AND LEARNING ANALYTICS

Assessment Resources: Sample Rubrics www.winona.edu/air/rubrics.htm

A rich collection of links from many universities for different subjects and types of assignments, hosted by Winona State University.

RubiStar http://rubistar.4teachers.org/

Rubric generating and sharing site from University of Kansas.

Rubrics http://teachingcommons.depaul.edu/How_to/Assess_learning/Assessment%20tools/Rubrics/rubrics.html

From DePaul University, general information and links to specialized rubrics for different areas, including those for collab_oration and teamwork, blog and wiki assignments, writing, etc.

Society for Learning Analytics Research (SoLAR) https://solaresearch.org/

Organization that hosts an annual conference and promotes research into learning analytics, publishes the *Journal of Learning Analytics.*

Special issue on learning analytics, *Online Learning Journal* (OLJ) (Vol. 20, No. 2) June 2016. http://onlinelearningconsortium.org/read/online-learning-journal/

Using Scoring Rubrics www.calstate.edu/itl/resources/assessment/rubrics.shtml

Explains the principles behind rubrics. From Mary Allen of California State University.

LEARNING MANAGEMENT, SOCIAL MEDIA, AND SOFTWARE TOOLS

Learning Management Systems

Blackboard Learn blackboard.com

Commercial, institutional LMS, also provides a free hosted service.

Canvas www.canvaslms.com

Commercial, institutional LMS, also has a hosted service where free open courses or MOOCs can be offered (instructors must apply and be affiliated with institution or organization), www. canvas.net

D2L BrightSpace www.d2l.com/
Commercial, institutional LMS.

Schoology www.schoology.com
An LMS popular with K–12 sector but also for higher education.

OpenSource, Free, or Low-Cost LMSs or Software for Courses

Blogger google.com
Free blogging sites, login through Google apps.

CourseSites www.coursesites.com
Free hosted version of Blackboard LMS, for individual instructors to create their own course sites. Instructors can have up to five classes running at the same time. Also MOOC environment for institutions interested in offering open courses.

Edublogs www.edublogs.org
Free hosted blogging sites for the educator community; for fee version provides added features.

Foliospaces https://www.foliospaces.org
Free individual ePortfolio software, also available on institutional level for small administrative fee to create.

MediaWiki www.mediawiki.org/wiki/MediaWiki
Free, open source wiki software that can be downloaded to be hosted on your own institutional server. Same type of wiki software used on Wikipedia. For individual users, try PBworks or Wikispaces.

Moodle http://moodle.org
The Moodle community home page. Free, open source software that can be downloaded to run on institutional servers. There are also paid hosting partners/affiliates available.

Open EdX https://open.edx.org/
Open source version of EdX software for MOOCs for institutional use.

PBworks www.pbworks.com/education.html
Previously PB Wiki, for creating hosted wiki sites for education.

Sakai www.sakaiproject.org
The portal for Sakai open source software. Can be downloaded to run on an institutional server. Paid partners/affiliates are also available to host.

Schoology www.schoology.com
Limited individual accounts are available for free.

Weebly www.weebly.com
Template-driven, easy-to-use website builder, free version available, has Weebly branding but no ads.

Wikispaces www.wikispaces.com/content/classroom
Free hosted wikis for education, with many tools, easy to use.

Wordpress.com https://wordpress.com/
Free, hosted Wordpress software for creating blogs or websites.

Quizmaking, Polls, and Survey Tools with Free Versions

ClassMarker www.classmarker.com
Allows for hosted quizzes, emails reports of results, creates links from your own site.

EasyTestMaker www.easytestmaker.com
Free hosted quizzes.

Hot Potatoes http://hotpot.uvic.ca
A useful, freeware suite of software that can be downloaded for creating web-based quizzes and exercises. Tutorials are included on the site.

Kahoot https://getkahoot.com
Game-based real-time quizzing program.

Polldaddy polldaddy.com
For polls and surveys, can add media or images to questions, integration with Wordpress.com.

Poll Everywhere   polleverywhere.com
> Designed for real-time response—good for synchronous online sessions or blended classes.

ProProfs Quiz School   www.proprofs.com/quiz-school
> Enables one to create and have quizzes hosted, offers many options, and allows for tagging and sharing and embedding the quiz on your own site. Free and for fee versions available.

Quizrevolution.com
> Hosts and provides templates to create multimedia quizzes and automatic feedback, and features scoreboards so that you can see how students have done. Free and for fee versions available.

Socrative   www.socrative.com
> Real-time quizzing program.

SurveyMonkey   www.surveymonkey.com
> Free survey for up to a hundred responses.

Zoho   www.zoho.com/survey
> For creating and hosting quizzes. Free and for fee versions available.

Social Bookmarking

Delicious   http://del.icio.us/
> Popular social-bookmarking tool, easy to use. Has changed ownership hands several times so check status. You can annotate and share bookmarks selectively or with the public.

Diigo   www.diigo.com
> Social bookmarking, annotating and sharing, plus highlighting and sticky notes directly on web pages, create separate private groups.

Evernote   https://evernote.com/
> While primarily an individual note, organizer, and research tool, can also be used to clip web pages, annotate, and share notes with others or create a group notebook for students to collaborate, all within the free version.

Social Networking Sites Just for Educators

Classroom 2.0   www.classroom20.com

A social networking site for educators interested in using Web 2.0 technologies in education, created on Ning. Great place to hear from and share ideas and examples with other educators. Also, see bottom of home page for quick search of discussion concerning specific Web 2.0 tools.

Edmodo   www.edmodo.com

Focused on K–12 educators and their students, teachers can create and control class groups.

The Educators's PLN   http://edupln.ning.com/

A site for individual educators and interest groups.

Creating and Sharing Video, Audio, and Images

DoInk   www.doink.com

Create and share animated movies.

Flickr   www.flickr.com

The photo-sharing site.

Kaltura   http://corp.kaltura.com/

No free version, commercial video hosting service popular with education sector, institutional adoption so check to see if your institution has it if interested.

Panopto   www.panopto.com

No free version, commercial video hosting service popular with education sector, institutional adoption so check to see if your institution already has it.

Teacher Tube   www.teachertube.com

A free community and video-sharing site that is aimed at K–12 educators.

Vimeo   www.vimeo.com

Free version allows one to upload and share videos, free version has lower limits on storage size than for fee versions.

VoiceThread   http://voicethread.com

No free version for educators but individual and institutional education pricing, can upload videos, images, and other content with built-in discussion by text, audio, or video cam. Can be integrated with many LMS so check to see if your institution already has it.

YouTube www.youtube.com

Free hosting, with different privacy options available and no limits on uploads. Simple verification of account needed for videos longer than fifteen minutes. Easy-to-use caption maker. Create your channel through your Google account.

Screencast Video

Camtasia Studio www.techsmith.com

Sophisticated screencasting software with editing tools; version available for both PC and Mac. Free thirty-day trial only, no free version but available in education pricing.

Jing www.techsmith.com

Free, five-minute recording limit, easy to use, allows you to take screen grabs as well as video captures. Requires a download but can be used with either Windows or Mac.

Screencast-o-Matic www.screencast-o-matic.com

Free, accessed through browser with Java applets. Allows you to make and host your screen-recorded video on their website up to fifteen minutes, without download of software or save and post on YouTube. You can provide a link for your students to their site to view the video or embed it in your own site. Low-cost Pro version for group license provides more tools and capabilities, longer recording time.

Free Livestreaming Video

Facebook Live

Available through Facebook, thirty-minute limit on length. Video can remain on your Facebook page for replay or can be downloaded to save on your own device.

Periscope https://www.periscope.tv/

Owned by Twitter but you can sign up using your phone number if you do not want a Twitter account. Broadcast can be public or private. Videos can also be saved.

Avatar and Cartoon Creation with Free Versions

Voki www.voki.com

Easy to create 3-D talking avatars and make one-minute recordings using free version. Educator premium subscriptions provide more tools, greater selection of avatars.

DoppelMe http://doppelme.com/

Create very simple, cartoon-like avatar with face and body.

Faceyourmanga www.faceyourmanga.com/

Create manga-style avatar face.

Makebeliefs Comix www.makebeliefscomix.com/

Free comic creation site, also available in mobile app format.

WittyComics www.wittycomics.com/

Free, register only to save comics made on the site.

Interactive Video Lessons and Animations

EDpuzzle www.edpuzzle.com

Free and fee versions, edit videos and add assessments.

GoAnimate https://goanimate4schools.com/public_index

Animated videos, educational pricing, free trial only.

PlayPosit www.playposit.com

Formerly known as eduCanon. Edit videos, add assessments, embed in LMS.

PowToon www.powtoon.com/edu-home/

To create animated videos with narration, hosted on site, limited free version or low-cost educational plans.

VideoScribe www.videoscribe.co/

Write on whiteboard-style animation, must be downloaded, educational pricing, free trial only.

Free Communication and Screensharing Tools

Join.me https://www.join.me

Offers free version of screensharing and video conferencing software to download.

Skype www.skype.com

Make free calls and video conference over the internet. Good for communicating with students at a distance. Screensharing is also possible.

Twitter www.twitter.com

Features micro-blogging (short messages of up to 140 characters, known as "tweets") that can be received via mobile device or on a website. Users can "follow" other users and share with a small group or the public.

Infographics and Posters

Canva www.canva.com

Offers templates for creating infographics and posters.

Glogster http://edu.glogster.com/

Interactive multimedia posters, education version.

Piktochart http://piktochart.com/

For creating infographics, available in both a free and paid education version.

Timeline Creation

Dipity www.dipity.com/

Timelines can be created by one or more people, working collaboratively. Free and premium versions.

HSTRY www.hstry.co

Is specifically geared toward the education sector, free and premium versions.

Timeline JS http://timeline.knightlab.com/#fileformat

Free tool, allows one to start building a timeline from a simple Google spreadsheet template.

Other Software Tools and Websites

Google google.com

Free software for word processing, spreadsheets, slide shows, etc. Allows for collaboration on documents, forms, downloading documents to your own computer, or exporting for conversion into many Microsoft applications and other software formats. Your institution might have adopted Google Apps for Education which while still free, provides more privacy, no ads, and Google Classroom, which can be used like an LMS.

Storybird   Storybird.com
A visual story-building program, create books and share, using its image library (geared to K–12), free.

TagCrowd   http://tagcrowd.com/
Site for creating word clouds, free, no registration required.

Thinglink   www.thinglink.com
Create interactive media images, basic account free for educators, also premium education versions.

Prezi   Prezi.com
An alternative to the basic slide show, good for those who use a lot of images and a minimum of text in their presentations.

Wordle   www.wordle.net/
Site for creating word clouds, free, no registration required.

Web Page Editors: Free, Cross-Platform

CoffeeCup   www.coffeecup.com/free-editor/
HTML editor.

KomPozer   www.kompozer.net
Free and open source.

Screenshot/Grab Software

Snagit   www.techsmith.com/screen-capture.asp
Easy to use, not free but available for a free trial.

Snipping Tool: free screenshot tool included in Windows (starting with Windows Vista version).

Image Editing Software

Aviary   www.aviary.com
Free image editing software, mobile app.

Canva   https://photo-editor.canva.com/
  Free online photo editor that does not require you to download a software program.

GIMP   www.gimp.org
  Free, cross-platform, open source image editing software.

Google Photos   photos.google.com
  Basic image editing and storage in the cloud.

Paint.NET   www.getpaint.net
  It is available in many languages and requires a download to a Windows computer.

Aggregators and Curation Tools

Feedly   feedly.com
  Aggregates content from RSS feeds, a news reader available for mobile devices or browser based.

Flipboard   www.flipboard.com
  Mobile app to collect news, articles, photos, videos, provides support for Twitter and Facebook feeds or other social media.

Pinterest   pinterest.com
  Popular tool for collecting and annotating

Padlet   https://padlet.com
  Collect, annotate, share, offered in both free and educator (free trial) versions, can create a class "wall."

Storify   storify.com
  To curate tweets from Twitter and images, add annotations, free and for fee versions.

Virtual Worlds

How to Transform Your Classroom With Augmented Reality
https://www.edsurge.com/news/2015–11–02-how-to-transform-your-classroom-with-augmented-reality
  Article from EdSurge which introduces concept of using augmented reality in education and provides examples of tools current at the time of this November 2015 article.

Minecraft Education Edition http://education.minecraft.net/
Version of Minecraft for educational use. Successor to MinecraftEDU.

OpenSim http://opensim-edu.org/blog/
For information and resources (some public worlds you can visit) for those who are able and willing to create their own virtual worlds, using open source platform. See also the wiki for OpenSimulator developers, administrators, and creators at http://opensimulator.org/wiki/Main_Page

Second Life http://secondlife.com
Requires download of software, basic membership is free. Many education institutions still exist in Second Life, see its wiki, Second Life Education at http://wiki.secondlife.com/wiki/Second_Life_Education

Mind-Mapping/Concept Mapping

Bubble.us https://bubbl.us/
Free but limited version, for fee versions with more features, no download needed.

Coggle https://coggle.it/
Free and educator pricing, online, no downloads of software needed.

Mindomo www.mindomo.com
Mind-mapping software and sharing. Education pricing.

Sound and Podcasting

Audacity www.audacityteam.org/
Free, easy-to-use editing and recording software, must be downloaded, is cross-platform.

CLYP https://clyp.it/
Free, upload a recording but also record directly to its site. Provides you with a URL and embed code to share your audio clips.

Podomatic http://podomatic.com
A hosting service that allows you to create podcasts for free. It also features Web 2.0 types of sharing on the site.

Open Educational Resource (OER) or Open Courses/ Courseware, Including MOOCs

College Open Textbooks www.collegeopentextbooks.org/

A site geared to the community college community, for those looking to adapt an open textbook.

Curriki www.curriki.org

Open courseware with an emphasis on K–12.

Gooru www.gooru.org/

OER database for K–12.

MERLOT II https://www.merlot.org/merlot/index.htm

Peer-reviewed course materials, content, and lesson plans for reuse from one of the earliest established content sharing sites, sponsored by California State University system. As a member, you can join a subject area community and contribute content, become a peer reviewer.

MIT OpenCourseWare http://ocw.mit.edu

OER Commons https://www.oercommons.org

A great place to start a search through OER material collections, also connect with others of similar interests through the OER Groups or create a Hub with your colleagues to share resources on this site. Also offers professional development for using OER, and authoring tools for OERs.

OpenCourseWare Consortium www.ocwconsortium.org

More than 200 higher education institutions share course materials in this consortium.

Open Learn http://openlearn.open.ac.uk

Site gives access to courseware from the Open University in the UK.

Open Learning Initiative http://oli.stanford.edu/courses/ and http://oli.cmu.edu/

Originating at Carnegie Mellon and now at Stanford University, whole self-paced courses in such subjects as Elementary French and Intro to Biology, expertly designed using research-based learning design. You can sign up as an instructor to use OLI courses in conjunction with your own blended class, with options to customize the OLI course for your teaching and LMS integration. Generally free and open courses, there may be a small fee to use some OLI courses in this way.

OpenStax CNX   http://cnx.org

A site for sharing content, OERs, based out of Rice University. Formerly known as Connexions. Modules and collections that can be remixed and used for your courses.

Open Yale Courses   http://oyc.yale.edu

WikiMedia Commons   http://commons.wikimedia.org/wiki/Main_Page

Repository of freely accessible images and multimedia objects.

MOOC Platforms Offering Free Courses

Coursera   www.coursera.org

MOOC provider, offering free course enrollments from variety of universities.

EdX   www.edx.org

MOOC provider, offering free course enrollments from a variety of universities.

Canvas   www.canvas.net

MOOC provider, offering free course enrollments from a variety of universities.

WEB RESOURCES FOR INSTRUCTION

Collections and Portals

The Atlas Image Database of the Louvre in Paris   www.louvre.fr/en/moteur-de-recherche-oeuvres

Click on databases for the Atlas, an English database which offers views of 35,000 works in the museum. Other databases available in French for other collections.

Clipart ETC   http://etc.usf.edu/clipart

A collection of clipart sponsored by Florida's Educational Technology Clearinghouse, containing tens of thousands of pieces of clipart suitable for students and teachers, offered free for educational use of up to fifty items without permission.

EcEdWeb: Economic Education Web   http://ecedweb.unomaha.edu/home.cfm

Links to resources and lesson plans for incorporating web resources on economics and related topics.

Europeana   www.europeana.eu/portal

A portal that provides access to millions of digital materials from different sources in Europe, including text, images, video, and sound. Go to Exhibitions for artifacts organized around a particular theme.

Flickr   www.flickr.com

Image collections, many royalty free.

Free Music Archive   http://freemusicarchive.org

A curated collection of music as well as a social networking site. All music here is free to download and policy on reuse is clearly stated for each, many under Creative Commons licenses.

Khan Academy   https://www.khanacademy.org/

Free tutorials with emphasis on math and science, some materials on other subjects as well. Mostly videos with some text and image modules. Excellent resource for illustrating a concept or taking students through a process.

The Internet Archive   www.archive.org/index.php

A free library resource of collections, some unusual, of texts, music, television archives, and other digital content as well as its Wayback Machine collection of websites, with historical views of old web pages.

iTunes U   www.apple.com/itunes

Visit the iTunes site to download the software that enables you to access the university areas of the iTunes store for free education material. Many universities have made audio and video lecture materials freely available through iTunes.

Fine Arts Museums of San Francisco   https://art.famsf.org/

A searchable collection of art, several different parameters to search by.

National Geographic MapMaker Interactive   http://mapmaker. nationalgeographic.org/

Allows one to search for maps worldwide, with street, birds-eye, satellite, and 3-D maps available, then you can layer on data for population, climate, history, and many other data sets. Google Earth can similarly allow one to interactively explore the globe and the oceans.

National Palace Museum in Taiwan   www.npm.gov.tw/en/

Provides generous samples of Chinese art from different periods, helpful commentary and even 3-D views, all in English, French, and several other languages.

Metropolitan Museum of Art in New York   www.metmuseum.org/ art/collection

Has a large searchable collection of world art, searchable by time, place, artist, and object type or material (for example, "copper" or "drinking vessels").

Math Forum   http://mathforum.org

Now part of the National Council of Teachers of Mathematics (NCTM), offers math resources for teachers and students, mostly for K–12, some higher education.

New York Public Library Digital   http://digitalcollections.nypl.org/

Images, texts, audio, and video. Permissions for use vary.

National Archives Online Exhibit Hall   www.archives.gov/exhibits

Documents and objects from the US National Archives collection, most can be freely used in education.

Office of Teaching Resources in Psychology   http://teachpsych.org/ otrp/index.php

Society for Teaching of Psychology provides peer-reviewed teaching materials for different areas of the psychology field.

Science Education Resource Center (SERC)   http://serc.carleton. edu/index.html

Course materials, lessons, and multimedia for science education. Areas for higher education and K–12, Geoscience, etc.

TED Talks   ted.com

Video talks on wide variety of subjects.

TED-Ed http://ed.ted.com/

Lesson creation and sharing with a Ted Talk video.

Library of Congress/UNESCO's World Digital Library www.wdl.org

Available in seven languages, offers primary source cultural materials from all over the world—manuscripts, recordings, photographs, maps, timelines, drawings, etc.

Tricklar http://tricklar.com/

An international news site that can be sorted by country or topic to produce word clouds that reflect a current news story. Free, registration not required to generate word clouds.

The World Radio Network www.wrn.org/listeners/#home-listeners

Carries streaming audio programs from radio stations all over the world, in English or broadcast in several other languages.

World Wide Internet TV http://wwitv.com

A portal featuring direct links to live online streaming from television stations worldwide, in the language of diverse countries but also sometimes in English.

YouTube EDU www.youtube.com/edu

Videos from higher education institutions or schools on YouTube.

WEBSITES, BLOGS , AND ONLINE JOURNALS

Australasian Journal of Educational Technology http://ajet.org.au/index.php/AJET/index

Peer-reviewed scholarly articles on educational technology in higher education, with most contributions from areas of Australia, New Zealand, Asia.

Educational Technology & Society www.ifets.info/index.php

An English language journal with international reach, with emphasis on intersection of technology and educational systems. Good journal for those interested in what is happening with educational technology and open education in Asia, Europe, Canada, Middle East.

EdITLib www.editlib.org

Sponsored by AACE, offers "peer-reviewed papers and articles on the latest research, developments, and applications related to Educational Technology and E-Learning"—articles from AACE publications. It also has organized "collections"—compiled writings on a particular subject—that are very useful.

EdSurge www.edsurge.com

EdTech news and information, product reviews, K–12 and some higher ed.

Educause Publications www.educause.edu/research-and-publications

Periodicals and newsletters, many available online, from the organization concerned with information technology use in higher education. See also the Library page (https://library.educause.edu/library) to search for topical materials.

Edudemic www.edudemic.com/

Current trends in education and technology, teaching and learning issues, focus on K–12.

Edutopia www.edutopia.org/

Lucas Foundation sponsored site with news and information about teaching and learning strategies for K–12.

Elearnspace www.elearnspace.org/blog/

Blog by George Siemens good for those interested in current research into technology and learning, learning analytics, short reports from those conferences you can't attend yourself...

EURODL (European Journal of Open, Distance and E-Learning) www.eurodl.org

Covers research and practice, peer-reviewed scholarly journal with focus on Europe but includes many articles covering other parts of the world.

Faculty Focus www.facultyfocus.com/free-reports

Free short reports on pedagogical issues from Magna publications.

Hack Education http://hackeducation.com/

The thought-provoking blog by Audrey Watters on educational technology.

International Review of Research in Open and Distance Learning www.irrodl.org/index.php/irrodl

A refereed electronic journal covering theory, research, and practice in distance learning.

Hastac (Humanities, Arts, Science, and Technology Alliance and Collaboratory) https://www.hastac.org

An interdisciplinary, open academic community with thought-provoking blogs, for educators, students, researchers, organizations—interested in new ideas in teaching and learning, the future of higher education, as well as in the digital humanities, technology in learning.

Jane Hart's Top 100 Tools http://c4lpt.co.uk/top100tools/

Continually updated annual list of tools for learning, compiled from contributors in education and workplace. See also http://c4lpt.co.uk/directory-of-learning-performance-tools/.

Journal of Educators Online www.thejeo.com/

Peer-reviewed scholarly journal, open access.

Journal of Learning Analytics http://epress.lib.uts.edu.au/journals/index.php/JLA/about

An open access journal from the Society of Learning Analytics.

Journal of Interactive Media in Education http://www-jime.open.ac.uk/

From Open University, UK, journal with focus on educational technology.

Larry Ferlazzo's Websites of the Day http://larryferlazzo.edublogs.org

English teacher's blog highlights and critiques resources on the internet and new technology tools—although aimed at K–12 teachers of ESL and EFL, the resources and Ferlazzo's commentary are nearly always equally valuable to those in other subject areas and higher education.

Instructional Design and Development Blog www.iddblog.org

From DePaul University, an ongoing, lively blog concerning instructional design and technology issues.

OLDaily www.downes.ca/news/OLDaily.htm

A newsletter from Stephen Downes, brief postings on latest research, trends in education, including MOOCs, learning analytics, comments on recent articles in the field.

Online learning and distance education resources

www.tonybates.ca

An excellent source of critical reviews and commentary on resources, news, publications, and trends in online and distance learning, with international scope, by Tony Bates.

Online Learning Journal (formerly JALN) http://onlinelearning consortium.org/read/online-learning-journal/

Sponsored by Online Learning (formerly Sloan) Consortium, peer-reviewed scholarly journal on current topics of interest in the field, special theme-based issues, strives to be international in scope. The former JOLT from MERLOT has now merged with this journal.

Online Learning Update Blog http://people.uis.edu/rschr1/online learning/

News and research curated by Ray Schroeder of the University of Illinois, Springfield.

Online Journal of Distance Education Administration www. westga.edu/~distance/ojdla/

For those involved in administration of online and other distance learning programs.

Online Learning Update http://people.uis.edu/rschr1/online learning/

Active blog featuring news and selected links to articles of interest concerning online education by Ray Schroeder of the University of Illinois at Springfield.

Sue Waters Blog http://suewaters.com

Sue Waters focuses on eLearning and educational technology, with emphasis on K–12 educators. Lots of "how-to" tips. She also has a site called The Edublogger at https://www.theedu blogger.com/ which has tips for other educators on blogging and technology.

Teach100 http://teach.com/teach100

Ranks and scores the best educator/education blogs, targeted for K–12 sector.

The Turkish Online Journal of Distance Education http://tojde. anadolu.edu.tr/

From Turkey's Anadalou University, an international journal on distance education.

COMPUTER-BASED SIMULATIONS

MERLOT II www.merlot.org

Collection offers a number of links to simulations and animations, with commentary about how they might be used in teaching. Many MERLOT materials are accompanied by peer reviews of the resource, pointing out the special features of an item or suggesting ways in which it can be incorporated into a course activity. Contains many OERs.

PhET http://phet.colorado.edu/index.php

Interactive, free simulations for physics, chemistry, biology, earth science, and math, from University of Colorado at Boulder.

SERC portal http://serc.carleton.edu/index.html

Based at Carleton College, an excellent collection of resources for the sciences, including computerized simulations and simple animations. Contains many OERs.

Solar System Simulator http://space.jpl.nasa.gov

Sponsored by the Jet Propulsion Laboratory of the National Aeronautics and Space Administration, this simulator allows one to view different parts of the solar system.

CASE STUDIES AND SCENARIO OR ROLE-PLAYING SIMULATIONS; DEBATES

Case Centre www.thecasecentre.org/educators/products/view? id=133460

Case studies for business education, both free and for fee

ChemCollective   www.chemcollective.org

Hosts a variety of simulations, virtual labs, and scenario-based activities for chemistry courses.

Debate Central   http://debate.uvm.edu/

Sponsored by University of Vermont, "everything about debates and debating," includes debate training resources, debate formats—helpful for those instructors who do not have background in debating.

Economist Debates   http://debates.economist.com/

The Economist magazine sponsors online debates on current topics of interest, using Oxford-style debating format.

International Debate Education Association (IDEA)   www.idebate. org/

Includes an online debate topic database (Debatabase), teaching resources and other helpful resources for educational debates.

MIT Sloan Teaching Innovation Resources   https://mitsloan.mit. edu/LearningEdge/Pages/default.aspx

Instructors can download and freely use case studies in such areas as industry evolution, sustainability, and global entrepreneurship.

National Center for Case Study Teaching in Science   http:// sciencecases.lib.buffalo.edu/cs/

Collection by the State University of New York at Buffalo. The Center not only provides cases but also includes instructor guideline notes.

Public Health Games   www.publichealthgames.com

Provides links to simulations and games in which scenarios such as a bioterrorism attack or a natural disaster striking a community are presented with the participant choosing a role to play and decisions to make in response.

GAMES

ClassCraft   www.classcraft.com/

Create online role-playing games, free or low fee for educators.

Jeopardy Labs   https://jeopardylabs.com/
Create a browser-based jeopardy-style game for reviewing fact-based materials.

Gamified wiki   http://gamifi-ed.wikispaces.com/
Operated by educators and students who contribute and invite reviews of learning games from educators and students.

Twinehttps://twinery.org/   An open source story writing tool.

COPYRIGHT AND INTELLECTUAL PROPERTY ISSUES

Copyright Clearance Center   www.copyright.com
One of several online services that will help you find a copyright owner and secure permission to use material.

Crash Course in Copyright   http://copyright.lib.utexas.edu/
Provided by the University of Texas, this is another well-designed and comprehensible site dealing with copyright and intellectual property. Take the online tutorial on copyright.

International Copyright Law   http://depts.washington.edu/uw copy/Copyright_Law/International_Copyright_Law
Section on international copyright law from the University of Washington copyright connection.

What is Intellectual Property?   www.wipo.int/about-ip/en
From the World Intellectual Property Organization (WIPO) links to resources for understanding IP rights on a global or country-to-country basis.

Preventing Plagiarism/Ensuring Academic Integrity

Academic Integrity tutorial site www.umuc.edu/students/academic-integrity/ai-tutorial/academic-integrity-tutorial.html
At University of Maryland University College; covers academic integrity issues.

Academic Integrity Quiz   https://www.reed.edu/registrar/academic_integrity/quiz.html
At Reed College; provides automatic feedback.

Indiana University—How to Recognize Plagiarism https://www.indiana.edu/~academy/firstPrinciples/index.html

Tutorial site for students, focused on plagiarism in writing, features clear explanations and lots of examples of plagiarism in writing and how to avoid it.

International Center for Academic Integrity www.academicintegrity.org/icai/home.php

Valuable curated resources and links to promote academic integrity, including sample policy statements, tutorials, etc.

Ryerson University, Academic Integrity http://ryerson.ca/academicintegrity/episodes/index.html

Entertaining "episodes" provide examples for students of different situations involving academic integrity.

Turnitin www.turnitin.com

Company that provides services to institutions and instructors to detect plagiarism by students.

PROFESSIONAL DEVELOPMENT AND STUDENT PREPARATION

Selected Conferences and Organizations That Offer Professional Development Opportunities in Online Teaching and Educational Technology

AACE www.aace.org

Offers online resources, publications, plus a number of different annual conferences, each aimed at different audience for educators involved with technology.

Annual Conference on Distance Education and Learning www.uwex.edu/disted/conference

Sponsored by University of Wisconsin–Madison.

EDEN www.eden-online.org/

European Distance and E-Learning Network offers several conferences, including one on the open classroom and another on research into the distance and eLearning areas as well as online discussion and publications.

International Council for Open and Distance Education   www.icde.org

> Global organization for open and distance higher education, international conference participation.

International Society for Technology in Education   www.iste.org

> For K–12 and teacher education sector.

League for Innovation in the Community College   https://www.league.org/

> Aimed at the community-college educator in the United States.

National University Technology Network (NUTN)   www.nutn.org/

> Offers resources and workshops at annual meeting.

Online Educa Berlin   www.online-educa.com

> Conference held each year in Berlin, Germany, focuses on education and corporate training areas, video.

Online Learning (formerly Sloan) Consortium   http://onlinelearningconsortium.org/

> Offers online workshops, publications as well as several annual conferences.

The TLT (Teaching, Learning, and Technology) Group   www.tltgroup.org

> The site offers resources, online symposia, and workshops.

WCET   www.wcet.info/2.0

> Offers online webinars and workshops at their annual conference.

Readiness Surveys and Orientation Materials for Students

Arizona State University, ASU Online Orientation   http://online-student-welcome.asu.edu/

> Series of videos introducing online learning, enrollment and preparation logistics, resources, etc. Sections aimed at both prospective as well as admitted students.

Blue Ridge Community and Technical College, Online Student Orientation   www.blueridgectc.edu/stu_ori/index.html

Simple click-through tutorial pages covering basics of online learning, expectations, navigating a course site, resources. First section includes a readiness quiz.

De Anza College, Online Education Center   https://www.deanza.edu/online-ed/prospective/index.html

A readiness page and quiz for prospective students and an online orientation for enrolled students that covers skills and strategies, resources and links to info about LMS and class site navigation.

Rio Hondo Virtual College Online Survival Guide   http://online.riohondo.edu/student/guide/web1aa.htm

Includes information on a variety of basic skills needed to take an online course.

Sierra   College   www.sierracollege.edu/distancelearning/help-center/getting-started/readiness-assessment.php

A readiness survey.

University of Arkansas   Online Course Readiness Quiz   https://online.uark.edu/students/readiness-quiz.php

University of Central Florida Learn Online   https://online.ucf.edu/learn-online/

Contains sections providing overview of online learning, what one needs to be successful in an online class plus expectations, logistics, and resources.

University of Memphis, Online Student Orientation   www.memphis.edu/oso/index.php

Covers areas of interest to both prospective as well as admitted students.

Washington Online, Is Online Learning for Me   https://www.waol.org/prospective_students/isonlineforme.aspx

A readiness quiz.

Xavier University, An Orientation for Online Students   www.xavier.edu/online/Student-Orientation.cfm

Series of orientation modules in Canvas, introducing online learning, showing examples of online courses, skills needed for success, resources. Ends in a quiz.

Some Online Training or Degree Programs in Online Teaching, Distance Education, or Educational Technology

Athabasca University, Master in Distance Education   http://cde. athabascau.ca/programs/index.php#mde
> Athabasca offers a variety of certificates and degrees in distance education and instructional design.

California Community Colleges @One Project www.onefor training.org/online-courses
> A well-established program targeted to California Community College faculty and staff, these low-cost online training courses and certificate program are also open to out of state educators for what is still a very low fee.

California State University, East Bay, Certificate in Online Teaching and Learning https://www.ce.csueastbay.edu/ce/programs/online-teaching-certificate/
> A well-established program that offers a certificate as well as an MEd with Option for Online Teaching and Learning, www.csueastbay.edu/ceas/departments/otl/index.html

Illinois Online Network, Making the Virtual Classroom a Reality www.ion.uillinois.edu/courses/students/index.asp
> Illinois public institutions and international partners receive discount—single workshops and a Master Online Teacher Certificate are offered. Also open to general public.

Indiana University, online certificate and degree programs   http:// iuconnected.iu.edu/CertificateDegreePrograms.aspx#isted
> Indiana U. offers online certificates, masters, and doctoral level (EdD) degree programs in instructional systems technology.

OLC (formerly Sloan Consortium) Online Teaching Certificate Program http://onlinelearningconsortium.org/learn/teaching-certificates/

OLC Workshops   http://onlinelearningconsortium.org/learn/workshops/
> Highly regarded certificate program with foundational course, electives, and specializations. The individual workshops are on

current trends and topics, and may be available to you for free through your college if your institution is a member of OLC and has a Workshop Pass.

Penn State University World Campus, Master of Education in Learning, Design, and Technology www.worldcampus.psu.edu/degrees-and-certificates/penn-state-online-masters-in-learning-design-technology/overview

San Diego State University, Online Certificate and Degree Programs https://www.ces.sdsu.edu/Pages/Engine.aspx?id=685

Online certificates and masters in instructional technology and learning design and technology, some requiring regular admission and some through their Open University.

University of British Columbia, Master of Educational Technology https://www.grad.ubc.ca/prospective-students/graduate-degree-programs/master-of-educational-technology

University of Colorado, Denver MA, Information and Learning Technologies with emphasis on eLearning Design and Implementation www.ucdenver.edu/academics/colleges/SchoolOf Education/Academics/MASTERS/ILT/Pages/eLearning.aspx

The University of Colorado, Denver; also has MA with emphasis in Instructional Design and Adult Learning.

University of Maryland University College www.umuc.edu/academic-programs/education-and-teaching.cfm

UMUC offers a Master of Education in Instructional Technology as well as a Master of Distance Education and E-learning.

 This guide is available as a downloadable eResource from: www.routledge.com/9780415832434

Index ●●●●●

Page numbers in *italics* denote tables, those in **bold** denote figures.

Made in the USA
Monee, IL
14 July 2020